Happiness and Poverty in Developing Countries

Happiness and Poverty in Developing Countries

A Global Perspective

John Malcolm Dowling
Department of Economics, University of Hawaii

Chin-Fang Yap

palgrave
macmillan

Northwest State Community College

First published 2013 by
PALGRAVE MACMILLAN

Palgrave Macmillan in the UK is an imprint of Macmillan Publishers Limited, registered in England, company number 785998, of Houndmills, Basingstoke, Hampshire RG21 6XS.

Palgrave Macmillan in the US is a division of St Martin's Press LLC, 175 Fifth Avenue, New York, NY 10010.

Palgrave Macmillan is the global academic imprint of the above companies and has companies and representatives throughout the world.

Palgrave® and Macmillan® are registered trademarks in the United States, the United Kingdom, Europe and other countries

ISBN: 978–0–230–28575–0

This book is printed on paper suitable for recycling and made from fully managed and sustained forest sources. Logging, pulping and manufacturing processes are expected to conform to the environmental regulations of the country of origin.

A catalogue record for this book is available from the British Library.

A catalog record for this book is available from the Library of Congress.

10 9 8 7 6 5 4 3 2 1
22 21 20 19 18 17 16 15 14 13

Transferred to Digital Printing in 2013

Contents

List of Tables

List of Figures

Acknowledgments

We would like to thank the Department of Economics, University of Hawaii, for support and the flexibility that allowed us to develop courses in the economics of poverty and happiness. In particular we want to thank Denise Konan and Byron Ganges for their ongoing encouragement and Timothy Halliday for his helpful comments and suggestions. We also would like to thank the Asian Development Bank for financial support. Douglas Brooks, Assistant Chief Economics and Research Department, Asian Development Bank and Guanghua, Principal Economist, Asian Development Bank were particularly helpful and supportive. We would also like to thank the editors at Palgrave Macmillan for their advice and continued encouragement and an anonymous referee who made many useful comments and suggestions.

1
Introduction

To begin our study of the determinants of well-being and happiness, it is useful to take a look at the history of ideas and how being happy as a goal in life has evolved. We start with the ancient Greeks, a good beginning point for readers steeped in the traditions of Europe. Fatalism pervaded the world of philosophy in the early days of the Greek empire. This was reflected in drama and in the writings of early historians such as Herodotus. As Greek civilization evolved and their wars with Sparta and the Persians came to an end, a fresh breath of freedom, greater wealth, security and tolerance emerged, along with the belief that individuals could, indeed, seek to be happy as individuals. These new attitudes found a voice in the writing of Socrates, who said that the search for happiness is a natural longing (see http://classics.mit.edu/Herodotus/history.html). Furthermore, "Socrates and Plato created a longing of tremendous power. Their happiness is the sum of all desires, the final resting place of Eros, the highest good" (McMahon 2004, p. 90). These ideas reached their zenith in the work of Aristotle. He argued that everything we do is in pursuit of some end result:

> *in medicine this is health, in generalship victory; in house building a house...in every action and decision it is the end, since it is for the sake of the end that everyone does the other things...everything that is pursued into action...will be the highest good...and to be a good human being is to be a happy human being and happiness is an activity of the soul expressing virtue.*
>
> *(Aristotle, Nichomachean Ethics 1.73 and 1.81, translated by Terence Irwin, 1985)*

1

and "Happiness is the meaning and the purpose of life, the whole aim and end of human existence" (Aristotle).

Following this Aristotelian logic, the purpose of research on happiness in the modern era is to investigate the sources of happiness for different people around the world. In this book we focus on developing countries, where deprivations and poverty are more widespread and where there has been less emphasis on the determinants of well-being and happiness.

In recent years the topics of happiness and well-being have become the subject of considerable research and economic policy discussions. There have been a growing number of studies of the determinants of well-being, which began with a focus on per capita income. It was soon realized that per capita income and living standards need to be augmented if we are to gain a fuller and more complete understanding of what motivates individuals and societies to lift their levels of well-being and happiness.

There are two major strands of research that characterize the search for a more robust measure of well-being that goes beyond the narrow concept of per capita income. The first research program into well-being is known as the capabilities approach. The focus is on the provision of social and economic goods and capabilities which contribute to raising levels of happiness and well-being. These include food, health, education and other social services necessary for leading a fulfilling life. The capabilities approach is closely related to basic needs and has been implemented in the Human Development Index (HDI), which has been compiled by the United Nations for countries around the globe for the past few decades. It is also closely associated with the work of Amartya Sen, who has written extensively on this approach. Originally couched in terms of income alone, such measures have been expanded to include indices of educational attainment and health outcomes. The HDI, developed by UNDP and incorporated in its influential Human Development Report beginning in the 1980s, is the first example of this sort of measure. It has been widely used and quoted as an alternative to a simple income measure of poverty. The index includes life expectancy and average years of schooling completed as supplements to per capita income, which is the third leg of the stool that the index stands on.

Recently Oxford University has developed a Multidimensional Poverty Index (MPI), which is highlighted in the UNDP Human Development Report of 2010. This index uses a similar approach to the HDI, but expands the database to include a variety of new health, education and standard of living components (the latter including but not exclusively relying on income) which rely on more detailed data sets than the HDI.

The Organisation for Economic Co-operation and Development (OECD) has also published an analysis of a variety of social and economic indicators for its member countries as a component of its semiannual outlook publication (see OECD 2011, which can be downloaded from the OECD website www.oecd.org). These well-being indicators include many additional variables in addition to those in the MPI index.

The Oxford MPI Index is briefly summarized as follows.

Health (each indicator weighted equally at 1/6): Child mortality, measured by whether any child has died in the family; nutrition, measured if any adult or child in the family is malnourished.

Education (each indicator weighted by 1/6): Years of schooling, if no member of the household has completed 5 years of schooling; child enrolment, measured by noting whether any school-aged child is out of school in years 1–8.

Standard of living (each indicator weighted at 1/18): Electricity, if a household does not have electricity; drinking water, if household does not meet Millennium Development Goals (MDG) definitions of less than a 30 minute walk to safe drinking water; sanitation, if it does not meet MDG definitions or if toilet is shared; flooring, if the floor is dirt, sand or dung; cooking fuel, if cooking is done with wood, charcoal or dung; assets, if household does not own more than one of the following: radio, TV, telephone, bike, motorbike.

The MPI is the product of two numbers – the headcount ratio, or the percentage of people who are poor, and the average intensity of deprivation. The average density of deprivation reflects the proportion of dimensions in which households are deprived.

Data are assembled at the country level and also include some analysis of different regions within countries. Both the MPI and the HDI draw conclusions about the breadth and depth of poverty drawn from an analysis of these surveys. Comparisons are drawn between the HDI and MPI indices, pointing out the importance of adding a richer source of data to the conventional income per day and HDI benchmarks. More recently the OECD has developed a *Better Life Index* (www.oecdbetterlifeindex.org), which measures 10 aspects of life for OECD countries in a broader context than poverty, as follows: income, housing, jobs, community, education, environment, health, government, life satisfaction and work-life balance.

To quote the *Economist* magazine:

> *Looking at many aspects of poverty at once has several benefits. One problem with considering just one indicator is that some deprivations may be a matter of choice.... Some, for instance, may prefer the earthiness of a mud*

floor to the coldness of a concrete one. But the number of people choosing to be malnourished, illiterate, lacking in basic possessions and drinkers of dirty water all at once is probably fleetingly small. A person deprived along many of these dimensions surely counts as poor. The Economist, July 31 2010 (p. 62)

However, one can question whether the poor will always provide unreliable and misleading information regarding their own well-being. When there is long-standing deprivation, the poor try to adapt to these parlous circumstances. They don't weep and wail. That doesn't mean they love squalor. They make do with what they have. When asked they may say they are doing OK even though they are poorly clothed, malnourished and in poor health while living in a slum. Yet it seems ludicrous to think that we should not ask them about their goals and aspirations and value their responses to these questions. We need to value their aspirations, goals and objectives in making a more prosperous, happy and fulfilling life for themselves and their families. It is vitally important to know what the poor and underprivileged want for themselves. Do they want better housing and secure clean water close by? Do they want better health and education facilities? Do they want more income and cleaner and safer working conditions? How do improvements in living conditions, health, education and income impact on the well-being of the poor and their level of happiness? These objectives seem to us an achievable and laudable objective for research into the living conditions of the poor. In whatever richness of detail possible, we can explore what effect changes in life circumstances of the poor will have on their level of happiness and well-being.

The second approach followed in searching for a better measure of happiness is known popularly as subjective well-being. Subjective well-being relies on the results of personal interviews with many thousands of individuals in different countries on all continents. The motivation for this focus on well-being is that individuals are the best judges of their own well-being and happiness. The most widely accessible database on well-being has been assembled by a group of researchers around the globe. The World Values Survey is organized as a network of social scientists coordinated by a central body, the World Values Survey Association. The hope is that a more robust and deeper understanding of the determinants of well-being and happiness can be obtained by assembling responses to questions about well-being and other pertinent socioeconomic and cultural variables which serve as possible determinants of well-being and happiness.

There is a deep philosophical difference between the two approaches. Subjective well-being relies on individuals to assess their own state of mind and to evaluate their life experience. It relies on direct observation of the individual valuation of his (or her) own experienced utility and serves as an important proxy measure for revealed preference where other measures of revealed preference are not possible. On the other hand, the capabilities approach relies on government and society to determine the appropriate level of basic goods and services that should be provided to its citizens. Although the United Nations has attempted to codify some of these entitlements, there are still differences of opinion as to the appropriate level and the mix of these goods and services. And, in the end, it is outside observers who determine what contributes to the well-being of citizens of the world. As Deaton (2008) observes,

> *The survey measures of life and health satisfaction are direct measures of an important aspect of human experience, and economists and other social scientists need to understand what they mean, how they relate to familiar objective measures such as income and life expectancy, whether they are superior, inferior, or just different measures of well-being.* (Deaton 2008, p. 13)

The research and policy agenda differs depending on which approach is followed. In the subjective well-being literature, the basic thrust is to achieve a better understanding of the determinants of subjective well-being by analyzing the questionnaire responses that have been compiled in different locations and at different times. There are many studies, some involving thousands of questionnaire responses for different countries and different time periods. Researchers have devoted their lives to sifting through these data sets to draw conclusions about the determinants of well-being using sophisticated empirical techniques. Policy conclusions often flow from these investigations, but only after careful analysis of the questionnaire responses.

The basic needs, entitlement or capability analysis is a policy-based approach that gives people freedom to make economic and other social choices by providing goods and services by which to achieve their individual and collective objectives. Not much stress is put on the analytical foundation for this approach, aside from the recognition that certain objectives, including access to food, health and sanitation, education and other public services in adequate measure, are assured.

A third approach, mentioned by Stiglitz *et al.* (2010) in their recent book, which summarizes the report of the Commission on the

Measurement of Economic Performance and Social Progress and which has been developed by economists, is based on concepts developed in the field of welfare economics and requires weighting the nonmonetary dimensions of the quality of life so that people's preferences are taken into account. This approach requires establishing some reference point for each of these dimensions and obtaining people's preferences with respect to the reference. So far, we are not aware of any studies that have developed a concrete application of such welfare measures.

1.1 Extensions and criticisms of the subjective well-being approach

As long as we can rely on responses to questions about well-being as reflecting the true state of the individual's well-being, then we are justified in using these responses and the associated responses to other questions in these surveys to build up an analysis of the determinants of well-being and to use this analysis to measure differences in the quality of life and well-being between individuals and across societies. But what if these responses are somehow biased or otherwise unreliable indicators of well-being and happiness? There are several comments.

Psychologists and economists have been studying the relationship between happiness and behavior for a long time. Daniel Kahneman won a Nobel prize for his work on decision-making and has recently published a book that explores well-being and how people arrive at a decision to answer survey questions. Others have made significant contributions to our understanding of utility and happiness. In this work a number of new discoveries have been made that demonstrate the complexity of decision-making and the difficulties encountered in developing a coherent theory of what makes people happy. Much research has been developed against a background of a rational decision-maker, which economists have embraced in much of their work on choice. We are not concerned here with exploring the full range of behaviors that have been discussed in the economic and psychological literature. Rather, we focus on the relationship between choice, well-being and public policy as they relate to surveys of well-being, and how public policy can be used to increase the level of happiness and well-being generally, and particularly among the poor.

Many behavioral patterns have been discovered which could aid in this endeavor. The first is that people react quickly to changes in circumstances and then return to some predetermined genetic or behavioral equilibrium after a short interlude of adjustment. This equilibrium is sometimes referred to as homeostasis or as a "set point." If this is indeed the case, then attempts to determine what factors lead to a higher level of well-being or happiness would be futile. After a short time the individual returns to the original state of well-being. There has been substantial research on this phenomenon of "adaptation." There is no question that such a process does go on. Accident victims and people with disabilities do recover a degree of well-being after a time, as do winners of the lottery. However, the adaptation is not complete. There is a permanent loss of well-being (see Brickman *et al.* 1978, Diener *et al.* 2003 and Lucas 2007). More generally, "affective forecasting," where individuals try to anticipate the satisfaction of something new in their life (relationship, promotion, vacation, etc.), shows generally that people overestimate the impact of these new anticipated developments on their well-being. This works in both directions: being sick, having an operation, losing your job or getting divorced is not as bad as it seems before the fact, and the same is true of the anticipated satisfaction of a vacation, a new purchase or a new relationship. In this sense, the return to the set point is a way that we all have of smoothing out our emotional reaction to short-term perturbations in our lives (see Diener *et al.* 2006, Gilovich 1991 and Wilson and Gilbert 2003). This does not mean that we can ignore these short-term movements. It does mean that they may not be as momentous as we believed them to be when they originally occurred.

The second observation is that adaptation by the peer group effect has an important impact on well-being. This is a more general, although similar, form of adaptation than the response to unexpected changes in life circumstances discussed above. It refers to how the life circumstances themselves affect our well-being and decision-making processes. This is commonly referred to as "keeping up with the Joneses," and has been observed when looking at the relationship between income and happiness in many different countries. More specifically, it refers to the hedonic process of adaptation to changes in levels of consumption and income over time. We get used to a bigger house, a nicer car, a quieter neighborhood, better proximity to schools, more varied entertainment or exercise facilities. So, no matter how much we accumulate, we are unable to lift our subjective well-being very much. And this adaptive mechanism also relates to how we see ourselves in relation to our neighbors, coworkers and friends. This form of social comparison can be a powerful influence on well-being and happiness. This phenomenon makes itself manifest in the importance of looking at relative income and its impact on happiness.[1] Economists have appreciated the importance of relative income for a long time. In the modern era this began with the relative income hypothesis of Dusenberry (1949) and the habit persistence theory of Friedman (1957). Frey and Stutzer (2002a) note that happiness as a result of higher consumption or income dissipates over time. The hedonic impact needs to be continually reinforced by more income, different goods and new experiences. Frank (1988) and Hirsch (1976) argue that some goods, which Hirsch refers to as positional goods, are demanded only because they are rare or expensive and are out of the reach of most consumers. The income and consumption pattern of the reference group also matters. Clark and Oswald (1994) observe that the higher the income of the reference group, the less satisfied workers are with their own jobs. The importance of social comparisons extends to all levels of society and to industrial as well as developing countries. Graham (2010), in a comparison between Chileans and Hondurans, who are both in the bottom income quintile of the global population distribution in terms of income, shows that, even though the poor Chilean is twice as wealthy as the poor Honduran, the distance of the poor Chilean from the mean Chilean income is far greater than that of the poor Honduran from the mean Honduran income. She speculates that the poor Honduran is happier than the relatively richer Chilean. She also notes that this same phenomenon is true at the higher end of the income distribution. The distance from the mean is much higher for the richer Chilean. So, the further from the mean, the less satisfaction is achieved by those who have less. While we don't want to push this analogy too far – many communist systems have failed despite a narrow income distribution – the importance of relative income can be a powerful determinant of well-being. Carrying the income and well-being analogy a bit further, Kasser and Kanner (2004) found that materialistic individuals experienced lower self-esteem, greater conflict in social situations and less empathy than those who were less driven by materialistic objectives. Csikszentmihalyi *et al.* (2003) found that adolescents in affluent suburbs were less happy than those in middle-class neighborhoods. Similar results are reported by Hagerty (2000) and Putnam (2001); see also discussion in Dowling and Yap (2007), chapter 6. Taken together, these research findings show that, while well-being can be enhanced by moving to higher rungs on the income ladder, there are also potential negative effects on well-being for those who had an inordinately high focus on material success.

There are also distinctions between what is remembered and what is experienced at the time. These differences are explored further by Nobel Prize winner Daniel Kahneman and his colleagues (see Kahneman 2011,

Kahneman and Riis 2005 and Kahneman *et al.* 1997). There are also surveys of daily experience that have been assembled and analyzed by Kahneman and others (see Kahneman 2011, pp. 392–393 and Kahneman and Krueger 2006). Kahneman and Krueger came up with a U index, which measures the amount of time spent in an unpleasant state. By looking at how much time individuals spend in the U state they were able to develop some idea of what percentage of time is spent there. For example, in a sample of 1,000 women in a Midwestern American city the U index was 29 percent for the morning commute, 27 percent for work, 24 percent for child care, 18 percent for housework, 12 percent for socializing and watching TV, and 4 percent for sex. Kahneman *et al.* (2004) describe the index in more detail. Kahneman (2011) suggests that, to increase their level of happiness and well-being, people should spend less time on activities where U is high, which makes a lot of sense but will depend upon schedules and commitments. Exploring these differences is difficult and costly, since moment-to-moment recorded assessments are expensive. Because of this, most researchers have relied upon questionnaire responses to assess subjective well-being as a method for judging happiness. There are also questions over whether subjects are concerned with how they are feeling at the moment when they answer the questionnaire or whether they are offering a reflection on their life experience. Kahneman refers to these as the two facets of memory and experience. He has a powerful insight into how these two interact. In responses to a questionnaire such as the Gallup or World Value Survey, Kahneman argues that the experiencing self has no voice at all. It is the remembered self who is responding. And the remembered self has an interesting screening mechanism, which Kahneman and others have explored in a variety of experiments (see Kahneman 2011, chapter 5). The main conclusion is that the duration of the experience is not important. What matters is the end and the high point or intensity of the experience. Experiences (hand dipped in cold water) which were long and painful were chosen over shorter pain periods because there was less pain at the end (water was warmed a bit). Generally, we remember the high points and the end of an experience. For people in chronic or extreme poverty, it could be that their responses to well-being questions have more to do with how they are feeling at the time and their memory of their worst episode of poverty rather than how long they have been poor. So, from the well-being point of view of those in poverty, a focus on chronic poverty may be misplaced. Greater emphasis should be placed on peak deprivation, such as extreme hunger or pain. The importance of the peak and the unimportance of duration can also help us to understand difference states of well-being. Paraplegics generally recover something close to their previous level of well-being. They get used to their new state. However, people who are chronically depressed or in pain are continually reminded of their "new" state, making it very difficult to return to a happy state. Behavior modification comes from what we learn from the remembered self, and such peak experiences or an uninterrupted continuation of an unhappy state will help policymakers to understand the motivation for individual decision-making and how to make policies more effective. It is impossible to say, without a more elaborate questionnaire which could be used to explore these nuanced distinctions. Such questionnaire designs are generally not part of the protocol for these data-gathering efforts that are widely available around the globe, although recent efforts by the UN, mentioned above, as well as by some European governments are a step in this direction.

Attitudes toward future outcomes are also subject to psychological factors. In subsequent chapters we will explore the impact that better future prospects have on well-being in developing countries. These prospects are reflected in a question about the chances of getting out of poverty. Interestingly enough, positive responses to this question by the poor and the nonpoor resulted in an increase in well-being for both groups. Better opportunities for the poor make everyone feel better!!

Looking at the economics of future choices, the standard model of discounting (see Samuelson 1937) assumes that utility is discounted at a constant rate over time. There are many documented cases where preferences are not consistent at different points in time. It is often observed that discount rates fall over time. Individuals are willing to pay higher rates of interest for immediate satisfaction, and this is one reason why consumers are willing to pay high rates of interest for credit card debt. Placing higher value on the current purchase and a lack of willingness to postpone consumption are consistent with hyperbolic discounting. The poor who literally live from hand to mouth do not have the ability to avoid hyperbolic discounting, and are therefore unable to take advantage of bulk buying or other efficiencies that come with more income.

Attitudes toward risk have been studied extensively. Generally, and for the analysis of well-being and happiness, researchers have concluded that people are more adversely affected by loss than they are by a commensurate gain, that people value what they have more than what others have, that how choices are framed has an impact on choices made, and that the probability of likely and highly unlikely events is weighed differently (see Dowling and Yap 2007, chapter 6 and Kahneman and Tversky 1979, 1982 and 1983). Briefly, the fear of loss prompts risk-averse behavior. The fear of loss is much greater than the attractiveness of gain. However, when subject to persistent fluctuations in income and/or where there is little income to lose, this fear may be less compelling (see Graham 2010, p. 153). Nevertheless, this behavior has been observed in many different situations. Framing choice has an impact on decision-making even if the choices offered have identical probability. A medical procedure framed as a possible positive outcome is chosen over an identical procedure framed as a negative outcome (probability of success is 0.7 in the first instance and probability of failure 0.3 in the second). Highly unlikely events are often seen as more likely than they really are because they are given so much press coverage. This is despite the series of catastrophic natural and terrorist events that occurred between 2000 and 2011. Controlling for the number of miles traveled, the probability of dying in an airplane crash is considerably lower than that of being killed in an automobile accident.

It is also possible that people are not aware of the consequences of their actions, or that they lack the discipline to stay away from unfavorable outcomes. Social engineering approaches, such as those suggested by Richard Thaler and Cass Sunstein (2009), are designed to help people choose what they would choose for themselves if they had the correct information. Addictions of various kinds fall into the second category. Societies have adopted many aspects of social engineering that are designed to guide people to make "good" choices which are designed to increase well-being and happiness. Legal sanctions on the sale of habit-forming drugs and taxes on cigarettes and liquor are common examples. In a more general way, a social engineering approach might be favored by behavioral economists yet rejected by libertarians, who are opposed to any infringement on personal freedom. A middle ground might be referred to as libertarian paternalism. In such a world, agents are given as much salient information as they need to make informed choices. In the process, we should become aware of the errors of judgment that arise from various fallacies or heuristics. Some of these have been discussed, and further reference can be found in Kahneman (2011) and Dowling and Yap (2007), chapters 3–7.

As well as these two approaches, subjective well-being and multidimensional poverty, that have been employed to establish well-being determinants, a more broadly based approach has been suggested by Dolan *et al.* (2006). This includes:

Preference satisfaction – uses income and other resources as a proxy for preferences. This approach assumes that agents are hedonistic and satisfaction is maximized when individuals have more resources.

Objective lists – defines an objective list of conditions from which well-being is regarded as emerging, such as education, freedom and safety.

Functioning accounts – this definition goes beyond physical goods and focuses on a "range of experiences and characteristics of life that are believed to be part and parcel of living well." These could include meaningful life pursuits, engagement and fulfilling social relationships.

Hedonic accounts – these are short-term measurements of states focusing on positive or negative emotional states at different points in time.

Evaluative accounting – these reactions are based on an individual's assessment of how well their life is going. These are judgments about feelings rather than the feelings themselves.

Our emphasis on subjective well-being is most akin to evaluative accounting, but is also related to preference satisfaction, and the United Nations/Oxford MPI approach is closely related to the objective lists approach. In a subsequent article, Thompson and Marks (2008) developed a model in which external conditions, such as income, employment and level of stability of income, interact with personal resources, such as health, and psychological factors, such as self-esteem and resilience, to impact on safety and security and hence on overall well-being. Given data limitations, it is difficult to measure the extent of these interactions in a dynamic behavioral model. In particular, it is challenging to assess psychological factors and needs such as autonomy, competence and relatedness when behavioral models have to depend on survey data based on a standard template of questions.

Taking all these factors into consideration, this book concentrates on responses to questions about life satisfaction as well as detailed data on socioeconomic, economic and political factors that have been suggested as determinants of subjective well-being. Data sets from national and international sources are analyzed, the main two sources being the Gallup organization polls and the World Value Surveys. These will be augmented by other sources and studies as required. The approach is based on estimation of a reduced form equation that incorporates many of the factors suggested by different researchers, including the New Economic Forum (NEF) and MPI approaches as well as the work of many others.

How, then, are we to set up the research agenda, and what is the general methodology for determining the factors that have the most important impact on the well-being of the poor? Rojas (2004) has explored this question by looking at the determinants of subjective well-being for the poor and the nonpoor in Mexico and Puerto Rico. He does this by looking at the lower and upper quartiles (quintiles) of the income distribution and running regressions for the poor and nonpoor groups as a function of a set of explanatory variables comprised of economic variables (job, income, employment status) and socioeconomic variables (marital status, age, gender, friendships, family size and ages, personal and community). He then explores how responses differ between the poor and nonpoor. At the outset he points out that some of those who would be categorized as being poor have higher subjective well-being scores than we would expect, given their low levels of income. Similarly, some individuals with incomes in the nonpoor category have lower values of subjective well-being. The point is that well-being and income are not necessarily correlated. There is more to well-being and happiness than the level of income. We turn to these issues in the next section.

1.2 Determinants of well-being

To begin, we survey the literature on the determinants of well-being and happiness. There are a number of studies reported looking at the determinants of subjective well-being, primarily for industrial countries (Deiner *et al.* 2010, di Tella and MacCulloch 2006, Easterlin 1974 and 2001, Layard 2005, and many others). These and other studies are summarized briefly below. However none of them, aside from the work by Rojas mentioned above, have tried to unravel the specific relationship between poverty and well-being, aside from commenting that poor countries have a generally lower average index score of well-being than richer countries We discuss briefly the main variables that have been suggested and analyzed in previous studies as determinants of well-being and happiness.

1.2.1 Health

Poor health and illness diminish well-being dramatically, as shown in several studies (see Deiner and Seligman 2004, Gerlach and Stephan 1996, Helliwell 2003, Packer *et al.* 1997 and www.worldvaluessurvey. org). Feelings of well-being are positively correlated with longer life expectancy and individuals' view of their own health. This creates a positive feedback loop that can cause an upward bias on the coefficient on the health variable, although there is independent evidence that those that are optimistic about their health have better health outcomes than those with a more pessimistic frame of mind (see Scheier *et al.* 1989). Furthermore, there is evidence that happy people are healthier. They have lower blood pressure and recover faster (see Diener and Seligman 2004, p. 14 and references in Dowling and Yap 2007), and show fewer signs of mental illness (Deiner and Seligman 2002). Depression and other psychiatric illnesses together make up 30 percent of the various causes of disability, compared with 10 percent for alcohol and drug addiction and 15 percent for respiratory illness, cancer and heart disease combined. It is true that studies of identical twins raised apart show that the bulk of interpersonal difference in personality is genetic (see Lykken and Tellegen 1996 and Tellegen *et al.* 1988), and this will reduce the gains from changes in mental attitudes. Nevertheless, there are surely beneficial health outcomes for all, healthy and the sick alike, if policies are pursued that contribute to raising the overall level of happiness. Furthermore, there is additional evidence (Baldacci *et al.* 2010, Barnett and Brooks 2010 and IMF 2010) that higher public expenditure on health increases household consumption rates. Cross-country evidence from econometric studies (see Baldacci *et al.* 2010) suggests that in Asia an increase in public health spending of 1 percent of GDP would result in a more than proportional increase in household consumption. Currently public health spending averages between 1 and 2 percent of GDP (about 2 percent in China, 1 percent in India and Pakistan, 2 percent in Malaysia and 1.5 percent in the Philippines), and consumption is less than 50 percent of GDP, whereas in advanced countries public health spending is between 7 and 8 percent of GDP and household consumption is over 60 percent of GDP (IMF, 2010, p. 41). Instead of saving in anticipation of a possible health emergency, developing countries can devote more of their resources to boosting living standards by increasing consumer spending. This shift would probably help the nonpoor more than the poor. Nevertheless, it would have a trickle-down effect on incomes and living standards of the poor as well. IMF (2010) also notes that the ability of countries to expand public health spending will depend upon current levels as well as projected economic growth. In Asia, public health spending is below the average of all emerging economies, and as a result some countries with higher than average growth potential will be able to increase public health expenditures (China, Indonesia, the Philippines and Thailand). In India and Malaysia, on the other hand, fiscal space is more limited and the environment is less conducive to rapid expansion.

1.2.2   Income

There is a widely held view, based on a number of empirical studies, that as the average income in a country increases its average subjective well-being does not change much after income has reached a threshold level. The seminal article was written by Richard Easterlin (1974) and there have been numerous subsequent contributions confirming this general conclusion (Deiner and Seligman 2004, Frey and Stutzer 2002, Graham 2009 and Inglehart and Klingemann 2000). The US General Social Survey found that in the US average happiness remained virtually unchanged from 1965 to 2005 while GDP per capita rose by over 50 percent. Similar results have been obtained in Japan and Europe (see Blanchflower 2009). However, some recent studies have provided some evidence that, while the strength of income's effect on well-being diminishes, there is still some positive slope to the relationship (see Deaton 2008 and Helliwell 2003 and 2008). A recent article by Dunn *et al.* (2011) argues that many people may think they are increasing their happiness when they get a raise or increase their income. However, this doesn't necessarily result in an uptick in happiness. They suggest several ways to strengthen the relationship between income and happiness, drawing on a variety of research studies. Briefly, they argue that consumers should (1) buy more experiences and fewer material goods, (2) use their money to benefit others rather than themselves by more pro-social spending (gifts for others and charitable donations generally), (3) buy many small pleasures instead of a few big ones, (4) buy less insurance, because we really don't need that much emotional protection from a potential loss, (5) pay now and consume later, since there is an emotional kick from delaying pleasurable consumption, (6) use the imagination in constructive ways so that we can get pleasure from everyday events as well as special occasions, (7) beware of the potential pitfalls of too much comparison shopping, which can overestimate the hedonic impact of goods rather than their extrinsic value, and (8) be aware of the satisfaction that others get from their purchases and mimic the behavior of the appropriate reference group. The authors conclude that money can buy many, if not all, of the things that make them happy. However, because of various misperceptions about what will make them happy, they are not as happy as they could be if they knew how to make more appropriate choices about spending their money. Be that as it may, we are left with individuals' perceptions of how income can make them happier. To determine this we have to look to perceived happiness and well-being and determine how it relates to income. Much of the research relating income to well-being is based on per capita income figures for aggregations of individual households and also on average per capita income for economies as a whole. In more disaggregated work the well-being variables are related to sample data for households which have been collected by survey. The World Value Surveys that constitute the main data source for our study do not generally ask questions about family income, but, rather, about where the family income lies in the income distribution. A conventional way to measure income poverty is to designate families below a poverty line as being poor. From the analysis of poverty statistics where this criterion has been used in Asia, Africa and Latin America, it is evident that the lowest quintile does not cover all the poor families in many countries. In Asia substantially more than 20 percent of the population of Cambodia, India, Lao PDR and Nepal are in poverty, while in Africa Ethiopia, Mali, Nigeria, Rwanda, Tanzania, Zimbabwe and Zambia fall into this category. For these countries it might even be appropriate to use the results for the entire sample to reflect the impact of income on well-being. Alternatively, an expanded quintile definition may be appropriate, say the lowest 40 percent or lowest 60 percent for the really poor countries in Africa and Asia (Mali, Nigeria, Rwanda, Zimbabwe and Zambia at over 50 percent and Cambodia, India, Lao PDR and Nepal at over 35 percent). We explore these issues in Chapters 2, 3 and 4.

1.2.3   Peer group effects

Peer group effects are invoked to explain why average well-being in a richer country (or within a group of richer countries) does not increase over time. People look at other families in their neighborhood and realize that their relative status has not changed. As a result, they are no happier than they were before their income went up. This continues over time as the average income of everyone rises. There are some who rise in the income distribution, and perhaps their well-being increases, but this is offset by those who perceive they now have lower relative income, and so their well-being decreases. Without additional data, it is hard to determine what is actually going on in terms of aggregate behavior (see Frank 1999, Lane 2000 and Layard 2005). Easterlin (2001) approaches this behavior in a slightly different way. He points out three observations from studies of well-being. First, those with higher incomes are happier than those with lower incomes. Second, people expect to be happier in the future than they are now. Finally, happiness tends to be constant over the life cycle. According to Easterlin, these three facts are explained by the fact that human aspirations change in proportion to their income, with the result that people don't become happier over time even as they believe they will (recall the concept of affective forecasting). Despite these findings, researchers have still included income and relative income as pertinent explanatory variables in models of subjective well-being. Furthermore, new research by Kahneman and

Deaton (2010) analyzing US data from a recent set of Gallup surveys (2010) suggests that income and well-being are positively related even at higher levels of income (see Figure 1.1).

1.2.4 Education

There is substantial evidence of a positive effect of education on happiness. Di Tella *et al.* 2003, Hayo and Seifert 2003, Helliwell 2003, Frey and Stutzer 2002a, Castriota 2006 and Checchi 2006 provide evidence and useful summaries. The main reasons relate to the benefits of education on employment, income and feelings of self-worth and prestige. Without education, beginning with the elementary ability to read and write, many jobs are out of reach. Individuals are embarrassed to admit

Figure 1.1 Global estimates of life satisfaction and income

Source: *New York Times* (April 16, 2008).

they do not have these skills. Education is also a signal that the individual is capable, and this alone can increase the probability of employment. Education also results in higher income and earnings (see Becker 1994 and Blanchflower and Oswald 1994). It increases job satisfaction and job mobility, raises chances of promotion, reduces the changes of unemployment and has a positive impact on health (Albert and Davia 2005). The educated can also impart the desire for knowledge in their children, increasing the well-being and happiness of the next generation. At the same time that education has been noted as being a potentially important determinant of well-being by some researchers, it has been ignored by many others, including Layard (2005), perhaps because of its close relationship with income in industrial countries. Deaton (2008) suggests that income and health are more important explanatory variables than education.

1.2.5   Work and employment

There is powerful evidence that unemployment has a strongly deleterious impact on well-being. Being unemployed has both economic and psychological impacts on well-being (see Clark and Oswald 1994, di Tella *et al.* 2001 and Frey and Stutzer 2002a and 2002b). Aside from the loss of income and the negative impact this has on well-being psychologically, unemployment results in a loss in self-esteem and lowers feelings of self-worth. This can lead to depression, desperation and hopelessness, all of which are associated with a precipitous fall in well-being. Work plays an instrumental role in establishing social position and status, which are critical in establishing a good feeling about one's self. Furthermore, the longer the spell of unemployment the greater the potential loss in skills, making it even harder to find a job. Being laid off or fired is different from 'voluntary' withdrawal from the labor force. Retirement or having withdrawn from the labor force has only minimal impact on well-being (see Layard 2005, p. 67). Youth unemployment in industrial countries is also highly correlated with sociopathic behavior such as street gangs and higher crime rates. There is also some evidence that when unemployment increases the rest of society feels worse, a kind of universal sympathetic reaction (see Di Tella *et al.* 2001 and 2003). However, when unemployment is high the impact is not as strong, since there is more widespread misery. The impact of increases in unemployment also seems to be nonlinear with income – those who have lost the most have the most severe displacement in well-being and happiness, and this goes beyond the loss of income. This is true of individuals and also of nations (see Helliwell 2003). There is also greater loss of well-being for men who have lost their job, as opposed to women. Conversely, a stable and satisfying work environment is a key ingredient for a high level of self-esteem, self-worth and well-being. Furthermore, happy workers are more productive. Turnover is lower, as well as absenteeism, and happy workers are more punctual (see Albert and Davia 2005, Deiner and Seligman 2004, Miner *et al.* 2005 and Spector 1997). Having happy employees also results in more satisfied consumers, leading to repeat business and more sales. Paying workers more than the norm of the industry also contributes to higher productivity and profit, according to the efficiency wage argument (Campbell 1993).

1.2.6 Family, community and friends

Rewarding social interactions are key components of well-being (Baumeister and Leary 1995). This entails frequent and pleasant interactions with a few people within the context of a stable, trusting and mutual caring environment (Zak and Knack, 2001). Ongoing relationships, within a framework of mutual concern, provide a stronger and more substantive bond and feeling of belonging than one based on self-interest alone (Clark 1984 and Clark and Mills 1979).

Furthermore, superficial social contacts cannot substitute for deeper and more intimate relationships (Baumeister and Leary 1995 and Weiss 1973 and 1979). Positive social bonds are associated with positive emotions and higher levels of well-being (see McAdams 1985 and Sternberg 1986). Conversely, the loss of friends leads to loneliness and depression (Leary 1990) as well as anxiety (Baumeister and Tice 1990). Other research shows that intimate relationships and close social and family ties are highly valued by respondents and, in the case of sexual intimacy, result in a significantly high increase in well-being (Blanchflower and Oswald 2004, Diener and Seligman 2002 and Kahneman *et al.* 2004). The importance of close relationships with others is illustrated by the importance that marriage has in raising well-being. Helliwell (2003) finds that married people are the happiest, followed by those living as married, widows or widowers, the divorced and the separated. Singles without partners are the least happy. Helliwell finds that the distinction between being married and separated accounts for more of a negative impact on well-being than being unemployed. Following on this train of thought, two specific events that have a strong impact on a person's need to belong are divorce and death. Even though marriages that end up in the divorce court may not have been joyful, divorce nevertheless results in negative feelings and reduced well-being (Price and McKenry 1988 and Weiss 1973). The death of a spouse, child or close friend ranks high on the list of stressful and difficult events and can result in a period of depression (Holmes and Rahe 1967 and Weiss 1973).

1.2.7   Age, gender and marital status

A number of other variables have been introduced to explain changes in levels of well-being. Some of these, such as gender and age, are social and demographic characteristics that are not subject to policy. However, it is still interesting to see their impact on well-being. Age and gender are the two most obvious. Age is interesting in its own right and also as a proxy for variations in age cohort effects on happiness or deterioration in health or other unobserved social factors. The World Values Study Group (1994) found a small positive effect, reflecting either that the happy live longer (Argyle 1999) or that they feel more in control of their environment (Ryff 1995) or have come to grips with life and have fewer expectations (Campbell *et al.* 1976). Other results show that a U-shaped pattern of well-being is observed over the life cycle, with a low point in the mid-forties to early fifties age groups for both men and women (Blanchflower and Oswald 2004, Frey and Stutzer 2002a and 2002b and Helliwell 2005), perhaps reflecting what is commonly referred to as the midlife crisis. However, Alesina *et al.* (2004) and Easterlin (2001) found that happiness increases with age up until between 40 and 45, after which happiness begins to decrease. The explanation given by Easterlin (2001) for differences between his result and the U-shaped pattern reported by Helliwell (2003), Blanchflower and Oswald and others is that these other studies included life cycle variables such as work, marital and economic status. In any event, the impact of age on well-being, while statistically significant, is never large. Likewise gender does not have a significant impact on well-being. Like age, gender plays a very small role in determining levels of well-being. Other things being equal, men are marginally less happy than women (Blanchflower and Oswald 2004, Di Tella *et al.* 2003 and Helliwell 2005), although, as Helliwell (2005) points out, the attempted suicide rate for women is higher. Marriage increases happiness. Those who are married are happier than singles, those cohabiting and those who are divorced or have lost a spouse.

1.2.8   Ethnicity

In most countries there is a strong relationship between well-being and ethnicity, however the latter is defined. Whether it is those of African descent in Latin America and the United States, minorities in the developing countries of Asia and Africa or other ethnic groups in the developing world in general, minorities are discriminated against. This has a distinct and measurable negative impact on well-being (see World Bank (2005) and FIDH (2011)).

1.2.9 Income distribution

According to data compiled by Richard Wilkinson and presented at the Singapore Economic Policy Forum 2010, countries with high levels of social capital, such as health and mental health, education, and social mobility, also had lower levels of income inequality. Poor people gain more from an additional dollar of income, so that, if there is a positive relationship between extra dollars and well-being, then if society wants a life of overall well-being it will redistribute income from the rich to the poor, which will raise overall well-being by reducing income inequality. To put it another way, a poor income distribution will lower well-being while a good income distribution will raise well-being (see Chappel, Forster and Martin 2009). However, in doing this, there is the risk of loss aversion. People weigh loss more heavily than gain, and so the rich might scream more than the poor applaud. In any event, the evidence for rich countries over the past few decades is that income distribution is getting worse, and this has had an adverse impact on well-being in industrial countries. While comparisons of income can have a negative impact on well being particularly if you observe that you are falling behind your peers, it could still have a positive impact on well being if it creates incentives to improve material well-being and prospects for social mobility are readily available. We find this in our empirical results, discussed in the next three chapters. People are particularly upset if the current status or changes in the income distribution are thought to be capricious or unfair.

1.2.10 Social organization and freedom of expression

Variables that measure aspects of these variables have a positive impact on well-being. Helliwell (2003 and 2005) concluded that people with the highest feeling of well-being are those who live in societies where social and political institutions are effective, with a high degree of mutual trust and a low level of corruption. Other studies (Inglehart and Klingmann 2000, Veenhoven 1994 and 2001 and Layard 2005) found that economic freedom was positively related to happiness, particularly in poorer countries. Diener *et al.* (1995) suggested that human rights and individual freedom are also correlated with well-being. Frey and Stutzer (2002) explored the relationship between democracy and indices of subjective well-being in Switzerland. They found a highly significant relationship between life satisfaction and democracy using data from Swiss cantons. Furthermore, they found that a stronger democratic environment raised the well-being coefficients across the board for a wide range of individuals in the entire society, not just a select few. Repressive regimes reduced the sense of well-being (Frey and Stutzer 2000 and Veenhoven 2001). On the other hand, stability in a society is also an important component in establishing a feeling of well-being. Such feelings are reinforced when there is widespread trust in others and institutions. Low happiness scores were reported in the Soviet Union in the unstable years following liberation from Soviet oppression (Inglehard and Klingemann 2000, Layard 2005 and Veenhoven 2001). The lowest happiness scores were recorded in countries that used to be part of the Soviet Union.

It is possible that widespread well-being is necessary for democracy to prosper, as suggested by Inglehart (1990), although high levels of well-being could legitimize democracy and promote its survival, as suggested by Doyle (2002). But democracy is not a necessary condition for happiness. For example, well-being in China (a communist state) is higher than in India (a parliamentary state). This implies a reverse causality between happiness and the establishment of democratic institutions, which tends to bias estimates in models where happiness is posited as a function of the institutional setting.

Another factor to consider in judging the importance of the institutional setting is how the organizational norms of society and the degree of tolerance of departures from these norms impact on well-being. For example, Arrindell *et al.* (1997) and Triandis (1994) argue that in tight societies with rigid enforcement of rules, such as Japan (Iwao 1993), people are more prone to experiencing high levels of anxiety. They fear that they will be sanctioned or even ostracized if they fail to adhere to proper behavioral norms. Ng (2002) argues that East Asian societies have lower happiness coefficients than industrial economies, even though living standards are comparable. He attributes this primarily to the high level of stress and anxiety, which is reinforced by high population density and the pressure to do well in school and at work. Asians also take fewer vacations and have less leisure time, which could also work to reduce well-being if leisure and well-being are correlated (see also Swinyard *et al.* 2001). However, it may be that leisure increases happiness only to the extent that time is spent in pleasurable activities. At the same time, there is no evidence that couch potatoes are less happy than those with fulfilling hobbies. Sex ranks at the top of the list of most pleasurable leisure activities, followed by socializing, eating and relaxing. Watching TV ranks only slightly below exercising. Commuting to and from work is at the bottom of the list (Kahneman *et al.* 2004). See also Blanchflower and Oswald (2004b).

1.2.11 Government policy

Recent work comparing Americans with Europeans suggests that the social context and government policy have important impacts on well-being, particularly for those in the lower levels of the income distribution. For example, Alesina *et al.* (2004) found that, when income in Europe is more unequally distributed, the level of happiness is reduced. This suggests that just observing greater income inequality makes Europeans unhappy. However, in the United States the distribution of income doesn't generally have a significant effect on happiness. Alesina *et al* (2004) suggest two possible explanations: Europeans prefer more equal societies, and social mobility is higher in the United States. Alesina *et al.* (2004) also found evidence in the US that only the rich liberals were unhappy about the level of income inequality, whereas in Europe both the poor and the rich liberals were unhappy about the level of inequality. The results suggest that there is greater popular demand for governments to fight inequality in Europe than in the United States. This could explain why the "dole" is generally less popular as a method for redistributing income in the United States than it is in Europe.

1.2.12 Meditation

The work of several scholars has demonstrated the impact that meditation can have on awareness and happiness, as well as providing beneficial feedback on health and wellness. The work of Kabat-Zinn is notable. He also has developed meditation courses to help relieve the stress of the modern pace of urban life (Kabat-Zinn 1994). He describes many different types of mindfulness: sitting, standing, lying down, walking and as an integral part of daily lives. By presenting meditation to the West as an effective way to cope with the stresses of everyday life, his work promotes peace, inner reflection, compassion and tolerance. There are other meditation traditions that are popular in the West, such as transcendental meditation (TM). The TM technique and TM movement were introduced in India in the mid-1950s by Maharishi Mahesh Yogi and had spread around the world by the 1960s. The TM technique is based on Indian philosophy and was passed on to Maharishi Mahesh Yogi by his Guru, Brahmananda Saraswati. There are a number of other spiritual leaders, such as the Dalai Lama, who teach mindfulness meditation or other techniques based on the teaching of Hinduism, Buddhism and other major religions as well. The difficulty in systematically exploring the impact of meditation on happiness for a large sample is that there is no systematic compilation of the relationship between meditation and well-being for large sample sizes such as the World Value Surveys, Gallup or other results from large sampling organizations. While the benefits of meditation have been mentioned and touted by many, we are not able to test the power of meditation in uplifting well-being in our models.

1.2.13 What can we test from the World Value Survey data bank?

While the previous few paragraphs have indicated a wish list and some previous research results for a number of variables that could potentially have an impact on well-being, we have chosen to stick to one large database which incorporates information from a wide range of developing countries for several waves of sample data. The World Value network of research institutions is global and relies on data collected by research institutes and scholars connected in a network that provides the data free of charge, enabling scholars to undertake research on a variety of pertinent topics. This puts certain restrictions on the variables available and models that can be constructed and tested empirically. In our view, these limitations are far outweighed by the breadth and scope of a single reliable database that has been providing quality information for many years. For more information go to www.worldvaluessurvey.org.

1.3 The model – Phase I

This study is keen to explore the determinants of well-being for the poor and the nonpoor, especially given that the poor and the rich have different roles for work, family and friends and differing extent of access to education and health services, and move in different cultural environment settings. Underemployment and low levels of education and health exist for the former group (that is, the poor). Previous studies have primarily focused on industrialized countries, where health and education were generally accessible to the citizens. For our study, we will primarily investigate three particular regions (Asia, Africa and Latin America economies) with differing extents of economic development and provision of basic services, and explore the determinants of well-being for three specific groups of poor people (i.e. those who are health poor, education poor and income poor). It could help to give further insights if determinants of well-being differ between the poor and the nonpoor. If so, we hope to throw some light on the role of government and how it could aid in improving the well-being of the poor in the society. A one-size-fits-all solution may not meet the needs of the poor, for the solution depends on their particular deprivation, be it of health, education, income or all three. The three poverty groups may require specific targeted assistance with what they find most pressing. Alternatively, those poor people may not find the need for assistance pressing, but it could prove to be critical to their well-being. The study finds that there are many dimensions to improving the well-being of the poor, and more could be explored by government.

Having briefly reviewed the well-being literature, we now turn to setting up a preliminary model that investigates the determinants of well-being for both the poor and the nonpoor of society. We begin with a simple model in which well-being is a function of a few key variables that are available for many developing countries and which have been found to be significant in previous studies. The statistical model is displayed in Equation 1.1. The age variable has been modified to reflect possible nonlinearities observed in several studies, as noted above (Alesina *et al.* 2004 and Easterlin 1974 and 2001). Notice that we have not included unemployment, freedom of expression or social variables. This is primarily because these variables are not available for a wide range of countries. In an expanded version of (1.1) we will add some of these variables as they are available.

$$WB = b0 + b1 \text{ Health} + b2 \text{ Income} + b3 \text{ Education} + b4 \text{ Gender} + b5 \text{ Age} + b6 \text{ Age Squared} + b7 \text{ Marital status} + b8 \text{ Family} + b9 \text{ Friends} \tag{1.1}$$

Variable definitions are displayed in Table 1.1.

Initially we begin by estimating this model for three alternative definitions of well-being/poverty:

(1) income poverty (WB_1), where the poor indicate that they belong to the first two deciles of the income distribution,
(2) education poverty (WB_2), where the poor are defined as those who have completed primary education only and
(3) health poverty (WB_3), where the poor themselves report either poor or very poor health.

These three poverty variables have been defined in the spirit of the MPI index developed by the United Nations Development Programme (UNDP)

Table 1.1   Definitions of selected WVS indicators

Satisfaction with your life (ladder formulation)
a170 Expanded state of happiness
1: Dissatisfied –
10 Satisfied

a008 State of happiness
1: Very happy
2: Quite happy
3: Not happy
4: Not at all happy

a008r Compacted state of happiness
0: Not at all happy, not happy
1: Happy, very happy

State of Health
1: Very good
2: Good
3: Fair
4: Poor
5: Very Poor
1–3: Health Nonpoor
4–5: Health Poor

Income level (country specific) 10th step
1st–2nd income decile: Income Poor
3rd –10th income decile: Income Nonpoor

Highest level of education attained
1: Inadequately completed elementary education
2: Completed (compulsory) elementary education
3: Inadequately completed secondary education
4: Completed secondary education (technical, vocational secondary)
5: Inadequately completed secondary, university preparatory education
6: Completed secondary education: university preparatory
7: Some university without degree
8: University with degree/ higher
1st–2nd levels: Education Poor
3rd–10th levels: Education Nonpoor
Gender
1: Male
2: Female

Age (3 intervals)
1: 15–29
2: 30–49
3: 50 years and above

Important in Life: Work
1: Very important
2: Rather important
3: Not very important
4: Not at all important

Important in Life: Religion
1: Very important
2: Rather important
3: Not very important
4: Not at all important

Most people can be trusted
1: Most people can be trusted
2: Can't be too careful

Confidence in the Civil Services
1: A great deal
2: Quite a lot
3: Not very much
4: None at all

Table 1.1 Continued

Marital Status 0: Not Married 1: Married or Living Together
Family important in life 1: Very important 2: Rather important 3: Not very important 4: Not at all important
Friends important in life 1: Very important 2: Rather important 3: Not very important 4: Not at all important

and Oxford University and discussed above. The poverty measures bridge the gap in measuring poverty which would require establishing some poverty line, however determined, which would put those below the line in poverty and those above the line out of poverty. To avoid this issue, we adopt three simple criteria. For income poverty, those who believe they are in the lowest 20 percent of the income distribution are poor. This probably understates income poverty for poor countries and overstates it for richer countries. However, it does set a relative poverty norm that is the same for all countries.[2] By using completion of elementary education as the dividing line for the education poor, we establish a criterion that can be compared from country to country, even though it ignores the question of comparability of what is learned. It may also understate the level of education poverty in richer countries, where many have completed secondary education or higher. For the health poor, there are no external guidelines or rules such as morbidity or mortality to separate the healthy from those who are not. The health indicator is self-reported from the World Value Survey responses. Those who report they are healthy could be deathly ill and those reporting poor health could be hypochondriacs. There is no way of knowing whether there are errors in variables or not. In our estimation we do not try to guess what the errors are, nor do we try different estimating techniques to account for these possible errors for the health variables, which are potentially larger than the errors in education variables, and also likely in the income estimates, which rely on where respondents think they are in the income distribution. In addition, it is possible that in a richer country someone could consider himself educationally deprived if he did not have a secondary school education. In this case, our uniformly applied standard of an elementary school education would be erroneous, and responses of well-being would have to be interpreted differently. However, without prior knowledge of such attitudes we have elected to proceed as if everyone at all levels of education believed that educational deprivation as having only an elementary school education or less.

We explore what factors influence the well-being of the poor and how these factors differ in scope and magnitude from the factors that impact the well-being of the nonpoor. By examining differences in the structure of behavior between the poor and the rest of the society, more appropriate policies can be formulated to raise the well-being of the poor.

Using a different estimation algorithm, it is possible to categorize the dependent variable as a series of integers. The first is a binary variable defined as 0 for not happy and 1 for happy. This kind of on/off switch has been used in many studies in which choice is binary in nature. In the simple model just described, the happiness variable is zero (0) if the person reports being not happy or not at all happy and one (1) if the person is happy or very happy. Another alternative would be to allow the variable to take four values of 1–4 for not at all happy, not happy, happy and very happy. More nuanced sample measures of overall happiness have been suggested, such as worst possible life (0) to best possible life (10). The questionnaire could include a picture of a ladder (sometimes called the Cantril ladder), where the bottom rung is the worst possible life and the top of the ladder represents the best possible life for you. The respondent is asked the question "Where on the ladder do you feel you personally stand at the present time?" (see Cantril 1965). Notice that this definition does not use the word happiness but, rather, the concept of life satisfaction. Some researchers make a distinction between happiness and life satisfaction. Our view is that these two definitions may contain subtle distinctions for the individual, but we are in no position to understand what they are from any systematic point of view. From a practical point of view they tend to move together. Since the two happiness variables are defined over a different space than the Cantril ladder definition of life satisfaction, there is no one to one correspondence that we can measure. The correlation between the two measures is not particularly high for Asia (see Table 1.2), further reinforcing the decision to use both measures as indices of well-being in the regional analysis that follows in Chapters 2–4. In the United States there is some evidence of a close correlation between happiness and well-being measures. See Easterlin *et al.* (2010).

Table 1.2 Correlations between WVS measure of happiness and life satisfaction

	Correlation between 1–4 and 1–10 measures of happiness and life satisfaction	No. of observations
South Asia	−0.4364	12,904
East NICs	−0.4244	12,475
South East Asia	−0.2325	10,444
Asia	−0.3946	35,823

Alternative definitions for the state of happiness have been suggested in the literature, and these are also reflected in the World Value Survey database. There are three different definitions of well-being that either appear in the World Value Survey questionnaire or are transformed to create a new variable. In the World Value Survey data that are used in this book, two questions are aimed at soliciting the respondent's state of well-being or happiness. The first has four recorded states of happiness, as noted in Table 1.1. In compacted form, there are two options, 0 indicating the respondent is not happy or not at all happy and 1 indicating the respondent is happy or very happy. These categories of happiness or well-being are used in the statistical analysis presented in discussions for Asia, Africa and Latin America that follow in Chapters 2, 3 and 4. The second question is a variation of the Cantril ladder: the respondent is asked "All things considered, how satisfied are you with your life as a whole these days?" The respondent can choose options from 1 to 10, where 1 is "Dissatisfied" and 10 is "Satisfied". Other studies have used variations of these two questions with different possible ranges of responses and quality of response, such as: not at all satisfied to very satisfied; terrible to delighted; completely dissatisfied to neutral to completely satisfied.

See also http://worlddatabaseofhappiness.eur.nl/hap_quer/examples. htm for further discussion of the categories of questions that exist in the literature on the determinants of well-being.

We began by considering the two World Value Survey questions and the compacted form of the four-response question described in Table 1.1 (three versions of well-being) for each of the three regions (Asia, Africa and Latin America) and with different sets of explanatory variables in the probit regressions. There are, therefore, several sets of results to be discussed for each region: one for responses to each form of the well-being/happiness question and another set of responses for the full sample of respondents in each region and also for each of the three poverty groups – the health poor, the education poor and the income poor. The results are discussed in three chapters, each dealing with one of the three geographical regions. We explored extensions of the standard model by adding four social control variables to Equation 1.2. These variables are trust in others; the importance of work in a person's life; confidence in the civil services provided by the government. We also added a variable designed to reflect the importance of religion as a determinant of well-being. We begin with the following expanded form of the model in (1.1) first:

$$
\begin{aligned}
WB = {} & b0 + b1 \text{ Health} + b2 \text{ Income} + b3 \text{ Education} + \\
& b4 \text{ Gender} + b5 \text{ Age} + b6 \text{ Age Squared} + b7 \text{ Marital status} + \\
& b8 \text{ Family} + b9 \text{ Friends} + b10 \text{ Work} + b11 \text{ Religion} + \\
& b12 \text{ Trust} + b13 \text{ Confidence in Civil Services} \quad\quad (1.2)
\end{aligned}
$$

Furthermore, we also explored attitudes toward the opportunity of realizing a better life style in the future and urban-rural difference in subjective well-being. There are some variables, such as peer group effects and adaptation as well as ethnicity and the role of income distribution, which were not included in the estimated models described in the next three chapters. The nature of the data set constrains us from considering other possible determinants of well-being, such as employment or wages or income inequality, and their impact on happiness and well-being. Furthermore, the variables for work and confidence in the civil service are not detailed enough to capture all the possible nuances that respondents could attribute to these variables. What level of the provision of civil services is being considered? Is it local, regional or national? Is it the police, the military or the village elders? What aspects of the work environment do the respondents consider? Is it the skill required, safety factors, the variety of challenges in the work environment, congeniality of relationships with colleagues or other factors that determine whether work has an uplifting impact on well-being? Without more information, it may be that the work variable's place in the constellation of factors having an impact on well-being is not strong enough to have uniformly strong impact on respondents as an important factor in determining well-being.

To summarize and explain the results, we organize the probit regressions according to independent variable. In addition, the variables designated as friends and family take on different meaning in different countries. As distinct from other questions that pertain more easily to each individual's demographic status, such as marital status, gender or age, these variables are subject to individual interpretation and valuation. A table for each independent variable is presented with results for each country as a row and the coefficients for each of the different fitted models in a separate column. For example, the results for the full sample and each of the three poverty groups are reported for the central ladder configuration (1 to 10) and are displayed in the first four columns of the table. The next four columns present the results for the 1–4 ranking of well-being. The final four columns look at the binary form of the well-being/happiness variable. In each chapter we begin with the model described in Equation 1.2 above. In subsequent discussion, social variables are added to the model. Before reviewing the probit results, we first introduce each region with a discussion of the general indicators of health, income and education in the region.

A note of caution is needed in the interpretation of the coefficients for health, income and education for the three poverty groups. For the health poor, the health variable is constrained since we are dealing only with those who report they are in poor or very poor health. Similarly, income for the income poor is constrained to the lowest two deciles of the income distribution and education is constrained to the completion of elementary school. These constraints hold only for each of the individual poverty groups. They don't hold for the other two poverty groups. The education poor could have any value for the health variable or the income variable, the health poor could have any value for education or income, and so on. For example, if the health poor variable has a significant coefficient this can be interpreted as implying that those in the poorest health would like to be healthier, even if this means moving up from very poor to poor health. What could happen is that the constrained poverty category is unlikely to have a lot of significant coefficients.

1.3.1 A word about the law of large numbers

Economists who are used to working with time series data on a quarterly or yearly basis are comfortable with sample sizes of 100 to 200 observations, or even fewer, and a few independent variables. In the absence of multicollinearity and using modern statistical time series techniques, the results can lead to strong conclusions about the significance of the explanatory variables. When working with cross section data, economists who are used to time series analysis are overjoyed to see sample sizes that are typically ten times as large or more as they were used to seeing with time series data. Of course, the coefficient of determination is much lower for the typical cross section model, and much more of the variation in the dependent variable is unexplained. That seems to be the nature of these cross section studies. In the work that we undertake in the next three chapters we have access to thousands of observations for Africa, Asia and Latin America – over 120,000 observations all told. However, through a process of disaggregation and analysis of over 30 countries and several different poverty groups and three measures of well-being, there are some cases where sample sizes are as small as 100 observations or fewer. To explore the potential richness of experience for small countries and poverty groups, we have sacrificed some of the power of having the law of large numbers on our side. We believe that the sacrifice is worth it. The results with smaller sample sizes may not be as statistically significant as more aggregated measures. There are, however, some very useful conclusions that can be drawn from a more micro-oriented approach stressing individual country experiences. However, we also report more aggregative results for each of the regions, which rely on grouping of countries together in each of the three larger continental regions.

2
Analysis for Asia

We begin this chapter with a general discussion of indicators of health, income and education for Asian economies. Looking at the last two decades, health indicators for the Asian economies are displayed in Table 2.1. Life expectancy, infant mortality and under-5 infant mortality have decreased in Asia over the last 18 years. The rate of improvement in these indicators has varied widely. In Bangladesh and Nepal, where life expectancy was only 54 years in 1990, there was an improvement of 12 and 13 years respectively by 2008. For other countries where health indicators were already higher, improvement has been more modest. Still, by 2008 several countries in Southeast and East Asia had a life expectancy of over 70. In South Asia and parts of the Mekong subregion the figures were still in the 60s. Infant mortality and under-5 mortality also fell, sometimes dramatically, over the sample period. Most notable was progress in Bangladesh and Lao PDR, where both infant mortality rates were over 100 per 1,000 in 1990. India also made good progress, while Pakistan, where infant mortality was also high, made less progress. The more prosperous countries also improved their performance, although from a lower base. The incidence of TB showed little change, suggesting a lack of monitoring as well as lack of awareness by public health officials. The access to improved water increased (an indication of reduced incidence of intestinal problems), suggesting a significant downward trend in several countries, particularly in the Mekong region. With the exception of Sri Lanka and Vietnam, access to better sanitation facilities in South Asia and the Mekong region is still lagging badly behind other countries in the Asian region. Comparisons with an earlier period are not available for dietary deficiencies such as the incidence of underweight, stunting and anemia. With the exception of Sri Lanka, the number of children suffering from these three

33

Table 2.1 Health indicators for Asia

Country	Life expectancy 1990	Life expectancy 2008	Infant mortality 1990	Infant mortality 2008	Under-5 mortality 1990	Under-5 mortality 2008
Bangladesh	54	66	103	43	149	54
Cambodia	55	61	85	69	117	90
China	68	73	37	18	46	21
India	58	64	83	52	116	69
Indonesia	62	71	56	31	86	41
Lao PDR	54	65	108	48	157	61
Malaysia	70	74	16	6	18	6
Nepal	54	67	99	41	142	51
Pakistan	61	67	101	72	130	89
Philippines	65	72	42	26	61	32
Sri Lanka	70	74	23	13	29	15
Thailand	69	69	26	13	32	14
Vietnam	65	74	39	12	56	14
East Asia	67	72	42	23	55	29
South Asia	58	64	89	58	125	76
Korea	71	80	8	5	9	5
Singapore	74	81	6	2	7	3

Source: World Development Indicators.

Table 2.1 continued Health indicators for Asia

Country	Access to improved water 1990	Access to improved water 2006	Access to improved sanitation 1990	Access to improved sanitation 2006	Health spending as % of GDP 2008	Health spending per capita $PPP 2008
Bangladesh	78	80	26	36	3.4	42
Cambodia	19	65	8	28	5.9	108
China	67	88	48	65	4.3	233
India	71	89	14	28	4.1	109
Indonesia	72	80	51	52	2.2	81
Lao PDR		60		48	4	84
Malaysia	98	99		94	4.4	604
Nepal	72	89	9	27	5.1	55
Pakistan	86	90	33	58	2.7	64
Philippines	83	93	58	78	3.9	130
Sri Lanka	67	82	71	86	4.2	179
Thailand	95	98	78	96	3.7	286
Vietnam	52	92	29	65	7.1	183
East Asia	68	87	48	66	4.1	208
South Asia	73	87	18	33	4	98
Korea		100			6.3	1,362
Singapore	100	100	100	0	3.1	1,643

Source: World Development Indicators.
Note: GDP, Gross Domestic Product; PPP, purchasing power parity.

Table 2.1   continued Health indicators for Asia

Country	Incidence of TB 2000	Incidence of TB 2008	Underweight	Stunting	Anemia under 5
Bangladesh	225	225	41.3	43.2	47
Cambodia	530	490	28.8	39.5	62
China	110	97	6.8	21.8	20
India	168	168	43.5	47.9	74
Indonesia	189	189	19.6	40.1	44
Lao PDR	160	150	31.6	47.6	48
Malaysia	110	102			32
Nepal	163	163	38.8	49.3	48
Pakistan	231	231	31.3	41.5	51
Philippines	330	285	26.2	27.9	36
Sri Lanka	66	66	21.1	17.3	30
Thailand	137	137	7	15.7	
Vietnam	200	200	20.2	35.8	34
East Asia		138			
South Asia		180			
Korea		88			
Singapore		39	3.3	4.4	19

deficiencies is still quite high in South Asia and the Mekong, where over a third of children are stunted, over 30 percent are undernourished and an even larger proportion are anemic. Poor performance in many areas of public health is evidence of the low priority that government spending on health has in the spending programs of many countries in the region. Most of South Asia and the Mekong spend around $100 or less per resident on health sector programs. In Southeast Asia spending is higher. However, Indonesia spends much less than its counterparts in Southeast Asia: $81 per capita (2.2 percent of GDP) compared with $286 (3.7 percent) and $604 (5.1 percent) for Thailand and Malaysia respectively.

If we consider the high-income countries in Asia, statistics are readily available for Korea and Singapore in the World Development Database. The health indicators for these two countries are displayed in the last two rows of Table 2.1. Life expectancy is longer and infant mortality is much lower than in most of the poorer countries, and also lower than most of the more prosperous countries in Southeast Asia, with the exception of Malaysia. Indicators of anemia and stunting, but not TB, are also much lower than most of the other countries in South Asia and also in Southeast Asia. Per capita spending on health is also significantly higher than in the poorer countries in the region.

Turning to education, summary statistics are presented in Table 2.2. Since the bulk of the poor would have either no education or only primary abilities to read and write as well as elementary math skills, stress is put on literacy and primary school completion rates rather than secondary and tertiary rates. We put more emphasis on recent figures since complete coverage for earlier years is not available. With the exception of Bangladesh and Pakistan, elementary completion rates are now 75 percent or higher. This is a significant improvement, given the evidence available from earlier years, and is further evidenced by higher youth literacy rates. Male adult literacy is low and female literacy (not reported) is even lower, particularly in Bangladesh, Nepal, Pakistan and India. The demand for education is strong in most countries, as reflected by the much higher rates of youth literacy *vis-à-vis* general educational attainment as well as improvements in youth education recorded since 1990. Enrolment rates have also increased at the primary level, although Bangladesh and Pakistan still lag. However, public spending per student has not increased at the primary level, suggesting that there is a possible deterioration in the quality of primary education as budget resources have not kept pace with increased enrolment. For Korea and Singapore, the two richer countries in the region, educational data are somewhat more limited than for the other countries in the region. Spending per capita on both primary and secondary education is higher than the average for the other countries, but not exceedingly out of line by comparison with Southeast and South Asia.

Considering income and poverty, the poverty levels in the 1990s and more recently are displayed in Table 2.3 along with income shares of the lowest 10 percent, the lowest 20 percent and the Gini coefficient of inequality. The results for the different measures of income inequality and poverty are not always consistent. Generally the Gini coefficient has decreased over time, suggesting an increase in income equality. However, in China, India and Indonesia, the three largest and two of the fastest-growing economies in the region and the world, the Gini coefficient has increased, resulting in a deterioration in income distribution and a greater spread between rich and poor. In the case of China, the deterioration in income distribution has been quite rapid, going from

Table 2.2 Education indicators for Asian economies

	Primary completion rate 1991	Primary completion rate 2008	Male youth literacy 1990	Male youth literacy 2005–8	Male adult literacy
Bangladesh	na	58	52	73	60
Cambodia	na	79		90	86
China	107	99	97	99	97
India	63	94	74	88	75
Indonesia	93	108	97	97	95
Lao PDR	45	75		89	82
Malaysia	91	96	96	98	94
Nepal	50	75	68	86	71
Pakistan		60		79	67
Philippines	88	92	96	94	93
Sri Lanka	101	105		97	92
Thailand	na	na		98	96
Vietnam	89	na	94	97	95
East Asia		100	97	98	96
South Asia		79	71	86	73
Korea	98	99	na	na	na
Singapore	na	na	na	na	na

Source: World Development Indicators.

a low in the region of 29 in 1980 to one of the highest at 41.5 around 20 years later. With the exception of Thailand and Pakistan, poverty rates have fallen. The rate of decline in poverty in China has been dramatic, although this is not adequately reflected in the data reported in Table 2.3. The income shares of the lowest 10 percent and the lowest 20 percent of the income distribution are generally, although not always, consistent with the size of the Gini coefficient. Bangladesh has the lowest Gini coefficient and also the highest income share of the bottom decile and lowest quintile. Bangladesh has also been able to lower poverty by nearly 9 percent between 2000 and 2005. Lao PDR also has a high share of the lowest income classes and has been able to reduce poverty between 1998 and 2003. India has a large share of income in

Table 2.2 continued Education indicators for Asian economies

	Primary net enrollment rate 1991	Primary net enrollment rate 2008	Public spending per student elementary 1999	Public spending per student elementary 2008	Public spending per student secondary 1999	Public spending per student secondary 2008
Bangladesh	70	88		10.5	13.6	14.3
Cambodia	72	89	5.9		11.5	
China					11.6	
India		90	11.9	8.9	24.7	16.2
Indonesia	98	95				
Lao PDR	60	82	2.2	10.8	4.5	
Malaysia	93	97	12.5		21.7	
Nepal			9.1	15.1	13.1	11.2
Pakistan	33	66				
Philippines	96	90	12.8		11	
Sri Lanka	83	100				
Thailand			17.8		15.9	
Vietnam	89			19.7		17.2
East Asia	96					
South Asia	68	88			13.6	
Korea	99	99	18.4	17.2	15.7	22.2
Singapore	na	na	na	na	11.2	16.6

Source: World Development Indicators.

the lowest quintile, but its progress in poverty reduction has been slow and its Gini coefficient has gone up. Other countries known for favorable pro-poor policies, such as Sri Lanka and Vietnam, have favorable relative shares of the lowest 20 percent but not for the lowest 10 percent. The Gini coefficient for Sri Lanka has decreased, although from a relatively high 47 in 1963. Furthermore, the reliability of poverty and income distribution is often questionable and perhaps investigated more intensively than other measures of poverty, such as school enrolment. For the two richest countries in the region (Korea and Singapore), the income shares and Gini ratios suggest that income distribution is relatively uneven. The share of the lowest 10 percent of the population is lower than for many other countries in the region, particularly the lowest 10 percent in Singapore. The Gini coefficient in Singapore is also over 40, comparable to the ratio for Cambodia, China, Sri Lanka and Thailand. Poverty figures are not available for Singapore from World Development Indicators. Other sources suggest that poverty has fallen substantially in both Korea and Singapore. Thus, on the surface it doesn't seem that a weak and unexceptional income distribution has held back their development. Human development, as registered by the HDI of the United Nations, has improved considerably in many countries, particularly the performance of lower and middle-income countries. All but a few countries were able to achieve average growth in the HDI index of over 1 percent per annum for the 30-year period from 1980 to 2010. Only Sri Lanka, the Philippines and Hong Kong fell short of 1 percent growth. The HDI is a measure that supplements income growth with education and health indicators. As such, it gives a more robust indication of progress in economic and social development. It is evident that HDI rankings and changes in these rankings are only loosely related to changes in income per capita. This reinforces the arguments made earlier that several measures of poverty need to be examined to gain a more thorough understanding of deprivation beyond the income dimension.

Summary

Poverty indicators in Asia have generally improved in step with the region's ability to grow rapidly and, in many instances, much more rapidly than other developing regions. Different measures of poverty have generally reflected this growth performance. However, progress has not been uniform. South Asia and the Mekong region have been slower to address poverty concerns than the more developed countries of East and Southeast Asia. There are, however, some encouraging surprises.

Table 2.3 Poverty, income distribution and Human Development Index (HDI)

Country	Income share of lowest 10%	Income share of lowest 20%	Early Gini	Later Gini after 2000	Poverty rate National early	Poverty rate National later	HDI rank 2010	Average annual % change in HDI between 1980 and 2010	Poverty rate ADB
Bangladesh	4.3	9.4	37 (1963)	31	48.9 (2000)	40.0 (2005)	129	1.99	
Cambodia	2.7	6.5		44.2	34.7 (2004)	30.1 (2007)	124	na	40.2
China	2.4	5.7	29 (1980)	41.5	3.5 (2000) rural	2.5 (2005) rural	89	1.96	15.9
India	3.6	8.1	33 (1960)	36.8	36 (1993)	28.6 (2000)	119	1.61	41.6
Indonesia	3.1	7.4	34 (1976)	37.6	17.6 (1996)	16.7 (2004)	108	1.43	21.4
Lao PDR	3.7	8.5		32.6	38.6 (1998)	33.5 (2003)	122	1.69*	35.7
Malaysia	2.6	6.4	51 (1970)	37.9	15.5 (1989)		57	1.06	15.5
Nepal	2.7	6.1	55 (1977)	47.3	41.8 (1996)	30.9 (2004)	138	2.37	54.7
Pakistan	3.9	9.1	38 (1964)	31.2	28.6 (1993)	32.6 (1999)	125	1.52	22.6

(Continued)

Table 2.3 Continued

Country	Income share of lowest 10%	Income share of lowest 20%	Early Gini	Later Gini after 2000	Poverty rate National early	Poverty rate National later	HDI rank 2010	Average annual % change in HDI between 1980 and 2010	Poverty rate ADB
Philippines	2.4	5.6	52 (1961)	44	32.1 (1994)	25.1 (1997)	97	0.66	22.6
Sri Lanka	2.9	6.8	47 (1963)	41.2	25 (1996)	22.7 (2002)	91	0.82	10.3
Thailand	2.6	6.1	44 (1969)	42.5	9.8 (1994)	13.6 (1998)	92	1.01	
Vietnam	3.1	7.1		37.8	37.4 (1998)	28.9 (2002)	113	1.70*	22.8
East Asia								1.73	
South Asia								1.65	
Korea	2.9	7.9		31.6			27	1.18	
Singapore	1.9	5		42.5			12	na	

* 1990–2010.

Source: World Development Indicators, Bauer et al. (2008) for poverty estimates from Asian Development Bank (ADB) and Hasan, and Quibria (2002) for early Gini.

Bangladesh has made impressive strides in improving its income distribution and reducing poverty. India has made slower progress, despite a recent acceleration in economic growth. China has grown rapidly, although its poverty record is not adequately reflected in the World Development Indicators database. Furthermore, it has suffered a significant deterioration in income distribution, according to the Gini coefficients in Table 2.3. Indonesia has also had a disappointing performance in the past decade or so following the Asian financial crisis. The Gini coefficient has increased and poverty levels have remained constant while health spending, particularly access to sanitation, has stagnated. This is not to say that Indonesia has not accomplished a lot in raising educational achievement and nearly universal literacy. Progress in Pakistan, Cambodia and Laos has been slower than might have been expected. Poverty has increased in Pakistan and has fallen slowly in Lao PDR and Cambodia. Health and educational completion in primary schools and various health indicators remain low, although Cambodia has made significant strides in improving access to clean water and adequate sanitation. Nevertheless, Vietnam remains far ahead of the other Mekong countries in the ability to raise educational and health outcomes.

2.1 Well-being in Asia

The World Value Survey data base assembles data from personal interviews with thousands of interview subjects worldwide. As an introduction to this data base we consider the average well-being statistics for the Asian economies including the five waves of the survey, which were conducted between 1990 and 2010. Not every country was sampled in each wave. These summary statistics are reported for the Asian economies in Table 2.4. In terms of well-being measured on a scale of 1 to 4 where 1 is registered as very happy, Thailand records the highest happiness score of 1.676 followed in descending order by Malaysia and Singapore (tie), Philippines, Vietnam, Indonesia, Taiwan, India, Pakistan, Bangladesh, China, Korea and Hong Kong. With the exception of Hong Kong, Korea and Taiwan, these rankings roughly follow the level of development and per capita income of the countries in Asia. The richer countries have the highest level of average well-being and the poorer countries the lower levels of average well-being. The rankings are often quite close and two of the lowest scores are that of Bangladesh and China while Malaysia and Singapore are tied. It is notable that China has one of the lowest well-being score despite its per capita income being higher than India and Pakistan. As noted above,

Table 2.4 Average well-being from World Value Surveys of selected Asian economies

Country	Well-being (scale of 1–4)	Life satisfaction (scale of 1–10)	Wave(s)	Wave 2 Average happiness	Wave 2 Life Satisfaction	Wave 2 Obs	Wave 3 Average happiness	Wave 3 Life Satisfaction	Wave 3 Obs	Wave 4 Average happiness	Wave 4 Life Satisfaction	Wave 4 Obs	Wave 5 Average happiness	Wave 5 Life Satisfaction	Wave 5 Obs	Total no. of obs.
Bangladesh	2.041	6.092	3–4			na	1.986	6.406	1,525	2.098	5.775	1,500			na	3,025
China	2.042	6.833	2–5	2.054	7.292	1,000	1.948	6.828	1,500	2.132	6.525	1,000	2.061	6.762	2,015	5,515
India	2.017	6.077	2–5	2.073	6.702	2,500	1.956	6.532	2,040	2.047	5.142	2,002	1.981	5.793	2,001	8,543
Indonesia	1.826	6.925	4–5			na			na	1.847	6.958	1,004	1.816	6.909	2,015	3,019
Malaysia	1.689	6.839	5			na			na			na	1.689	6.839	1,201	1,201
Pakistan	2.016	4.851	3–4			na	1.97	na	733	2.062	4.851	2,000			na	2,733
Philippines	1.708	6.746	3–4			na	1.682	6.84	1,200	1.733	6.652	1,200			na	2,400
Thailand	1.676	7.213	Wave 5			na			na			na	1.676	7.213	1,534	1,534
Vietnam	1.748	6.863	4–5			na			na	1.59	6.517	1,000	1.853	7.094	1,495	2,495
Hong Kong	2.096	6.408	5			na			na			na	2.096	6.408	1,252	1,252
Singapore	1.689	7.235	4			na			na	1.689	7.235	1512			na	1,512
Korea	2.043	6.433	2–5	2.138	6.686	1,251	2.001	na	1,252	2.044	6.214	1,200	1.991	6.387	1,200	3,652
Taiwan	1.892	6.623	3 and 5			na	1.805	6.56	780			na	1.947	6.662	1,227	2,007
Average	1.883	6.549		2.088	6.893		1.907	6.633		1.916	6.208		1.901	6.674		

Note: Wave 2: 1989–93, Wave 3: 1994–9, Wave 4: 1999–2004 and Wave 5: 2005–7.

Korea and Hong Kong's well-being are quite low given its high per capita income. Another question asked respondents to rank their life satisfaction on a scale from 1 to 10, the higher the score the greater the satisfaction. These results are also reported in Table 2.4. The rankings for this question were somewhat different, but still similar, to the 1 to 4 rankings. Singapore, Thailand, Indonesia and Vietnam were the highest followed by Malaysia and China. Bangladesh India and Pakistan ranked at the bottom. These rankings more consistently rate South Asian countries lower than the 1–4 rankings. Korea and Hong Kong are still ranked lower than we would expect given their standards of living. Other things equal perhaps the pressure to succeed and make money is so strong it has a negative impact on well-being. Somehow Singapore has been able to avoid this kind of pressure.

Over time there is no consistent pattern of changes in well-being for individual countries. In China, India and Korea, where there are averages of 1 to 4 well being scores reported for four waves, well being goes up, then down then up again. In Taiwan and Bangladesh well-being went down from wave 3 to 5 and went up in Indonesia and Pakistan.

A separate analysis of well-being has been conducted by the Gallup organization. In 2006, Gallup conducted a World Poll using samples of people in each of 132 countries. With the exceptions of a few countries (Angola, Cuba, and Myanmar) where the samples are urban, the samples are nationally representative of people aged 15 and older. The questionnaire covered many aspects of well-being, including an overall measure of life satisfaction, as well as several aspects of health and economic status. Because the survey used the same questionnaire in all countries, it provides an opportunity to make cross-country comparisons. No previous poll has provided national samples of so many countries, particularly poor countries and has been reported in the *Human Development Report* of 2010 and in Table 2.5 (see also Angus Deaton 2008 and http://www.gallupworldpoll.com/content/24046/About.aspx for more details of the survey and evidence on the level of well-being and health around the world.) Deaton points out that the World Value Surveys were prone to sample more literate and urban dwellers than the poor and so there could have been an urban and wealth bias in these surveys. He also notes that there is good reason to believe that the two surveys yield essentially similar conclusions about the nature and differences in well-being around the world.

In the Gallup analysis, there was generally widespread agreement that people were satisfied with their health status – over 70 percent in all countries and over 80 percent in 7 countries (see Table 2.5).

Table 2.5 Well-being, job and life satisfaction from Human Development Report

Country	Life Satisfaction		Purposeful life		Treated with respect		Social support network		Satisfied with job	Satisfied with living standard	Satisfied with health
	Total	Female	Total	Female	Total	Female	Total	Female			
Bangladesh	5.3	5.4	94	93	87	86	53	51	76	63	73
Cambodia											
China	6.4	na	na	na	87	86	79	78	78	60	80
India	5.5	5.4	91	90	72	79	66	65	74	61	85
Indonesia	5.7	5.6	95	95	92	94	78	78	63	62	83
Lao PDR	6.2	6.3	98	98	43	42	81	83	91	80	89
Malaysia	6.6	6.6	95	94	88	86	79	79	86	68	87
Nepal	5.3	5.5	93	93	48	44	80	80	80	51	84
Pakistan	5.4	5.5	72	73	89	81	44	50	77	53	75
Philippines	5.5	5.5	96	96	94	95	77	76	83	68	77
Sri Lanka	4.7	4.8	91	91	76	75	82	84	85	58	77
Thailand	6.3	6.3	95	94	75	80	82	87	91	63	79
Vietnam	5.4	5.4	98	98	98	92	79	77	72	59	79
East Asia											
South Asia											
Korea	6.3	6.5	80	81	63	67	79	82	68	71	71
Singapore	6.7	6.7	90	89	81	81	84	83	88	77	95
Japan	6.8	7	76	77	60	65	89	92	73	64	68

Source: United Nations, *Human Development Report* 2011 raw data from Gallup Organization.

There seems to be little correlation with living standards as measured by per capita income and satisfaction with health. The results of the Gallup poll responses will be compared with similar questions in the World Value Surveys later in this chapter. Several previous studies have explored nonlinearities in the health and age variables, arguing that there could be a slump in well-being in middle age and that well-being and health could be nonlinearly related in old age. For now we are entering both variables in a linear fashion. This assumption will be relaxed in a more expanded model in the next section.

The generally positive, yet not always strong, relationship between income and well-being has also been noted by a number of researchers (see Figure 1.1, and also Dowling and Yap 2009, chapter 6, Inglehart and Klingmann 2000 and Frey and Stutzer 2002a), particularly at lower levels of income. At the higher end of the income scale the relationship is not as strong and many studies have noted that income changes have very little, if any, impact on well-being. However, recent results reported by Deaton (2008) using the Gallup data do find a positive relationship between average life satisfaction and the logarithm of per capita income for 123 countries in 2008. Furthermore, Easterlin (2001) has noted that much of the relationship between income and well-being remains unexplained, as the simple correlation between these two variables is only 0.20 for a sample of industrial and developing countries.

The gender comparisons from the Gallup analysis confirm results from other studies that report women are happier than men. In seven countries in Asia (including Japan) female life satisfaction was higher, and in three others they were the same. Men were more satisfied on average in only two countries. These Gallup surveys also report responses to a variety of questions about satisfaction with job, with living standards and with health. Questions were also asked about whether respondents felt they were living a purposeful life, whether they were being treated with respect and whether they had a helpful support network. Generally the responses to job and living standard questions were correlated with life satisfaction. Satisfaction with living standards was ranked lower than job satisfaction by as much as 20 to 30 percent. Singapore reported the highest life satisfaction average of 6.7 for both males and females. Malaysia, Korea and China followed closely behind. Lao PDR presents a seemingly interesting contradiction. It ranked highest in both job and living standard satisfaction and also had a relatively high life satisfaction report, even though it is one of the poorest economies in Asia. It also ranked below India on the HDI, ranking 122 out of 169 countries in 2010. Turning to job and living standards, responses are broadly ranked in generally the same order as life satisfaction. Lao PDR and Thailand at were at the top of the job satisfaction ranking, followed by Singapore and Sri Lanka. Living standards were ranked lower. Over 70 percent of respondents were satisfied with living standards in only three countries – Lao PDR, Korea and Singapore.

We compared the average well-being values from the Human Development Report (obtained from the Gallup organization) and the well-being values from the world value surveys, where the options are 1 to 10 – lowest to highest well-being. These comparisons are displayed for the comparable Asian economies in Table 2.4.

The average Gallup well-being values are lower than the World Value Survey values.[1] This is reflected in the correlation and simple regression relationship between the two variables, where the coefficient on the Gallup values is statistically significant at a relatively low level (refer to Figure 2.1).

Interesting additional insights to the Cantril ladder ranking of well-being in Asia are evident from histograms for the World Value Survey summaries of well-being. Each Asian country is aggregated over all available wages of the survey. These are displayed in Figure 2.3.

It is somewhat surprising that there is no apparent overall consistency among the various histograms. As a result, summary statistics of central tendency and variance do not fully capture the richness of the variation in how respondents' well-being varies across countries. We can see from Table 2.4 which countries reported the highest average level of well-being, and yet there is still much to be gained by looking at the country histograms. Pakistan, Bangladesh and India have the lowest

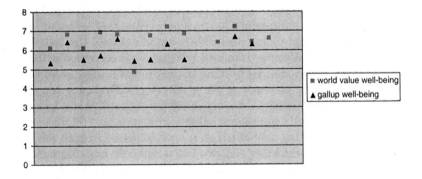

Figure 2.1   Well-being data from WVS and Gallup

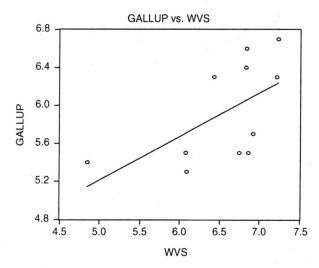

Figure 2.2 Correlation between Gallup and WVS well-being data for Asian countries

average well-being of the nine countries surveyed. The median is 5, the value most reported by around 30 percent of Indian and Bangladeshi respondents and over 40 percent of Pakistani respondents. The median in other countries was usually 7 or 8, but was as low as 6 in Hong Kong and Vietnam.

What distinguishes the South Asian data is the lack of strong reporting of responses above 6. Looking at the lower levels of satisfaction for the various countries, there were very few respondents in any country reporting well-being less than 4. Therefore, looking at regression results of probit analysis, it is probably more appropriate to focus on responses of 6 or above, except perhaps in the case of South Asia where 5 is the median. The Philippines is an interesting bimodal case, where close to 20 percent of respondents reported well-being of 5 and 10 respectively! It is extremely important to recognize the danger of placing too much reliance on results that rely on aggregation measures that group all Asian countries together in making policy recommendations for countries with widely varying levels of reported well-being as well as levels of poverty, average income, health and educational attainment. While the averages include a wide range of variation, there are certain regularities. Eight countries show positively skewed unimodal distributions (Taiwan, Malaysia, Thailand, Singapore, India, Bangladesh, Pakistan and Korea), while four others have bimodal distributions (Philippines, China, Indonesia and Vietnam).

The importance of disaggregation

Most of the studies relating happiness to a set of explanatory variables have focused on large data sets for individual industrial countries, such as the US, the UK, Canada or Germany, or for Europe. There have been few studies of developing countries, and those that have analyzed data for these groups of countries have tended to aggregate over a number of different countries. In this study we begin by considering individual countries in Asia. For each country we consider three different measures for well-being and poverty, as discussed in Chapter 1. We analyze both the responses of all the Asian countries to the values of the explanatory variables and the different country responses to the set of all explanatory variables. By cutting across both country and variable dimensions, we hope to get a more detailed and accurate picture of what factors are important in uplifting well-being for individual Asian countries.

This disaggregation protocol does gain specificity for individual countries while pointing out differences within the Asia region; however, there is also a price to be paid. There are fewer observations for each country to work with. Furthermore, when fitting the full statistical model more observations are lost. The full sample size picture is displayed in Table 2.6.

Who is poor?

Before looking at the probit results for Asia, we summarize the three different kinds of poverty for the Asian economies. We have designated three poverty groups:

(1) Those who have limited education, i.e. respondents who reported that they either had no education or have completed only elementary education as reported on the questionnaire.
(2) Those who have limited income, i.e. respondents who reported they are in the bottom quintile (20 percent) of the income distribution as reported on the questionnaire.
(3) Those who report being in poor health, i.e. respondents who reported they were in poor or very poor health on the questionnaire.

Note that all designations of poverty are taken from the distribution of responses to the questionnaire; poverty income from those who believe they are in the lowest 20 percent of the income distribution, education poverty from those who have completed primary education or less, and health poverty from those who reported being in either poor health or very poor health.

There are fewer health poor than education or income poor, and the overall sample size also varies widely among countries. Countries with larger populations generally have larger sample sizes. In some cases the sample sizes for the income poor are less than 100. This may make inferences difficult when there are as many as 12 independent variables. For the health poor, many countries did not have a survey response indicating health. Furthermore, the income poor figures for different countries are subject to large variations, since the

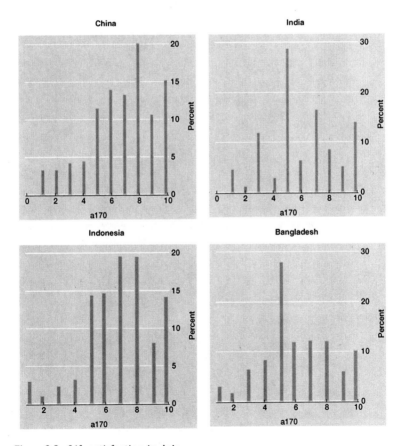

Figure 2.3 Life satisfaction in Asia.

Note: Sample size and average well-being are shown in Table 2.4.

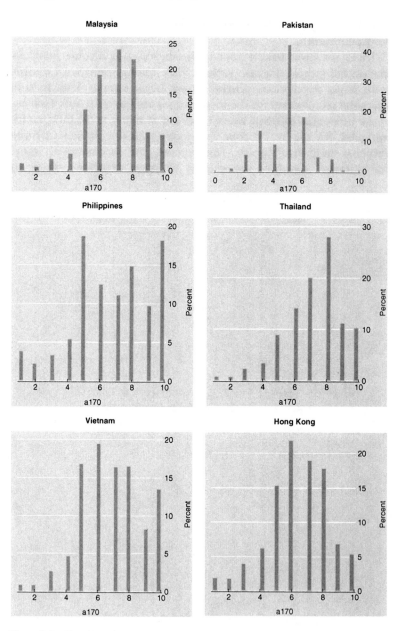

Figure 2.3 Continued

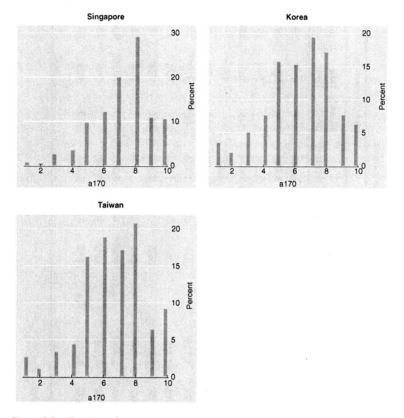

Figure 2.3 Continued

questions have been interpreted in widely different ways. For Indonesia (8 percent), Pakistan (5 percent), Thailand (8 percent) and Vietnam (3 percent), the small relative numbers of income poor do not reflect the spirit of the question, which is designed to identify those in the bottom two deciles of the income distribution. Similarly, Singapore's response could be an overestimate, as a third of the respondents believe they are in the lower two deciles. Despite these difficulties, the data do represent the spirit of identifying the income poor.

The distribution and intensity of these three poverty groups for the Asian region are reported in the Venn diagrams displayed in Figure 2.4.

The overlap among the groups is reasonably small (Table 2.7). The two largest groups – income and education poor – share less than 20 percent

Table 2.6 Sample size for the Asian region by country and poverty group (after fitting into the model)

	Total	a170 (Scale 1-10)*				a008 (Scale 1-4)*				a008r (Scale 0-1)*			
		Overall*	Health Poor	Edn Poor	Income Poor	Overall*	Health Poor	Edn Poor	Income Poor	Overall*	Health Poor	Edn Poor	Income Poor
China	5,515	1,630	375	662	244	1,639	371	668	246	1,643	193	669	246
India	8,543	5,918		1,819	1,476	5,927		1,813	1,475	5,952	376	1,826	1,482
Indonesia	3,019	2,253		364	187	2,281		365	195	2,294		364	199
Bangladesh	3,025	2,617	148	801	352	2,640	148	809	353	2,648	149	811	356
Malaysia	1,201	1,151		180	54	1,152		181	54	1,152		157**	
Pakistan	2,733	1,074		396	53	1,899	125	818	338	1,911	125	830	338
Philippines	2,400	1,156		316	175	1,154		314	175	1,156	80**	310**	172
Thailand	1,534	1,450		852	115	1,451		65	852	1,451		852	115
Vietnam	2,495	2,156		623	75	2,156		622	74	2,167	181	624	75
Hong Kong	1,252	990		214	147	989		213	147	994		215	147
Singapore	1,512	1,388**		389**	461**	1,386**		388**	461**	1,389**		389**	462
Korea	3,649	2,245		125	234	3,463		266	334	3,468		266	334
Taiwan	2,007	1,858	115	464	333	1,852	114	463	332	1,858	115	464	333
	38,885												

Note: * after fitting into the equation for the extended model.
** some variables dropped.

of the total for the two poverty groups in most cases, while the health poor group, although small, tends to have less than half the poor in common with the education and income poor. Finally, only a small proportion of the poor are common to all three groups. Therefore, it seems that making the distinctions of health, income and education poverty is important if we are to understand the multidimensional nature of poverty in Asia. And these remarks hold equally well for Africa and Latin America, as we shall see in Chapters 3 and 4.

2.2 Probit regression analysis for Asia

We begin with an extended version of the fundamental equation (1.1) introduced in the previous chapter and expanded to equation (1.2). Redefining 1.2 as 2.1, we have well-being as a function of the three policy variables health, education and income. To these we add the socioeconomic characteristics gender, age, marital status, family and friends. Finally we add the four social variables work, religion, trust and confidence in the provision of civil services.

$$\begin{aligned} WB = b_0 &+ b_1 \text{ Health} + b_2 \text{ Income} + b_3 \text{ Education} + b_4 \text{ Gender} + \\ &b_5 \text{ Age} + b_6 \text{ Age Squared} + b_7 \text{ Marital status} + b_8 \text{ Family} + \\ &b_9 \text{ Friends} + b_{10} \text{ Work} + b_{11} \text{ Religion} + b_{12} \text{ Trust} + \\ &b_{13} \text{ Confidence in Civil Services} \end{aligned} \quad (2.1)$$

We added last four social variables to reflect the potential impact of the work environment, belief in religion, trust in people and confidence in the civil service. These four variables, which were available for most countries in the World Value Survey database, reflect the ideas suggested in Chapter 1, where the importance of social organization and government policy were mentioned. There are several equations to report. These include well-being as a function of the independent variables for the overall sample and also for each of the poverty groups. Furthermore, there are three possible configurations of the dependent variable which we loosely define as well-being or happiness. They are 0 and 1 (unhappy and happy), 1,2,3,4 (very happy, happy, unhappy, very unhappy) and 1,2,3...10 (not at all happy...very happy). The third configuration is sometimes described in terms of satisfaction rather than happiness, and the literature sometimes uses these two terms interchangeably.

Variable definitions are shown in Table 2.8. We replicate Table 1.2 for ease of reference. We report the results by independent variable.

For the extended model described in equation 2.1, we analyze the results of the probit analysis variable by variable.

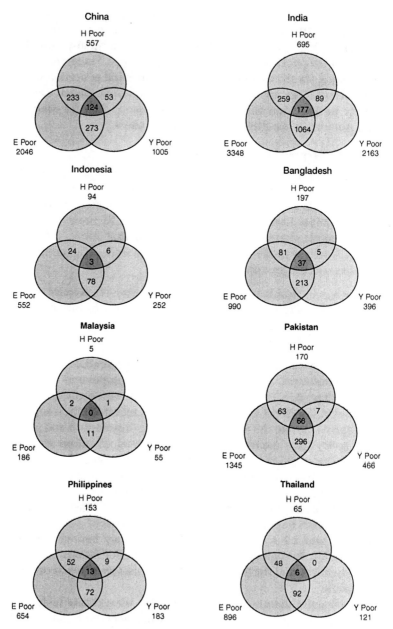

Figure 2.4   Venn diagrams for selected Asian countries

Notes: 1. H Poor stands for Health Poor, E Poor stands for Education Poor and Y Poor stands for Income Poor.
2. There are no WVS data on health status for Singapore. Hence we only show the overlap between education poor and income poor.

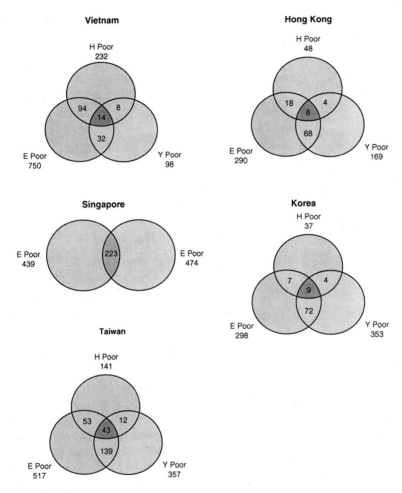

Figure 2.4 Continued

2.2.1 Policy variables

As reviewed earlier in Section 1.1, individuals' views of their health and income levels would impact their well-being and life satisfaction, although it was found that, beyond a certain threshold level of income, average subjective well-being did not change much. Education has also been noted as a potentially important determinant of well-being by some and ignored by others, possibly due to its close relationship with income in industrial countries. Deaton (2008) found that

Table 2.7 Overlap in poverty groups in Asia

Country	Education poor and income poor over total poor	Health poor that are not income poor or education poor over total	Intersection of three poverty categories as percent of total
India	22	46	0.02
China	13	26	3
Indonesia	10	65	0.03
Bangladesh	18	48	2
Malaysia	4	40	0
Pakistan	20	20	3
Philippines	10	52	0.13
Thailand	10	17	0.04
Vietnam	5	50	1.2
Hong Kong	17	47	1.3
Singapore	24	0	0
Korea	12	46	0.13
Taiwan	21	25	4.3

income and health are more important explanatory variables than education. Under the current model, we will investigate the importance of (self-reported) status of health, income and education on the individual respondent's well-being. We have deliberately labeled health, income and education under the category of policy, as the government could actively intervene to alter the status of health, education and income via provision of health care and education services, as well as income redistribution efforts via taxation and transfer payments. In addition, the government could actively intervene to promote greater demand for health and education services through provision of information and publicity campaigns, especially in lower-income countries where the public are not fully informed of the benefits of health and education.

   Health. Health status is significant in the overall probit regression for all 12 countries in Asia for well-being measured on a scale 1 to 10 (as can be seen in the first column of Table 2.9). The overall probit results

Table 2.8 Definitions of selected WVS indicators

Satisfaction with your life (ladder formulation)
1: Dissatisfied –10: Satisfied

a170 Expanded state of happiness
1: Very happy
2: Quite happy
3: Not happy
4: Not at all happy

a008 State of happiness
1: Very happy
2: Quite happy
3: Not happy
4: Not at all happy

a008r Compacted state of happiness
0. Not at all happy, not happy
1. Happy, very happy

State of Health
1: Very good
2: Good
3: Fair
4: Poor
5: Very Poor
1–3: Health Nonpoor
4–5: Health Poor

Income level (country specific) 10th step
1st–2nd income decile: Income Poor
3rd–10th income decile: Income Nonpoor

Highest level of education attained
1: Inadequately completed elementary education
2: Completed (compulsory) elementary education
3: Inadequately completed secondary education
4: Completed secondary education (technical, vocational secondary)
5: Inadequately completed secondary, university preparatory education
6: Completed secondary education: university preparatory
7: Some university without degree
8: University with degree/higher
1st–2nd levels: Education Poor
3rd–10th levels: Education Nonpoor

Important in Life: Work
1: Very important
2: Rather important
3: Not very important
4: Not at all important

Important in Life: Religion
1: Very important
2: Rather important
3: Not very important
4: Not at all important

Most people can be trusted
1: Most people can be trusted
2: Can't be too careful

Confidence in the Civil Services
1: A great deal
2: Quite a lot
3: Not very much
4: None at all

(Continued)

Table 2.8 Continued

Gender
1: Male
2: Female

Age (3 intervals)
1: 15–29
2: 30–49
3: 50 years and above

Marital Status
0: Not Married
1: Married or Living Together

Family important in life
1: Very important
2: Rather important
3: Not very important
4: Not at all important

Friends important in life
1: Very important
2: Rather important
3: Not very important
4: Not at all important

Table 2.9 Probit results for Asia – state of health

	a170 (Scale 1–10)				a008 (Scale 1–4)				a008r (Scale 0–1)			
	Overall	Health Poor	Edn Poor	Income Poor	Overall	Health Poor	Edn Poor	Income Poor	Overall	Health Poor	Edn Poor	Income Poor
China	-0.30* (-10.91)		-0.28* (-6.86)	-0.31* (-4.66)	0.45* (14.39)		0.42* (9.30)	0.39* (5.30)	-0.42* (-10.69)	-0.77 (-1.99)	-0.37* (-6.48)	-0.33* (-3.77)
India	-0.31* (-18.63)	-0.16 (-0.81)	-0.36* (-12.49)	-0.29* (-9.33)	0.51* (27.88)	0.16 (0.79)	0.55* (17.42)	0.48* (13.95)	-0.49* (-21.33)	-0.05 (-0.32)	-0.59* (-14.76)	-0.51* (-11.98)
Indonesia	-0.16* (-5.03)		-0.29* (-3.48)	-0.22 (-1.96)	0.47* (12.02)		0.45* (4.43)	0.38* (3.15)	-0.35* (-5.86)		-0.33* (-2.49)	-0.22 (-1.50)
Bangladesh	-0.25* (-9.05)	0.49 (1.33)	-0.22* (-4.58)	-0.19* (-2.49)	0.61* (18.55)	-0.23 (-0.59)	0.68* (11.93)	0.44* (5.05)	-0.52* (-12.48)	0.25 (0.96)	-0.52* (-8.00)	-0.45* (-4.35)
Malaysia	-0.22* (-4.30)		-0.29* (-2.44)	-0.22 (-0.84)	0.65* (10.44)		0.66* (4.35)	1.05* (2.96)	-0.57* (-5.27)		-0.59* (-2.21)	
Pakistan	-0.46* (-7.90)		-0.70* (-7.03)	-0.49 (-1.37)	0.43* (11.42)	-0.07 (-0.12)	0.50* (9.05)	0.35* (4.69)	-0.35* (-7.30)	0.00 (0.00)	-0.41* (-6.22)	-0.36* (-3.95)
Philippines	-0.19* (-5.09)		-0.07 (-0.97)	-0.21* (-2.10)	0.32* (7.81)		0.28* (3.42)	0.48* (4.40)	-0.34* (-5.49)	-0.16 (0.77	-0.31* (-2.52)	-0.52* (-3.39)
Thailand	-0.28* (-7.39)		-0.20* (-4.12)	-0.20 (-1.47)	0.46* (10.44)		0.38* (6.72)	0.62* (3.91)	-0.36* (-5.11)		-0.31* (-3.39)	-0.53* (-2.28)
Vietnam	-0.15* (-5.17)		-0.08 (-1.61)	-0.02 (-0.13)	0.33* (9.85)		0.13* (2.10)	0.30 (1.62)	-0.20* (-3.61)	0.18 (0.46)	-0.23* (-2.42)	-0.25 (-0.94)

(Continued)

Table 2.9 Continued

	a170 (Scale 1–10)				a008 (Scale 1–4)				a008r (Scale 0–1)			
	Overall	Health Poor	Edn Poor	Income Poor	Overall	Health Poor	Edn Poor	Income Poor	Overall	Health Poor	Edn Poor	Income Poor
Hong Kong	-0.42* (-7.87)		-0.46* (-4.01)	-1.01* (-6.76)	0.74* (10.37)		1.00* (6.06)	0.79* (4.47)	-0.74* (-8.95)		-0.90* (-5.05)	-0.56* (-2.86)
Singapore												
Korea	-0.32* (-8.68)		-0.36* (-2.43)	-0.66* (-6.25)	0.57* (15.53)		0.39* (3.44)	0.78* (7.34)	-0.42* (-9.13)		-0.44* (-3.13)	-0.44* (-3.70)
Taiwan	-0.33* (-10.58)	-0.09 (-0.18)	-0.35* (-6.42)	-0.21* (-3.17)	0.41* (11.54)	-0.50 (-0.93)	0.53* (8.47)	0.39* (5.22)	-0.34* (-6.82)	-0.22 (-0.48)	-0.52* (-6.13)	-0.32* (-3.32)

Notes: 1. Based on probit results for Equation (2.1) where z stats are displayed in parenthesis and * denotes statistical significance at the 5% level. For 1–10 and 0–1 definitions of well-being, a negative sign indicates healthier people are happier. For the 1–4 definition of well-being, a positive sign indicates healthier people are happier.
2. No WVS data on state of health and confidence in civil services and confidence in civil services for Singapore.
3. Variable dropped due to multicollinearity.

are also significant for all countries for the other two configurations of the well-being variable. This suggests that the form of well-being question has no significant impact on the level of well-being with respect to the health variable. For the sample as a whole, the coefficients vary in size from −0.15 in Vietnam to −0.46 in Pakistan for the 1 to 10 scale, from 0.32 to 0.74 for the 1 to 4 scale and from −0.34 to −0.74 for the 0 and 1 scale. These differences suggest that the response in well-being to changes in the individual respondent's health status varies from country to country even when the well-being response is quite strong. Given the importance of health to the individual's well-being, we can infer that programs to increase provision of health care services in countries would have strong positive impacts on well-being, and would be particularly effective if demand for such health services is present.

Next we turn our attention to the three poverty groups (i.e. those who report themselves to be in poor health, or in the lowest two income deciles, or with elementary education or less) in columns 2–4, 6–8 and 10–12. For the health poor there are a limited number of responses, and even for those few responding countries the sample size is small. As a result, there are no significant coefficients in the response of the health poor irrespective of the form of the well-being variable. Reading down columns 3, 7 and 11, the education poor are only slightly less responsive to variations in health than the overall sample, being significant in all but one of the possible 36 probit regressions. For the income poor (columns 4, 8 and 12), the well-being response is again only slightly lower than the overall response to variations in the status of health. Only a few countries have insignificant coefficients out of 36 possible cases.

The next question is whether the response of the poor to changes in health status is any stronger than it is for the full sample. The answer to this question is contained in Table 2.12. To be listed in Table 2.12 requires that the coefficient for the health variable among the poor in these two countries be approximately twice the size of the overall coefficient, and significance tests are confirmed by a z test. The three configurations of the dependent variable are displayed in the first column and the differential impact of the health variable is shown in the next three columns. The answer to the question of the response of the poor depends upon the form of the dependent variable. There is a significant difference for the 1 to 10 definition of well-being and for the income poor in Hong Kong and Korea and for the education poor in Indonesia and Pakistan. For 1 to 4 definitions, the impact on the education poor is strong in Hong Kong and in the Philippines, Thailand and Malaysia for the income poor. There are no significant differences for the 0 and 1 form.

We postpone further discussion of the other components of Table 2.12 until we discuss income and education. However, we can say now that the results for health are very strong and encouraging. The well-being of the poor is more responsive to improvements in the provision of health than that of the general population in seven different countries in the Asia region. This suggest that public policy can increase general well-being, and also the well-being of the poor, by increasing the provision of health services to all levels of society – well-to-do and poor alike.

Income.   Income appears to be a major determinant of well-being for all three different configurations of the well-being variable (see Table 2.10, where overall probit results are significant for most countries). This suggests that the form of well-being question has no significant impact on the effect of income on well-being. The results for income are similar to those for health, in the sense that the overall sample has significant coefficients for income in almost all countries for the three different responses for well-being. The coefficients vary about as much as the health coefficients (from 0.05 to 0.15 for 1 to 10 categories, from 0.03 to 0.09 for 1 to 4 categories and 0.07 to 0.23 categories). As with health, the variation in response of well-being can be as much as threefold across countries. It would be misleading not to take these variations into account when making public policy for individual countries.

Turning to the results of the three poverty groups, the health poor and the education poor both have significant coefficients in many reporting countries and for the three different definitions of well-being (51 of 66 possible coefficients). The results for the income poor are much less significant across the range of countries. Of 37 possible outcomes (around 13 countries and three definitions of well-being), there are only 13 significant income coefficients, mostly occurring in South Asian economies and Indonesia. This suggests that, once income reaches a certain level, well-being doesn't respond much to changes in income, even among the poor in the wealthier countries. From these probit results it seems that the well-being of the poor could respond to provision of better health and (perhaps) education.

Do the poor respond more to changes in income than the full sample? From Table 2.12 we see that, for Taiwan and Singapore, the income poor in all three well-being definitions responded more than the overall sample. For all of the three well-being definitions, Chinese health poor respond more to changes in income than the overall sample, while in two of the three definitions the poor in both India and Thailand respond

Table 2.10 Probit results for Asia – income level

	a170 (Scale 1–10)				a008 (Scale 1–4)				a008r (Scale 0–1)			
	Overall	Health Poor	Edn Poor	Income Poor	Overall	Health Poor	Edn Poor	Income Poor	Overall	Health Poor	Edn Poor	Income Poor
China	0.08* (6.31)	0.15* (3.91)	0.11* (5.05)	0.04 (0.26)	-0.08* (-5.58)	-0.15* (-3.73)	-0.09* (-3.93)	-0.25 (-1.69)	0.09* (5.04)	0.15* (3.06)	0.13* (4.34)	0.38* (2.18)
India	0.07* (9.00)	0.08* (2.82)	0.05* (3.85)	-0.34* (-6.14)	-0.03* (-4.33)	-0.10* (-3.30)	-0.04* (-2.61)	0.20* (3.50)	0.07* (7.17)	0.13* (3.41)	0.06* (2.92)	0.01 (0.12)
Indonesia	0.12* (10.26)	0.37* (4.95)	0.16* (5.58)	-0.41* (-2.50)	-0.07* (-4.95)	0.05 (0.67)	-0.13* (-3.95)	0.20 (1.13)	0.13* (5.86)		0.20* (4.11)	-0.09 (-0.42)
Bangladesh	0.14* (12.74)	0.18* (3.75)	0.06* (2.89)	0.12 (1.04)	-0.10* (-7.75)	-0.03 (-0.57)	-0.11* (-4.47)	0.09 (0.70)	0.11* (6.61)	0.05 (0.77)	0.13* (4.13)	-0.09 (-0.58)
Malaysia	0.08* (4.54)		0.14* (3.04)	0.01 (0.03)	-0.04* (-2.06)		-0.18* (-3.19)	1.16* (2.54)	0.13* (3.67)		0.18 (1.81)	
Pakistan	0.05 (1.75)	0.37 (1.83)	0.03 (0.69)		-0.08* (-5.38)	-0.15* (-2.36)	-0.08* (-3.07)	0.22 (1.67)	0.09* (4.45)	0.10 (1.33)	0.11* (3.34)	-0.08 (-0.50)
Philippines	0.14* (8.74)	0.19* (2.65)	0.12* (3.80)	-0.03 (-0.20)	-0.08* (-4.81)	-0.26* (-3.34)	-0.14* (-4.06)	-0.09 (-0.51)	0.10* (3.58)	0.19 (0.04)	0.16* (3.01)	0.30 (1.24)
Thailand	0.11* (7.35)	0.40* (4.14)	0.11* (5.86)	-0.20 (-0.90)	-0.08* (-4.89)	-0.30* (-2.87)	-0.11* (-4.95)	0.11 (0.46)	0.10* (3.49)		0.13* (3.50)	0.00 (0.01)
Vietnam	0.23* (14.57)	0.29* (4.88)	0.31* (9.96)	-0.31 (-1.14)	-0.06* (-3.13)	-0.12* (-2.00)	-0.07* (-2.25)	-0.11 (-0.35)	0.23* (7.98)	0.20* (2.34)	0.25* (5.00)	0.84 (1.70)

(Continued)

Table 2.10 Continued

	a170 (Scale 1–10)				a008 (Scale 1–4)				a008r (Scale 0–1)			
	Overall	Health Poor	Edn Poor	Income Poor	Overall	Health Poor	Edn Poor	Income Poor	Overall	Health Poor	Edn Poor	Income Poor
Hong Kong	0.07 (4.17)	0.41* (3.10)	0.26* (4.60)	0.46* (2.32)	-0.08* (-3.45)	-0.12 (-0.83)	-0.14 (-1.89)	-0.33 (-1.35)	0.11* (3.66)		0.21* (2.46)	0.65* (2.35)
Singapore	0.08* (5.41)		0.06 (1.67)	0.36* (3.14)	-0.03 (-1.90)		-0.05 (-1.13)	-0.42* (-3.15)	0.06 (1.89)		0.25* (2.42)	0.75* (3.58)
Korea	0.15* (11.46)		0.21* (3.54)	0.09 (0.64)	-0.07* (-5.62)		-0.03 (-0.74)	-0.09 (-0.67)	0.11* (6.95)		0.07 (1.37)	0.25 (1.58)
Taiwan	0.10* (9.44)	0.10* (2.59)	0.10* (4.80)	0.34* (2.92)	-0.09* (-7.09)	-0.12* (-2.84)	-0.08* (-3.28)	-0.29* (-2.23)	0.11* (6.15)	0.08 (1.59)	0.12* (3.52)	0.40* (2.49)

Notes: 1. Based on probit results for extended model where z stats are displayed in parenthesis and * denotes statistical significance at the 5% level. For 1–10 and 0–1 definitions of well-being, a positive sign indicates that higher income results in higher well-being. For the 1–4 definition of well-being, a negative sign indicates higher income results in higher well-being.

2. No WVS data on state of health and confidence in civil services for Singapore.

3. Variable dropped due to multicollinearity.

Table 2.11 Probit results for Asia – education level

	a170 (Scale 1-10)				a008 (Scale 1-4)				a008r (Scale 0-1)			
	Overall	Health Poor	Edn Poor	Income Poor	Overall	Health Poor	Edn Poor	Income Poor	Overall	Health Poor	Edn Poor	Income Poor
China	0.01 (0.62)	-0.01 (-0.34)	-0.10 (-1.14)	0.02 (0.59)	-0.03 (-1.73)	0.00 (0.08)	-0.09 (-0.96)	-0.11* (-2.67)	0.07* (3.73)	0.02 (0.30)	0.25* (2.11)	0.14* (2.88)
India	0.04* (7.71)	0.10* (4.23)	0.14* (2.71)	0.08* (7.31)	-0.01 (-1.90)	0.01 (0.40)	-0.12* (-2.13)	-0.02 (-1.93)	0.03* (4.26)	0.01 (0.21)	0.28* (4.09)	0.05* (3.75)
Indonesia	0.04* (3.78)	-0.03 (-0.42)	-0.03 (-0.28)	0.10* (2.61)	-0.05* (-3.73)	-0.08 (-1.03)	0.25 (1.69)	-0.09* (-2.07)	0.09* (4.16)		-0.15 (-0.69)	0.13* (2.39)
Bangladesh	0.04* (3.79)	-0.01 (-0.21)	0.25* (3.11)	0.09* (2.75)	-0.04* (-3.53)	-0.09 (-1.92)	-0.19* (-2.12)	-0.22* (-5.86)	0.10* (6.29)	0.10 (1.66)	0.35* (3.16)	0.26* (5.14)
Malaysia	-0.01 (-0.50)		-0.06 (-0.31)	0.04 (0.49)	-0.04 (-1.71)		0.06 (0.24)	-0.10 (-0.93)	0.10* (2.49)		0.32 (0.77)	
Pakistan	0.07* (4.29)	0.00 (0.03)	0.16 (1.25)	-0.55* (-2.37)	0.00 (0.03)	-0.08 (-1.13)	-0.08 (-0.88)	0.04 (0.84)	0.05* (2.81)	0.08 (1.04)	0.33* (2.95)	0.02 (0.29)
Philippines	-0.01 (-0.63)	-0.04 (-0.72)	0.15 (1.26)	-0.02 (-0.66)	0.01 (0.70)	0.05 (0.90)	0.02 (0.16)	-0.02 (-0.46)	-0.02 (-0.71)	-0.05 (-0.47)	0.13 (0.66)	-0.05 (-0.82)
Thailand	0.02 (1.18)	-0.09 (-1.19)	-0.05 (-0.63)	0.16* (2.16)	0.05* (2.89)	0.16 (1.81)	-0.03 (-0.28)	-0.08 (-0.94)	-0.07* (-2.63)		0.07 (0.46)	0.17 (1.19)
Vietnam	0.02 (1.73)	-0.02 (-0.31)	0.02 (0.24)	0.15 (1.58)	-0.04* (-2.29)	0.04 (0.70)	-0.10 (-0.97)	-0.14 (-1.19)	0.09* (3.02)	0.02 (0.21)	0.00 (0.03)	0.22 (1.16)

(Continued)

Table 2.11 Continued

	a170 (Scale 1-10)				a008 (Scale 1-4)				a008r (Scale 0-1)			
	Overall	Health Poor	Edn Poor	Income Poor	Overall	Health Poor	Edn Poor	Income Poor	Overall	Health Poor	Edn Poor	Income Poor
Hong Kong	0.07* (3.28)	0.06 (0.55)	0.02 (0.10)	0.18* (3.29)	-0.05 (-1.87)	-0.09 (-0.70)	-0.40 (-1.59)	-0.12 (-1.86)	0.08* (2.48)		0.52 (1.84)	0.24* (2.91)
Singapore	-0.07* (-4.04)		0.09 (0.63)	-0.06 (-1.70)	-0.01 (-0.52)		-0.16 (-1.00)	-0.03 (-0.61)	0.03 (0.71)		-0.20 (-0.73)	0.08 (0.97)
Korea	-0.02 (-1.59)		-0.17 (-0.70)	0.01 (0.22)	0.01 (0.40)		0.49* (2.71)	0.13* (3.20)	0.07* (4.31)		-0.09 (-0.40)	0.02 (0.54)
Taiwan	0.01 (0.82)	0.06 (1.19)	0.25* (2.22)	-0.01 (-0.53)	0.01 (0.84)	-0.05 (-1.01)	-0.12 (-1.02)	-0.01 (-0.48)	0.05* (2.64)	0.01 (0.24)	0.24 (1.46)	0.06 (1.56)

Notes: 1. Based on probit results for extended model where z stats are displayed in parenthesis and * denotes statistical significance at the 5% level. For 1–10 and 0–1 definitions of well-being, a positive sign indicates that education results in higher well-being. For the 1–4 definition of well-being, a negative sign indicates education results in higher well-being.
2. No WVS data on state of health and confidence in civil services for Singapore.
3. Variable dropped due to multicollinearity.

more than the overall sample. In India, Indonesia and Pakistan the health poor respond more to changes in income than the overall sample. For Hong Kong, education and income poverty groups respond for at least two definitions of well-being, while India, China and Malaysia also record significant differences between the income poor and the overall sample. Overall, the income variable for the three poor groups is significantly different from the income coefficient for the overall sample in 10 countries. Taken as a whole, these results suggest that increased income has a stronger impact on well-being among some poor groups in selected countries when compared with the well-being response of the full sample. However, more detailed research is necessary to delve further into the well-being response to changes in income in individual countries.

Education. With the exception of South Asia, where illiteracy is high, education is significant in fewer countries than income or health for the overall sample. However, education is significant in the three poverty categories, particularly in South Asia and China. Education appears much more often and with greater significance in these countries than in the richer countries of Southeast and East Asia (see Table 2.11). For the education poor group, the significance level of education and the size of the coefficient are notable in the poor countries of South Asia. The coefficients are much larger than they are for the sample as a whole. For example, in the binary form of well-being (0, 1), the coefficients for the education poor are 0.28 for India, 0.25 for China, 0.35 for Bangladesh and 0.33 for Pakistan. These compare with values of 0.03, 0.07, 0.10 and 0.05, respectively, for these countries in the full sample. The differences are dramatic – between two and 10-fold – and statistically significant.[2] We suspect that the strength of the education variable in the poorest countries reflects a deep and abiding thirst for knowledge among families where the breadwinner is either illiterate or with a few years of primary education at most. The significance differences for these and other countries are displayed in Table 2.12. Education appears most often for the countries in South Asia (India and Bangladesh six times and Pakistan three times).

As noted in the earlier review of the determinants of well-being in Chapter 1, the significance of education in well-being research has often been ignored or treated superficially. Layard (2007) did not include education as an explanatory variable in his review of the literature of the determinants of well-being, and Helliwell (2008) includes education as an afterthought. This may be understandable for richer countries where education and income tend to be correlated. Furthermore, aggregation has tended to cover up the strong impact on well-being that education exerts for the poor. This result is only possible for disaggregated date by poverty categories and is evident from the results of comparisons between the full sample and the poor. The lessons for policy are clear. To increase the well-being of the poor in the poorest countries in South Asia and China, greater stress must be put on education. Whatever educational attainment the poor have realized, they are still thirsty for more. Also, the education coefficients for the income poor and health poor are also small. So the impact of education is reflected much more strongly among those with little or no education and not necessarily among the health or income poor groups. These results offer strong evidence that programs to increase literacy and education in general have very strong positive effects on well-being in countries where the poor suffer from a widespread lack of educational opportunities.

2.2.2   Sociological and demographic variables

We now turn to the results for the control variables of Gender, Age and Marital status that are displayed in Tables 2.13 to 2.16.

Age.   Easterlin (1974 and 2001) suggests that age enters the happiness equation in a nonlinear fashion, with well-being declining until the mid-40s and increasing afterward. We explore this possibility for the Asian economies by including both age and age squared. This nonlinear functional form receives limited support for the Asian economies, and the results are sensitive to the form of the well-being variable. Looking at Tables 2.14 and 2.15 together, China, Philippines, Vietnam and Taiwan have significant nonlinear coefficients for age in the full sample – five for the 0 and 1 designation of well-being (India, Indonesia, Pakistan, Singapore and Taiwan) and four for 1 to 10 (China, Philippines, Vietnam and Taiwan). For the 1 to 4 range, Bangladesh and Vietnam have a significant nonlinear relationship between age and well-being. It is obvious that the results are quite sensitive to the definition of well-being. We explored an alternative formulation (results not reported) where age was entered in a linear fashion without the age squared term; age and well-being were positively related, suggesting that older people are happier. For the three poor categories, far fewer nonlinearities are observed in the relationship between age and well-being.

Gender and Marital Status.   Results for gender and marital status are broadly consistent with the results reported in the literature, although we can gather almost nothing about the response of the three poverty groups (see Tables 2.13 and 2.16). Women are happier than men in about a third of the countries for well-being definitions of 1 to 10 and 1 to 4.

Table 2.12 Differential impact of variations in health, education and income on well-being of three poverty groups

Dependent variable	Health Variable			Education Variable			Income Variable		
	Impact on Health poor	Impact on Education poor	Impact on Income Poor	Impact on Health poor	Impact on Education poor	Impact on Income poor	Impact on health poor	Impact on education poor	Impact on Income poor
1 to 10	India	Indonesia Pakistan	Hong Kong Korea	India	India Bangladesh Taiwan	India Indonesia Bangladesh Pakistan Hong Kong Thailand	China Indonesia Thailand Hong Kong	Hong Kong	India Indonesia Thailand Hong Kong Singapore Taiwan
1 to 4		Hong Kong	Philippines Thailand Malaysia		India Bangladesh Korea	China Indonesia Bangladesh Korea	China India Pakistan Philippines Thailand Vietnam	Indonesia Malaysia	India Malaysia Taiwan Singapore
0 and 1					China India Bangladesh Pakistan	China India Bangladesh Hong Kong	China India	Hong Kong Singapore	China Hong Kong Taiwan Singapore

Note: The requirement to be listed in Table 2.12 is that the coefficient for the health variable among the poor in these two countries should be twice the size of the overall coefficient, and significance tests are confirmed by a z test in Table 2.9. This is done likewise for the income and education variables for Tables 2.10 to 2.11.

Table 2.13 Probit results for Asia – gender

	a170 (Scale 1–10)				a008 (Scale 1–4)				a008r (Scale 0–1)			
	Overall	Health Poor	Edn Poor	Income Poor	Overall	Health Poor	Edn Poor	Income Poor	Overall	Health Poor	Edn Poor	Income Poor
China	0.03 (0.54)	−0.14 (−0.88)	0.03 (0.31)	0.19 (1.39)	−0.13* (−2.13)	0.28 (1.65)	−0.08 (−0.91)	−0.31* (−2.00)	0.24 (3.23)*	−0.35 (−1.66)	0.02 (0.16)	0.10 (0.53)
India	0.07* (2.31)	0.13 (1.10)	0.10 (1.97)	0.01 (0.09)	−0.08* (−2.75)	−0.05 (−0.44)	−0.02 (−0.35)	0.02 (0.30)	0.23* (5.91)	0.08 (0.58)	0.10 (1.57)	0.13 (1.75)
Indonesia	0.05 (1.20)	−0.36 (−1.23)	−0.07 (−0.63)	0.18 (1.08)	−0.14* (−2.58)	0.17 (0.55)	0.08 (0.60)	−0.17 (−0.96)	0.21* (2.37)		0.22 (1.10)	0.15 (0.64)
Bangladesh	0.19* (4.40)	0.05 (0.25)	0.03 (0.37)	−0.06 (−0.49)	−0.03 (−0.59)	0.04 (0.21)	0.20* (2.30)	0.15 (1.17)	0.09 (1.47)	−0.20 (−0.81)	−0.09 (−0.94)	−0.07 (−0.46)
Malaysia	0.13* (2.11)		0.36* (2.14)	−0.10 (−0.29)	−0.10 (−1.39)		−0.16 (−0.78)	0.80 (1.89)	0.23 (1.69)		−0.11 (−0.31)	
Pakistan	0.05 (0.64)	0.78 (1.87)	−0.08 (−0.71)	0.01 (0.03)	0.01 (0.12)	−0.36 (−1.51)	0.07 (0.78)	0.09 (0.66)	0.11 (1.53)	0.57 (1.98)	0.05 (0.48)	0.27 (1.65)
Philippines	0.06 (0.93)	−0.13 (−0.50)	0.18 (1.48)	0.34* (2.04)	−0.10 (−1.52)	−0.28 (−1.01)	0.12 (0.94)	−0.13 (−0.75)	0.22* (2.15)	0.19 (0.56)	−0.28 (−1.35)	0.10 (0.42)
Thailand	−0.03 (−0.63)	−0.49 (−1.72)	−0.01 (−0.09)	0.12 (0.59)	−0.10 (−1.64)	−0.32 (−1.03)	−0.02 (−0.27)	0.22 (0.93)	0.01 (0.14)		−0.12 (−0.82)	−0.14 (−0.40)
Vietnam	−0.05 (−1.07)	−0.31 (−1.83)	−0.05 (−0.58)	−0.05 (−0.20)	−0.02 (−0.39)	0.29 (1.56)	−0.01 (−0.12)	0.04 (0.15)	0.08 (0.86)	−0.43 (−1.68)	0.05 (0.29)	−0.18 (−0.39)

Hong Kong	0.20*	1.13*	0.28	0.06	−0.34*	0.43	−0.36	−0.35	0.46*		0.52*	0.52
	(3.04)	(2.45)	(1.89)	(0.34)	(−3.87)	(0.84)	(−1.84)	(−1.55)	(4.35)		(2.31)	(1.89)
Singapore	0.03		−0.02	0.08	−0.23*		−0.38*	−0.30*	0.31*		0.41	0.22
	(0.45)		(−0.15)	(0.83)	(−3.50)		(−2.97)	(−2.62)	(2.72)		(1.92)	(1.05)
Korea	−0.03		−0.28	0.15	0.04		0.07	−0.32*	0.23*		0.08	0.37*
	(−0.60)		(−1.36)	(1.02)	(0.82)		(0.46)	(−2.29)	(3.96)		(0.42)	(2.22)
Taiwan	0.24*	0.09	0.18	0.11	−0.24*	−0.02	−0.31*	−0.19	0.33*	0.07	0.44*	0.31
	(4.96)	(0.42)	(1.75)	(0.97)	(−4.42)	(−0.10)	(−2.78)	(−1.46)	(4.14)	(0.27)	(2.82)	(1.83)

Notes: 1. Based on probit results for extended model where z stats are displayed in parenthesis and * denotes statistical significance at the 5% level. For 1–10 and 0–1 definitions, a positive sign indicates that women are happier. For 1–4 definition, a negative sign indicates women are happier.
2. No WVS data on state of health and confidence in civil services for Singapore.
3. Variable dropped due to multicollinearity.

Table 2.14 Probit results for Asia – age

	a170 (Scale 1–10)				a008 (Scale 1–4)				a008r (Scale 0–1)			
	Overall	Health Poor	Edn Poor	Income Poor	Overall	Health Poor	Edn Poor	Income Poor	Overall	Health Poor	Edn Poor	Income Poor
China	−0.51* (−2.21)	0.80 (0.92)	−1.00* (−2.23)	−1.21 (−1.77)	0.34 (1.30)	−0.94 (−1.02)	0.49 (1.00)	−0.19 (−0.25)	0.65* (2.60)	1.83 (1.50)	0.50 (1.33)	0.62 (1.11)
India	0.02 (0.14)	−0.12 (−0.24)	0.14 (0.65)	0.01 (0.04)	−0.02 (−0.16)	−0.61 (−1.14)	−0.32 (−1.36)	0.18 (0.70)	1.19* (9.78)	0.65 (1.16)	1.20* (5.60)	0.82* (3.38)
Indonesia	0.14 (0.67)	−3.14* (−2.05)	−1.45* (−2.20)	0.08 (0.10)	−0.09 (−0.34)	1.84 (1.12)	2.03* (2.55)	−0.95 (−1.22)	1.51* (4.48)		0.80 (1.06)	1.22 (1.39)
Bangladesh	−0.33 (−1.87)	−1.13 (−1.44)	−0.48 (−1.61)	−0.41 (−0.88)	0.80* (4.01)	1.09 (1.28)	1.33* (3.97)	1.21* (2.30)	0.13 (0.59)	−2.06* (−2.17)	0.03 (0.08)	−0.96 (−1.73)
Malaysia	−0.20 (−0.73)		−1.37 (−1.97)	−1.61 (−1.14)	0.18 (0.56)		0.61 (0.72)	3.55* (2.10)	0.63 (1.24)		0.30 (0.27)	
Pakistan	−0.14 (−0.53)	−25.92* (−3.62)	−1.61* (−3.04)	−5.01* (−2.70)	0.28 (1.26)	−0.84 (−0.80)	0.73* (2.10)	0.09 (0.16)	0.44* (2.02)	−0.36 (−0.30)	−0.21 (−0.67)	1.10* (2.13)
Philippines	−0.62* (−2.38)	−0.85 (−0.68)	−0.15 (−0.28)	0.05 (0.07)	0.27 (0.92)	0.18 (0.13)	0.55 (0.88)	−1.01 (−1.33)	0.11 (0.25)	−0.14 (0.93)	0.82 (1.11)	−0.56 (−0.59)
Thailand	−0.45 (−1.81)	1.99 (0.78)	−0.87 (−1.60)	0.63 (0.60)	0.46 (1.59)	0.54 (0.19)	0.42 (0.67)	2.24 (1.83)	1.14* (3.29)		0.57 (0.98)	−0.05 (−0.05)
Vietnam	−0.49* (−2.43)	0.46 (0.53)	−0.32 (−0.82)	0.92 (0.84)	0.72* (3.08)	−0.31 (−0.33)	−0.16 (−0.35)	−0.53 (−0.43)	0.08 (0.25)	0.12 (0.09)	0.68 (1.24)	2.24 (1.44)

Hong Kong	0.16 (0.50)	-5.80* (-2.54)	-0.66 (-0.24)	-0.62 (-0.50)	0.09 (0.24)	-7.22* (-2.51)	0.44 (0.10)	1.93 (1.25)	1.02* (2.70)		0.84 (0.81)	-0.33 (-0.29)
Singapore	-0.31 (-1.17)		-0.90 (-1.56)	-0.05 (-0.11)	0.26 (0.87)		0.31 (0.47)	-0.23 (-0.43)	0.82* (2.05)		0.97 (1.14)	0.25 (0.34)
Korea	-0.11 (-0.57)		0.52 (0.22)	0.49 (0.74)	-0.11 (-0.53)	-2.12 (-1.36)	0.49 (0.76)	1.33* (6.09)			2.48* (2.98)	1.31* (2.25)
Taiwan	-0.56* (-2.51)	0.19 (0.13)	-0.72 (-0.39)	-1.42* (-2.31)	-0.16 (-0.62)	-2.84 (-1.84)	2.63 (1.24)	-0.43 (-0.64)	0.85* (3.07)	2.45 (1.54)	1.71* (2.57)	1.19* (2.05)

Notes: 1. Based on probit results for extended model where z stats are displayed in parenthesis and * denotes statistical significance at the 5% level. For 1–10 and 0–1 definitions, a positive sign indicates that older people are happier and vice versa. For 1–4 definition, a negative sign indicates older people are happier.

2. No WVS data on state of health and confidence in civil services for Singapore.

3. Variable dropped due to multicollinearity.

Table 2.15 Probit results for Asia – age squared

	a170 (Scale 1–10)				a008 (Scale 1–4)				a008r (Scale 0–1)			
	Overall	Health Poor	Edn Poor	Income Poor	Overall	Health Poor	Edn Poor	Income Poor	Overall	Health Poor	Edn Poor	Income Poor
China	0.15* (2.75)	-0.15 (-0.77)	0.27* (2.72)	0.33* (2.12)	-0.13* (-2.11)	0.17 (0.82)	-0.16 (-1.51)	-0.06 (-0.33)	-0.10 (-1.63)	-0.32 (-1.22)	-0.06 (-0.62)	-0.05 (-0.37)
India	0.01 (0.20)	0.02 (0.17)	-0.02 (-0.39)	0.02 (0.26)	0.00 (0.04)	0.17 (1.37)	0.05 (0.97)	-0.05 (-0.73)	-0.27* (-8.80)	-0.16 (-1.18)	-0.25* (-4.71)	-0.18* (-2.83)
Indonesia	-0.02 (-0.40)	0.72 (1.98)	0.30* (2.07)	0.00 (-0.02)	0.01 (0.22)	-0.48 (-1.22)	-0.44* (-2.48)	0.25 (1.32)	-0.33* (-4.00)		-0.18 (-0.96)	-0.33 (-1.51)
Bangladesh	0.11* (2.38)	0.31 (1.64)	0.12 (1.64)	0.14 (1.10)	-0.22* (-4.34)	-0.32 (-1.55)	-0.35* (-4.11)	-0.33* (-2.40)	-0.01 (-0.17)	0.51* (2.20)	0.01 (0.12)	0.29 (1.88)
Malaysia	0.07 (0.98)		0.35* (2.13)	0.44 (1.12)	-0.06 (-0.76)		-0.16 (-0.80)	-0.89 (-1.95)	-0.11 (-0.80)		-0.04 (-0.12)	
Pakistan	0.05 (0.79)	5.54* (3.72)	0.37* (3.00)	1.02* (2.53)	-0.06 (-1.08)	0.24 (1.00)	-0.17* (-2.08)	0.00 (0.02)	-0.10 (-1.82)	0.07 (0.26)	0.07 (0.88)	-0.26* (-2.00)
Philippines	0.18* (2.83)	0.24 (0.81)	0.10 (0.81)	0.03 (0.20)	-0.02 (-0.29)	0.05 (0.15)	-0.07 (-0.51)	0.32 (1.72)	-0.09 (-0.83)	-0.03 (0.94)	-0.28 (-1.60)	0.03 (0.12)
Thailand	0.11 (1.94)	-0.30 (-0.56)	0.19 (1.69)	-0.13 (-0.52)	-0.10 (-1.46)	-0.14 (-0.23)	-0.10 (-0.74)	-0.51 (-1.83)	-0.28* (-3.35)		-0.13 (-0.94)	0.00 (0.01)
Vietnam	0.13* (2.59)	-0.08 (-0.40)	0.07 (0.79)	-0.13 (-0.48)	-0.18* (-3.20)	0.07 (0.31)	0.00 (0.01)	0.06 (0.20)	-0.04 (-0.53)	-0.04 (-0.13)	-0.13 (-1.00)	-0.39 (-1.01)

Hong Kong	0.02 (0.34)	1.56* (2.85)	0.20 (0.36)	0.26 (0.90)	-0.07 (-0.70)	1.51* (2.30)	-0.15 (-0.17)	-0.48 (-1.34)	-0.19* (-2.01)		-0.13 (-0.55)	0.10 (0.35)
Singapore	0.08 (1.16)		0.21 (1.54)	0.03 (0.26)	-0.04 (-0.54)		-0.04 (-0.23)	0.07 (0.57)	-0.22* (-2.13)		-0.28 (-1.31)	-0.05 (-0.24)
Korea	0.02 (0.31)		-0.09 (-0.18)	-0.12 (-0.80)	0.04 (0.77)		0.44 (1.33)	-0.07 (-0.46)	-0.31* (-5.60)		-0.48* (-2.52)	-0.29 (-1.99)
Taiwan	0.15* (2.81)	-0.06 (-0.18)	0.16 (0.43)	0.32* (2.34)	0.04 (0.62)	0.67 (1.99)	-0.49 (-1.15)	0.12 (0.79)	-0.20* (-2.95)	-0.60 (-1.69)	-0.43* (-2.79)	-0.30* (-2.14)

Notes: 1. Based on probit results for extended model where z stats are displayed in parenthesis and * denotes statistical significance at the 5% level.

2. No WVS data on state of health and confidence in civil services for Singapore.

3. Variable dropped due to multicollinearity.

Table 2.16 Probit results for Asia – marital status

	a170 (Scale 1–10)				a008 (Scale 1–4)				a008r (Scale 0–1)			
	Overall	Health Poor	Edn Poor	Income Poor	Overall	Health Poor	Edn Poor	Income Poor	Overall	Health Poor	Edn Poor	Income Poor
China	0.31* (3.97)	0.26 (1.03)	0.32* (2.33)	0.23 (1.24)	-0.32* (-3.63)	-0.35 (-1.30)	-0.29 (-1.99)	-0.36 (-1.74)	0.32* (2.93)	0.53 (1.55)	0.33 (1.81)	0.36 (1.39)
India	0.07 (1.92)	0.18 (1.32)	0.08 (1.03)	0.20* (2.76)	-0.16* (-3.97)	-0.05 (-0.35)	-0.20* (-2.52)	-0.30* (-3.90)	0.10 (1.96)	0.02 (0.11)	0.21* (2.14)	0.24* (2.53)
Indonesia	-0.02 (-0.25)	0.33 (0.87)	-0.07 (-0.49)	-0.14 (-0.70)	-0.07 (-1.02)	-0.34 (-0.84)	0.08 (0.47)	0.08 (0.40)	0.02 (0.15)		-0.13 (-0.50)	0.01 (0.04)
Bangladesh	0.11* (2.00)	0.14 (0.58)	0.22 (1.81)	0.39* (2.66)	-0.12 (-1.84)	-0.34 (-1.29)	-0.23 (-1.71)	-0.50* (-3.04)	0.17* (2.03)	0.39 (1.22)	0.40* (2.57)	0.52* (2.55)
Malaysia	0.19* (2.61)		0.06 (0.30)	-0.23 (-0.58)	0.09 (1.01)		-0.05 (-0.20)	0.76 (1.47)	0.05 (0.29)		0.24 (0.49)	
Pakistan	0.15 (1.62)	5.46* (3.40)	0.61* (3.04)	0.59 (0.92)	-0.09 (-1.29)	0.04 (0.11)	-0.07 (-0.55)	-0.15 (-0.82)	0.05 (0.58)	0.29 (0.64)	0.15 (0.99)	0.07 (0.31)
Philippines	0.00 (-0.05)	-0.13 (-0.39)	-0.18 (-1.12)	-0.54* (-2.50)	-0.22* (-2.52)	-0.58 (-1.55)	0.05 (0.29)	0.21 (0.87)	0.23 (1.80)	0.70 (0.11)	0.11 (0.42)	0.35 (1.04)
Thailand	0.17* (2.43)	0.29 (0.84)	0.21* (2.00)	0.28 (1.09)	-0.07 (-0.90)	0.08 (0.20)	-0.25* (-2.06)	-0.90* (-3.04)	0.16 (1.20)		0.54* (3.00)	0.48 (1.11)
Vietnam	0.30* (4.80)	0.28 (1.24)	0.28* (2.44)	0.68* (2.36)	-0.70* (-9.59)	-0.47 (-1.91)	-0.68* (-5.18)	-0.71* (-2.18)	0.89* (8.33)	0.66* (2.22)	0.79* (4.55)	0.82 (1.48)

Hong Kong	0.22* (2.63)	0.82 (1.65)	0.31 (1.56)	0.18 (0.96)	0.02 (0.21)	0.60 (1.04)	0.10 (0.38)	-0.07 (-0.30)	0.02 (0.14)		-0.13 (-0.47)	0.00 (0.00)
Singapore	0.27* (3.66)		0.46* (2.89)	0.30* (2.45)	-0.39* (-4.42)		-0.55* (-2.99)	-0.40* (-2.75)	0.10 (0.64)		0.21 (0.70)	0.37 (1.42)
Korea	0.17* (2.80)		-0.22 (-0.94)	0.07 (0.40)	-0.23* (-3.90)		0.01 (0.03)	-0.39* (-2.47)	0.13 (1.72)		0.05 (0.22)	0.46 (2.47)
Taiwan	0.20* (3.20)	0.07 (0.30)	0.18 (1.42)	0.21 (1.52)	-0.16* (-2.25)	-0.25 (-0.96)	-0.20 (-1.46)	-0.22 (-1.48)	0.24* (2.47)	0.18 (0.61)	0.46* (2.63)	0.39* (2.11)

Notes: 1. Based on probit results for extended model where z stats are displayed in parenthesis and * denotes statistical significance at the 5% level. For the 1–10 and 0–1 definitions of well-being, a positive sign indicates that married or living together couples are happier and vice versa. For 1–4 well-being, a negative sign denotes the positive effects of marriage/living together.
2. No WVS data on state of health and confidence in civil services for Singapore.
3. Variable dropped due to multicollinearity.

Table 2.17 Probit results for Asia – importance of family

	a170 (Scale 1–10)				a008 (Scale 1–4)				a008r (Scale 0–1)			
	Overall	Health Poor	Edn Poor	Income Poor	Overall	Health Poor	Edn Poor	Income Poor	Overall	Health Poor	Edn Poor	Income Poor
China	−0.10* (−2.24)	−0.04 (−0.36)	−0.03 (−0.42)	0.02 (0.14)	0.21* (4.10)	−0.05 (−0.35)	0.15* (2.00)	−0.14 (−0.91)	−0.03 (−0.50)	−0.01 (−0.03)	−0.04 (−0.39)	0.24 (1.31)
India	0.09* (2.56)	0.11 (0.91)	0.13 (1.92)	−0.02 (−0.23)	0.06 (1.45)	0.07 (0.59)	−0.06 (−0.83)	0.06 (0.81)	−0.02 (−0.39)	−0.15 (−1.02)	0.08 (0.96)	−0.07 (−0.85)
Indonesia	−0.32* (−2.07)	0.08 (0.14)	0.24 (0.53)	−0.20 (−0.50)	0.30 (1.70)	0.91 (1.49)	−0.99* (−2.17)	−0.02 (−0.06)	−0.23 (−1.07)			0.09 (0.17)
Bangladesh	0.00 (−0.03)	−0.11 (−0.26)	0.03 (0.20)	0.13 (0.68)	0.04 (0.37)	0.10 (0.19)	0.03 (0.22)	−0.16 (−0.74)	0.23 (1.88)	−0.13 (−0.25)	0.30 (1.61)	0.43 (1.57)
Malaysia	0.05 (0.31)		0.49 (1.16)	−2.17 (−1.73)	0.10 (0.55)		−0.07 (−0.14)	−0.44 (−0.29)	0.24 (0.74)			
Pakistan	−0.07 (−0.72)	−3.42* (−3.60)	−0.01 (−0.06)	0.32 (0.41)	0.10 (1.52)	0.26 (1.53)	−0.05 (−0.50)	0.01 (0.06)	0.04 (0.57)	−0.20 (−0.98)	0.32* (2.66)	0.16 (1.07)
Philippines	0.21 (0.92)		−0.25 (−0.56)	−0.11 (−0.17)	−0.33 (−1.21)		−0.20 (−0.41)	−0.39 (−0.56)	1.49* (2.86)			
Thailand	−0.31* (−3.94)	−0.01 (−0.02)	−0.30* (−3.19)	−0.27 (−1.15)	0.06 (0.68)	0.07 (0.24)	−0.02 (−0.18)	−0.22 (−0.81)	0.41* (2.34)		0.32 (1.52)	0.48 (0.84)
Vietnam	−0.26* (−4.32)	−0.54* (−2.73)	−0.22* (−2.30)	−0.42 (−1.47)	0.19* (2.77)	0.26 (1.22)	0.18 (1.74)	0.59 (1.61)	−0.27* (−2.57)	−0.28 (−1.03)	−0.26 (−1.71)	−1.39* (−2.49)

Hong Kong	−0.11	−0.28	−0.14	−0.11	0.21*	−0.17	0.23	−0.08	−0.14		−0.22	0.12
	(−1.56)	(−0.78)	(−0.96)	(−0.65)	(2.27)	(−0.42)	(1.26)	(−0.38)	(−1.24)		(−1.06)	(0.49)
Singapore	−0.35*		−0.36	−0.21	0.42*		0.33	0.39	−0.16		−0.05	−0.02
	(−3.07)		(−1.99)	(−1.26)	(3.15)		(1.56)	(1.93)	(−0.84)		(−0.17)	(−0.07)
Korea	−0.15		−0.53	−0.26	0.37*		0.32	0.66*	−0.42*		−0.61*	−0.69*
	(−1.91)		(−1.55)	(−1.08)	(5.10)		(1.35)	(3.16)	(−4.90)		(−2.14)	(−2.82)
Taiwan	−0.10	0.07	−0.12	−0.07	0.11	−0.09	−0.01	−0.03	0.13	0.26	0.17	0.07
	(−1.43)	(0.38)	(−1.09)	(−0.58)	(1.42)	(−0.41)	(−0.08)	(−0.22)	(1.32)	(1.04)	(1.12)	(0.43)

Notes: 1. Based on probit results for extended model where z stats are displayed in parenthesis and * denotes statistical significance at the 5% level. For 1–10 and 0–1 definitions, a negative sign indicates that people who value family are happier. For 1–4 definition, a positive sign indicates people who value family are happier.

2. No WVS data on state of health and confidence in civil services for Singapore.

3. Variable dropped due to multicollinearity.

Table 2.18 Probit results for Asia – importance of friends

	a170 (Scale 1–10)				a008 (Scale 1–4)				a008r (Scale 0–1)			
	Overall	Health Poor	Edn Poor	Income Poor	Overall	Health Poor	Edn Poor	Income Poor	Overall	Health Poor	Edn Poor	Income Poor
China	-0.11* (-2.89)	-0.17 (-1.54)	-0.15* (-2.52)	-0.13 (-1.36)	0.12* (2.87)	-0.10 (-0.84)	0.12 (1.86)	0.28* (2.65)	-0.09 (-1.60)	0.20 (1.40)	-0.13 (-1.50)	-0.38* (-2.92)
India	-0.03 (-1.60)	-0.10 (-1.47)	-0.06 (-1.97)	-0.10* (-2.62)	0.10* (5.41)	0.10 (1.54)	0.12* (3.49)	0.21* (5.44)	-0.09* (-3.85)	-0.08 (-1.06)	-0.11* (-2.72)	-0.18* (-3.80)
Indonesia	0.08* (2.00)	0.34 (1.42)	0.26* (2.79)	0.04 (0.31)	-0.02 (-0.35)	-0.20 (-0.77)	-0.14 (-1.26)	0.03 (0.17)	0.02 (0.27)		0.09 (0.52)	0.19 (0.88)
Bangladesh	-0.05 (-1.64)	-0.23 (-1.69)	-0.23* (-4.65)	-0.12 (-1.63)	0.01 (0.18)	0.08 (0.59)	0.03 (0.62)	0.04 (0.42)	0.14* (3.16)	-0.14 (-0.79)	0.09 (1.38)	0.09 (0.88)
Malaysia	-0.04 (-0.85)		0.10 (0.77)	0.47 (1.57)	0.09 (1.48)		-0.06 (-0.39)	0.20 (0.52)	-0.01 (-0.06)		0.06 (0.23)	
Pakistan	-0.07 (-1.54)	-0.38 (-1.74)	-0.15* (-2.19)	-0.31 (-1.41)	0.08* (2.45)	-0.02 (-0.12)	0.12* (2.48)	0.16* (2.18)	-0.08 (-1.90)	0.05 (0.33)	-0.07 (-1.21)	-0.11 (-1.26)
Philippines	0.00 (0.07)	-0.31 (-1.72)	-0.06 (-0.67)	0.09 (0.81)	0.20* (4.10)	0.15 (0.78)	0.14 (1.55)	0.10 (0.82)	-0.17* (-2.35)	-0.03 (0.89)	-0.02 (-0.14)	-0.24 (-1.47)
Thailand	-0.04 (-0.93)	0.22 (0.88)	-0.04 (-0.62)	-0.17 (-1.08)	-0.08 (-1.62)	-0.36 (-1.31)	-0.08 (-1.22)	0.07 (0.42)	0.27* (3.06)		0.22 (1.96)	0.11 (0.46)
Vietnam	-0.01 (-0.34)	0.16 (1.28)	-0.02 (-0.34)	0.19 (1.04)	0.05 (1.18)	-0.07 (-0.53)	0.08 (0.97)	0.09 (0.43)	-0.04 (-0.51)	0.00 (0.00)	-0.20 (-1.68)	-0.02 (-0.07)

Hong Kong	0.11 (1.50)	0.71 (1.83)	0.00 (−0.02)	−0.27 (−1.29)	0.09 (0.95)	0.86 (1.92)	0.05 (0.25)	0.35 (1.39)	0.03 (0.26)		0.11 (0.46)	−0.17 (−0.56)
Singapore	−0.15* (−3.41)		−0.04 (−0.54)	−0.18* (−2.53)	0.16* (3.07)		0.15 (1.66)	0.27* (3.29)	−0.22* (−2.50)		−0.23 (−1.48)	−0.44* (−3.03)
Korea	−0.04 (−1.14)	0.27 (1.82)	−0.07 (−0.56)		0.10* (2.66)		0.16 (1.34)	0.34* (2.81)	−0.08 (−1.59)		−0.07 (−0.45)	−0.24 (−1.64)
Taiwan	−0.05 (−1.31)	−0.34* (−2.20)	0.11 (1.40)	−0.13 (−1.50)	0.14* (2.93)	0.25 (1.50)	0.11 (1.35)	0.19 (1.92)	−0.03 (−0.48)	−0.29 (−1.43)	−0.06 (−0.55)	−0.25 (−1.97)

Notes: 1. Based on probit results for extended model where z stats are displayed in parenthesis and * denotes statistical significance at the 5% level. For 1–10 and 0–1 definitions, a negative sign indicates that people who value friends are happier. For 1–4 definition, a positive sign indicates people who value friends are happier.

2. No WVS data on state of health and confidence in civil services for Singapore.

3. Variable dropped due to multicollinearity.

However, when the well-being is a binary choice between happy and unhappy (0 and 1), gender is significant in 8 of 13 countries. Women are happier than men in most cases where gender is significant. For the poor, the results are less conclusive. Gender is significant in only a few countries, poverty categories or well-being scales (10 out of 104 cases, a result that would be expected by chance). The results on gender are, therefore, sensitive to the definition of well-being, and there is no evidence for the poor. From the overall sample results for marital status, those who are married seem to be happier in about half the countries, and the results in the other countries are generally not significant. This result is consistent with other studies that find marriage increases well-being compared with other marital status variables (single, divorced, widow or widower). However, these results do not generally hold in any of the poor categories. It is, therefore, hard to draw any conclusions about the impact of marriage on the well-being of the poor.

The final two social variables, **Family and Friends**, are displayed in Tables 2.17 and 2.18. Here our results are not fully consistent with previous research. Previous research (see literature review in Chapter 1) suggests that valuing friends and family is important and a critical source of support, resulting in a positive influence on well-being. According to psychologists, a lack of friends and family can lead to a sense of isolation and result in feelings of loneliness and depression. This is the simple explanation for the inclusion of these variables in well-being analysis in industrial countries, and finding them significant provides support for such conclusions. However, in developing countries, where there is a greater sense of belonging to a community as opposed to a sense of separateness and a strong ego combined with the importance of individuality of personality, these two variables could have less significance in the determination of well-being and happiness. This is what seems to be happening in the probit analysis of well-being for Asia. Tabulating the significance of friends and family for the Asian economies suggests these two variables are not highly significant determinants of variations in well-being, either for the full sample or for the three poverty groups. Reading down the overall sample column in Tables 2.18 (columns 1, 5 and 9), friends are significant in three, seven and five countries depending on the definition of well-being. Reading down columns 2, 3, 4, 6, 7, 8 and 10, 11, 12, no more than four countries have any statistically significant poverty coefficient. For family, the results appear to be similar to the importance of friends – fewer than six countries are significant for the overall probit regressions, but no more than two countries have significant family coefficients in each column of the nine different regressions for the three poverty categories. Looking at these results in a more positive light, they suggest that family and friends can have a positive impact on well-being. However, the impact is probably not generally as strong as the impact of variations in health, education and income.

2.2.3 Other social variables

Turning to the four social variables in Tables 2.19 to 2.22, **Trust** is significant for the overall sample in more than half of the countries (seven countries) if we use the 1–10 and 1–4 definition, but only four countries out of 13 based on the binary definition. For the poverty categories, there are only eight countries with significant coefficients on trust out of the possible 103 cases. The significance of **Religion** for the overall sample is limited to a few countries: three, four or seven out of 13 depending on the definition of the dependent variable. The significance for the poverty groups is likewise limited, although there are a few more cases of significance than in the case of trust (21 out of 102 available possibilities). There is no apparent pattern to the countries where religion plays a significant role in well-being, either for the overall sample or for the three poverty groups. Nevertheless, religion has a significant impact on Indian (Hindu) well-being for all three versions of the dependent variable and for two versions in Thailand (Buddhist), Singapore (Buddhist/Muslim/Hindu/Christian) and Korea (Buddhist/Christian). There are no significant coefficients in China aside from the impact of religion on the health poor.

On the surface, it would seem that **Work** should be an important determinant of well-being. Those who enjoy work might be happier. Looking at Table 2.19, there are only 13 significant coefficients out of 143 possible cases for the overall sample and poverty groups! The results for the overall sample are no more significant than for the poverty categories. What is the explanation for this nearly universal denial of the impact of work satisfaction on well-being? What seems to be happening is that well-being is determined by other influences other than work, except in a few particular circumstances. Most respondents don't consider work a source of well-being or happiness but rather as a source of income to feed their families.

Finally, a variable denoting confidence in the provision of **civil services** was included to reflect the faith in the government to deliver the appropriate level of government services. The results were disappointing. For the overall sample, only a few of the civil service variables were significant: in the 1–10 definition, three out of 12; in the 1–4 definition, five out of 12 with

Table 2.19 Probit results for Asia – importance of work

	a170 (Scale 1–10)				a008 (Scale 1–4)				a008r (Scale 0–1)			
	Overall	Health Poor	Edn Poor	Income Poor	Overall	Health Poor	Edn Poor	Income Poor	Overall	Health Poor	Edn Poor	Income Poor
China	0.06 (1.62)	-0.03 (-0.27)	0.03 (0.53)	0.07 (0.82)	0.08 (1.91)	0.11 (1.03)	0.12 (1.90)	0.05 (0.52)	0.01 (0.18)	-0.08 (-0.57)	-0.02 (-0.29)	-0.03 (-0.27)
India	-0.04 (-1.26)	-0.10 (-1.01)	0.05 (1.01)	0.03 (0.46)	0.04 (1.28)	0.07 (0.64)	0.00 (-0.01)	-0.05 (-0.81)	0.03 (0.66)	-0.11 (-0.88)	0.03 (0.50)	0.20* (2.48)
Indonesia	-0.09 (-1.61)	-0.64 (-1.56)	-0.18 (-1.47)	-0.06 (-0.25)	-0.05 (-0.74)	-0.47 (-1.03)	0.10 (0.67)	-0.17 (-0.64)	0.18 (1.53)		0.01 (0.03)	0.70 (1.26)
Bangladesh	0.06 (1.08)	-0.20 (-0.82)	0.21 (1.59)	-0.18 (-1.05)	0.15* (2.27)	0.29 (1.09)	0.11 (0.79)	-0.04 (-0.24)	-0.14 (-1.64)	-0.32 (-1.02)	-0.15 (-0.91)	-0.20 (-0.89)
Malaysia	0.02 (0.33)		0.06 (0.46)	0.13 (0.47)	0.12* (2.08)		-0.13 (-0.76)	-0.03 (-0.08)	0.03 (0.25)		0.37 (1.07)	
Pakistan	0.00 (0.01)	-1.11* (-2.98)	0.07 (0.83)	-0.13 (-0.58)	0.04 (0.99)	0.29 (1.84)	-0.04 (-0.62)	0.02 (0.17)	0.10 (1.82)	-0.14 (-0.78)	0.16* (2.07)	-0.01 (-0.06)
Philippines	0.06 (0.61)	-0.12 (-0.68)	-0.12 (-0.66)	0.32 (1.23)	-0.07 (-0.69)	-0.21 (-1.11)	0.17 (0.85)	-0.31 (-1.09)	0.16 (1.13)	0.13 (0.57)	-0.05 (-0.20)	1.33* (2.01)
Thailand	0.07 (1.44)	-0.04 (-0.20)	0.03 (0.45)	0.34* (2.34)	0.14* (2.66)	0.26 (1.13)	0.11 (1.62)	0.20 (1.30)	-0.20* (-2.51)		-0.13 (-1.25)	-0.15 (-0.74)
Vietnam	0.03 (0.70)	0.05 (0.47)	0.08 (1.18)	-0.16 (-0.97)	0.30* (7.21)	0.19 (1.50)	0.33 (4.63)	0.40 (1.88)	-0.11 (-1.57)	0.10 (0.57)	0.00 (-0.03)	-0.62* (-2.04)

Hong Kong	0.10 (1.95)	-0.11 (-0.40)	0.06 (0.56)	0.54* (4.00)	-0.12 (-1.79)	-0.17 (-0.55)	-0.17 (-1.27)	-0.21 (-1.30)	0.27* (3.20)		0.16 (1.01)	0.13 (0.63)
Singapore	0.01 (0.23)		0.01 (0.19)	0.02 (0.34)	0.06 (1.16)		0.09 (1.24)	0.06 (0.71)	0.11 (1.23)		0.02 (0.19)	0.02 (0.13)
Korea	0.00 (0.04)		-0.07 (-0.64)	0.24* (2.31)	-0.02 (-0.47)		-0.03 (-0.34)	0.02 (0.18)	0.10* (2.32)		0.13 (1.14)	-0.01 (-0.10)
Taiwan	0.02 (0.57)	0.09 (0.74)	-0.06 (-0.89)	0.01 (0.17)	0.00 (-0.05)	0.08 (0.64)	0.06 (0.86)	-0.03 (-0.41)	0.06 (1.13)	-0.01 (-0.06)	-0.04 (-0.42)	0.09 (0.88)

Notes: 1. Based on probit results for extended model where z stats are displayed in parenthesis and * denotes statistical significance at the 5% level. For 1–10 and 0–1 definitions, a negative sign indicates that people who value work are happier. For 1–4 definition, a positive sign indicates people who value work are happier.

2. No WVS data on state of health and confidence in civil services for Singapore.

3. Variable dropped due to multicollinearity.

Table 2.20 Probit results for Asia – importance of religion

	a170 (Scale 1–10)				a008 (Scale 1–4)				a008r (Scale 0–1)			
	Overall	Health Poor	Edn Poor	Income Poor	Overall	Health Poor	Edn Poor	Income Poor	Overall	Health Poor	Edn Poor	Income Poor
China	-0.02 (-0.82)	0.01 (0.16)	0.05 (1.08)	0.03 (0.42)	0.01 (0.19)	-0.26* (-2.58)	-0.10 (-1.94)	-0.04 (-0.54)	0.07 (1.70)	0.20 (1.68)	0.11 (1.80)	0.01 (0.05)
India	-0.08* (-5.37)	-0.09 (-1.59)	-0.11* (-3.49)	-0.11* (-3.43)	0.11* (6.50)	0.01 (0.14)	0.12* (3.69)	0.12* (3.62)	-0.05* (-2.19)	-0.06 (-0.88)	-0.11* (-2.81)	-0.03 (-0.78)
Indonesia	-0.18 (-1.85)		-0.29 (-1.52)	-0.07 (-0.22)	0.19 (1.75)		0.13 (0.73)	-0.07 (-0.26)	-0.34* (-2.45)		-0.46* (-2.11)	-0.56 (-1.50)
Bangladesh	-0.05 (-0.90)	-0.14 (-0.59)	-0.13 (-0.97)	-0.12 (-0.54)	0.28* (4.87)	0.00 (0.01)	0.09 (0.65)	0.34 (1.38)	-0.33* (-4.67)	-0.08 (-0.28)	-0.14 (-0.84)	-0.35 (-1.17)
Malaysia	-0.05 (-0.76)		0.13 (0.83)	0.34 (0.74)	0.21* (2.99)		0.18 (0.98)	0.22 (0.39)	-0.11 (-0.98)		-0.49 (-1.72)	
Pakistan	0.01 (0.17)	1.17* (2.80)	0.09 (0.65)	-1.86* (-2.62)	0.08 (1.72)	0.18 (1.05)	0.10 (1.15)	0.18 (1.43)	-0.01 (-0.24)	-0.30 (-1.47)	-0.06 (-0.50)	-0.27 (-1.80)
Philippines	-0.12 (-1.82)	0.22 (0.98)	-0.32* (-2.04)	0.00 (-0.01)	0.13 (1.71)	-0.15 (-0.58)	0.07 (0.42)	0.03 (0.10)	-0.16 (-1.59)	0.07 (0.83)	-0.05 (-0.17)	0.16 (0.42)
Thailand	-0.17* (-3.41)	-0.49 (-1.79)	-0.27* (-3.78)	-0.12 (-0.66)	0.27* (4.56)	0.60 (1.99)	0.36* (4.44)	0.32 (1.64)	0.01 (0.12)		0.06 (0.41)	0.05 (0.16)
Vietnam	0.01 (0.31)	-0.05 (-0.53)	0.05 (0.95)	0.15 (0.95)	0.02 (0.50)	-0.03 (-0.27)	-0.05 (-0.86)	0.07 (0.36)	0.19* (3.58)	0.00 (0.01)	0.20* (2.30)	0.05 (0.16)

Hong Kong	-0.06	-0.34	0.01	-0.13	0.17*	0.78*	0.01	-0.01	0.00		0.05	0.14
	(-1.28)	(-1.27)	(0.05)	(-0.97)	(2.76)	(2.29)	(0.08)	(-0.06)	(-0.03)		(0.29)	(0.69)
Singapore	-0.16*		-0.23*	-0.16*	0.21*		0.18*	0.17*	-0.12		-0.18	-0.09
	(-4.71)		(-3.35)	(-2.55)	(5.39)		(2.28)	(2.31)	(-1.76)		(-1.39)	(-0.67)
Korea	-0.14*		-0.42*	-0.10	0.17*		0.20*	-0.03	-0.02		-0.04	0.12
	(-6.36)		(-4.22)	(-1.40)	(7.51)		(2.64)	(-0.46)	(-0.75)		(-0.46)	(1.51)
Taiwan	-0.01	-0.07	0.05	-0.01	0.05	0.06	-0.02	0.01	-0.08	-0.29*	-0.13	-0.08
	(-0.24)	(-0.63)	(0.81)	(-0.17)	(1.54)	(0.52)	(-0.27)	(0.11)	(-1.57)	(-2.00)	(-1.31)	(-0.86)

Notes: 1. Based on probit results for extended model where z stats are displayed in parenthesis and * denotes statistical significance at the 5% level. For 1–10 and 0–1 definitions, a negative sign indicates that people who value their religion are happier. For 1–4 definition, a positive sign indicates people who value their religion are happier.
2. No WVS data on state of health and confidence in civil services for Singapore.
3. Variable dropped due to multicollinearity.

Table 2.21 Probit results for Asia – trust

	a170 (Scale 1–10)				a008 (Scale 1–4)				a008r (Scale 0–1)			
	Overall	Health Poor	Edn Poor	Income Poor	Overall	Health Poor	Edn Poor	Income Poor	Overall	Health Poor	Edn Poor	Income Poor
China	−0.13* (−2.45)	−0.20 (−1.26)	−0.13 (−1.59)	−0.30* (−2.20)	0.11 (1.91)	0.08 (0.46)	0.15 (1.67)	0.18 (1.18)	−0.10 (−1.34)	0.04 (0.22)	−0.14 (−1.20)	−0.24 (−1.35)
India	−0.06* (−2.08)	0.04 (0.32)	0.03 (0.61)	0.14* (2.35)	−0.03 (−0.87)	0.00 (−0.01)	−0.03 (−0.52)	−0.17* (−2.81)	0.11 (2.91)*	−0.18 (−1.28)	0.12 (1.80)	0.36* (4.92)
Indonesia	−0.15* (−3.43)	−0.20 (−0.67)	−0.18 (−1.61)	−0.11 (−0.62)	0.17* (3.23)	0.05 (0.14)	0.19 (1.38)	0.09 (0.50)	−0.17 (−1.81)		0.04 (0.22)	−0.23 (−0.91)
Bangladesh	0.25* (4.93)	0.38 (1.87)	0.16 (1.96)	0.49* (3.29)	−0.13* (−2.23)	−0.34 (−1.57)	0.03 (0.35)	−0.59* (−3.48)	0.39* (5.62)	0.43 (1.70)	0.16 (1.46)	0.81* (4.30)
Malaysia	−0.20 (−1.88)		−0.60* (−2.16)	−0.05 (−0.09)	0.32* (2.53)		0.84* (2.34)	0.40 (0.66)	0.21 (1.05)			
Pakistan	−0.20* (−2.95)	0.70 (1.27)	0.00 (−0.04)	−0.16 (−0.43)	0.14* (2.39)	0.66* (2.59)	0.16 (1.82)	0.22 (1.47)	0.16* (2.23)	−0.36 (−1.26)	0.16 (1.57)	−0.06 (−0.40)
Philippines	0.05 (0.43)	−0.03 (−0.07)	0.08 (0.37)	−0.12 (−0.41)	0.08 (0.66)	−0.33 (−0.79)	0.01 (0.05)	−0.45 (−1.35)	0.06 (0.37)	0.03 (0.96)	0.44 (1.42)	0.65 (1.82)
Thailand	0.02 (0.32)	−0.36 (−1.11)	0.04 (0.57)	−0.16 (−0.70)	−0.01 (−0.13)	1.25* (3.01)	−0.08 (−0.93)	−0.37 (−1.44)	−0.03 (−0.26)		−0.04 (−0.24)	0.08 (0.22)
Vietnam	0.09 (1.89)	0.00 (−0.02)	−0.01 (−0.08)	0.07 (0.23)	−0.18* (−3.41)	0.09 (0.48)	−0.03 (−0.35)	0.02 (0.06)	0.06 (0.68)	0.01 (0.03)	−0.12 (−0.78)	0.42 (0.92)

Hong Kong	-0.11	0.08	-0.05	-0.07	0.07	0.04	0.06	-0.20	0.04		-0.16	0.30
	(-1.66)	(0.18)	(-0.31)	(-0.36)	(0.78)	(0.08)	(0.32)	(-0.87)	(0.35)		(-0.70)	(1.11)
Singapore	-0.21*		-0.30	-0.22	0.14		0.01	0.12	0.42*		0.38	0.19
	(-2.59)		(-1.80)	(-1.29)	(1.46)		(0.06)	(0.59)	(3.05)		(1.30)	(0.62)
Korea	-0.24*		-0.28	0.07	0.22*		0.22	0.24	-0.08		-0.15	-0.14
	(-4.90)		(-1.17)	(0.43)	(4.51)		(1.20)	(1.53)	(-1.20)		(-0.66)	(-0.75)
Taiwan	-0.04	0.06	-0.04	-0.09	0.17*	0.17	0.14	0.21	-0.13	-0.09	-0.25	-0.14
	(-0.81)	(0.23)	(-0.34)	(-0.71)	(2.75)	(0.65)	(1.10)	(1.49)	(-1.46)	(-0.29)	(-1.34)	(-0.75)

Notes: 1. Based on probit results for extended model where z stats are displayed in parenthesis and * denotes statistical significance at the 5% level. For 1–10 and 0–1 definitions, a negative sign indicates that people who trust others are happier. For 1–4 definition, a positive sign indicates people who trust others are happier.

2. No WVS data on state of health and confidence in civil services for Singapore.

3. Variable dropped due to multicollinearity.

Table 2.22 Probit results for Asia – confidence in civil services

	a170 (Scale 1–10)				a008 (Scale 1–4)				a008r (Scale 0–1)			
	Overall	Health Poor	Edn Poor	Income Poor	Overall	Health Poor	Edn Poor	Income Poor	Overall	Health Poor	Edn Poor	Income Poor
China	-0.22* (-5.57)	-0.26* (-2.37)	-0.15* (-2.36)	-0.11 (-1.12)	0.14* (3.25)	0.41* (3.52)	0.11 (1.64)	0.14 (1.31)	-0.11 (-1.95)	-0.43* (-3.01)	-0.13 (-1.51)	-0.16 (-1.15)
India	-0.12* (-7.75)	-0.08 (-1.51)	-0.15* (-5.59)	-0.13* (-4.42)	0.07* (4.14)	0.10 (1.83)	0.08* (2.90)	0.08* (2.56)	-0.03 (-1.45)	-0.06 (-0.88)	-0.06 (-1.80)	-0.02 (-0.63)
Indonesia	0.03 (0.90)	0.09 (0.45)	0.01 (0.15)	0.13 (1.29)	-0.02 (-0.41)	0.29 (1.30)	-0.06 (-0.70)	0.13 (1.16)	0.03 (0.46)		0.28* (2.18)	-0.11 (-0.83)
Bangladesh	0.04 (1.37)	0.04 (0.34)	0.15* (2.74)	0.02 (0.24)	-0.11* (-3.16)	-0.23 (-1.83)	-0.16* (-2.63)	-0.05 (-0.55)	0.16* (3.46)	0.26 (1.72)	0.16* (2.08)	0.07 (0.61)
Malaysia	-0.04 (-0.96)		0.01 (0.11)	-0.11 (-0.44)	-0.01 (-0.16)		-0.26 (-1.74)	0.04 (0.13)	0.02 (0.20)		0.41 (1.55)	
Pakistan	-0.01 (-0.32)	0.10 (0.36)	-0.01 (-0.21)	0.15 (0.81)	0.02 (0.70)	-0.02 (-0.10)	0.03 (0.54)	0.04 (0.47)	0.05 (1.31)	0.05 (0.28)	0.04 (0.80)	0.16 (1.64)
Philippines	-0.05 (-1.37)	0.01 (0.05)	0.11 (1.43)	-0.20 (-1.86)	0.03 (0.68)	0.01 (0.06)	-0.11 (-1.27)	-0.01 (-0.11)	0.02 (0.27)	-0.07 (0.76)	0.26* (2.00)	0.06 (0.38)
Thailand	-0.07 (-1.95)	-0.10 (-0.38)	-0.03 (-0.56)	0.34* (2.48)	-0.13* (-2.91)	-0.52 (-1.82)	-0.17* (-2.90)	-0.41* (-2.63)	0.10 (1.46)		0.02 (0.20)	0.51* (2.23)
Vietnam	-0.18* (-5.83)	-0.51* (-4.78)	-0.26* (-4.57)	-0.28 (-1.77)	0.10* (2.91)	0.20 (1.79)	0.07 (1.16)	0.14 (0.78)	-0.12* (-2.00)	-0.28 (-1.78)	-0.20 (-1.96)	-0.64* (-2.01)

Hong Kong	-0.06 (-1.09)	0.45 (1.32)	-0.07 (-0.50)	-0.27 (-1.73)	0.18* (2.59)	0.32 (0.83)	0.29 (1.61)	0.54* (2.77)	-0.13 (-1.55)		-0.15 (-0.74)	-0.57* (-2.40)
Singapore												
Korea	-0.04 (-1.24)		-0.11 (-0.83)	0.08 (0.87)	0.03 (0.94)		0.12 (1.19)	-0.05 (-0.62)	0.03 (0.66)		-0.16 (-1.32)	0.05 (0.52)
Taiwan	-0.06 (-1.80)	-0.04 (-0.24)	-0.09 (-1.27)	-0.03 (-0.39)	0.08* (2.01)	0.01 (0.08)	0.16 (1.91)	0.09 (0.92)	-0.01 (-0.19)	-0.15 (-0.79)	-0.09 (-0.75)	-0.12 (-1.07)

Notes: 1. Based on probit results for extended model where z stats are displayed in parenthesis and * denotes statistical significance at the 5% level. For 1–10 and 0–1 definitions, a negative sign indicates that people with confidence in civil services are happier. For 1–4 definition, a positive sign indicates people with confidence in civil services are happier.

2. No WVS data on state of health and confidence in civil services for Singapore.

3. Variable dropped due to multicollinearity.

two significant and a perverse sign; and only two in the 0 and 1 form for well-being. [3] For the three poverty categories, the results were equally weak. Only a few coefficients were significant for any of the three poverty categories. The results for the education poor in the 1–10 well-being category were the most encouraging, as four countries had significant coefficients. Apart from this, there were three coefficients at most reaching a significant level for the various poverty groups and definitions of well-being.

Results for the nonpoor. The results for the full sample of Asian economies are mirrored in the results for the more well-to-do segments of society that are not income poor, health poor or education poor. To conserve space, these results have not been reported. Although we did not test for the significance of differences, the coefficients of the variables are also similar in size to the total probit results. The same can be said for the other explanatory variables as well. Aside from a few education variables – India and Pakistan, where the poorly educated were recorded in large numbers – these results are consistent with intuition, since the sample sizes do not change that much when the poor are excluded from the full sample.

2.3　Country results

Further insights can be gained by considering the results on a country by country basis.

In **India**, health is important for the overall sample and also for the poverty groups, with the exception of the health poor, for whom there were limited observations. Income and education were also important as determinants of well-being for all the poor groups as well as the full sample, except in a few cases in which there were limited observations and in one case of the income poor. As noted above, the importance of education for the poorly educated is highly significant, with a coefficient that is much higher than for the nonpoor. This suggests that increasing the availability of education for the poor would provide a significant boost in their well-being in India. Gender and marital status are also generally significant for the overall sample, but less so for the poverty groups. Females are happier, as are those who are married. The effect of marriage is particularly strong for the poor, as its regression coefficient is larger than the coefficient for the full sample. Age was not significant for either the full sample or the poverty groups, and marital status was weakly significant for the full sample and for two of the poverty groups. As we might expect from other studies, those married are happier than those in the other categories. Women are happier than men in the full sample results, but not for any of the poverty groups. For both the poor and the full sample, family is not a significant explanatory variable. On the other hand, friends were significant among the income and educated poor, and also for the full sample in most cases, although some of the impacts were only marginally significant. The civil service variable was an important determinant of well-being in India, significant in two forms of the well-being probit regression and also for the health and education poor (twice), and it was marginally significant in several other instances. Significantly, religion was important in all three of the overall probit regressions, and also for the education and income poor. Trust was important for the full sample two out of three times, and also for the income poor in all three cases. The results for the work variable were disappointing. Work was not an important determinant of well-being either in the full sample or in the poverty regressions.

Turning to **China**, health is extremely important as a way to uplift well-being. It is significant for the full sample and also for each of the poverty groups, except where there is a lack of data for the heath poor. Income is also important for lifting well-being, both overall and for the health poor, but particularly for the latter, where the coefficient is much stronger than for the sample as a whole (see Table 2.12). The response for education is not as strong as that of health or income in raising well-being. The results are similar for both the poor and the nonpoor. Education is not significant for the overall sample or among the income poor. On the other hand, education is significant among the health and education poor. Age is significant in nonlinear form for the full sample (1–10 version) and also for the education poor. In the full sample, those who are married are happier than those who are not. However, there is not much evidence for marriage increasing well-being among the poor. For the impact of gender on well-being, the evidence suggests that women are generally happier than men for the full sample, but not among the poor. For the overall sample, both family and friends are significant in two out of the three definitions of well-being. However, neither variable is particularly important among the poor. Turning to the social variables, trust is significant in two of three overall sample results but is not generally important among the poor. Civil society is significant in all three aggregate formulations and also among the health poor (twice) and education poor (once). Neither work nor religion has much of an impact on well-being. To summarize, for the income deprived health and income are important explanatory variables, while for the education poor income has a powerful impact on well-being, similar to the highly significant impact we noted in India. This is an important result with strong policy implications. In summary, the most important result is the significance of education and income on the well-being of the full sample and of income on the health and income poor. One interesting observation has been made by Brockmann *et al.* (2009), who show that average life satisfaction fell between 1990 and 2000 while average incomes were rising rapidly. This trend is confirmed by glancing at Table 2.4 and also the tables provided by Brockmann *et al.* As they suggest, there is a time series puzzle which is not apparent from the cross-section results taken at several points of time and then aggregated over several survey waves. When we looked at the time trend of well-being earlier, these trends for China were not particularly evident, perhaps because we didn't compare end points and also because the earlier waves showed lower well-being. Be that as it may, it is important to realize that time trends in well-being may be overlooked by considering the response to changes in the independent variables which are significant yet overlook time series tendencies. Brockmann *et al.* offer three possible explanations, the most persuasive of which is that rapid growth is overwhelming psychologically, resulting in a feeling of powerlessness and lower well-being despite higher income. A lack of political freedom is also suggested as a possible explanation. This is not particularly persuasive, as there were few changes in the regime over this decade and no evidence that higher incomes translated into political dissatisfaction. The incident in Tianamen square occurred earlier. They also suggest that the relative deprivation theory may apply in China. What could be occurring is that the relative income distribution has become more skewed over this period and this increasing inequality could have resulted in a decline in overall well-being. This has been observed in Peru and Russia and is driven by a growth in "top-down" inequality as the proportion of mean income in the country grows rapidly, creating an environment of general dissatisfaction even in the face of rising incomes.

For **Bangladesh**, the three policy variables (health, income and education) are significant for the full sample, although health is only marginally important, probably because of data limitations. Women are happier than men, and there is evidence that those married are happier than those unmarried for the overall sample and in the case of the income poor. Happiness increases with age in linear form (not reported) and also in nonlinear form in one overall result and in one result each for the education, health and income poor. Family is not important, while friends are significant in one overall regression and marginally (z value between 1.5 and 2) in another. and friends are both important, but with the wrong a priori sign. Turning to the three poverty groups, the significance of education and income continues to be important for the poor. For those in poor health, none of the variables aside from education are statistically significant. For the income poor, only education is highly significant, while income is not. For those in the education-ally deprived group, education, health and income are all statistically significant. Health has the highest significance, and income and education are also significant. Turning to the social variables, civil service is significant in two of the three overall regressions and marginally significant in the third. The civil service variable is also important for the education poor in all three configurations of well-being. This is an interesting result and suggests that even those who are poorly educated are still interested in the provision of civil services. Trust is important in the overall regressions and also in all three cases for the income poor. Work is not significant for the poor, but is important in two of the three overall results. Religion is significant twice for the overall sample results but not for any of the poverty probit results. The lesson to be drawn from this analysis for Bangladesh is that for the complete sample all three policy variables are significant. When the sample is broken down into poor and nonpoor groups, education emerges as the most important variable in increasing the well-being of the poor. Income is significant only in the case of the educationally deprived. Policy interventions need to take into account which of the poverty groups is being targeted, since each of the three poverty groups responds to different incentives. Furthermore, some of the social variables are selectively important – civil services for the education poor and trust for the income poor – while religion is important for increasing overall well-being.

Looking at **Indonesia**, health and education are both significant for all versions of well-being in the full sample, while income is significant only once. Age is significant in nonlinear form in three countries and happiness is an increasing function of age in linear form (results not reported) for the other countries. There is some evidence for the full sample that women are happier than men, but this is not the case for the poverty regressions, in which the gender coefficient is not significant. There is no evidence that marital status has any impact on well-being, and friends and family are both significant for only the 1 to 10 version of well-being for the full sample. None of the other results for the full sample or the three poverty categories are significant for the marital status variable. For the four social variables, trust and religion are both significant for the full sample in all three formulations but at marginal levels of significance (z values between 1.5 and 2) in some cases. Civil service and work are not significant and have no appreciable impact on well-being in Indonesia. In general, the poverty regressions are rather disappointing. For the health poor there are only a relatively few observations (94) and none of the independent variables are statistically significant. For a larger sample of 250 respondents who are income poor, education is the only significant variable. The marriage variable shows married people are happier. There are no results for the education poor in Indonesia.

For **Pakistan**, the overall results are similar to some other countries where health, income and education are important for the overall sample. However, there are only scattered significant results for the poverty groups. The health variable is significant in lifting the well being of those with low income and the well-being of the education poor. Similarly, income is generally a significant variable in uplifting the well-being of the income poor or the education poor. Gender and marital status are not generally significant variables in raising well-being. However, well-being is a monotonically increasing function of age in the linear form of the model (not reported) and there is evidence that all poverty groups have a nonlinear fit with a dip in well-being in middle age. Family is sometimes significant in raising the well-being of the poor, but not at all for the overall sample. The same can be said of friends. The importance placed on having friends raised well-being in only a few cases among the poorly educated and in the overall sample. The value of friends was slightly more significant among the poorly educated and once (out of three) for the overall sample. Trust is significant in all three cases for the overall sample but not at all for the poor categories, suggesting that trust is more relevant as a variable that raises well-being for the nonpoor but not the poor. Work and religion were significant not at all for the overall sample and in only a few poverty categories. The civil service variable is never significant.

In the **Philippines**, health is statistically significant for the full sample and also for the poorly educated and those with low incomes. There are limited results for the health poor because of a lack of observations. Income is also an important determinant for the full sample and for the poorly educated and those in poor health. Strangely enough, income was not significant in uplifting well-being among the income poor. Educational attainment was not an important source of well-being, either for the entire sample or for any poverty groups. Similarly, there is little evidence that marriage raises well-being either for the overall sample or for the poverty groups. Results for gender are neutral aside from two instances out of 12 possibilities where the coefficient is significant, suggesting women are happier. Contrary to results from other countries, well-being is a declining function of age (not reported) and the nonlinear form is significant only for the overall sample with 1–10 ranking for well-being. Friends are important for the overall sample in two out of three formulations but in none of the poverty groups. Family is significant in one case for the full sample, but nowhere else. Both of these results suggest that the well-being of the nonpoor rather than the poor is more likely to benefit from the strong presence of family and friends. Work is significant only once, for the income poor, while trust is never significant. Religion and civil services are each significant only once, among the poorly educated, and not at all among the other poor groups or the overall sample.

The **Thailand** results are similar to those in the Philippines. For the health variable, education and income poor have significant health coefficients in determining well-being, while the coefficient for the health poor is not significant, perhaps because of a limited sample size. Income is also a significant determinant of well-being both for the full sample and for the health and education poor groups. As in the Philippines, income is not an important source of uplifting well-being for the income poor. Education was a significant source that uplifted well-being in the overall sample. Education was not that significant for the poor groups, with the exception of income poor in one instance. Marriage increases well-being for the overall sample in one case, and also for the income poor and education poor in one and two cases respectively. There is no evidence that gender plays a role in uplifting well-being and age enters linearly (not reported). There is little to support the importance of family and friends in uplifting well-being. Family is significant in one case for the full sample and once for the poorly educated, while friends are not significant with the correct a priori sign.[4] Work is significant for the full sample in two formulations and is marginally significant in the third ($z = 1.44$), but is not important for any of the poor groups. This provides additional evidence for Thailand that the work variable is more important for the nonpoor. Trust is not significant for the overall sample and is significant in only one poor group. The results provide evidence that religion is a source of well-being in Thailand. The religion variable is significant in two of the three regressions for the overall sample, and also among the poorly educated in two cases. Finally, the importance of confidence in civil society is weak, as several coefficients have the wrong sign. Only the coefficient for the full sample is close to significance ($z = 1.95$) for the 1 to 10 definition of well-being.

In **Vietnam**, the policy variables of health, income and education are all significant determinants of well-being for the full sample.

For health there is only one significant coefficient among the poor groups, while for income the results are much stronger. The health and education poor both benefit from higher income. Turning to the education variable, there are no significant results for the poverty groups. Looking at the other explanatory variables, marital status is important. Nearly all variables for both the poor and the overall sample suggest that those married are happier than the other groups. The gender variable is never significant, suggesting that men and women are equally happy, other things being equal. Age enters nonlinearly for the overall sample but not for the poor. Family is significant for the full sample in Vietnam for all three definitions of well-being, providing strong evidence for the importance of family in raising well-being. On the other hand, friends are not important, either for the full sample or for the poor. Work doesn't generally lift well-being in Vietnam. Work is significant once for the overall sample and once for the income poor. Religion doesn't lift well-being in Vietnam, a result we might have predicted given the lack of significance in China as well as its atheistic orientation. Trust is not significant either. However, confidence in civil services is highly significant, as it was in China. All three regressions for the overall sample have a significant coefficient for civil services, and there are also some significant results for the health, income and education poor (one out of three in each case).

There were limited results for **Singapore**. To begin with, there are no World Value Survey data on health. Income is significant at the overall level (although at a low level in two cases) and also for the income poor. The well-being of the education poor also responds significantly to changes in income in Singapore. The education variable is significant once for the overall sample, but not for any of the poverty groups. Marriage has a positive impact on well-being for the overall sample as well as the education and income poor. There is also evidence that women are happier than men, both for the full sample and for the income and education poor. Furthermore, there is some evidence of a nonlinear relationship between age and well-being, but only from one of the three different well-being regressions. There is no evidence of age nonlinearity among the poverty groups. Family is significant for the full sample, but not for any of the poverty groups, while friends are important for the full sample and for the income poor group. Given the priority that Singaporeans place on work, we would expect work to be a significant factor of well-being in Singapore. This is not borne out by the probit analysis. Singapore does not have a single significant coefficient for the work variable. The civil service question was not included in the Singapore sample. Trust was significant for the full sample in Singapore, but not among any of the poverty groups. The importance of religion, on the other hand, was strong for the sample as a whole and also for the education and income poor.

For the full sample in **Korea**, health is significant for the overall sample in all three definitions of well-being and also for all of the poverty categories, a very strong result indeed. For income, the results are not as comprehensive as those for the health variable. Income is again significant for the three overall probit regressions, but for only one of the education poor groups and none of the other poor group regressions. Education is only significant for one version of well-being for the overall sample and once each for the education poor and the income poor. Turning to the control variables, those who are married are happier in the full sample and (once) among the income poor. There is little evidence that gender makes a difference in Korea. Women are happier in two out of 12 possible regressions, and there is no indication of gender preference in the others. For age, there is limited evidence of nonlinearity in the 0 and 1 definition of well-being and (once) for the income and education poor. For a linear version (not reported), well-being is a linear function of age. Family is significant for all the full sample results and a few for the education and income poor. Friends, on the other hand, are significant for only one of the full sample probit regressions and once for the income poor. Turning to the four social variables, there is nothing to suggest that confidence in the civil service raises well-being, and a slight indication that work is important – for one overall probit regression and one for the income poor. Religion is significant in two overall regressions and also for two of the education poor regressions. Trust is also significant for two of the overall regression results, but not for any of the poor categories or different definitions of well-being.

In **Taiwan**, the health coefficient is significant for all three well-being regressions and also for the different poverty group regressions, with the lone exception of the health poor. Similarly, all the income coefficients are significant, even for the health poor. For education, the overall results are significant, but only once among the poverty groups. This result is similar to that observed for other countries, suggesting that well-being among the poor responds to short-term concerns about health and income and not about education, even among those who would like more education in the longer run for themselves or their families. Turning to the control variables, the married are happier than others for the full sample, but not generally for the poor. Gender results confirm that women are happier in the overall sample, but not generally for the poor. Age enters in a nonlinear way for the full sample and also for the poor, twice for the income poor and once for the poorly educated. Family is not important, while friends are significant once for the overall sample and once for the health poor. There was little evidence that the social variables have an impact on well-being in Taiwan. Work was not significant, while both trust and confidence were significant for only one overall probit regression and religion was significant for the health poor.

Tentative conclusions from the explanatory variables and country perspectives

Aside from the strong overall health findings and the education results for the poorest countries in South Asia and China, what are we to make of these rather disappointing findings for the rest of the explanatory variables? Looking on the bright side, the major explanatory variables of health, income and education are significant for many countries, but not across the board for all countries. Some further insights were obtained by looking at the size of the significant coefficients in the poverty probit regressions and comparing them with the results for the entire sample sets for all countries, and these results are reported in Table 2.12. This analysis suggests that, to uplift the well-being of the poor in South Asia and in Southeast and East Asia, greater emphasis should be put on providing primary health care and health services for the poor as well as making primary education more available. Better health has a significant impact on the education poor and the income poor as well. From a policy point of view, more spending on health has a more significant impact on the poor than the nonpoor in these countries. This result is consistent with several studies cited by Gupta *et al.* (2001). These studies found that public spending on health may matter more for the poor (see also Bidani and Ravallion 1997). For the richer countries in the region (Hong Kong, Singapore, Korea and Taiwan, as well as India and China), the poor are more responsive to improvements in income than the overall sample. Perhaps this is because of the demonstration effect, as the poor observe the lifestyle of those who are better off and see some opportunities for lifting their own well-being. Raising incomes would lift more poor families out of health poverty and enhance their well-being greatly.[5] These suggestions are consistent with the suggestion made by Gupta *et al.* (2001). Improving the provision of primary education would provide a significant boost to well-being as a result of a much higher elasticity of well-being with respect to education than for health or income poverty. We explore this in the next experiment by including a variable to reflect the probability of the poor exiting poverty. Finally, for those in poor health, there are no notable differences in the response of well-being to changes in the explanatory variables compared with the total sample. This could be a result of the small sample of the health poor, which depends on self-reporting. Most people don't report being in poor health. There were more observations in these two poverty groups of income and education poor. This could be due to those in poor health not even partaking in the questionnaire in the first place.[6]

If we consider the results from the perspectives on the countries, several tentative conclusions can be drawn. Health is consistently the most significant policy variable, followed closely by income. Education is generally less important, perhaps for reasons outlined in the country analysis discussion of Taiwan earlier on, namely the longer-term nature of education compared with the other two policy variables. Another interesting observation is that there are wide disparities in how well-being in different countries responds to the control and social variables in different ways. Studies that aggregate over many countries are missing out on the richness of individual country experiences, and may fail to see the importance of developing tailor-made policies for individual countries rather than making general conclusions about what is significant and what is not.

It is also useful to make some simple comparisons between the size of the coefficients for health, education and income for the poor and for the full sample. In the case of education, for most countries, the well-being of the poor is uplifted more than the well-being of the general population when there are more educational opportunities. This is true for those countries where education is significant in the probit regressions and also in countries where education has a less significant impact on well-being. The latter cases are usually the richer countries, where the level of education is generally higher and the poorly educated constitute a smaller proportion of the population. As noted above, the results are particularly striking for South Asia and the Mekong countries. In India the education coefficient for the full sample (8543 observations) is 0.01, 0.03 or 0.04 depending on the form of the well-being variable, whereas for those with only an elementary education (2440 observations) the coefficients are 0.12, 0.28 and 0.14, each several times the size of the overall coefficient for the full sample! All coefficients are statistically significant. Similar results are found for Bangladesh and Pakistan for some formulations of the well-being variable. Comparisons of the health and income poor coefficients with the full sample results are not as dramatically different, either because of lack of significance or because of the limited sample size for the poor groups in these two categories.

For the four social variables of confidence, meaningful work, trust and religion, results are generally mixed. For the social variable of confidence in the civil service the significance is generally low, particularly in Southeast Asia and Pakistan. It is also low in the richer countries of East Asia – Hong Kong, Korea and Taiwan. Confidence is higher in China and Vietnam, the only centrally planned countries in our sample, and also, somewhat surprisingly given the reputation for high levels of bureaucratic red tape, in India and Bangladesh. Second, meaningful work is almost never important in uplifting the level of happiness and well-being in Asia. Of 140 possible chances to register an important impact on well-being over the different formulations of well-being and for different poverty groups, the meaningful work variable is significant only eight times, even less than we might expect it to be significant by chance. In this study, we were limited by the data, in that there was no information on type of work or job characteristics that impacted the well-being of the poor. Warr (1990) argued that jobs can have a substantial impact on the well-being of the individual. The quality of well-being on the job influences the behavior and decisions of the worker and their interactions with colleagues, family and social life. From our study, it would be an understatement to say that the types of job available and future employment prospects in a more developed Asian economy like Singapore or Hong Kong would be rather different from a developing Asian country. Hence, the current work estimate could be somewhat biased, given the difference in job characteristics between different Asian countries. However, it could still give us a general picture of how Asia feels about work and its impact on well-being. Third, trust is important for the full sample in about half the countries but is much less significant for the poverty groups, particularly the health and education poor. We can only speculate why this might be so, perhaps because of a limited sample size and the large number of explanatory variables in the regression equations. It could be that the poor are subject to discrimination and corruption to a greater degree than the nonpoor. Lastly, religion is significant for the overall sample in about half the countries, but not in the centrally planned economies or among the health and income poor.

2.4 Aggregation results for three Asian subregions

To explore the findings further, we aggregated the results for three subregions of Asia as well as for the entire Asian region. These results are reported in Table 2.23. We review these results by independent variable and by subregion as well as by poverty group. As we reported for results for individual countries, there are probit coefficients for each of the three designations for the dependent variable well-being or happiness, and results are reported for each of the three poverty groups and for the overall sample. In general, aggregation results in a better fit of the model and generally greater significance of the independent variables, and provides us with information about the importance of the explanatory variables in the different Asian regions.

Health
On the regional level, results for health are consistent with the summaries of regressions for the individual countries reported above. The overall sample coefficients are highly significant (z values over 20 in many cases for all three measures of well-being and for all the subregions – South Asia, Southeast Asia and East Asia – as well as Asia as a whole and the aggregate of East Asia and Southeast Asia). The health results are displayed in the first 10 lines of Table 2.23. All the coefficients are statistically significant, with the exception of a few coefficients for the health poor, where there are fewer data observations. Coefficients for the education poor and income are also highly significant for all subregions. However, it should be noted that none of the health coefficients for the different regions are significantly larger than the coefficients for the overall regressions. This suggests that the poor are responding to changes in the provision of health facilities in much the same way as the nonpoor. The results for health also suggest that the well-being of all the Asian subregions, as well as the region as a whole, would benefit from the provision of better health facilities.

Income
On the regional level, income provides a boost to happiness and well-being, with only a few exceptions. The overall sample coefficients on income are all statistically significant, with high z values, and these results generally carry over to the poor as well. Only the well-being of the income poor is not improved by higher income in a few cases, particularly in Southeast Asia, where income is not significant in any of the three well-being models. Income also fails to be significant in one case each in South Asia and East and Southeast Asia. This result echoes the findings for some of the countries in the richer countries in East and Southeast Asia, where we noted that the results for the income poor are much less significant across the range of developing countries in Asia.

Table 2.23 Aggregated probit results for Asia

	a170 (Scale 1-10)				a008 (Scale 1-4)				a008r (Scale 0-1)			
	Overall	Health Poor	Edn Poor	Income Poor	Overall	Health Poor	Edn Poor	Income Poor	Overall	Health Poor	Edn Poor	Income Poor
STATE OF HEALTH												
South Asia	-0.30* (-21.98)	0.04 (0.26)	-0.35* (-15.08)	-0.29* (-10.33)	0.52* (36.46)	0.05 (0.28)	0.58* (24.01)	0.45* (15.94)	-0.45* (-25.28)	0.00 (-0.03)	-0.54* (-18.28)	-0.45* (-13.10)
East and Southeast Asia	-0.25* (-22.19)	0.24 (0.52)	-0.23* (-11.53)	-0.29* (-9.37)	0.43* (33.44)	-0.67 (-1.32)	0.36* (16.09)	0.44* (13.02)	-0.36* (-20.21)	0.13 (0.85)	-0.36* (-11.53)	-0.35* (-8.37)
East Asia and Singapore	-0.33* (-19.56)	0.06 (0.13)	-0.30* (-10.25)	-0.35* (-8.77)	0.49* (26.44)	-0.74 (-1.45)	0.46* (13.96)	0.45* (10.27)	-0.42* (-17.35)	-0.33 (-1.43)	-0.43* (-10.27)	-0.34* (-6.62)
Southeast Asia excluding Singapore	-0.19* (-12.14)		-0.16* (-5.70)	-0.24* (-4.62)	0.40* (22.46)		0.28* (8.78)	0.46* (8.01)	-0.31* (-11.40)	0.35 (1.50)	-0.28* (-5.90)	-0.38* (-5.11)
Asia	-0.27* (-31.61)	0.06 (0.39)	-0.29* (-18.96)	-0.28* (-13.50)	0.47* (50.15)	0.06 (0.37)	0.47* (28.86)	0.45* (20.66)	-0.41* (-33.12)	-0.01 (-0.11)	-0.46* (-22.02)	-0.41* (-15.79)
INCOME												
South Asia	0.07* (12.24)	0.10* (4.05)	0.05* (4.36)	-0.29* (-5.96)	-0.05* (-8.54)	-0.08* (-3.69)	-0.06* (-4.97)	0.19* (3.91)	0.10* (12.44)	0.10* (3.75)	0.08* (5.82)	-0.01 (-0.19)
East and Southeast Asia	0.12* (27.23)	0.19* (10.10)	0.13* (15.50)	0.08* (1.44)	-0.08* (-17.65)	-0.15* (-7.89)	-0.11* (-11.71)	-0.10 (-1.82)	0.13* (18.16)	0.15* (6.30)	0.15* (11.49)	0.30* (4.38)
East Asia and Singapore	0.10* (16.14)	0.12* (5.02)	0.12* (9.27)	0.26* (3.91)	-0.08* (-11.44)	-0.12* (-4.59)	-0.08* (-5.69)	-0.23* (-3.23)	0.10* (10.82)	0.10* (3.22)	0.11* (5.87)	0.35* (4.17)

Southeast Asia excluding Singapore	0.14* (21.38)	0.27* (8.91)	0.15* (12.61)	-0.17 (-1.94)	-0.07* (-9.93)	-0.15* (-4.83)	-0.11* (-8.55)	0.10 (1.11)	0.14* (12.29)	0.17* (4.31)	0.17* (8.21)	0.13 (1.13)
Asia	0.11* (33.23)	0.16* (11.13)	0.12* (18.98)	-0.10* (-2.76)	-0.08* (-22.46)	-0.13* (-9.35)	-0.10* (-14.94)	0.07* (2.06)	0.13* (25.98)	0.14* (8.46)	0.14* (14.78)	0.10* (2.41)
EDUCATION LEVEL												
South Asia	0.05* (11.67)	0.09* (4.32)	0.19* (4.50)	0.09* (8.76)	-0.02* (-4.19)	-0.03 (-1.34)	-0.13* (-3.12)	-0.05* (-4.50)	0.04* (6.83)	0.04 (1.60)	0.32* (6.29)	0.07* (5.40)
East and Southeast Asia	0.00 (-0.23)	-0.01 (-0.66)	0.02 (0.53)	0.01 (1.16)	0.03* (6.00)	0.02 (0.79)	0.00 (-0.05)	-0.01 (-0.44)	0.04* (5.92)	-0.02 (-0.82)	0.17* (3.07)	0.07* (3.94)
East Asia and Singapore	-0.01* (-2.10)	-0.01 (-0.24)	0.00 (-0.08)	-0.01 (-0.32)	0.01 (0.95)	-0.02 (-0.74)	-0.06 (-0.99)	-0.01 (-0.44)	0.07* (7.43)	0.02 (0.62)	0.26* (3.32)	0.07* (3.20)
Southeast Asia excluding Singapore	0.01 (1.74)	-0.02 (-0.66)	0.03 (0.56)	0.04* (2.06)	0.01 (0.82)	0.04 (1.37)	0.00 (0.02)	-0.04 (-1.63)	0.04* (3.69)	-0.05 (-1.25)	0.06 (0.81)	0.08* (2.55)
Asia	0.02* (7.34)	0.03* (2.37)	0.18* (6.88)	0.06* (7.35)	0.00 (1.51)	-0.01 (-0.39)	-0.12* (-4.25)	-0.04* (-4.37)	0.04* (8.98)	0.01 (0.50)	0.32* (9.03)	0.07* (7.49)
SEX												
South Asia	0.10* (4.44)	0.10 (1.10)	0.09* (2.37)	0.00 (0.00)	-0.06* (-2.48)	-0.05 (-0.54)	0.04 (1.12)	0.04 (0.83)	0.18* (6.08)	0.10 (0.97)	0.07 (1.39)	0.11 (1.92)
East and Southeast Asia	0.05* (3.24)	-0.16* (-2.12)	0.05 (1.52)	0.14* (2.67)	-0.08* (-4.12)	0.04 (0.52)	-0.05 (-1.44)	-0.14* (-2.56)	0.21* (7.78)	-0.17 (-1.73)	0.09 (1.68)	0.21* (2.98)
East Asia and Singapore	0.10* (3.80)	-0.05 (-0.46)	0.07 (1.26)	0.15* (2.27)	-0.12* (-4.29)	-0.01 (-0.10)	-0.16* (-2.66)	-0.25* (-3.48)	0.28* (7.76)	-0.03 (-0.24)	0.22* (2.90)	0.27* (3.06)

(Continued)

Table 2.23 Continued

	a170 (Scale 1–10)				a008 (Scale 1–4)				a008r (Scale 0–1)			
	Overall	Health Poor	Edn Poor	Income Poor	Overall	Health Poor	Edn Poor	Income Poor	Overall	Health Poor	Edn Poor	Income Poor
Southeast Asia excluding Singapore	0.02 (0.79)	−0.24* (−2.26)	0.03 (0.60)	0.16 (1.82)	−0.09* (−3.24)	0.02 (0.15)	−0.01 (−0.29)	−0.02 (−0.21)	0.15* (3.54)	−0.24 (−1.64)	−0.04 (−0.49)	0.10 (0.85)
Asia	0.08* (6.29)	0.01 (0.12)	0.09* (3.73)	0.05 (1.28)	−0.08* (−5.47)	−0.04 (−0.73)	−0.02 (−0.88)	−0.03 (−0.87)	0.23* (11.44)	0.03 (0.40)	0.10 (2.84)	0.17* (3.74)
AGE												
South Asia	−0.10 (−1.17)	−0.32 (−0.77)	−0.13 (−0.83)	−0.11 (−0.54)	0.17 (1.81)	−0.20 (−0.50)	0.26 (1.62)	0.26 (1.26)	0.87* (9.46)	−0.19 (−0.45)	0.58* (3.88)	0.59* (2.98)
East and Southeast Asia	−0.13 (−1.90)	−0.48 (−1.24)	−0.39 (−2.09)*	−0.27 (−1.17)	−0.01 (−0.19)	−0.35 (−0.86)	0.19 (0.91)	−0.08 (−0.31)	1.23* (13.98)	0.51 (1.05)	1.13* (5.99)	1.10* (4.93)
East Asia and Singapore	−0.35* (−3.04)	0.21 (0.33)	−0.46 (−1.18)	−0.63 (−1.83)	0.02 (0.14)	−1.42* (−2.15)	−0.23 (−0.54)	−0.02 (−0.05)	0.99* (7.66)	1.72* (2.21)	1.01* (3.62)	0.81* (2.71)
Southeast Asia excluding Singapore	−0.22* (−2.22)	−0.91 (−1.61)	−0.48* (−2.13)	0.13 (0.34)	0.31* (2.66)	0.40 (0.66)	0.28 (1.11)	−0.14 (−0.35)	0.85* (5.76)	−0.58 (−0.75)	0.70* (2.50)	1.00* (2.44)
Asia	−0.24* (−4.30)	−0.57* (−2.00)	−0.27* (−2.27)	−0.23 (−1.52)	0.23* (3.78)	−0.04 (−0.13)	0.24 (1.89)	0.21 (1.35)	0.89* (13.74)	−0.06 (−0.19)	0.57* (5.08)	0.67* (4.62)

AGE SQUARED

South Asia	0.04 (1.68)	0.07 (0.75)	0.05 (1.19)	0.05 (0.89)	-0.05* (-2.13)	0.06 (0.64)	-0.08* (-2.11)	-0.07 (-1.35)	-0.20* (-8.53)	0.04 (0.39)	-0.11* (-3.00)	-0.12* (-2.44)
East and Southeast Asia	0.06* (3.29)	0.14 (1.61)	0.11* (2.72)	0.08 (1.48)	0.00 (-0.13)	0.07 (0.77)	-0.05 (-1.16)	0.03 (0.44)	-0.28* (-12.16)	-0.09 (-0.78)	-0.24* (-5.16)	-0.25* (-4.40)
East Asia and Singapore	0.10* (3.63)	-0.02 (-0.16)	0.13 (1.55)	0.16* (2.09)	-0.02 (-0.68)	0.30* (2.01)	0.02 (0.18)	-0.01 (-0.13)	-0.21* (-6.45)	-0.34 (-1.96)	-0.18* (-2.76)	-0.16* (-2.19)
Southeast Asia excluding Singapore	0.07* (2.97)	0.25 (1.89)	0.13* (2.48)	0.00 (-0.03)	-0.07* (-2.49)	-0.08 (-0.56)	-0.07 (-1.22)	0.06 (0.62)	-0.21* (-5.65)	0.13 (0.73)	-0.16* (-2.33)	-0.26* (-2.53)
Asia	0.08* (5.85)	0.15* (2.30)	0.10* (3.46)	0.08* (2.03)	-0.06* (-4.21)	0.01 (0.13)	-0.08* (-2.67)	-0.05 (-1.35)	-0.20* (-12.02)	0.03 (0.44)	-0.10* (-3.62)	-0.14* (-3.86)

MARITAL STATUS

South Asia	0.12* (4.27)	0.16 (1.44)	0.14* (2.39)	0.23* (3.67)	-0.13* (-4.46)	-0.10 (-0.89)	-0.14* (-2.51)	-0.31* (-4.80)	0.09* (2.30)	0.13 (0.97)	0.24* (3.51)	0.26* (3.36)
East and Southeast Asia	0.15* (8.41)	0.21* (2.52)	0.13* (3.41)	0.14* (2.56)	-0.17* (-8.96)	-0.15 (-1.77)	-0.18* (-4.24)	-0.14* (-2.41)	0.24* (8.34)	0.17 (1.64)	0.20* (3.46)	0.14 (1.89)
East Asia and Singapore	0.22* (6.56)	0.33* (2.32)	0.22* (2.98)	0.18* (2.31)	-0.18* (-4.92)	-0.23 (-1.55)	-0.14 (-1.75)	-0.26* (-3.12)	0.16* (3.32)	0.11 (0.62)	0.21* (2.19)	0.32* (3.18)
Southeast Asia excluding Singapore	0.12* (4.02)	0.13 (0.95)	0.13* (2.20)	-0.13 (-1.28)	-0.24* (-7.12)	-0.34* (-2.34)	-0.25* (-3.73)	-0.16 (-1.44)	0.32* (6.12)	0.55* (3.02)	0.42* (4.50)	0.16 (1.07)
Asia	0.13* (7.57)	0.21* (2.86)	0.11* (3.20)	0.14* (3.23)	-0.17* (-8.88)	-0.18* (-2.46)	-0.14* (-3.72)	-0.26* (-5.76)	0.13* (5.18)	0.21* (2.39)	0.24* (4.95)	0.24* (4.41)

(Continued)

Table 2.23 Continued

	a170 (Scale 1–10)				a008 (Scale 1–4)				a008r (Scale 0–1)			
	Overall	Health Poor	Edn Poor	Income Poor	Overall	Health Poor	Edn Poor	Income Poor	Overall	Health Poor	Edn Poor	Income Poor
FAMILY												
South Asia	0.10* (3.09)	0.07 (0.63)	0.13* (2.43)	0.01 (0.16)	0.07* (2.20)	0.12 (1.30)	-0.05 (-1.04)	0.06 (0.99)	0.00 (0.04)	-0.17 (-1.46)	0.20* (3.09)	0.00 (0.02)
East and Southeast Asia	-0.15* (-6.64)	-0.09 (-1.23)	-0.15* (-4.09)	-0.08 (-1.33)	0.28* (11.03)	0.16* (2.00)	0.17* (4.20)	0.08 (1.27)	-0.16* (-4.86)	-0.11 (-1.22)	-0.11 (-1.94)	-0.06 (-0.74)
East Asia and Singapore	-0.07* (-2.51)	0.04 (0.47)	-0.08 (-1.67)	-0.03 (-0.41)	0.22* (7.05)	0.00 (0.02)	0.13* (2.37)	0.03 (0.35)	-0.11* (-2.73)	0.03 (0.25)	-0.06 (-0.93)	0.00 (-0.02)
Southeast Asia excluding Singapore	-0.21* (-4.96)	-0.22 (-1.57)	-0.22* (-3.58)	-0.12 (-0.85)	0.12* (2.61)	0.14 (0.94)	0.05 (0.78)	-0.07 (-0.42)	0.04 (0.60)	-0.10 (-0.49)	0.04 (0.41)	0.17 (0.79)
Asia	-0.02 (-0.85)	-0.01 (-0.14)	0.00 (-0.14)	-0.01 (-0.32)	0.15* (7.68)	0.13* (2.11)	0.04 (1.37)	0.05 (1.06)	-0.06* (-2.53)	-0.12 (-1.70)	0.06 (1.37)	-0.03 (-0.54)
FRIENDS												
South Asia	-0.07* (-5.15)	-0.12* (-2.18)	-0.13* (-5.61)	-0.11* (-3.40)	0.09* (6.05)	0.06 (1.17)	0.11* (4.60)	0.18* (5.80)	-0.04* (-2.09)	-0.05 (-0.78)	-0.06* (-2.19)	-0.11* (-2.94)
East and Southeast Asia	-0.01 (-0.55)	-0.08 (-1.50)	-0.01 (-0.20)	-0.02 (-0.58)	0.03 (1.78)	0.08 (1.44)	0.04 (1.55)	0.14* (3.23)	-0.02 (-0.79)	-0.05 (-0.75)	-0.01 (-0.24)	-0.15* (-2.85)
East Asia and Singapore	-0.05* (-2.16)	-0.22* (-2.83)	-0.02 (-0.47)	-0.07 (-1.41)	0.10* (4.50)	0.16* (2.08)	0.11* (2.45)	0.25* (4.59)	-0.07* (-2.25)	-0.14 (-1.48)	-0.09 (-1.54)	-0.27* (-3.98)

Southeast Asia excluding Singapore	0.00 (0.11)	0.10 (1.19)	0.00 (0.08)	0.03 (0.50)	0.03 (1.36)	-0.02 (-0.20)	0.00 (0.13)	0.03 (0.39)	-0.01 (-0.37)	0.06 (0.57)	0.04 (0.73)	-0.02 (-0.18)
Asia	-0.07* (-7.34)	-0.13* (-3.51)	-0.11* (-6.51)	-0.07* (-2.89)	0.09* (8.58)	0.10* (2.64)	0.11* (6.14)	0.17* (7.04)	-0.07* (-5.25)	-0.07 (-1.55)	-0.08* (-3.48)	-0.14* (-4.67)
WORK												
South Asia	-0.07* (-3.19)	-0.16 (-1.99)	0.02 (0.55)	-0.01 (-0.19)	0.05* (2.12)	0.10 (1.36)	-0.03 (-0.96)	-0.03 (-0.63)	0.03 (1.07)	-0.07 (-0.81)	0.07 (1.61)	0.11 (1.74)
East and Southeast Asia	0.02 (1.80)	-0.02 (-0.49)	-0.01 (-0.37)	0.11* (2.88)	0.07* (4.41)	0.06 (1.22)	0.10* (3.64)	0.01 (0.23)	0.05* (2.25)	-0.04 (-0.60)	0.01 (0.32)	0.02 (0.44)
East Asia and Singapore	0.05* (2.60)	-0.02 (-0.33)	-0.01 (-0.28)	0.12* (2.67)	0.00 (0.11)	0.13 (1.73)	0.08* (2.05)	-0.02 (-0.36)	0.08* (3.16)	-0.11 (-1.25)	0.01 (0.12)	0.03 (0.45)
Southeast Asia excluding Singapore	0.01 (0.27)	-0.05 (-0.62)	0.02 (0.51)	0.15 (1.92)	0.14* (5.81)	0.04 (0.56)	0.15* (3.64)	0.01 (0.08)	-0.04 (-1.10)	-0.03 (-0.24)	-0.03 (-0.50)	0.05 (0.48)
Asia	0.01 (1.30)	-0.05 (-1.20)	0.03 (1.43)	0.09* (2.90)	0.04* (3.36)	0.06 (1.33)	0.03 (1.43)	-0.03 (-0.92)	0.08* (4.55)	-0.01 (-0.27)	0.06* (2.09)	0.09* (2.45)
RELIGION												
South Asia	-0.03* (-2.17)	-0.08 (-1.42)	-0.04 (-1.51)	-0.09* (-3.03)	0.11* (7.92)	0.02 (0.36)	0.11* (3.95)	0.11* (3.73)	-0.10* (-5.77)	-0.11 (-1.82)	-0.12* (-3.76)	-0.08* (-2.09)
East and Southeast Asia	-0.04* (-4.42)	-0.05 (-1.45)	0.00 (0.12)	-0.06* (-2.33)	0.12* (13.18)	0.09* (2.31)	0.09* (4.56)	0.11* (4.14)	-0.08* (-5.70)	-0.10* (-2.23)	-0.09* (-3.60)	-0.07 (-1.91)
East Asia and Singapore	-0.04* (-2.70)	0.00 (0.05)	0.00 (0.07)	0.00 (-0.09)	0.09* (5.98)	0.00 (-0.02)	0.02 (0.76)	0.01 (0.37)	-0.03 (-1.63)	-0.07 (-1.00)	-0.05 (-1.12)	0.00 (0.03)

(Continued)

Table 2.23 Continued

	a170 (Scale 1–10)				a008 (Scale 1–4)				a008r (Scale 0–1)			
	Overall	Health Poor	Edn Poor	Income Poor	Overall	Health Poor	Edn Poor	Income Poor	Overall	Health Poor	Edn Poor	Income Poor
Southeast Asia excluding Singapore	0.00 (−0.32)	−0.08 (−1.44)	−0.05 (−1.75)	−0.01 (−0.10)	−0.04* (−2.45)	0.01 (0.09)	−0.01 (−0.42)	−0.01 (−0.21)	0.07* (2.54)	0.00 (0.04)	0.02 (0.41)	−0.05 (−0.54)
Asia	−0.01 (−0.79)	0.00 (0.11)	0.03* (2.46)	−0.07* (−3.75)	0.09* (11.72)	0.00 (−0.17)	0.05* (3.74	0.10* (5.16)	−0.03* (−3.13)	−0.01 (−0.26)	−0.05* (−2.50)	−0.04 (−1.59)
TRUST												
South Asia	0.00 (0.08)	0.06 (0.66)	0.08 (1.96)	0.17* (3.15)	−0.01 (−0.43)	0.02 (0.21)	0.02 (0.57)	−0.14* (−2.70)	0.21* (6.96)	−0.06 (−0.51)	0.14* (2.86)	0.36* (5.94)
East and Southeast Asia	−0.10* (−5.86)	−0.16 (−1.98)	−0.07* (−2.12)	−0.17* (−3.04)	0.06* (3.26)	0.15 (1.74)	0.08 (1.99)	0.10 (1.63)	−0.02 (−0.73)	−0.12 (−1.10)	−0.08 (−1.42)	−0.03 (−0.39)
East Asia and Singapore	−0.19* (−7.11)	−0.21 (−1.79)	−0.15* (−2.68)	−0.19* (−2.72)	0.18* (6.17)	0.14 (1.16)	0.13* (2.16)	0.20* (2.61)	−0.07 (−1.95)	−0.01 (−0.09)	−0.15 (−1.94)	−0.16 (−1.75)
Southeast Asia excluding Singapore	−0.05* (−2.17)	−0.11 (−0.95)	−0.04 (−0.92)	−0.16 (−1.61)	−0.03 (−0.93)	0.12 (0.98)	0.02 (0.42)	−0.02 (−0.17)	0.00 (−0.11)	−0.21 (−1.27)	−0.04 (−0.52)	0.09 (0.67)
Asia	−0.07* (−5.36)	−0.08 (−1.30)	−0.02 (−0.77)	0.00 (−0.11)	0.04* (2.97)	0.09 (1.46)	0.05 (1.94)	−0.04 (−0.96)	0.07* (3.43)	−0.08 (−1.07)	0.02 (0.70)	0.20* (4.22)

CIVIL SERVICES

South Asia	-0.10* (-8.29)	-0.07 (-1.63)	-0.09* (-4.74)	-0.10* (-3.71)	0.02* (2.00)	-0.01 (-0.24)	0.01 (0.52)	0.05 (1.90)	-0.01 (-0.94)	0.04 (0.81)	-0.01 (-0.42)	0.01 (0.17)
East and Southeast Asia	-0.08* (-7.52)	-0.14* (-2.87)	-0.05* (-2.46)	-0.01 (-0.21)	0.07* (5.34)	0.15* (2.99)	0.01 (0.21)	0.04 (1.04)	-0.02 (-0.93)	-0.20* (-3.23)	0.00 (-0.09)	-0.03 (-0.78)
East Asia and Singapore	-0.11* (-6.33)	-0.13 (-1.67)	-0.13* (-3.39)	-0.06 (-1.31)	0.05* (2.51)	0.15 (1.92)	0.09* (2.25)	0.02 (0.49)	-0.01 (-0.49)	-0.18 (-1.93)	-0.07 (-1.40)	-0.06 (-1.02)
Southeast Asia excluding Singapore	-0.06* (-3.83)	-0.19* (-2.75)	-0.03 (-0.95)	0.06 (1.07)	0.03 (1.70)	0.12 (1.72)	-0.07* (-2.21)	0.03 (0.51)	0.01 (0.37)	-0.21* (-2.26)	0.06 (1.16)	-0.01 (-0.16)
Asia	-0.09* (-11.82)	-0.13* (-4.07)	-0.08* (-5.75)	-0.08* (-3.96)	0.05* (5.49)	0.07* (2.16)	0.02 (1.05)	0.06* (2.70)	-0.02 (-1.73)	-0.08* (-2.05)	-0.03 (-1.41)	-0.01 (-0.51)

Notes:
1. Based on probit results for extended model where z stats are displayed in parenthesis and * denotes statistical significance at the 5% level.
2. Variable dropped due to multicollinearity.
3. South Asia includes India, Bangladesh and Pakistan.
4. East Asia includes China, Hong Kong, Korea and Taiwan.
5. Southeast Asia includes Indonesia, Malaysia, Philippines, Thailand and Vietnam.

Education

Considering all the subregions and configurations of the well-being variable, education is again of generally less significance in raising well-being than the other two policy variables of income and health. Education is extremely important in raising well-being, mainly for South Asia. Education is much less important in raising well-being in East and Southeast Asia, both in these regions as a whole and among the poverty groups in these two regions. For Asia as a whole, education is also significant in the majority of cases. It is also notable that the education poor coefficient is significantly greater than the overall coefficient both in South Asia and for Asia as a whole (0.18 versus 0.02 for Asia and 0.19 versus 0.05 for South Asia). This result mirrors the findings on the importance of education in India and Bangladesh, which was discussed in the country results and also reported in Table 2.12, and confirms our earlier conclusion that education is highly valued in South Asia. The coefficient for the health poor is significant only once and the overall coefficient two out of three times. The limited significance of education among the poor in Southeast and East Asia suggests that in these two regions economic development may have reached the point of diminishing returns to further education even among the poorly educated. Whether or not this is true certainly bears further investigation. It should be noted that there is some evidence from the table that the income poor do value education, and this is reflected in significant coefficients for income poverty in Southeast Asia in two of the three models of well-being.

Gender

For the overall regional sample, women are generally happier than men for the three different forms of the dependent variable. This is also true for three different regions when the overall sample is disaggregated. However, with the possible exception of the income poor in East Asia, the significance of gender is much reduced when we examine the poverty groups. Of 45 possible coefficients for gender, only 13 are statistically significant.

Age

The age variable in its nonlinear form is statistically significant for all versions of the overall regression for Asia, and also for the health and education poor, but only for the 1 to 10 specification of the dependent variable. The inflection point in this relationship is reported for the aggregate form of the model along with the other results for country

Table 2.24 Effect of age on life satisfaction and well-being in Asia

| Country | Overall | a170 (Scale 1–10) | | a008r (Scale 0–1) | |
		Health Poor	Edn Poor	Income Poor	Health Poor
China	1.70		1.85		
Indonesia		2.42			
Bangladesh					2.02
Pakistan		2.34	2.18	2.46	
Philippines	1.72				
Vietnam	1.88				
Hong Kong		1.86			
Taiwan	1.87			2.22	

Notes: 1. Age is defined as 1: 15–29, 2: 30–49 and 3: 50 years and above.
2. Data are shown only for available cases. The age at which the minimum occurs is given by the coefficient of linear age divided by twice the coefficient of age-squared.

probit regressions in Table 2.24. There are nonlinear relationships in eight of the Asian countries for some of the overall sample, and some poor subgroup results for the 1–10 scale of well-being and one case for the 0 to 1 scale. These results provide partial support for the nonlinear hypothesis. The inflection point is generally in a younger age group than the midlife crisis scenario suggested by Easterlin. This could be because life expectancy is somewhat shorter for Asian countries, or it could be the result of having fewer intervals for age. Most of the inflection points are in the late 20s or 30s.

Marital status
Those who are married are generally happy, overall, in the subregions, and for the different poverty groups in Asia.

Family
The results for the significance of family are mixed. For the overall Asian region, family is significant in two of the three forms for happiness/ well-being, and this result holds true for the South Asia and Southeast Asia subregions. For East Asia, family is significant in all three cases for the overall sample. For the poverty groups, family is not important at all for the income poor in any of the regions or for Asia as a whole, whereas for the education poor it is important in two of three cases in

East and Southeast Asia and South Asia, and in one case in Southeast Asia. For the health poor, family is significant only once for East and Southeast Asia.

Friends

The importance of friends is more evident in South Asia and the region as a whole than in East and Southeast Asia. Only a few poverty groups value friends in these two regions, as opposed to much higher significance in South Asia and the region as a whole. The only exception to this is in East Asia, where all three poverty groups are significant for the 1 to 4 designation of well-being and for the income poor in East and Southeast Asia. To some extent the aggregate results mirror the country results, which also highlight the importance of these two variables in South Asia.

Work

In many, but not all, cases work is a significant explanatory variable in all three regions and for the overall sample in all subregions. However, for the poor work is generally not significant in any of the subregions or for any of the three poverty groups, except for a few cases of the income poor. It should be noted that the aggregate results for work tend to obscure the fact that this variable was not significant in a number of countries. We have noted the caveat for work earlier in the discussion of country perspectives.

Religion

Religion is generally significant for the overall sample in Asia and all the subregions. However, for the poor the results on religion are mixed. In South Asia, religion is important for the income and education poor but not for the health poor. Looking at the region as a whole, religion is important for the education and income poor but not for the health poor. For East Asian and Southeast Asian regions respectively, religion is not important for any of the poverty groups. Disaggregation into subregions reduces the significance of religion, particularly in East Asia and Southeast Asia when measured separately.

Trust

For the region as a whole, trust is significant for all three measures of well-being, and also for the East and Southeast Asia aggregate. However, few poverty coefficients are significant aside from East Asia and East and Southeast Asia, where there are a few significant coefficients for the health and income poor.

Confidence in civil services

Civil services are generally important in the overall regression for Asia and for the three subregions as well. However, there is little evidence of the importance of civil services in raising the well-being of the poor, with the exception of the health poor in Asia as a whole and in East and Southeast Asia.

Conclusions from aggregation exercise

Even though aggregation results in a better fit of the model and generally greater significance of the independent variables, aggregate data analysis does very little to improve our understanding of what is going on at the micro level in terms of the impact on the well-being of the three poverty groups. Furthermore, aside from the results already displayed in Table 2.23 and discussed earlier, there is virtually no evidence that the poor respond more vigorously to changes in the four social variables of Trust, confidence in civil services, Religion or Work. What is needed are more detailed surveys on individual countries to explore how the different social, demographic and policy variables work and interact to improve well-being and the measures that can be adopted to increase the response of well-being to variations in the provision of health and education services, as well as steps to increase income to the poorest segments of society.

2.5   Extensions of the model

2.5.1   *Probability of escaping poverty or possibility of a better lifestyle*

We next explored a simplified version of equation 2.1 to include attitudes toward realizing a better lifestyle and how this impacted on the well-being of the poor. World Value Survey provides data on the chance to escape poverty; respondents are to indicate whether they believe that they have a chance to get out of poverty and lead a better life. However, such data are only available for one particular wave, so available data are limited. Hence equation 2.2 is simplified by taking out the last four social variables.

$$WB = b_0 + b_1 \text{ Health} + b_2 \text{ Income} + b_3 \text{ Education} + b_4 \text{ Gender} + b_5 \text{ Age} + b_6 \text{ Age Squared} + b_7 \text{ Marital status} + b_8 \text{ Family} + b_9 \text{ Friends} + b_{10} \text{ Chance to Escape Poverty} \qquad (2.2)$$

The motivation for this exercise is the work of di Tella and MacCulloch (2006), who found a significant impact of beliefs on well-being using the third wave of the World Value Survey for 36 countries around the globe. The regression included all income levels and

43,700 sample observations. Di Tella and MacCulloch found that lower income affects one's happiness in a negative way if it is accompanied by a belief that poverty tends to be a permanent state. They did this by using an interaction term of real income times the chance of escaping poverty.

Our results provide more focus on the poor in Asia, and are summarized in Table 2.25.

For the World Value Surveys, we analyzed probit results for several countries where the question was part of several waves of the survey for individual countries. It seems to us that it is more useful to focus our attention on the poor rather than on all respondents, most of whom are nonpoor. We do not believe that the nonpoor know how the well-being of the poor would be impacted by responses to this variable. For brevity, only the coefficient and significance of the chance of escaping poverty variable are reported. The other variables are controls for personal characteristics. If the respondent thought there was a chance of escaping poverty, a one (1) was recorded in the response sheet. If there was very little chance of escaping poverty, the value was entered as two (2). Simply, if the coefficient on the variable is positive, then the respondent's positive attitude about escaping has a negative impact on well-being for the 0 to 10 and 0 and 1 designations for well-being and a positive impact for the 1 to 4 designation.

In China, the escaping poverty variable is significant for the full sample in all three forms of well-being, and also for the education poor in two of three and the income poor in all three designations of well-being. This is a very important result for both the poor and the overall sample, and suggests that there is a widespread belief that there is upward mobility, which has a positive impact on well-being. In India, there is little evidence that a higher chance of escaping poverty uplifts well-being, either for the poor or for the entire sample. Only for the overall sample in the 1 to 10 version of well-being is the coefficient for this variable significant with the correct a priori sign. In Bangladesh and Pakistan, the results are more encouraging for both the full sample and the three poor groups as well as for the two forms of well-being. In the 1 to 4 and 0 and 1 designations of poverty, all three poverty group coefficients are significant or close to significance, as well as the probit results for the overall sample. In Taiwan, the chance of escaping poverty variable is significant only for the overall sample and the 1 to 4 form of well-being. In the Philippines, only the health and education poor have significant coefficients, suggesting that the poor see a better chance of escaping poverty and lifting their well-being, as opposed

Table 2.25 Significance of coefficient on chance to escape from poverty

	a170 (Scale 1–10)				a008 (Scale 1–4)				a008r (Scale 0–1)			
	Overall	Health Poor	Edn Poor	Income Poor	Overall	Health Poor	Edn Poor	Income Poor	Overall	Health Poor	Edn Poor	Income Poor
China	-0.44* (-5.17)	0.10 (0.30)	-0.48* (-3.54)	-0.49* (-2.18)	0.31* (3.27)	-0.47 (-1.35)	0.30* (2.02)	0.94* (3.81)	-0.32* (-2.80)	0.23 (0.55)	-0.18 (-1.06)	-0.66* (-2.30)
India	-0.25* (-4.19)	-0.08 (-0.31)	0.04 (0.39)	0.09 (0.73)	-0.01 (-0.13)	-0.67* (-2.43)	-0.10 (-0.90)	-0.21 (-1.53)	0.12 (1.49)	1.02* (2.95)	0.18 (1.42)	0.41* (2.42)
Bangladesh	0.02 (0.33)	-0.28 (-1.12)	0.00 (0.00)	-0.01 (-0.09)	0.48* (7.00)	0.55* (2.00)	0.50* (3.58)	0.59* (3.51)	-0.38* (-4.05)	-0.52 (-1.60)	-0.43* (-2.54)	-0.45* (-2.24)
Pakistan					0.31* (3.37)	0.52 (1.68)	0.32* (2.37)	0.45* (3.04)	-0.21 (-1.81)	-0.74 (-1.90)	-0.38* (-2.24)	-0.52* (-2.90)
Philippines	-0.07 (-1.06)	-0.48 (-1.67)	-0.34* (-2.45)		0.12 (1.50)	0.68* (2.19)	0.00 (-0.03)		0.05 (0.44)	-0.94* (-2.31)	0.25 (0.96)	
Taiwan	-0.24 (-1.74)	-0.54 (-1.44)	-0.10 (-0.42)	-0.15 (-0.60)	0.41* (2.57)	0.60 (1.43)	0.13 (0.46)	0.16 (0.57)	-0.22 (-0.97)	-0.13 (-0.26)	-0.12 (-0.36)	-0.22 (-0.63)
Overall	-0.14* (-4.33)	-0.01 (-0.11)	-0.11 (-1.86)	0.06 (0.79)	0.20* (5.92)	0.03 (0.23)	0.14* (2.58)	0.16* (2.38)	-0.19* (-4.35)	-0.02 (-0.14)	-0.17* (-2.55)	-0.12 (-1.51)

Notes: 1. Chance to escape from poverty ranges from 1 to 3. 1 indicates they have a chance; 2 indicates they have very little chance; 3 indicates other answer.
2. Based on probit results for original equation model (1.1) and inclusion of new variable – chance to escape from poverty. This is due to such data being available only in Wave 3 and hence unable to incorporate other social variables as in the extended model (1.2).
3. z stats are displayed in parenthesis and * denotes statistical significance at the 5% level.
4. No data available for a170 for Pakistan.
5. No data available for income level for Philippines in Wave 3.

to the respondents in the overall sample. The aggregate overall sample results, which pool the findings for all countries, are significant in all three cases, along with two cases for the education poor and one for the income poor. This suggests that belief in the chance of escaping poverty is an important influence on well-being for both the rich and the poor.

However, the aggregate results regarding the probability of achieving a better life cover up the significant difference in country responses between India and its neighbors. Only in China, Bangladesh and Pakistan are there high levels of significance of the better lifestyle variable for the poor – for health and education in Bangladesh and for health, education and poverty in Pakistan and China. These results are encouraging for China, Pakistan and Bangladesh, and, selectively, for the Philippines and India. We are tempted to conjecture that the nature of society in India may have a direct impact on the failure of this variable to have an impact on the probability of escaping poverty. To establish a stronger case for the importance of attitudes toward poverty on well-being, further research is needed. In our view it is not enough to establish gross aggregate relationships with data from many countries. As we see from the individual country results, there are significant differences in the reaction to the chance of escaping poverty across countries among those who are poor, and we gain little insight into country differences in the reactions of the poor by focusing only on the overall results. Furthermore, the attitudes of the nonpoor are not particularly helpful in establishing the impact of escaping poverty on the well-being of the poor.

2.5.2   Urban–rural differences in subjective well-being

There has been very little work done on comparing life satisfaction between different regions in the same country. Whatever research there is has tended to focus on differentials between income in rural and urban areas and the impact this has had on migration patterns. The impact on migration and the lure of higher income in urban areas is well documented. Those suffering the largest differential in earnings from others in their own communities, as well as between urban and rural areas, are also well documented. Even as income limitations keep them from thinking of international migration, those in the lowest quintiles of the income distribution are more likely to migrate internally. These incentives are directly related to the perceived potential income to be gained from migration, and also are increased if the cost of migration is small and knowledge of opportunities is extensive. These conditions are more likely to be true for rural locations in proximity to large urban areas. We also know that young males are the most likely to migrate.

The lack of research on well-being as opposed to income differentials partly reflects the lack of studies focusing on well-being and happiness rather than on income and earnings. Furthermore, happiness research has not put particular emphasis on geographical differences in well-being, for instance by incorporating regional variables which would permit such comparisons.

There are a few exceptions. Berry and Okulicz-Kozaryn (2009) look at data from 80 countries from the World Value Surveys wave taken in the year 2000 and compare life satisfaction in urban areas of 500,000 with life satisfaction in small rural villages of fewer than 2,000 residents. They control for socioeconomic characteristics and then ask the question whether people prefer to live in rural or urban environments. They conclude that, for their full sample, city living is not a critical determinant of well-being. Asia is the exception. In Asia, income differentials outweigh the costs associated with city living. The pull of the city in Asia is further reflected by more rural to urban migration than in other regions. The rapid growth of industry and higher wages in the region, along with better employment and income prospects, provide a strong magnet for young rural residents. More work needs to be done to consider the various migration hypotheses and to consider changes over a longer time period.

Relying on the Gallup database, Easterlin *et al.* (2010) systematically look at whether there are differences in happiness between rural and urban residents for a number of countries. All three of these studies (Easterlin *et al.*, Berry and Okulicz-Kozaryn and Brockmann *et al.*) draw similar conclusions. Changes in migration and growth in income lead to a shrinking of income differentials and happiness differentials (urban dwellers happier than rural dwellers) over time, and the allure of the city tends to fade over time.

According to Easterlin *et al.*, this conclusion is consistent with happiness research, which finds well-being highly correlated with income but not with growth in income above a certain point. However, the impact of urbanization on well-being in cross-section regressions remains high in some societies but not in others. This might be because, in a modern developed country setting, the disadvantages of living in a congested, noisy and polluted environment could outweigh any income advantage, and the retreat to the suburbs could be a way to bring about a partial return to a more relaxed and quiet lifestyle with less stress.

Certainly, the rapid and continued migration to the cities and the growing income differentials between the rural home base and the city would be reflected in higher levels of well-being if income and well-being are closely correlated and are not overwhelmed by other factors. This relationship could hold for many poorer countries, and would tend to be moderated only after income has reached a certain level. However, it is not clear that the data support this conclusion, simply because there are so few studies of the impact of urbanization on well-being, and the example of China is a cautionary tale, suggesting that well-being may not be so closely related to income.

The pattern on migration from rural to urban areas in Asia over the past several decades is the result of the rapid industrialization of the Asian region, combined with the decline in the importance of agriculture as a primary source of employment and income, as well as the rise of the service sector as a necessary component of the industrialization process. Differences in subjective well-being between these two sectors reflect these time trends as well as possible improvements in well-being as a result of higher income in urban areas as the industrial sector has grown, as well as advances in health care and the spread of education to a large segment of urban society. Over time, large differences in perceived well-being between the two sectors, along with more rapid growth in urban income and employment, contributed to high rates of migration from the countryside to cities. As industrialization continues into the twenty-first century, many of the richer Asian economies in East and Southeast Asia (Singapore, Hong Kong, Korea, Taiwan) have become largely urban in nature, and the differences between urban and rural well-being could be expected to shrink. Looking at income differentials between rural and urban areas as the key driving force behind the growth of cities, it is logical that the rate of migration between the two sectors would be roughly proportional to the differences in living standards. See, for example, the work of Easterlin *et al.* 2010).

Our database is not detailed enough to test this hypothesis. What we can do is investigate the World Value Survey database to examine whether subjective well-being is higher in urban areas than in rural areas, and also possibly see whether the differences tends to decrease in countries with higher per capita income. The probit model discussed earlier (equation 2.2) can be modified by replacing the last variable with a dummy variable to reflect urban versus rural residence. Since the model already includes a variety of explanatory variables that have an impact on well-being, the significance of this dummy variable would be strong evidence that urban sector residents have higher average levels of

Table 2.26 Probit results for Asia – rural–urban

	a170 (Scale 1–10)				a008 (Scale 1–4)				a008r (Scale 0–1)			
	Overall	Health Poor	Edn Poor	Income Poor	Overall	Health Poor	Edn Poor	Income Poor	Overall	Health Poor	Edn Poor	Income Poor
China	0.15 (1.37)	0.66 (1.01)	0.40 (1.80)	−0.61 (−1.69)	−0.19 (−1.51)		−0.33 (−1.34)	−0.01 (−0.02)	−0.13 (−0.71)		0.42 (1.00)	−0.71 (−1.30)
India	0.44* (7.56)	0.66* (2.42)	0.36* (3.66)	0.48* (4.39)	0.23* (3.81)	0.33 (1.17)	0.21* (2.06)	0.24* (2.03)	−0.24* (−2.97)	−0.39 (−1.20)	−0.23 (−1.81)	−0.14 (−1.04)
Indonesia	0.18 (1.89)	−0.52 (−0.89)	0.75* (3.59)	0.08 (0.29)	−0.13 (−1.13)		−0.18 (−0.75)	−0.24 (−0.75)	0.19 (1.09)	−0.24 (−0.21)		−0.32 (−0.71)
Bangladesh	0.17 (1.40)	−1.58 (−0.93)	0.10 (0.38)		−0.50* (−3.51)	0.70 (0.34)	−1.00* (−2.96)		0.48* (2.21)			
Malaysia	−0.29 (−1.66)		0.27 (0.41)		0.01 (0.06)		−0.30 (−0.32)		−0.60 (−0.86)			
Pakistan	0.27 (1.66)	−0.57 (−0.30)	0.03 (0.12)		−0.17 (−1.31)	−0.01 (−0.01)	−0.14 (−0.87)	−0.25 (−0.70)	0.41* (2.69)	0.51 (0.59)	0.25 (1.21)	0.31 (0.70)
Philippines									1.82 (1.20)			
Thailand	0.70* (2.14)		1.33* (2.31)		1.62* (4.33)		2.64* (4.49)		−2.03* (−4.03)		−2.84* (−4.04)	
Vietnam	−0.46 (−0.48)											
Korea					0.16 (1.58)		0.23 (0.99)	0.41 (1.32)	−0.16 (−1.13)		−0.07 (−0.26)	−0.38 (−0.99)
Taiwan									3.01* (2.84)			−0.72 (−0.19)

* Denotes significance at 5% level.

1. The rural–urban variable ranges from 0: rural (2,000 and fewer residents) to 1: urban (500,000 and more residents). Under the 1–10 and 0–1 definitions of well-being, a positive sign indicates that urban residents are happier. Under the 1–4 definition, a negative sign indicates that urban residents are happier.
2. Based on probit results for inclusion of added dummy variable for rural–urban variable into original equation (1.1) and z stats are displayed in parenthesis.
3. No WVS data on size of town for Singapore and Taiwan.
4. Variable dropped due to multicollinearity.

well-being than rural sector residents, other things being equal. We can use the differences in levels of development between East–Southeast Asia and South Asia to explore whether richer countries have smaller or less significant differences in urban and rural well-being. We segregated the sample into two groups, those residing in towns with fewer than 2,000 residents and large cities with more than 500,000 residents. Residents from smaller cities were deleted. This results in a reduction in the size of the sample, by about half in China and India.

The overall and poverty group results for India strongly suggest the presence of rural–urban well-being differentials. All three configurations of well-being in the probit regressions reported in Table 2.26 record significant differences, and these differences are reinforced by the results for the education and income poverty groups for the 1 to 10 definition of well-being. However, for the other two definitions results are different. For the 0 and 1 and 1–4 well-being definitions, the signs for the rural–urban dummy variable suggest that rural residents are happier. However, for other countries there is also support for greater well-being in big cities, particularly for the full sample. This is the case in Bangladesh, Pakistan, Taiwan, Thailand and Indonesia for the overall sample and the 1–10 definition of well-being.

There is less evidence to support the hypothesis for the other versions of well-being, particularly in Thailand, where several coefficients suggest rural residents are happier. In China, where there are more observations and more restriction on migration because of the *hukou* system,[7] there is no support for the hypothesis that urban residents are happier. This could be the result of policies implemented to make it difficult to migrate, which have a potential negative impact on well-being for migrants. Although the overall results for the 1 to 10 configuration of well-being strongly suggest urban residents are happier in South Asia, these findings are weakened by the lack of support for urban happiness among poverty groups in East and Southeast Asia. Greater support for the hypothesis may be possible by exploring a greater degree of aggregation within the Asian region.

3
Analysis for Africa

We begin the discussion of Africa with a review of health, income and education of African economies in general. Despite having a much smaller total population base, Africa has made more modest strides in human resource development than Asia. There are many reasons for this, which have been discussed by the academic community and international development agencies including the United Nations, the World Bank and the African Development Bank. At the risk of oversimplification, there are a few fundamental causes of slow growth and limited progress in poverty alleviation. Africa has been unable to create enough jobs to bring large numbers of families out of poverty. The labor supply has been increasing rapidly despite efforts to reduce family size and increase awareness. There has been slow growth in labor productivity as well as total factor productivity.

The slow growth in technology, particularly in the industrial sector, has been compounded by the lack of rapid transformation from agriculture to industry and services. Slow industrial growth has meant that the region has not been able to raise productivity quickly enough to sustain rapid growth momentum and raise incomes. This failure has been compounded by the inability to generate dynamic export sectors that can take advantage of low wages while developing niche markets for industrial exports. Trade and foreign direct investment policy has also constrained the ability to develop comparative advantage and move into global markets. Africa's share of world trade has fallen and its exports remain heavily concentrated in oil and other minerals. This is reflected by a shift in the pattern of trade, as China, India, Korea, Brazil and Turkey have increased their share of African exports. Emerging economics now account for 40 percent of Africa's total trade. The lack of strong and dynamic industrial growth is reflected in a low level of total factor productivity and low investment rates in all but a few high-performing economies (South Africa, Ghana and a few others).

Agriculture still employs over half of the labor force, and, while some labor demand has been generated by increased mining activity, this has not created the kind of employment that has characterized growth in Asia and, to a lesser extent, in Latin America. About three-quarters of the foreign direct investment in Africa has gone to the oil-rich countries and to other extractive industries. There are few linkages to the rest of the economy where the bulk of the poor reside. As a result, the elasticity of poverty reduction to changes in income is limited. The latest *African Development Report* notes that, between 2001 and 2008, only three of the 14 African countries where the annual growth rates were above the regional average had substantial rates of poverty reduction. At the same time domestic resource mobilization has remained low. Lacking an environment that attracts foreign investors in manufacturing industries, domestic savings have not been augmented sufficiently by foreign direct investment. FDI is a major contributor to raising the skill of the labor force in other regions, allowing firms to make rapid gains in productivity and build up exports. This has not happened in Africa.

The HIV/AIDS epidemic has also drawn valuable scarce resources away from investment in education and in building up labor force skills needed for a dynamic industrial economy. However, the pharmaceutical sector could, given its experience in treating HIV/AIDS, be the focus of industrial policy to produce generic medicines at the local level, creating employment and providing needed drugs to fight the HIV/AIDS epidemic, as well as other diseases. This has not happened yet. While remittances have augmented domestic resources, they are not yet sufficient to make a tangible difference in the balance of saving and investment needed to accelerate growth and slow the spread of poverty.

Despite these difficulties, there have been some improvements in economic growth in recent years, beginning around 2000, as a result of an increase in raw materials prices and exports, primarily to China and India. Africa has 10 percent of global oil reserves, 40 percent of gold and up to 90 percent of chromium, platinum and rare earth metals (see McKinsey Global Institute 2010). Arbache *et al.* (2008) suggest that these developments, along with improved terms of trade, have played a major role in raising growth. Between 2000 and 2009 Africa grew faster than Latin America and the Middle East (see McKinsey Global Institute 2010). The acceleration in demand for raw materials has been reinforced by improvements in the policy and political environments in several countries, as well as a cessation of domestic and international conflicts that sapped resources and created an unsettled environment for potential foreign investment. Work by Arbache *et al.* (2008) suggest that major conflicts result in a low level equilibrium trap of sustained low growth even after the conflict has ended. Low growth also has a detrimental impact on human development, including infant mortality and life expectancy.

There has also been an upswing in wholesale and retail trade and growth in agricultural output and productivity. Transportation and telecommunications have also shown signs of accelerating as overall growth prospects for the region have improved. However growth in manufacturing has not been as strong, contributing only 9 percent to growth between 2002 and 2007 (Mc Kinsey Global Institute 2010). Furthermore, the initial impact on employment was limited. However, there has been an uptick in employment generation in the last three or four years and the macroeconomic policy environment has also improved, particularly the ability to keep inflation in check since 1995. Between 1980 and 2006, 10 or more countries had experienced hyperinflation episodes (more than 50 percent per year increase in prices). Many more countries are now able to control inflation than in the 1980s and 1990s (see Arbache *et al.* 2008). Foreign debt has also been reduced and some state enterprises have been privatized; trade taxes have been lowered and the regulatory environment strengthened. Where reforms took place, GDP growth accelerated around three times faster than where there were limited reforms (see McKinsey Global Institute 2010). Furthermore, labor productivity has begun to increase for the first time in several decades. Regional cooperation in parts of Africa are also developing the potential for greater investment flows. The East African Community (EAC) of Kenya, Uganda, Tanzania, Burundi and Rwanda has formed a customs union which will eventually allow free movement of products and services as well as capital and labor. Growth has begun to accelerate, and there are plans to further expand the common market in East Africa to Southern Africa, so that it could eventually involve 26 African countries. An additional challenge is created by the recent development of purchasing land in Africa by business interests outside the region. To the extent that these land deals constrain development by those interested in African farming and other local interests, they could slow economic progress in the region (see the Future Agricultures Consortium website http://www.future-agricultures.org/index.php and Deininger *et al.* 2011 for further details).

To sustain growth in the future, Africa will have to make progress on several fronts. The high cost of doing business will have to be brought down. Eifert, Gelb and Ramachandran (2005) conclude that, while the top African enterprises can compete with Chinese and Indian firms in direct costs of production, they are much less competitive in keeping down indirect costs, particularly infrastructure. As a result of this and other factors such as bureaucratic red tape and corruption, the business environment is difficult; Africa generally is a high-cost and risky place to do business, and this has had an adverse impact on foreign direct investment. Supply chain analysis by Subramanian and Matthijs (2007) suggests that import logistics, lack of timely delivery to foreign markets and poor quality control are additional deterrents to efficient operations and greater penetration into foreign markets. In addition, infrastructure spending will have to continue at a rapid rate in order to cut transportation and other overhead costs. Foreign direct investment and greater access to foreign capital will also help in boosting efficiency and total factor productivity. Further progress in raising the depth and quality of education will also be required to raise worker skills and productivity.

While an autocratic ruler and lack of human rights progress can be partly blamed for the spread of demand for more democratic institutions and the ouster of strongmen such as Zine El Abidine in Algeria, Mubarak in Egypt and Khadafy in Libya, as well as other dictators or sovereigns, unrest also has been generated by a failure to spread income and wealth to the poorer echelons of society. Higher food prices and continued high youth unemployment have also been contributing factors. As a result of slow growth, low incomes and limited budget resources, many African economies may fail to meet the millennium development goals (see Arbache *et al.* 2008).

Our data bank for Africa is comprised of a subset of the more than 40 countries that make up the African continent. McKinsey Global Institute (2010) has developed a suggested segmentation method for grouping the region into four groups: (i) oil exporters; (ii) diversified economies that produce a range of manufactured and other products; (iii) pre-transition economies that are very poor and have yet to develop strong public institutions, viable and enforceable public policy and sustainable agricultural development; and, finally, (iv) the transition economies that are building on a base to diversity their economies and build up an export base of manufactured goods and stronger agricultural growth.

Looking at the rankings of countries in the Asian region in the UN Human Development Index (HDI), the profile of Africa is low. Countries in sub-Saharan Africa rank below nearly all other developing countries.

All but three countries in North Africa listed in Table 3.1, for which we will undertake further analysis of poverty and well-being, are in the bottom 20 percent of the distribution of countries for which the HDI was compiled in 2010. A similar ranking for gender inequality shows a somewhat better performance. A few countries escape the low ranks, yet most of the countries are in the bottom 30 percent of the distribution. Rwanda has made significant progress in reducing gender inequality compared with its overall HDI ranking. Furthermore, improvements in the ranking, as measured by annual increases in the HDI, show that several countries had either very low or negative scores. North Africa did well – each of the three countries in our sample grew by around 1.5 percent per annum between 1980 and 2010. Uganda, Ethiopia and Mali also did very well – averaging over 2 percent growth per annum. Zambia made little improvement, and Zimbabwe and South Africa lost ground in the struggle to increase health, income and education. The average improvement for all of sub-Saharan Africa was just under 1 percent per annum, less than South Asia and East Asia but better than Latin American and the Caribbean.

In terms of human development, the pre-transition economies have furthest to go, while the diversified economies and oil exporters have a firmer foundation in raising levels of health, education and income. The list of countries and their appropriate grouping is shown in Table 3.1, along with some measures of human development.

Because of our focus on poverty and well-being, we begin with an assessment of the problems of effective human resource development. Looking at Table 3.2, life expectancy has generally increased in the 18 years between the two sample years. The biggest improvement occurred in Rwanda, which had a life expectancy in 1990 of only 32, by far the lowest of any country in the region and, indeed, the globe. In South Africa, Zimbabwe and Zambia, life expectancy fell by between five and 15 years in the period between 1990 and 2008. In Zimbabwe the decline is directly attributed to the repressive regime of Robert Mugabe, the decline of health workers, many of whom have fled the country, and the rapid spread of AIDS. The Kaiser Foundation estimates that nearly 25 percent of the population has HIV/AIDS. If AIDS were not so prevalent (16.5 percent of the population, according to the Kaiser Foundation), the decline in life expectancy in Zambia would be puzzling. Although the level of rural poverty remains high, there has been significant progress in many areas of the economy, including increased fiscal discipline and privatization of the mining sector in the late 1990s. However, the reforms have had limited impact outside this highly

Table 3.1 Human development

Country	Human development Index (HDI) rank	Average annual HDI growth rate 1980–2010	Gini 2010	Poverty rate 1991–5 National estimate	Poverty rate 2000–8 National estimate	Gender Inequality rank	Category
Algeria	84	1.42	35.3	22.6		70	oil exporter
Egypt	101	1.52	32.1	22.9	16.7	108	diversified
Ethiopia	157	2.73*	29.8	45.5	44.2	135	pre-transition
Mali	160	2.1	39	13.1			pre-transition
Morocco	114	1.59	40.9	13.1		104	diversified
Nigeria	142	na	42.9	34.1			oil exporter
Rwanda	152	1.45	46.7	51.2	56.9	33	pre-transition
South Africa	110	−0.03*	57.8		22	82	diversified
Tanzania	148	0.95	34.5	38.6	35.7		transition
Uganda	143	2.03*	42.6		31.1	109	transition
Zambia	150	−0.34	50.7		68	124	transition
Zimbabwe	169	−1.81	50.1	25.8		105	pre-transition
Sub-Saharan Africa		0.94					
Arab states		1.32					

Note: 169 countries ranked for Human Development Index and 137 for Gender Inequality Index
* 1990–2010

urbanized economy, and the AIDS epidemic continues to claim lives. In South Africa much of the decline in life expectancy can be attributed to the AIDS epidemic, which is the leading cause of death among children under 5 and the leading cause of death in almost all South African provinces. At the end of 2003 there were an estimated 5 million people living with HIV/AIDS out of a total population of around 50 million, and some estimates are as much as double this rate.

Turning to infant mortality, there have been significant reductions in many African economies, including South Africa and Zambia. Infant mortality remained over 80 per thousand in Mali, Nigeria, Uganda and Zambia. Infant mortality increased in Zimbabwe from 54 to 58 per thousand population. Under-5 infant mortality remained at over 100 per 1,000 children in seven countries. More than one in 10 children were dead by age 5 in Ethiopia, Mali, Nigeria, Rwanda, Tanzania, Uganda and Zambia. Nevertheless, the decline in infant mortality is notable in North Africa (35, 30 and 20 per 1,000 live births respectively in Morocco, Algeria and Egypt). However, it has increased in South Africa due to HIV/AIDS and remains stubbornly high in Uganda, Tanzania, Zambia and Zimbabwe, partly because of HIV/AIDS and also from neglect. There has been little progress in control of TB, with the incidence increasing in more than half the countries in the sample. In 2008 the incidence of TB remained over at 30 percent of all residents in Ethiopia, Mali, Nigeria, Rwanda, South Africa, Uganda and Zimbabwe. In South Africa TB is widespread. A large percentage of children are underweight or anemic or their growth has been stunted by lack of food. In five countries over 40 percent of the residents were stunted, while in 10 countries over 30 percent were anemic and in three countries over 60 percent of the population was anemic. In North Africa the rate of anemia is low and has been for some time (see Table 3.2). In sub-Saharan Africa the rate of undernourishment has improved somewhat in a few countries. Ethiopia has cut the level of undernourishment from 71 percent to 44 percent, while in Mali the undernourishment rate is now only 10 percent. In several countries there has been little progress, or even a reduction in the average caloric intake (Zambia, Zimbabwe and Tanzania).

Access to improved water sources is estimated to have increased in all but a few countries. However, access remains far below levels in higher-income developing countries in other regions. By 2008 only four countries reported that more than 80 percent of households had access to good water. Three countries recorded more than 70 percent of families with access to improved sanitation. In seven of the 13 countries

Table 3.2 Health indicators for Africa – life expectancy and infant mortality

Country	Life expectancy 1990	Life expectancy 2008	Infant mortality 1990	Infant mortality 2008	Under-5 mortality 1990	Under-5 mortality 2008
Algeria	67.07	72.39	50.50	30.00	60.90	33.50
Egypt, Arab Republic	62.89	70.14	65.50	19.80	89.50	23.00
Ethiopia	46.95	55.20	124.30	69.40	209.50	108.50
Mali	42.98	48.43	138.80	102.50	249.70	193.80
Morocco	64.14	71.29	68.90	34.60	88.80	39.20
Nigeria	44.55	47.91	125.50	88.60	211.70	142.90
Rwanda	32.68	50.13	102.90	73.80	170.70	116.90
South Africa	61.41	51.48	47.80	44.70	61.70	65.30
Tanzania	50.83	55.65	99.20	69.90	162.00	111.40
Uganda	47.91	52.67	111.20	81.00	184.20	130.40
Zambia	51.10	45.40	107.50	87.90	178.60	145.10
Zimbabwe	60.80	44.21	54.20	58.20	81.30	93.40

Source: World Bank, World Development Indicators.

Table 3.2 continued Health Indicators for Africa – water and sanitation

Country	Access to improved water 1990	Access to improved water 2008	Access to improved sanitation 1990	Access to improved sanitation 2008	Health spending as % of GDP 2007	Health spending per capita $PPP 2008
Algeria	94.00	83.00	88.00	95.00	4.36	337.92
Egypt, Arab Republic	90.00	99.00	72.00	94.00	6.26	309.95
Ethiopia	17.00	38.00	4.00	12.00	3.79	29.69
Mali	29.00	56.00	26.00	36.00	5.72	66.93
Morocco	74.00	81.00	53.00	69.00	4.98	215.26
Nigeria	47.00	58.00	37.00	32.00	6.63	131.05
Rwanda	68.00	65.00	23.00	54.00	10.32	90.48
South Africa	83.00	91.00	69.00	77.00	8.62	819.40
Tanzania	55.00	54.00	24.00	24.00	5.32	63.05
Uganda	43.00	67.00	39.00	48.00	6.28	74.49
Zambia	49.00	60.00	46.00	49.00	6.16	79.06
Zimbabwe	78.00	82.00	43.00	44.00	8.95	2.00

Table 3.2 continued Health indicators for Africa – incidence of TB, underweight and anemia

Country	Incidence of TB 2000	Incidence of TB 2008	Underweight 2002–8	Stunting 2002–8	Anemia under 5 1993–2008	Undernourished 1990–2 (%)	Undernourished 2004–6 (%)
Algeria	47.78	57.93	11.10	23.30	42.80	<5	<5
Egypt, Arab Republic	27.36	20.35	6.80	30.70	34.20	<5	<5
Ethiopia	330.00	370.00	34.60	50.70	62.68	71	44
Mali	300.00	320.00	27.90	38.50	73.40	14	10
Morocco	130.00	120.00	9.90	23.10	37.20	5	<5
Nigeria	270.00	300.00	27.20	43.00	66.70	15	8
Rwanda	350.00	390.00	18.00	51.70	10.60	45	40
South Africa	580.00	960.00			58.20	<5	<5
Tanzania	240.00	190.00	16.70	44.40	21.84	28	35
Uganda	340.00	310.00	16.40	38.70	64.40	19	15
Zambia	600.00	470.00	14.90	45.80	46.90	40	45
Zimbabwe	680.00	760.00	14.00	35.80	47.00	40	30

Source: World Development Indicators and United Nations, *Human Development Report* 2010.
Note: incidence of TB per 100,000.

Table 3.2 continued Health indicators in Africa – incidence of HIV/AIDS and victims of war and social disruption

	Percent of adults living with HIV/AIDS (end 2003)	Number of people living with HIV/AIDS in thousands (end 2003)	Battle deaths resulting from wars	Period	African refugees (2006)
Algeria	na	na			
Egypt, Arab Republic	na	na	1,347	1992–8	
Ethiopia	6.6				74,026
Mali	1.5	1,000			
Morocco	na	na	13,000	1975–89	
Nigeria	5.5	3,600	75,000	1967–70	
Rwanda	na				92,966
South Africa	21.6	5,300			
Tanzania	8.8	1,600			
Uganda	4.1	530	107,000	1981–90	
Zambia	16.5	920			
Zimbabwe	24.6	1,800			
Sub-Saharan Africa	7.5	25,000			
Global		37,800			

Source: Kaiser Foundation for HIV/AIDS and *African Development Report 2008/2009* for battle deaths and refugees.

reported, fewer than half of the households had improved sanitation. Government spending on health per capita (purchasing power parity – PPP) in 2008 was less than $100 in seven countries, and more than $300 per capita in North Africa (Algeria and Egypt) and in South Africa ($819). As a percentage of GDP, average health spending was nearly 50 percent higher than spending in Asia (average 6.45 percent of GDP compared with 4.3 percent in Asia), probably as a result of the increased spending required to treat HIV/AIDS sufferers. On a country by country basis, health spending per capita varied dramatically throughout the African region (see Table 3.2). Zambia spent around $20 per capita while South Africa spent over $800.

Turning to education, summary statistics are presented in Table 3.3. Primary school enrollment and primary school completion rates are more relevant for the poor, since only a small cohort was able to move on to secondary or tertiary levels. By 2007, primary enrollment rates had reached fairly high levels for most countries in Africa. Only Ethiopia, Mali and Nigeria had enrollment levels below 70 percent. This is particularly encouraging in South Africa and its neighbors, which have been struggling with health issues for some time. Primary school completion rates are much lower, and available for a more limited sample of countries. For those countries reporting completion rates for primary school graduation, rates in 2008 ranged from around 50 percent, over 60 percent to 76 percent in South Africa (1991 data), 81 percent in Morocco and over 90 percent in Zambia and Zimbabwe (1991 data). The primary education program in Rwanda is particularly encouraging, since the primary completion rate was negligible in 1991 during the civil war period. Statistics on public spending on elementary education are limited to a few countries, and the limited information suggests that spending, where data is available, fell between 1999 and 2008. In most countries spending was between $10 and $16 per student, somewhat higher in Morocco ($16.33) and Tanzania ($22.90). In all cases spending was much lower than the budget for health.

Poverty statistics are not widely available for Africa. Only a few countries report Gini coefficients, and the income share of the lowest 10 percent of the population is not published. Gini coefficients for years before 2000 show ratios of over 50 in three countries and over 40 percent in two others. Tanzania, which has a socialist government, had a much lower ratio of 34 percent. Poverty rates calculated by national governments for the 1990s and the current decade are available for most countries, compiled by the United Nations in its Human Development Report. Comparing with results from an earlier period, there have been some minimal improvements in income distribution. In terms of poverty reduction, a few countries have shown modest progress in reducing poverty. Poverty rates are still over 50 percent in Rwanda and Zambia. North Africa has lower poverty rates, along with Zimbabwe.

Many factors are responsible for the poor performance of Africa in human development. The failure to reach the AIDS targets set as part of the Millennium Development Agenda has resulted in a shortage of international assistance. The pledge of $26 billion for Africa made at the Gleneagles summit in 2005 has not been fulfilled. As of 2010, only $9 billion has been allocated. Furthermore, the pledge to commit 0.7 percent of GDP to development assistance has also failed to materialize. The United States' share is only 0.2 percent, and only five countries in northern Europe have met their full pledge commitment as a percentage of GDP. The global crisis has hurt as well. The World Bank estimates that there are now 64 million more poor people in the world than there would have been before the crisis. Several other Millennium Development Goals are unlikely to be met, including cutting maternal mortality by 75 percent and reducing infant mortality. While recent growth in China and India has increased the demand for mineral exports from Africa, raising GDP growth, manufactured exports have stagnated. As a result, employment growth has remained modest throughout Africa. In this connection, the textile sector has been hit by the 2005 agreement on textiles and clothing. Higher food prices in 2008 created food

Table 3.3 Education indicators for Africa – literacy and school completion rate

Country	Primary completion rate 1991	Primary completion rate 2008	Male youth literacy 1990	Male youth literacy 2008	Male adult literacy
Algeria	79.51	113.86	NA	94.38	81.28
Ethiopia		52.07	NA	62.20	50.00
Mali	11.96	56.76	NA	47.38	34.86
Morocco	48.09	81.32	NA	84.80	69.40
Nigeria			NA	78.30	71.50
Rwanda	0.00	53.98	NA	77.10	74.80
South Africa	75.95		NA	96.10	89.90
Tanzania			NA	78.70	79.00
Uganda		56.13	NA	89.10	82.40
Zambia		92.98	NA	82.10	80.60
Zimbabwe	97.40		NA	98.30	94.40

Table 3.3 continued Education indicators for Africa – enrollment

Country	Primary net enrollment rate 1991	Primary net enrollment rate 2007	Public spending per student elementary 1999	Public spending per student elementary 2008	Public spending per student secondary 1999	Public spending per student secondary 2008	Primary net enrollment rate 1999
Algeria	88.85	95.54	11.96	NA	NA	NA	90.69
Egypt, Arab Republic	80.87	93.62	NA	NA	NA	NA	85.39
Ethiopia	23.96	74.80	NA	NA	NA	NA	36.25
Mali	23.13	66.40	13.54	10.38	52.97	34.49	44.36
Morocco		88.85	17.01	16.33	44.48		70.34
Nigeria		61.40					60.04
Rwanda	67.29	97.25		8.24		34.32	
South Africa	90.03	87.47	14.21	13.69	20.04	16.00	92.02
Tanzania	50.69	95.54		22.90			49.33
Uganda		95.46		8.48		27.05	
Zambia	76.90	93.10					69.33
Zimbabwe	82.85	89.92					83.16

insecurity, and domestic conflicts in Zimbabwe and elsewhere have contributed to a lack of progress in reducing poverty and improving health and education. There has been some progress in improving the delivery of primary education, yet Africa is unlikely to meet the Millennium target of 100 percent completion rates by 2020. Africa has two characteristics that distinguish it from other developing regions – the high incidence of HIV/AIDS and the amount of social disruption caused by wars as well as social and political disruption. For the countries in our World Value Surveys for Africa, these two statistics are displayed in Table 3.2. There are many other countries in Africa which have large numbers of individuals infected with HIV/AIDS and where wars and internal conflicts have broken out. They are not discussed here, since our focus is on health and well-being in the countries where World Value Surveys were conducted. The interested reader can refer to *African Development Report* (2009) and the Kaiser Foundation website www.kff.org. From a global standpoint, Africa has about two-thirds of the HIV/AIDS cases. While Asia had more battle deaths than Africa from the period 1960 to 2005 because of the Vietnam, Iraq and Afghanistan conflicts (3.5 million), Africa has had many more than other regions (1.6 million compared with around 200,000 in Europe and the Americas: Uppsala Conflict Data Program / Centre for the Study of Civil Wars, International Peace Research Institute, Oslo (UCDP/PRIO) armed conflict data set) over the same period. In Africa there were conflicts and deaths reported in at least 13 countries, a far greater overall regional involvement than in other regions. The Congo and neighboring Rwanda were particularly notable for the level of violence and the number of interlocking conflicts (see Stearns 2011). Most HIV/AIDS cases are found in sub-Saharan Africa. The incidence of HIV/AIDS is much lower in North Africa, as are the number of wars and internal conflict. Both armed conflicts and HIV/AIDS draw resources away from other activities, creating environments of distrust and hopelessness. It would not be surprising if well-being was lower as a result.

3.1 Well-being in Africa

Life satisfaction and other aspects of human development assembled in the Human Development Report of the United Nations for 2011 using raw data from the Gallup Organization are displayed in Table 3.4 for a panel of African economies that is similar to the panel of countries assembled in previous tables from the World Bank and also the countries sampled in the World Value Surveys. On a scale of 1 to 10, life satisfaction was particularly low in several countries (Tanzania and Zambia

Table 3.4 Life satisfaction, life purpose and satisfaction

Country	Life satisfaction		Purposeful life		Treated with respect		Social support network		Satisfied with job	Satisfied with living standard	Satisfied with health
	Total	Female	Total	Female	Total	Female	Total	Female			
Algeria	5.6	5.9			84	86	87	90	66	61	87
Egypt	5.8	6.2	86	87	90	84	74	75	84	82	86
Ethiopia	4.2	na	89	87	74	47	76	77	50	33	79
Mali	3.8	3.9	99	98	86	91	75	74	30	30	71
Morocco	5.8	6	90	91	85	87	85	87	69	71	88
Nigeria	3.8	4.9	92	90	81	80	72	69	65	40	80
Rwanda	4.2	4.1	88	95	77	75	56	56	41	37	64
South Africa	5	4.7	97	96	83	83	88	89	66	42	79
Tanzania	2.4	2.4	95	88	74	77	76	87	45	21	67
Uganda	4.5	4.7	96	96	79	83	85	85	53	35	64
Zambia	2.8	2.8	91	92	81	84	81	81	49	27	72

Source: United Nations *Human Development Report 2011* raw data from Gallup Organization.

under 3, and also Mali and Nigeria at 3.8). While life satisfaction was higher in North Africa (between 5 and 6), none of the African economies reported life satisfaction greater than 5.8, a little more than halfway up the scale. These negative attitudes were reflected in average responses to questions about jobs and living standards. Fewer than half of respondents were satisfied with their job in five countries, and Egypt was the only country where more than 70 percent were happy with their job. There was a similar or even greater dissatisfaction with living standards. The North African economies were reasonably satisfied with living standards (over 60 percent in Algeria, Egypt and Morocco).

Despite these attitudes toward living standards and life satisfaction, most respondents throughout Africa reported they were relatively satisfied with their health. Graham (2009) reports on results for Africa from an Afrobarometer survey. While the Afrobarometer survey does not have a direct question on well-being, Graham (2010) suggests that optimism, for which Afrobarometer does supply some data, and well-being are positively correlated. She suggests that optimism can be defined as having positive expectations for one's children. Making this assumption, she reports that African respondents' views about their own economic situation improving in the near future were positively correlated with income education and other socioeconomic variables which are associated with higher economic status. This is a result that we would expect, even though there might be generally low levels of life satisfaction.

Gender comparisons suggest that women are either happier or on an equal par with men in all but two countries (Rwanda and South Africa). A similar result was observed in Asia (see Table 2.4) and is consistent with other findings that found women to be happier. Furthermore, despite these relatively low levels of life satisfaction, satisfaction and living standards, nearly all respondents, both men and women, reported that they were living a purposeful life. Furthermore, with the exception of Ethiopia, where significantly fewer women (47 percent) reported a positive outcome, a majority reported being treated with respect. In addition (aside from Rwanda at 56 percent), a significant proportion reported having a supportive social network. The sense of these findings for Africa is that respondents were generally dissatisfied with their economic status, and this was reflected in a lower life satisfaction. At the same time, there were positive feelings about their health, their life purpose and how they were treated in their communities. These latter feelings seem to be relatively unrelated to their economic status.

The summary of life satisfaction from the various waves of the World Value Survey for Africa is displayed in Table 3.5. Well-being is calibrated

Table 3.5 Average well-being from World Value Surveys of African economies

Country	Well-being (scale of 1–4)	Life satisfaction (scale of 1–10)		Wave 2			Wave 3			Wave 4			Wave 5			Total no. of observations
				Average happiness	Life satisfaction	Obs	Average happiness	Life satisfaction	Obs	Average happiness	Life satisfaction	Obs	Average happiness	Life satisfaction	Obs	
Algeria	2.041	5.671	Wave 4							2.041	5.671	1,282				1,282
Egypt	2.009	5.564	Wave 4–5							1.937	5.353	3,000	2.078	5.772	3,051	6,051
Ethiopia	2.118	4.997	Wave 5										2.118	4.997	1,500	1,500
Mali	1.797	6.092	Wave 5										1.797	6.092	1,534	1,534
Morocco	1.966	5.781	Wave 4–5							1.962	6.061	2,264	1.972	5.252	1,200	3,464
Nigeria	1.656	6.705	Wave 2–4	2.024	6.586	1,001	1.719	6.592	1,996	1.422	6.874	2,022				5,019
Rwanda	2.048	4.965	Wave 5										2.048	4.965	1,507	1,507
South Africa	1.864	6.603	Wave 1–5	2.032	6.724	2,736	1.845	6.083	2,935	1.782	6.313	3,000	1.768	7.201	2,988	13,255
Tanzania	1.497	3.866	Wave 4							1.497	3.866	1,171				1,171
Uganda	1.994	5.651	Wave 4							1.994	5.651	1,002				1,002
Zambia	2.224	6.059	Wave 5										2.224	6.059	1,500	1,500
Zimbabwe	2.326	3.945	Wave 4							2.326	3.945	1,002				1,002

Data for South Africa are selected from Wave 2 onwards.

Note: Wave 2: 1989–93, Wave 3: 1994–9, Wave 4: 1999–2004 and Wave 5: 2005–7.

for the scale 1 to 4 and also for 1 to 10. For life satisfaction, the two scales of 1 to 4 and 1 to 10 are not quite as highly correlated for Africa as they were for Asia (Table 3.6). One obvious difference is that Tanzania had the lowest well-being scale on the 1 to 10 ranking and close to the highest on the 1 to 4 ranking. However, other countries had similar rankings, including the countries of North Africa (Algeria, Egypt and Ethiopia) and also in Central and Southern Africa (Nigeria, Rwanda, South Africa and Zimbabwe). At the same time, Zambia joined Tanzania in having a quite different ranking in the two scales. Turning to comparisons of well-being and per capita income, there is an even lower correlation (Table 3.7). North and South Africa have much higher per capita income than the rest of the continent. However, higher levels of well-being are spread more evenly through the continent. Well-being in Nigeria and Mali is higher than in North Africa, despite the fact that these countries have lower per capita incomes. Furthermore, the average well-being for African countries is more than one point lower than that for Asia (5.48 versus 6.55).

Life satisfaction has a different distribution for each country (see Figure 3.1). For several countries there is a peak at different levels of satisfaction – at 2 and 9 for Egypt, at 1 for Zimbabwe and Tanzania, at 5 for Uganda and Rwanda and at 8 and 10 for South Africa. Generally, the poorer countries have average life satisfaction that is considerably lower than life satisfaction for richer countries.

3.1.1 Sample size for Africa

Table 3.8 displays the sample sizes for various components of well-being for the full sample, for the three poverty groups and for the various countries in the region. South Africa has the largest sample size by far, followed by Egypt, and then Nigeria and some of the smaller countries. The three poverty groups contain as few as 56 observations in the case of the education poor in Uganda. Most sample sizes for the poor range from 200 to more than 4,000 in Egypt, Nigeria and South Africa. Nevertheless, small samples could be one reason why the full model with 12 independent variables fails to find significant coefficients for some of the social variables in the probit regressions discussed below. We explore the aggregation results in the next section. There we aggregate over a few countries for several regions. In the final section we look at overall results for Africa as a region. Notice that, by comparison with Asia, where there were many missing observations, the health poor are more often reported. One reason for this is the difference in the reporting of health outcomes in Africa *vis-à-vis* the other two regions. In Africa

Table 3.6 Correlations between WVS measure of happiness and life satisfaction

	Correlation between 1–4 and 1–10 measures of life satisfaction and happiness	No. of observations
North Africa	−0.2669	10,687
South Africa	−0.4913	13,088
East Africa	−0.1611	7,407
West Africa	−0.3956	6,363
Africa	−0.3656	37,545

Table 3.7 Correlations between WVS measure of happiness and income

	Correlation between well-being 1–10 and income level (self-reported scale)	No. of observations
North Africa	0.1487	9,309
South Africa	0.3573	11,530
East Africa	0.2936	6,546
West Africa	0.2655	5,612
Africa	0.2903	32,997

the healthy are in categories 1 and 2 while "we defined" health poor "to be" categories 3, 4 and 5. Individuals self-report 3 if they feel that they are in fair health, 4 if they feel that they are in poor health and 5 for very poor health. The expanded definition of health outcome took into account the general lower level of health conditions in Africa as compared with other regions. For instance, what an African respondent feels to be fair health could be differently interpreted under different conditions – it could possibly mean poor health for a respondent in the other two regions of Asia and Latin America. Hence, we have used the expanded definition of health outcomes for African economies only.

The variation in the response to the poverty level question is wide and has little relation to living standards. Over 40 percent of respondents said they were in the lowest two deciles of the income distribution in four countries (Algeria, Tanzania, Uganda and Zimbabwe), while in Ethiopia, Mali and Rwanda responses indicated that fewer than 15 percent believed they were in the lowest two deciles.

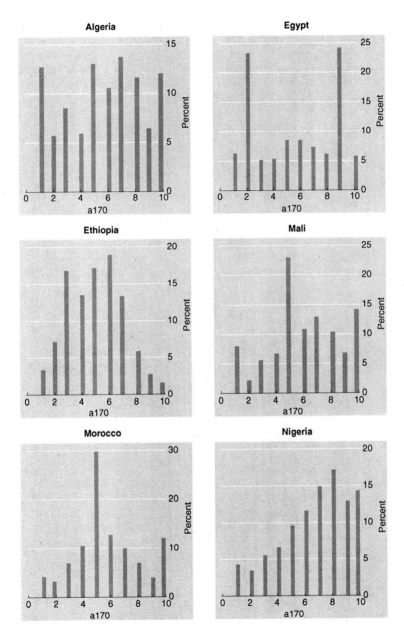

Figure 3.1 Life satisfaction in Africa

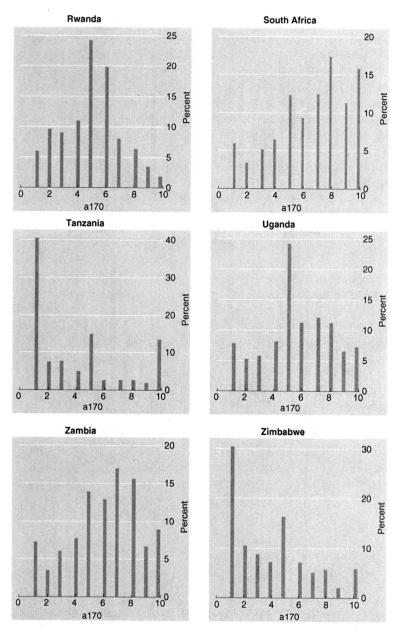

Figure 3.1   Continued

Table 3.8 Sample size for Africa region by country and poverty group (after fitting into model)

			a170 (Scale 1–10)*				a008 (Scale 1–4)*				a008r (Scale 0–1)*		
	Total	Overall	Health Poor	Edn Poor	Income Poor	Overall*	Health Poor	Edn Poor	Income Poor	Overall*	Health Poor	Edn Poor	Income Poor
Algeria	1,282	916	513	147	388	895	495	144	378	923	518	148	391
Egypt	6,051	4,981	1,637	2,283	1,016	4,984	1,637	2,286	1,018	4,988	1,638	2,286	1,018
Ethiopia	1,500	1,112	356	363	103	1,116	356	365	103	1,119	358	365	
Mali	1,534	701	217	438	97	719	220	452	104	728	224	458	105
Morocco	3,464	2,294	530	1,556	337	2,296	529	1,558	338	2,298	530	1,559	338
Nigeria	5,019	4,094	732	916	519	4,079	730	915	518	4,101	734	918	521
Rwanda	1,507	1,285	829	883	502	1,278	825	877	501	1,288	831	884	504
South Africa	13,255	9,052	2,043	2,151	2,634	9,047	2,043	2,149	2,635	9,067	2,052	2,155	2,640
Tanzania	1,171	799	283	369	328	801	282	368	329	807	286	372	333
Uganda	1,002	508	125	56	203	507	124	56	203	508			203
Zambia	1,500	1,040	282	236	147	980	247	214	138	1,053	286	239	150
Zimbabwe	1,002	743	284	301	296	739	283	301	297	745	284	302	297
	38,287												

*After fitting into the equation for the extended model (1.2).

3.1.2   Who is poor?

Before looking at the probit results for Africa, we summarize the three different kinds of poverty for the African economies. As we introduced in the discussion of Asia, there are three poverty groups:

(1) Those who have limited education, i.e. respondents who reported that they either had no education or have completed only elementary education as reported on the questionnaire.
(2) Those who have limited income, i.e. respondents who reported they are in the bottom quintile (20 percent) of the income distribution as reported on the questionnaire.
(3) Those who report being in poor health, i.e. respondents who reported they were in poor or very poor health on the questionnaire.

Note that the answers to all three questions are self-reported, based on responses to personal questions about these three variables. Countries with larger populations generally have larger sample sizes. There are generally fewer health poor than education or income poor, and the overall sample size also varies widely among countries. In some cases the sample sizes for the income poor are less than 100. This may make empirical inferences difficult. Furthermore, the income poor figures for different countries are subject to large variations, since the questions have been interpreted in widely different ways. For Algeria, Tunisia, Uganda and Zimbabwe there are estimates of poverty in the lowest two deciles of over 40 percent, while in several other countries (Mali, Rwanda, Ethiopia and Zambia) the estimates are under 15 percent. Despite these difficulties, the data do represent the spirit of identifying the income poor.

The distribution and intensity of these three poverty groups for the African region are reported in the Venn diagrams displayed in Figure 3.2. There is somewhat more overlap among the three poverty groups in Africa than there was in Asia. However, in most cases fewer than half of the health poor are also education and income poor. In the case of the education poor and income poor, more than 50 percent are shared in some cases, particularly because the education poor are a larger pool. Nevertheless, the overlap is not so large as to ignore any of these three important poverty subgroups.

3.2   Probit regression analysis for Africa

The definitions of the World Value Survey variables are shown in Table 3.9. We replicate Table 1.1 for ease of reference. We report the

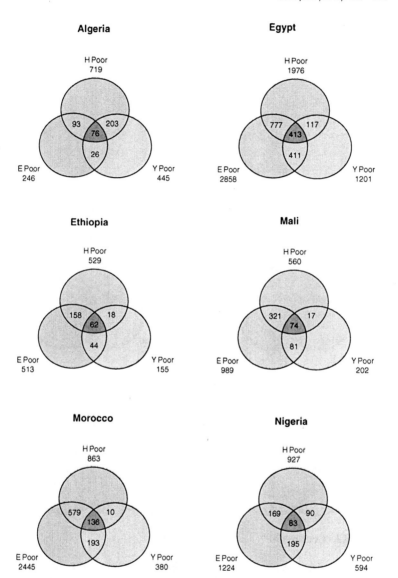

Figure 3.2 Venn diagrams for selected African countries

Note: H Poor stands for Health Poor, E Poor stands for Education Poor and Y Poor stands for Income Poor.

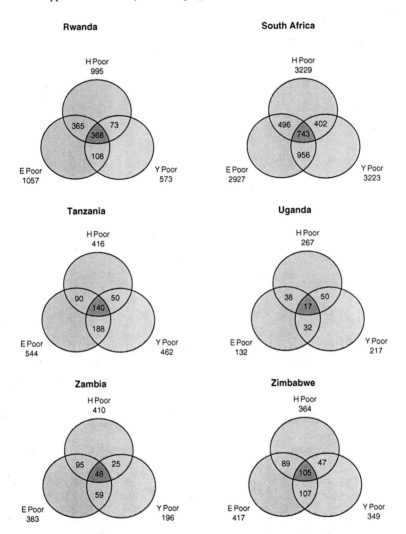

Figure 3.2 Continued

results by independent variable. Probit regressions are displayed in Tables 3.10 – 3.23 for the full sample of five waves of World Value Surveys by fitting Equation 1.2 for each country. The results are displayed for each independent variable, the three definitions of well-being (1 to 10, 1 to 4 and 0 and 1), and the probit regression overall as well as for each of the three poverty groups. This is the same setup that was used in the discussion for Asia in Chapter 2. The motivations for including variables were discussed in Chapter 1.

3.2.1 *Policy variables*

Health is a significant independent variable for all three configurations of happiness and well-being. It is most important among the income and education poor, being significant in all but a few countries for all three different definitions of well-being. It is less significant for the health poor, probably because of the smaller sample size for this poverty group.

Health. Starting with the independent variable health, the results confirm its overwhelming importance as a determinant of well-being in Africa. It is statistically significant in all 12 countries at high levels, with z value varying from 3 to 30. While the range of coefficients is large, their size suggests that the poorest countries would benefit with the most sizeable increase in well-being from having improved health. For the health poor (Table 3.10), all but two countries (Nigeria and Zambia) had a significant coefficient on health for the 1 to 4 scale of well-being. The pattern of response of well-being to improved health was not closely related to income. Algeria and Rwanda both had large coefficients. Rwanda, one of the poorest countries in Africa, has the highest coefficient, while Egypt and Morocco have the smallest coefficients. This finding is consistent with results mentioned in Chapter 2 for the Asian experience, and reinforces the importance of health for uplifting the well-being of the poor. It also conveys an added bonus of reducing child mortality among the poor (see Gupta *et al.* 2001, page 10). There is also evidence that the richer segments of society rely more on private resources, which strengthens the argument that public health spending has an appropriate focus on the poor.

Income. Income is the next most significant explanatory variable. For the overall sample, income is statistically significant in 11 countries for the 1–10 definition of life satisfaction, and in fewer countries where the happiness form for well-being (1 to 4 and 0 to 1) is used (Table 3.11). There is a much weaker association between the strength of the income effect on well-being than is observed for improvements in health services, and the coefficients vary over a smaller range. Among the poor, income is significant primarily among the health and education poor and less important among the income poor. This result seems counterintuitive, but could reflect the relatively higher importance placed on health and education among the income poor as a way to get out of poverty. There is a much weaker association between the strength of the income effect on well-being than is observed for improvements in health, and the coefficients vary over a smaller range. Levels of significance are generally lower for income than for health. Yet it is still a generally strong positive variable in lifting well-being across the African region.

Table 3.9 Definitions of selected WVS indicators

a170 Satisfaction with your life
1: Dissatisfied
10: Satisfied

a008 Feeling of happiness
1: happy
2: quite happy
3: not very happy
4: not at all happy

a008r
0: not very happy or not at all happy
1: happy or quite happy

State of Health
1: Very good
2: Good
3: Fair
4: Poor
5: Very Poor
1–2: Health Nonpoor
3–5: Health Poor (for African countries)

Income level (country specific) 10th step
1st–2nd income decile: Income Poor
3rd–10th income decile: Income Nonpoor

Gender
1: Male
2: Female

Age (3 intervals)
1: 15–29
2: 30–49
3: 50 years and above

Marital Status
0: Not Married
1: Married or Living Together

Family important in life
1: Very important
2: Rather important
3: Not very important
4: Not at all important

Friends important in life
1: Very important
2: Rather important
3: Not very important
4: Not at all important

Important in Life: Work
1: Very important
2: Rather important
3: Not very important
4: Not at all important

Important in Life: Religion
1: Very important
2: Rather important
3: Not very important
4: Not at all important

Most people can be trusted
1: Most people can be trusted
2: Can't be too careful

Confidence in the Civil Services
1: A great deal
2: Quite a lot
3: Not very much
4: None at all

Highest level of education attained

1: Inadequately completed elementary education
2: Completed (compulsory) elementary education
3: Inadequately completed secondary education
4: Completed secondary education (technical, vocational secondary)
5: Inadequately completed secondary, university preparatory education
6: Completed secondary education: university preparatory
7: Some university without degree
8: University with degree/higher

1st–2nd levels: Education Poor
3rd–10th levels: Education Nonpoor

Table 3.10 Probit results for Africa – state of health

	a170 (Scale 1-10)				a008 (Scale 1-4)				a008r (Scale 0-1)			
	Overall	Health Poor	Edn Poor	Income Poor	Overall	Health Poor	Edn Poor	Income Poor	Overall	Health Poor	Edn Poor	Income Poor
Algeria	-0.22* (-4.94)	-0.49* (-3.52)	0.04 (0.33)	-0.18* (-2.56)	0.46* (8.79)	0.63* (3.95)	0.43* (3.06)	0.48* (5.69)	-0.36* (-5.47)	-0.49* (-3.39)	-0.63* (-2.64)	-0.38* (-3.46)
Egypt	-0.14* (-7.64)	-0.19* (-3.06)	-0.17* (-6.34)	-0.26* (-6.56)	0.43* (18.92)	0.30* (4.36)	0.43* (13.49)	0.43* (9.25)	-0.36* (-12.33)	-0.17* (-2.39)	-0.38* (-9.82)	-0.48* (-8.51)
Ethiopia	-0.38* (-9.91)	-0.01 (-0.06)	-0.29* (-4.31)	-0.36* (-2.75)	0.82* (17.83)	0.88* (5.01)	0.77* (9.50)	1.02* (5.27)	-0.77* (-13.36)	-0.47* (-2.68)	-0.71* (-7.26)	
Mali	-0.42* (-8.59)	-0.27 (-1.19)	-0.52* (-8.40)	-0.68* (-4.95)	0.54* (9.79)	0.42 (1.81)	0.52* (7.61)	0.86* (5.93)	-0.38* (-5.23)	-0.42 (-1.87)	-0.38* (-4.34)	-0.58* (-3.44)
Morocco	-0.23* (-8.28)	-0.23 (-1.84)	-0.18* (-5.46)	-0.25* (-3.55)	0.54* (16.90)	0.40* (3.03)	0.55* (14.47)	0.47* (5.90)	-0.39* (-9.78)	-0.20 (-1.56)	-0.40* (-8.48)	-0.42* (-4.43)
Nigeria	-0.28* (-14.75)	-0.10 (-1.37)	-0.31* (-7.08)	-0.27* (-5.61)	0.48* (22.13)	0.13 (1.68)	0.60* (12.09)	0.47* (8.62)	-0.45* (-16.51)	-0.06 (-0.73)	-0.63* (-9.68)	-0.52* (-7.69)
Rwanda	-0.69* (-15.67)	-0.98* (-10.55)	-0.70* (-13.62)	-0.85* (-12.26)	0.59* (11.36)	0.90* (8.63)	0.59* (9.80)	0.54* (7.05)	-0.68* (-9.73)	-0.79* (-7.82)	-0.74* (-9.18)	-0.67* (-6.72)
South Africa	-0.28* (-22.05)	-0.39* (-9.01)	-0.29* (-12.62)	-0.26* (-12.39)	0.41* (29.54)	0.34* (7.48)	0.39* (15.97)	0.40* (17.83)	-0.38* (-21.29)	-0.23* (-4.83)	-0.39* (-13.39)	-0.38* (-14.28)

Tanzania	−0.20*	−0.27	−0.21*	−0.20*	0.34*	0.43*	0.24*	0.26*	−0.22*	−0.25	−0.11	−0.44*
	(−4.13)	(−1.33)	(−2.97)	(−2.63)	(6.23)	(2.18)	(3.02)	(3.18)	(−2.54)	(−1.12)	(−0.89)	(−3.08)
Uganda	−0.31*	−0.28	−0.05	−0.37*	0.97*	1.71*	1.42*	1.09*	−0.98*			−1.07*
	(−4.73)	(−0.62)	(−0.22)	(−3.71)	(11.80)	(2.99)	(4.50)	(8.37)	(−8.29)			(−6.15)
Zambia	−0.31*	−0.64*	−0.29*	−0.26*	−0.08	0.05	−0.19*	−0.13	−0.17*	0.06	−0.10	0.01
	(−8.17)	(−4.32)	(−3.79)	(−2.87)	(−1.91)	(0.27)	(−2.13)	(−1.33)	(−3.70)	(0.44)	(−1.13)	(0.05)
Zimbabwe	−0.08	−0.69*	−0.07	0.01	0.23*	0.84*	0.31*	0.28*	−0.24*	−0.34	−0.33*	−0.31*
	(−1.68)	(−3.68)	(−0.99)	(0.11)	(4.89)	(4.45)	(4.24)	(3.84)	(−4.38)	(−1.96)	(−3.85)	(−3.54)

Notes: 1. Based on probit results for extended model where z stats are displayed in parenthesis and * denotes statistical significance at the 5% level. For 1–10 and 0–1 definitions of well-being, a negative sign indicates healthier people are happier. For the 1–4 definition of well-being, a positive sign indicates healthier people are happier.
2. Variable dropped due to multicollinearity.

Table 3.11 Probit results for Africa – income level

	a170 (Scale 1–10)				a008 (Scale 1–4)				a008r (Scale 0–1)			
	Overall	Health Poor	Edn Poor	Income Poor	Overall	Health Poor	Edn Poor	Income Poor	Overall	Health Poor	Edn Poor	Income Poor
Algeria	0.08* (4.28)	0.08* (3.01)	0.12* (2.66)	0.08 (0.62)	−0.04 (−1.87)	−0.06 (−1.94)	−0.07 (−1.23)	−0.19 (−1.20)	0.06* (2.01)	0.08 (1.80)	0.18 (1.48)	0.12 (0.61)
Egypt	0.05* (7.45)	0.08* (6.84)	0.06* (6.02)	0.29* (4.44)	−0.10* (−11.67)	−0.10* (−7.28)	−0.10* (−8.10)	−0.35* (−4.63)	0.13* (11.39)	0.12* (7.55)	0.13* (8.15)	0.53* (5.98)
Ethiopia	0.21* (11.51)	0.21* (6.41)	0.21* (7.07)	0.34 (1.25)	−0.10* (−4.89)	−0.10* (−2.70)	−0.06 (−1.95)	0.12 (0.36)	0.14* (5.91)	0.14* (3.44)	0.09* (2.33)	
Mali	0.17* (8.62)	0.19* (5.39)	0.15* (6.19)	0.11 (0.43)	−0.13* (−6.44)	−0.18* (−4.88)	−0.12* (−4.65)	0.24 (0.90)	0.14* (5.23)	0.20* (4.36)	0.14* (4.21)	−0.37 (−1.11)
Morocco	0.22* (15.85)	0.23* (7.84)	0.21* (12.13)	0.04 (0.33)	−0.15* (−9.61)	−0.10* (−3.33)	−0.15* (−7.86)	0.06 (0.44)	0.18* (8.48)	0.10* (2.84)	0.15* (6.27)	0.09 (0.57)
Nigeria	0.08* (11.10)	0.06* (3.53)	0.08* (4.74)	−0.13 (−1.38)	−0.06* (−6.62)	−0.08* (−4.53)	−0.08* (−4.19)	0.07 (0.70)	0.09* (7.82)	0.11* (4.92)	0.08* (3.13)	0.06 (0.48)
Rwanda	0.14* (8.88)	0.18* (8.37)	0.15* (7.55)	0.03 (0.32)	−0.03 (−1.73)	−0.03 (−1.00)	−0.02 (−0.97)	0.03 (0.25)	0.07* (2.50)	0.08* (2.50)	0.05 (1.65)	0.16 (1.16)
South Africa	0.12* (22.29)	0.11* (9.70)	0.16* (11.67)	0.10* (2.41)	−0.09* (−15.21)	−0.09* (−7.22)	−0.11* (−7.57)	0.00 (−0.09)	0.13* (15.91)	0.11* (7.55)	0.13* (6.97)	0.12* (2.33)

Tanzania	0.07*	0.05	0.07	0.22	0.01	0.03	0.06	-0.05	0.00	0.08	-0.04	0.19
	(3.02)	(1.20)	(1.69)	(1.67)	(0.37)	(0.62)	(1.27)	(-0.37)	(0.01)	(1.06)	(-0.62)	(0.84)
Uganda	0.05	0.06	0.05	0.10	-0.03	-0.13	-0.07	0.09	0.15*			(0.28)
	(1.59)	(0.88)	(0.35)	(0.65)	(-0.84)	(-1.59)	(-0.43)	(0.53)	(2.63)			(1.26)
Zambia	0.09*	0.14*	0.15*	0.10	0.04*	0.00	0.07*	0.14	-0.03	-0.03	-0.05	0.04
	(6.55)	(4.48)	(5.30)	(0.55)	(2.41)	(0.10)	(2.15)	(0.67)	(-1.60)	(-0.95)	(-1.34)	(0.19)
Zimbabwe	0.09*	0.05	0.06	0.00	-0.03	-0.06	-0.08	-0.05	0.06*	0.09	0.08	0.29
	(3.79)	(1.16)	(1.14)	(0.03)	(-1.45)	(-1.39)	(-1.48)	(-0.42)	(2.05)	(1.75)	(1.34)	(1.84)

Notes: 1. Based on probit results for extended model where z stats are displayed in parenthesis and * denotes statistical significance at the 5% level. For 1–10 and 0–1 definitions of well-being, a positive sign indicates that higher income results in higher well-being. For the 1–4 definition of well-being, a negative sign indicates higher income results in higher well-being.
2. Variable dropped due to multicollinearity.

Table 3.12 Probit results for Africa – education level

	a170 (Scale 1–10)				a008 (Scale 1–4)				a008r (Scale 0–1)			
	Overall	Health Poor	Edn Poor	Income Poor	Overall	Health Poor	Edn Poor	Income Poor	Overall	Health Poor	Edn Poor	Income Poor
Algeria	0.01 (0.62)	0.00 (−0.10)	0.02 (0.10)	0.00 (0.15)	0.00 (−0.22)	−0.01 (−0.34)	0.21 (0.90)	−0.01 (−0.20)	0.03 (1.12)	0.05 (1.40)	−0.04 (−0.12)	0.01 (0.20)
Egypt	0.01 (1.47)	0.02 (1.34)	−0.11* (−2.03)	−0.01 (−0.67)	−0.01 (−1.57)	−0.02 (−1.60)	0.04 (0.70)	−0.01 (−0.31)	0.04* (3.58)	0.04* (2.46)	0.12 (1.57)	0.01 (0.46)
Ethiopia	−0.01 (−0.29)	0.01 (0.28)	−0.02 (−0.20)	−0.09 (−1.02)	−0.03 (−1.62)	0.00 (−0.13)	0.03 (0.20)	−0.12 (−1.06)	0.04 (1.63)	0.06 (1.34)	0.04 (0.23)	
Mali	0.01 (0.39)	0.11* (2.87)	0.17 (1.14)	0.03 (0.37)	−0.01 (−0.48)	−0.01 (−0.37)	−0.09 (−0.60)	0.02 (0.26)	0.05 (1.70)	0.06 (1.15)	0.06 (0.26)	0.02 (0.18)
Morocco	0.03* (2.71)	−0.06* (−2.23)	0.13 (1.55)	−0.01 (−0.18)	0.00 (0.13)	0.04 (1.24)	0.15 (1.57)	0.04 (0.78)	0.02 (1.03)	0.02 (0.49)	0.12 (1.00)	0.00 (−0.05)
Nigeria	0.03* (3.84)	0.04* (2.24)	−0.04 (−0.63)	0.06* (2.72)	0.00 (0.52)	0.01 (0.42)	−0.14 (−1.69)	−0.05 (−1.79)	0.02* (2.09)	0.03 (1.19)	0.30* (2.77)	0.03 (0.96)
Rwanda	0.02 (1.13)	0.00 (0.16)	0.12 (1.62)	0.07 (1.65)	0.00 (0.09)	0.02 (0.64)	0.07 (0.85)	0.02 (0.37)	0.01 (0.31)	0.03 (0.71)	0.03 (0.28)	−0.01 (−0.11)
South Africa	0.03* (4.60)	0.04* (3.65)	0.06 (1.33)	0.05* (4.36)	−0.02* (−3.28)	−0.04* (−2.88)	−0.03 (−0.56)	−0.06* (−5.30)	0.06* (6.54)	0.07* (4.34)	0.09 (1.45)	0.08* (5.51)

Tanzania	-0.03 (-1.56)	-0.04 (-0.99)	-0.19 (-1.18)	-0.15* (-2.93)	0.03 (1.09)	0.03 (0.74)	-0.17 (-0.97)	0.05 (0.97)	0.06 (1.38)	0.07 (0.89)	0.51* (2.04)	0.05 (0.65)
Uganda	0.00 (-0.14)	-0.09 (-1.30)	0.00 (-0.01)	-0.06 (-1.37)	0.04 (0.95)	0.01 (0.11)	0.23 (0.57)	0.06 (1.21)	0.03 (0.52)			-0.04 (-0.63)
Zambia	0.04* (2.17)	0.02 (0.69)	0.24 (1.69)	0.03 (0.52)	0.01 (0.69)	0.06 (1.40)	0.23 (1.36)	-0.06 (-1.00)	0.00 (0.07)	-0.01 (-0.15)	-0.01 (-0.03)	0.08 (1.24)
Zimbabwe	0.02 (0.56)	0.00 (-0.02)	-0.07 (-0.51)	0.00 (0.05)	0.00 (-0.12)	0.02 (0.37)	0.06 (0.44)	-0.02 (-0.30)	0.02 (0.37)	0.06 (0.84)	0.00 (-0.02)	-0.01 (-0.12)

Notes: 1. Based on probit results for extended model where z stats are displayed in parenthesis and * denotes statistical significance at the 5% level. For 1–10 and 0–1 definitions of well-being, a positive sign indicates that education results in higher well-being. For the 1–4 definition of well-being, a negative sign indicates education results in higher well-being.

2. Variable dropped due to multicollinearity.

Education. Surprisingly, education is not a crucially important variable in raising levels of well-being (Table 3.12), and African respondents appear to value raising health and income more. It is significant with the correct a priori sign in only five countries of 12 in the sample. As a result, education is not generally important in uplifting well-being in Africa. Education is not generally valued as a contributor to well-being among the poor, being statistically significant in only 14 cases out of 106 possible outcomes across 12 countries and the three poverty categories. This is a strongly negative result, suggesting that the poor and even the nonpoor do not put as high a value on education. Aside from the higher value placed on these alternatives, it could also reflect the poor quality of education offered throughout Africa and the low returns expected from education in a region with few employment opportunities in the modern sector of industry and services. Furthermore, the poor may be interested in wanting returns from variables, such as income and health, that are more short-term in nature.

Comparison of aggregate and poverty group results – where are impacts on well-being strongest?

To analyze differences in the response of the poor *vis-à-vis* the entire sample to changes in the three major decision variables of health, income and education, we compared the regression coefficients for the 1 to 10 Cantril ladder results. There are nine possible comparisons of overall well-being of the full sample with the well-being of the health, education and income poor. We arranged the results in a 3 by 3 matrix and summarize the significant differences between the poverty response and the overall response in Table 3.13. There is a significant difference if the poverty coefficient is around two standard deviations above the corresponding full sample coefficient.[1] Looking at the health variable in the overall and three poverty regressions and comparing the poverty coefficients with the overall coefficient, there is a significant difference (poverty coefficient higher than overall) in four countries (Algeria, Rwanda, Zambia and Zimbabwe) and a significant coefficient on income in three countries (Egypt, Malawi and Rwanda). The health poor and the income poor would respond more than the overall sample to changes in the provision of health services.

The income poor and education poor also respond more than the overall sample in Egypt and Zambia. However, the most interesting result is the number of cases in which the well-being of the poor is lifted much more than that of the rich when it comes to better health outcomes. Reading across the bottom row of Table 3.13, there are six countries where the poverty response is higher for the poor than for the

Table 3.13 Significant differences between poverty coefficients and full sample coefficients in 13 African countries for probit analysis of determinants of well-being – scale of 1 to 10 for well-being

	Significant income poverty coefficient	Significant education poverty coefficient	Significant health poverty coefficient
Income poor sample	Egypt, Egypt*, Egypt**	Zambia	Zambia
Education poor sample			Morocco
Health poor sample	Egypt, Mali, Rwanda		Algeria, Rwanda, Zambia, Zimbabwe***

*for 1 to 4 scale.
**0 to 1 scale.
***Tanzania and Zambia are close to significant using this rough rule of thumb.

sample as a whole among the health and income poor. This suggests that actions to raise the level of delivery of health service would have a strong impact on raising well-being across Africa.

3.2.2 Sociological and demographic variables

Gender For the sample as a whole, women are happier than men in just over half the economies in Africa, with gender difference being insignificant in the rest. Women are never unhappier than men. This result is consistent with the findings from other studies and also from the results for Asia reported in Chapter 2. For the poor, the gender results are less compelling. Women are happier than men in 30 out of 106 possible cases, and in the rest the gender variable has an insignificant impact on well-being (Table 3.14).

Age. For the overall sample, age shows a well-being dip in midlife and increases in later life for a few countries, primarily in South Africa and West Africa (Nigeria and South Africa in particular). However, for the majority of countries age does not seem to have an important impact on well-being, as the variable is not significant for most countries in either linear or nonlinear form (Tables 3.15 and 3.16).

Marital status. Married couples are happier than those who remain single or are divorced, widowed, etc. in a few countries, and the variable is insignificant in the remaining African countries (Table 3.17).

Table 3.14 Probit results for Africa – gender

	a170 (Scale 1–10)				a008 (Scale 1–4)				a008r (Scale 0–1)			
	Overall	Health Poor	Edn Poor	Income Poor	Overall	Health Poor	Edn Poor	Income Poor	Overall	Health Poor	Edn Poor	Income Poor
Algeria	0.22* (3.20)	0.15 (1.59)	0.45* (2.21)	0.26* (2.34)	-0.34* (-4.14)	-0.41* (-3.62)	-0.21 (-0.82)	-0.40* (-2.92)	0.54* (5.17)	0.64* (4.84)	0.52 (1.37)	0.67* (4.11)
Egypt	0.08* (2.43)	0.05 (0.82)	0.03 (0.58)	0.01 (0.08)	-0.17* (-4.36)	-0.19* (-2.85)	-0.23* (-3.75)	-0.29* (-3.36)	0.40* (7.91)	0.30* (3.95)	0.44* (5.97)	0.45* (4.37)
Ethiopia	0.07 (1.07)	0.08 (0.70)	0.05 (0.40)	-0.15 (-0.58)	0.11 (1.52)	0.15 (1.17)	0.13 (1.07)	-0.25 (-0.76)	0.13 (1.54)	0.00 (-0.03)	0.20 (1.43)	
Mali	0.02 (0.29)	0.05 (0.37)	-0.01 (-0.06)	-0.03 (-0.12)	-0.13 (-1.40)	-0.19 (-1.19)	-0.12 (-1.11)	-0.33 (-1.46)	0.40* (3.32)	0.50* (2.56)	0.35* (2.43)	0.54 (1.97)
Morocco	0.08 (1.79)	0.27* (2.87)	0.09 (1.75)	0.14 (1.17)	-0.12* (-2.37)	-0.25* (-2.41)	-0.10 (-1.66)	-0.16 (-1.23)	0.31* (4.73)	0.34* (2.97)	0.28* (3.67)	0.36* (2.36)
Nigeria	0.09* (2.70)	0.09 (1.20)	0.02 (0.26)	0.07 (0.81)	-0.12* (-3.06)	-0.12 (-1.41)	-0.11 (-1.34)	-0.38* (-3.58)	0.35* (6.97)	0.20* (2.08)	0.26* (2.44)	0.69* (5.25)
Rwanda	-0.06 (-0.96)	-0.05 (-0.63)	-0.11 (-1.57)	-0.08 (-0.87)	0.23* (3.25)	0.19* (2.20)	0.31* (3.62)	0.36* (3.33)	0.02 (0.23)	0.04 (0.38)	-0.02 (-0.20)	-0.12 (-0.90)
South Africa	0.05* (2.11)	-0.04 (-0.80)	0.04 (0.98)	0.06 (1.33)	-0.11* (-4.48)	-0.07 (-1.43)	-0.07 (-1.34)	-0.11* (-2.47)	0.17* (5.12)	0.08 (1.34)	0.07 (1.26)	0.13* (2.55)

Tanzania	0.33* (4.01)	0.38* (2.62)	0.49* (3.99)	0.40* (3.00)	0.02 (0.19)	0.00 (0.01)	-0.03 (-0.25)	-0.02 (-0.13)	0.15 (0.96)	0.28 (1.12)	0.32 (1.46)	0.55* (2.10)
Uganda	0.12 (1.17)	0.30 (1.32)	0.54 (1.69)	0.10 (0.64)	-0.23 (-1.94)	-0.45 (-1.77)	-0.44 (-1.17)	-0.01 (-0.04)	0.33* (2.01)			0.26 (1.09)
Zambia	0.17* (2.60)	0.16 (1.28)	0.23 (1.67)	-0.04 (-0.20)	0.03 (0.45)	-0.06 (-0.43)	0.11 (0.69)	-0.05 (-0.22)	0.01 (0.07)	0.06 (0.44)	-0.12 (-0.72)	0.04 (0.19)
Zimbabwe	0.24* (2.88)	0.26 (1.93)	0.36* (2.59)	0.24 (1.84)	-0.12 (-1.46)	0.05 (0.35)	0.03 (0.23)	-0.02 (-0.12)	0.25* (2.58)	0.19 (1.20)	0.20 (1.30)	0.05 (0.34)

Notes: 1. Based on probit results for extended model where z stats are displayed in parenthesis and * denotes statistical significance at the 5% level. For 1–10 and 0–1 definitions, a positive sign indicates that women are happier. For 1–4 definition, a negative sign indicates women are happier.
2. Variable dropped due to multicollinearity.

Table 3.15 Probit results for Africa – age

	a170 (Scale 1–10)				a008 (Scale 1–4)				a008r (Scale 0–1)			
	Overall	Health Poor	Edn Poor	Income Poor	Overall	Health Poor	Edn Poor	Income Poor	Overall	Health Poor	Edn Poor	Income Poor
Algeria	0.00 (0.00)	0.09 (0.23)	0.26 (0.22)	0.55 (1.21)	0.37 (1.09)	0.80 (1.65)	1.43 (0.99)	0.50 (0.93)	0.54 (1.41)	0.14 (0.27)	0.47 (0.38)	0.72 (1.20)
Egypt	-0.22 (-1.77)	-0.04 (-0.16)	-0.23 (-1.13)	-0.24 (-0.85)	0.62* (4.11)	0.85* (3.07)	0.87* (3.63)	0.70* (2.15)	0.58* (3.46)	0.07 (0.27)	0.31 (1.29)	-0.35 (-1.00)
Ethiopia	-0.56 (-1.83)	-1.22* (-2.15)	0.22 (0.46)	0.76 (0.50)	0.95* (2.73)	1.38* (2.18)	0.71 (1.35)	-4.10 (-1.94)	1.08* (3.15)	0.60 (0.95)	0.93 (1.87)	
Mali	-0.58 (-1.73)	-1.84* (-2.77)	-0.71 (-1.70)	-1.48 (-1.45)	0.38 (1.03)	0.46 (0.68)	0.73 (1.63)	0.89 (0.88)	-0.11 (-0.27)	-0.51 (-0.66)	-0.49 (-1.00)	0.02 (0.02)
Morocco	-0.05 (-0.28)	-0.52 (-1.30)	-0.14 (-0.63)	0.19 (0.39)	0.32 (1.50)	1.08* (2.48)	0.39 (1.57)	-0.77 (-1.40)	0.54* (2.33)	-0.20 (-0.46)	0.56* (2.04)	1.25* (2.20)
Nigeria	-0.36* (-2.34)	-0.81* (-2.32)	-0.24 (-0.82)	0.21 (0.50)	0.64* (3.60)	0.85* (2.26)	0.58 (1.72)	0.31 (0.68)	0.43* (2.31)	-0.09 (-0.26)	0.64 (1.80)	0.81 (1.79)
Rwanda	-0.12 (-0.48)	-0.26 (-0.81)	0.19 (0.64)	-0.23 (-0.57)	0.12 (0.37)	0.36 (0.97)	0.01 (0.03)	0.27 (0.58)	1.42* (3.82)	1.52* (3.60)	1.52* (3.53)	1.85* (3.46)
South Africa	-0.43* (-4.58)	-0.33 (-1.58)	-0.11 (-0.56)	-0.31 (-1.82)	0.56* (5.46)	1.00* (4.57)	0.31 (1.47)	0.69* (3.79)	0.23* (2.10)	-0.43* (-2.07)	0.49* (2.60)	0.07 (0.41)

Tanzania	−0.53	−1.30*	−0.41	−0.19	1.19*	0.61	0.93	0.97	1.07*	0.79	0.61	1.55
	(−1.56)	(−2.13)	(−0.81)	(−0.33)	(3.16)	(0.97)	(1.70)	(1.56)	(2.10)	(0.90)	(0.83)	(1.81)
Uganda	−0.04	−0.08	−0.25	0.22	1.01	1.44	0.86	1.30	−0.04			0.27
	(−0.08)	(−0.07)	(−0.17)	(0.28)	(1.91)	(1.18)	(0.50)	(1.44)	(−0.06)			(0.25)
Zambia	−0.25	0.14	−0.68	0.65	−0.16	−0.42	−0.07	0.96	0.09	−0.31	−0.45	−1.11
	(−0.79)	(0.25)	(−1.10)	(0.81)	(−0.45)	(−0.62)	(−0.10)	(1.03)	(0.28)	(−0.52)	(−0.76)	(−1.40)
Zimbabwe	−0.52	−0.96	−0.79	−0.63	0.97*	1.05	0.87	−0.09	−1.09*	−0.33	−0.47	−0.81
	(−1.52)	(−1.77)	(−1.46)	(−1.16)	(2.80)	(1.90)	(1.58)	(−0.16)	(−3.08)	(−0.57)	(−0.84)	(−1.43)

Notes: 1. Based on probit results for extended model where z stats are displayed in parenthesis and * denotes statistical significance at the 5% level. For 1–10 and 0–1 definitions, a positive sign indicates that older people are happier and vice versa. For 1–4 definition, a negative sign indicates older people are happier.
2. Variable dropped due to multicollinearity.

Table 3.16 Probit results for Africa – age squared

	a170 (Scale 1–10)				a008 (Scale 1–4)				a008r (Scale 0–1)			
	Overall	Health Poor	Edn Poor	Income Poor	Overall	Health Poor	Edn Poor	Income Poor	Overall	Health Poor	Edn Poor	Income Poor
Algeria	0.01 (0.10)	-0.01 (-0.10)	-0.05 (-0.20)	-0.13 (-1.12)	-0.11 (-1.21)	-0.24 (-1.93)	-0.41 (-1.28)	-0.14 (-0.99)	-0.07 (-0.65)	0.07 (0.47)	0.09 (0.31)	-0.15 (-0.91)
Egypt	0.06 (1.91)	0.03 (0.44)	0.06 (1.27)	0.09 (1.28)	-0.17* (-4.55)	-0.22* (-3.41)	-0.24* (-4.20)	-0.18* (-2.32)	-0.10* (-2.45)	0.03 (0.38)	-0.01 (-0.25)	0.11 (1.29)
Ethiopia	0.17 (1.99)	0.37* (2.33)	-0.03 (-0.26)	-0.24 (-0.52)	-0.29* (-2.98)	-0.47* (-2.67)	-0.22 (-1.60)	1.48* (2.30)	-0.24* (-2.44)	-0.07 (-0.38)	-0.19 (-1.43)	
Mali	0.15 (1.83)	0.45* (2.85)	0.18 (1.79)	0.40 (1.59)	-0.09 (-0.96)	-0.11 (-0.65)	-0.17 (-1.51)	-0.30 (-1.18)	-0.01 (-0.07)	0.11 (0.59)	0.08 (0.65)	0.05 (0.19)
Morocco	0.03 (0.61)	0.14 (1.46)	0.05 (0.86)	-0.01 (-0.06)	-0.14* (-2.53)	-0.31* (-2.92)	-0.16* (-2.51)	0.14 (1.04)	-0.07 (-1.21)	0.11 (1.02)	-0.07 (-1.00)	-0.24 (-1.63)
Nigeria	0.09* (2.24)	0.18 (1.96)	0.07 (1.02)	-0.01 (-0.13)	-0.15* (-3.13)	-0.18 (-1.83)	-0.14 (-1.62)	-0.05 (-0.44)	-0.11* (-2.23)	-0.01 (-0.12)	-0.14 (-1.58)	-0.22 (-1.81)
Rwanda	0.01 (0.18)	0.05 (0.56)	-0.05 (-0.70)	0.03 (0.31)	0.00 (-0.05)	-0.07 (-0.70)	0.02 (0.22)	-0.06 (-0.49)	-0.41* (-4.28)	-0.43* (-3.95)	-0.42* (-3.87)	-0.48* (-3.49)
South Africa	0.13* (5.76)	0.11* (2.31)	0.06 (1.29)	0.11* (2.45)	-0.16* (-6.39)	-0.28* (-5.33)	-0.11* (-2.21)	-0.21* (-4.60)	-0.02 (-0.79)	0.16* (3.12)	-0.07 (-1.50)	0.02 (0.55)

Tanzania	0.14	0.33*	0.10	0.03	−0.28*	−0.14	−0.22	−0.22	−0.26*	−0.19	−0.14	−0.38
	(1.64)	(2.16)	(0.80)	(0.17)	(−2.99)	(−0.91)	(−1.59)	(−1.35)	(−2.00)	(−0.88)	(−0.75)	(−1.70)
Uganda	−0.02	−0.06	0.15	−0.03	−0.27	−0.43	−0.28	−0.36	0.05			−0.06
	(−0.18)	(−0.18)	(0.37)	(−0.15)	(−1.78)	(−1.21)	(−0.60)	(−1.38)	(0.23)			(−0.18)
Zambia	0.08	−0.03	0.17	−0.17	0.06	0.15	0.04	−0.25	−0.03	0.05	0.12	0.28
	(0.91)	(−0.20)	(1.07)	(−0.82)	(0.66)	(0.84)	(0.21)	(−1.04)	(−0.41)	(0.28)	(0.75)	(1.36)
Zimbabwe	0.13	0.22	0.18	0.12	−0.22*	−0.21	−0.21	0.01	0.27*	0.08	0.15	0.22
	(1.48)	(1.63)	(1.41)	(0.91)	(−2.49)	(−1.54)	(−1.63)	(0.05)	(2.85)	(0.53)	(1.05)	(1.49)

Notes: 1. Based on probit results for extended model where z stats are displayed in parenthesis and * denotes statistical significance at the 5% level.

2. Variable dropped due to multicollinearity.

Table 3.17 Probit results for Africa – marital status

	a170 (Scale 1–10)				a008 (Scale 1–4)				a008r (Scale 0–1)			
	Overall	Health Poor	Edn Poor	Income Poor	Overall	Health Poor	Edn Poor	Income Poor	Overall	Health Poor	Edn Poor	Income Poor
Algeria	0.21* (2.71)	0.22* (2.06)	−0.04 (−0.17)	0.11 (0.87)	−0.41* (−4.44)	−0.41* (−3.19)	−0.17 (−0.62)	−0.51* (−3.48)	0.35* (2.90)	0.38* (2.52)	0.22 (0.55)	0.37 (1.97)
Egypt	0.10* (2.89)	0.06 (0.93)	0.05 (1.00)	−0.14 (−1.82)	−0.31* (−7.34)	−0.33* (−4.61)	−0.32* (−5.03)	−0.27* (−3.02)	0.32* (5.82)	0.31* (3.73)	0.40* (5.11)	0.30* (2.86)
Ethiopia	0.07 (0.95)	−0.08 (−0.67)	0.23 (1.71)	0.01 (0.02)	−0.08 (−1.06)	−0.15 (−1.11)	−0.06 (−0.44)	−0.93* (−2.30)	0.18 (1.79)	0.22 (1.34)	0.12 (0.66)	
Mali	0.17 (1.73)	0.43* (2.06)	0.17 (1.27)	0.14 (0.50)	−0.11 (−0.97)	−0.03 (−0.14)	−0.22 (−1.55)	0.06 (0.20)	0.28 (1.80)	0.48 (1.84)	0.33 (1.73)	−0.11 (−0.32)
Morocco	0.20* (3.85)	0.38* (3.41)	0.26* (4.17)	0.12 (0.84)	−0.17* (−2.93)	−0.27* (−2.28)	−0.15* (−2.23)	−0.02 (−0.13)	0.17* (2.11)	0.15 (1.10)	0.16 (1.77)	−0.03 (−0.13)
Nigeria	0.04 (1.02)	0.08 (0.79)	0.06 (0.69)	−0.14 (−1.31)	−0.04 (−0.90)	−0.01 (−0.11)	−0.09 (−0.85)	−0.02 (−0.14)	−0.04 (−0.61)	0.03 (0.23)	−0.14 (−0.98)	−0.25 (−1.58)
Rwanda	0.03 (0.41)	0.02 (0.26)	−0.07 (−0.90)	−0.03 (−0.29)	−0.03 (−0.42)	−0.10 (−1.03)	0.01 (0.09)	0.03 (0.29)	0.11 (1.03)	0.13 (1.10)	0.08 (0.68)	0.06 (0.37)
South Africa	0.11* (4.40)	0.11* (2.15)	0.11* (2.32)	0.07 (1.63)	−0.13* (−4.65)	−0.18* (−3.45)	−0.11* (−2.25)	−0.10* (−2.11)	0.09* (2.51)	0.18* (2.86)	0.09 (1.50)	0.08 (1.35)

Tanzania	0.15 (1.67)	0.19 (1.13)	0.16 (1.17)	0.17 (1.18)	-0.11 (-1.12)	0.14 (0.84)	-0.20 (-1.36)	-0.30 (-1.90)	0.17 (0.99)	-0.17 (-0.63)	0.12 (0.54)	0.38 (1.51)
Uganda	-0.16 (-1.47)	-0.21 (-0.94)	-0.23 (-0.63)	-0.12 (-0.72)	-0.07 (-0.56)	0.07 (0.28)	-0.10 (-0.24)	0.05 (0.28)	-0.01 (-0.04)			-0.04 (-0.16)
Zambia	0.06 (0.82)	0.04 (0.33)	0.19 (1.33)	0.10 (0.51)	-0.04 (-0.54)	0.07 (0.46)	-0.14 (-0.83)	-0.31 (-1.46)	0.03 (0.31)	-0.17 (-1.10)	0.12 (0.68)	0.22 (0.99)
Zimbabwe	-0.02 (-0.23)	0.00 (0.02)	-0.01 (-0.09)	0.20 (1.49)	-0.09 (-1.05)	-0.10 (-0.69)	0.16 (1.05)	-0.02 (-0.14)	0.04 (0.38)	0.02 (0.09)	-0.14 (-0.74)	0.05 (0.33)

Notes: 1. Based on probit results for extended model where z stats are displayed in parenthesis and * denotes statistical significance at the 5% level. For the 1–10 and 0–1 definitions of well-being, a positive sign indicates that married or living together couples are happier and vice versa. For 1–4 well-being, a negative sign denotes the positive effects of marriage/living together.
2. Variable dropped due to multicollinearity.

Table 3.18 Probit results for Africa – importance of family

	a170 (Scale 1–10)				a008 (Scale 1–4)				a008r (Scale 0–1)			
	Overall	Health Poor	Edn Poor	Income Poor	Overall	Health Poor	Edn Poor	Income Poor	Overall	Health Poor	Edn Poor	Income Poor
Algeria	-0.27 (-1.82)	-0.15 (-0.80)	-0.15 (-0.35)	-0.32 (-1.37)	0.33 (1.94)	0.17 (0.77)	0.55 (1.02)	0.42 (1.44)	-0.39* (-2.04)	-0.31 (-1.31)	-0.22 (-0.32)	-0.28 (-0.95)
Egypt	-0.16 (-1.90)	-0.18 (-1.34)	-0.19 (-1.73)	-0.05 (-0.25)	0.33* (3.57)	0.40* (2.71)	0.21 (1.70)	-0.45 (-1.94)	-0.05 (-0.48)	-0.23 (-1.44)	-0.10 (-0.69)	1.37* (3.83)
Ethiopia	-0.16 (-1.24)	-0.55* (-2.09)	0.11 (0.33)	-1.21* (-2.11)	-0.07 (-0.50)	0.39 (1.34)	0.05 (0.13)	2.14* (2.93)	0.38 (1.89)	-0.05 (-0.14)	0.52 (1.19)	
Mali	0.10 (0.82)	0.35 (1.93)	0.01 (0.06)	0.12 (0.41)	0.24 (1.81)	0.20 (1.07)	0.19 (1.12)	-0.10 (-0.33)	-0.08 (-0.49)	0.13 (0.55)	-0.12 (-0.57)	0.60 (1.58)
Morocco	0.05 (0.72)	-0.08 (-0.55)	0.03 (0.34)	0.28 (1.62)	0.19* (2.36)	0.15 (0.98)	0.23* (2.28)	0.10 (0.53)	-0.04 (-0.39)	-0.08 (-0.46)	-0.10 (-0.86)	-0.02 (-0.09)
Nigeria	-0.09 (-1.10)	-0.38* (-2.29)	-0.04 (-0.21)	-0.20 (-1.08)	0.16 (1.80)	0.35* (2.00)	-0.06 (-0.33)	0.06 (0.30)	0.26* (2.28)	-0.12 (-0.62)	0.52* (2.03)	0.15 (0.62)
Rwanda	-0.07 (-0.95)	-0.05 (-0.56)	-0.05 (-0.56)	-0.06 (-0.57)	0.18* (2.15)	0.20* (2.07)	0.19 (1.95)	0.31* (2.39)	-0.21 (-1.97)	-0.19 (-1.59)	-0.13 (-0.97)	-0.38* (-2.38)
South Africa	-0.01 (-0.33)	-0.01 (-0.17)	-0.04 (-0.67)	-0.02 (-0.40)	0.09* (2.18)	0.02 (0.31)	0.09 (1.37)	0.05 (0.92)	0.06 (1.24)	0.07 (0.94)	-0.03 (-0.43)	0.03 (0.44)

Tanzania	-0.02	0.12	-0.06	-0.10	0.51*	0.29	0.63*	0.74*	-0.29	-0.14	-0.24	-0.58*
	(-0.13)	(0.51)	(-0.34)	(-0.55)	(3.98)	(1.26)	(3.42)	(3.92)	(-1.63)	(-0.46)	(-0.93)	(-2.23)
Uganda	-0.49*	-0.35	-0.78	-0.58*	-0.12	-0.39	-0.39	-0.02	0.41*			0.40
	(-3.93)	(-1.55)	(-1.95)	(-3.21)	(-0.86)	(-1.54)	(-0.84)	(-0.10)	(2.09)			(1.55)
Zambia	-0.03	-0.24	0.12	0.31	0.11	0.18	0.00	-0.61	-0.12	-0.19	0.05	0.30
	(-0.28)	(-1.24)	(0.54)	(1.23)	(0.99)	(0.77)	(0.00)	(-1.88)	(-1.01)	(-0.82)	(0.18)	(0.88)
Zimbabwe	-0.11	-0.24	-0.48	-1.00	-0.20	-0.18	0.48	-0.23	0.55*	0.56	0.09	0.56
	(-0.56)	(-0.96)	(-0.97)	(-1.99)	(-1.02)	(-0.76)	(1.04)	(-0.82)	(2.32)	(1.87)	(0.20)	(1.39)

Notes: 1. Based on probit results for extended model where z stats are displayed in parenthesis and * denotes statistical significance at the 5% level. For 1–10 and 0–1 definitions, a negative sign indicates that people who value family are happier. For 1–4 definition, a positive sign indicates people who value family are happier.
2. Variable dropped due to multicollinearity.

Table 3.19 Probit results for Africa – importance of friends

	a170 (Scale 1–10)				a008 (Scale 1–4)				a008r (Scale 0–1)			
	Overall	Health Poor	Edn Poor	Income Poor	Overall	Health Poor	Edn Poor	Income Poor	Overall	Health Poor	Edn Poor	Income Poor
Algeria	-0.06 (-1.22)	-0.05 (-0.70)	-0.13 (-1.07)	-0.08 (-1.08)	0.13* (2.17)	0.20* (2.42)	0.11 (0.75)	-0.03 (-0.38)	-0.10 (-1.27)	-0.15 (-1.58)	0.01 (0.04)	-0.01 (-0.09)
Egypt	0.03 (1.52)	0.08* (2.45)	0.05 (1.72)	0.07 (1.64)	0.05* (2.21)	-0.01 (-0.37)	0.06 (1.77)	-0.10 (-1.91)	0.00 (0.02)	0.04 (0.93)	-0.01 (-0.30)	0.11 (1.82)
Ethiopia	-0.27* (-4.07)	-0.15 (-1.23)	-0.22* (-2.03)	-0.81* (-2.35)	0.25* (3.46)	0.32* (2.37)	0.17 (1.41)	0.49 (1.20)	-0.05 (-0.57)	-0.25 (-1.52)	-0.02 (-0.12)	
Mali	-0.11 (-1.55)	-0.12 (-1.05)	-0.12 (-1.34)	-0.20 (-1.10)	0.08 (1.05)	0.04 (0.34)	0.21* (2.35)	0.19 (1.02)	-0.08 (-0.81)	-0.10 (-0.67)	-0.17 (-1.42)	-0.37 (-1.56)
Morocco	-0.01 (-0.46)	-0.06 (-1.11)	-0.03 (-0.89)	-0.11 (-1.79)	0.10* (3.59)	0.20* (3.46)	0.09* (2.60)	0.18* (2.59)	-0.15* (-4.06)	-0.19* (-2.78)	-0.16* (-3.66)	-0.19* (-2.29)
Nigeria	-0.03 (-1.54)	0.03 (0.51)	-0.12* (-2.33)	-0.12 (-1.89)	0.10* (3.71)	0.01 (0.17)	0.10 (1.65)	0.06 (0.83)	-0.08* (-2.32)	0.05 (0.85)	-0.07 (-0.84)	-0.09 (-0.98)
Rwanda	-0.03 (-0.39)	-0.05 (-0.64)	-0.06 (-0.67)	0.04 (0.38)	-0.09 (-1.13)	-0.10 (-1.04)	-0.16 (-1.66)	-0.27* (-2.06)	0.13 (1.16)	0.07 (0.57)	0.13 (0.97)	0.16 (0.92)
South Africa	-0.05* (-3.73)	-0.01 (-0.39)	-0.02 (-0.93)	-0.04 (-1.90)	0.09* (6.40)	0.08* (2.90)	0.06* (2.49)	0.06* (2.58)	-0.05* (-2.88)	-0.06* (-2.08)	-0.04 (-1.32)	-0.03 (-1.01)

Tanzania	0.07 (1.24)	0.05 (0.57)	0.05 (0.65)	0.01 (0.15)	0.03 (0.51)	-0.01 (-0.06)	0.07 (0.79)	0.02 (0.22)	0.11 (1.08)	0.16 (1.06)	-0.06 (-0.45)	0.00 (-0.01)
Uganda	-0.13 (-1.48)	-0.12 (-0.66)	0.18 (0.64)	-0.11 (-0.80)	0.08 (0.79)	0.00 (-0.02)	0.11 (0.33)	0.01 (0.07)	0.03 (0.19)			0.20 (0.94)
Zambia	-0.10* (-2.03)	-0.01 (-0.09)	0.04 (0.44)	-0.16 (-1.22)	0.04 (0.73)	-0.12 (-1.14)	0.15 (1.25)	0.37* (2.27)	-0.09 (-1.48)	0.06 (0.59)	-0.20 (-1.68)	-0.32 (-1.96)
Zimbabwe	0.02 (0.35)	-0.11 (-1.42)	-0.12 (-1.60)	-0.01 (-0.18)	0.01 (0.22)	0.07 (0.86)	0.03 (0.35)	-0.03 (-0.36)	-0.02 (-0.41)	-0.08 (-0.89)	-0.05 (-0.59)	-0.07 (-0.76)

Notes: 1. Based on probit results for extended model where z stats are displayed in parenthesis and * denotes statistical significance at the 5% level. For 1–10 and 0–1 definitions, a negative sign indicates that people who value friends are happier. For 1–4 definition, a positive sign indicates people who value friends are happier.
2. Variable dropped due to multicollinearity.

The positive impact of married life is more apparent in North Africa (Algeria, Egypt and Morocco) and also in South Africa, and this result tends to hold for the overall sample as well as for the poor. These results are consistent with other studies and with the results for Asia reported in Chapter 2, and tend to debunk the idea that family life is not as viable in Africa as it might be elsewhere.

Family and friends. Family and friends are not as important as previous research for industrial economies suggests (Tables 3.18 and 3.19). For the overall sample, friends are significant in about a third of the possible cases (12 out of 36), and are even less important for the poor (19 out of 106 possibilities). Significance is highest among the health and income poor for the 1–4 well-being definition. For family, the results are somewhat less significant – 10 out of 36 for the overall sample and 15 out of 106 possibilities for the three poor groups. The results are scattered among different countries, and there is no apparent pattern of importance for individual countries or geographic regions. As observed in the Asian economies, family and friends are not as important as we might have been expected to believe from results for industrial countries. Around half of the countries recorded significant coefficients for these two variables. There were only three countries where both family and friends were statistically significant determinants for the 1 to 4 definition of well-being (Egypt, Morocco and South Africa).

3.2.3 Other social variables

For the four social variables, there are only a few notable results to suggest that these variables have any systematic impact on well-being.

Work. There is very little to suggest that meaningful work has any significant positive impact on well-being in Africa (Table 3.20). For the full sample, 10 out of 36 coefficients are statistically significant, with no discernible geographic trends. For the three poverty groups, the results are even weaker. Coefficients are significant in fewer than a third of possible cases (24 of 106 cases). The incidence of significance is highest among the income poor in the 1 to 4 and 1 to 10 designations of well-being. Nevertheless, the findings on work are still very weak.

Again, this needs to be investigated further, since work is often an important factor in uplifting well-being in industrial economies.

Religion For the sample as a whole, religion plays a role in uplifting well-being in few countries in North Africa (Egypt, Morocco) and also in Tanzania, Nigeria and South Africa. Both Christianity and Islam seem to be important in uplifting well-being in Africa. Egypt and Morocco are predominantly Moslem, Tanzania is 45 percent Christian and 35 percent Moslem, South Africa is 75 percent Christian, and Nigeria is split between Moslem and Christian.

For the poor, the results are similar in nature to the full sample results in the sense that there are a few countries where the poor are positively impacted by religion in their lives. Among the poor, religion plays a bigger role in Egypt, Nigeria and South Africa (Table 3.21).

Trust Aside from a few countries, there is very little evidence that trust is a factor in the determination of well-being in Africa (Table 3.22). Trust is important for lifting well-being in Morocco for the overall sample and for all three poverty groups. The results for Rwanda also reflect the importance of trust, but only for one form of the dependent variable (0 and 1). For the rest of Africa, trust is generally not significant in raising well-being. This could be because there is no hope that a trustworthy environment could be possible, and the failure of the variable to be significant could simply reflect a resignation to accept a pervasive distrust in society.

Civil services Confidence in the provision of civil services provides a boost to well-being in over half the countries in Africa, a particularly interesting result in view of the results for trust (Table 3.23). Perhaps there is greater trust in institutions than in personal contacts. More research is needed to explore the interaction of these two important social variables and their impact on well-being and happiness. The civil service variable is most often significant in North and East Africa (Algeria, Egypt, Morocco), Southern Africa (South Africa, Zimbabwe) and also West Africa (Nigeria). Since all of these countries are former colonies of European powers, it is unclear why some governments seem to be more trustworthy than others. For the poor, the results are less significant; the civil service variable matters for well-being in only a few instances.

Summary The probit results for Africa for a model with three policy variables and a few socioeconomic characteristics provide persuasive evidence that improving health is the most powerful variable in uplifting well-being in Africa, no matter how the dependent variable is configured or what poverty group is being considered. Income is less significant and significant in fewer countries. Its significance is also sensitive to the configuration of the well-being variable. Education is even less important to Africans in poverty, no matter which poverty group is being considered. The poor are more interested in short-term policies to uplift well-being as opposed to investments in education that will manifest in the future. The control variables of gender, age, marital

Table 3.20 Probit results for Africa – importance of work

	a170 (Scale 1–10)				a008 (Scale 1–4)				a008r (Scale 0–1)			
	Overall	Health Poor	Edn Poor	Income Poor	Overall	Health Poor	Edn Poor	Income Poor	Overall	Health Poor	Edn Poor	Income Poor
Algeria	-0.03 (-0.28)	-0.04 (-0.38)	-0.05 (-0.25)	0.14 (1.11)	0.01 (0.06)	-0.09 (-0.62)	0.07 (0.28)	0.15 (1.00)	0.04 (0.30)	0.04 (0.25)	-0.26 (-0.89)	-0.19 (-1.08)
Egypt	0.06* (2.98)	0.18* (5.30)	0.07* (2.52)	-0.03 (-0.58)	0.02 (0.86)	-0.05 (-1.30)	0.02 (0.60)	0.04 (0.85)	0.01 (0.19)	0.07 (1.57)	0.01 (0.18)	-0.08 (-1.27)
Ethiopia	0.02 (0.23)	0.03 (0.13)	0.28 (1.39)	0.79* (2.21)	-0.02 (-0.21)	0.64* (2.58)	-0.28 (-1.27)	-1.27* (-2.92)	0.16 (1.11)	-0.49 (-1.62)	0.35 (1.25)	
Mali	-0.07 (-0.74)	0.19 (1.14)	-0.11 (-0.98)	0.79* (2.19)	-0.06 (-0.58)	-0.26 (-1.45)	-0.15 (-1.17)	-0.13 (-0.37)	0.27 (1.63)	0.24 (1.03)	0.29 (1.48)	0.34 (0.68)
Morocco	0.00 (0.01)	0.01 (0.10)	-0.02 (-0.33)	-0.12 (-0.87)	-0.04 (-0.69)	0.00 (-0.01)	-0.04 (-0.70)	0.08 (0.51)	0.03 (0.41)	0.05 (0.49)	0.07 (0.83)	-0.10 (-0.58)
Nigeria	-0.03 (-0.92)	0.01 (0.08)	-0.09 (-1.31)	0.03 (0.28)	-0.04 (-0.98)	-0.02 (-0.23)	0.00 (-0.04)	-0.06 (-0.45)	0.21* (3.37)	-0.01 (-0.06)	0.19 (1.52)	0.14 (0.80)
Rwanda	0.01 (0.09)	-0.02 (-0.29)	0.02 (0.26)	-0.02 (-0.19)	0.01 (0.16)	-0.03 (-0.28)	0.02 (0.21)	0.18 (1.38)	0.23* (2.04)	0.24 (1.94)	0.10 (0.74)	0.06 (0.37)
South Africa	0.03 (1.94)	0.08* (2.22)	0.07* (2.00)	0.11* (3.20)	-0.07* (-3.48)	-0.10* (-2.63)	-0.13* (-3.20)	-0.12* (-3.21)	0.21* (7.04)	0.17* (3.60)	0.17* (3.41)	0.23* (4.69)

Tanzania	-0.05	-0.12	0.03	-0.01	0.34*	0.04	0.45*	0.37*	-0.19	0.18	-0.31	-0.33
	(-0.39)	(-0.58)	(0.15)	(-0.05)	(2.56)	(0.17)	(2.40)	(2.15)	(-1.14)	(0.52)	(-1.33)	(-1.48)
Uganda	-0.10	-0.07	0.20	-0.35*	0.29*	0.15	0.17	0.42*	-0.06			-0.35
	(-0.87)	(-0.24)	(0.32)	(-2.05)	(2.26)	(0.47)	(0.24)	(2.19)	(-0.30)			(-1.43)
Zambia	0.14*	0.24*	0.26*	0.16	0.04	-0.15	0.05	0.00	-0.07	-0.11	-0.20	-0.26
	(2.15)	(2.23)	(2.04)	(0.92)	(0.57)	(-1.00)	(0.30)	(0.02)	(-0.90)	(-0.80)	(-1.29)	(-1.19)
Zimbabwe	0.21	0.67*	0.46*	-0.05	-0.29*	-0.35	-0.33	-0.42*	0.63*	0.42	0.78*	0.59*
	(1.79)	(3.35)	(2.01)	(-0.29)	(-2.45)	(-1.70)	(-1.43)	(-2.45)	(4.05)	(1.77)	(2.88)	(2.78)

Notes: 1. Based on probit results for extended model where z stats are displayed in parenthesis and * denotes statistical significance at the 5% level. For 1–10 and 0–1 definitions, a negative sign indicates that people who value work are happier. For 1–4 definition, a positive sign indicates people who value work are happier.
2. Variable dropped due to multicollinearity.

Table 3.21 Probit results for Africa – importance of religion

	a170 (Scale 1–10)				a008 (Scale 1–4)				a008r (Scale 0–1)			
	Overall	Health Poor	Edn Poor	Income Poor	Overall	Health Poor	Edn Poor	Income Poor	Overall	Health Poor	Edn Poor	Income Poor
Algeria	0.09 (0.78)	-0.20 (-1.16)	0.88 (1.86)	-0.19 (-0.96)	0.03 (0.27)	0.24 (1.21)	-0.03 (-0.05)	0.29 (1.23)	-0.05 (-0.32)	0.04 (0.16)	0.29 (0.41)	-0.05 (-0.19)
Egypt	-0.17* (-2.35)	-0.01 (-0.07)	-0.16 (-1.51)	-0.31* (-2.33)	0.29* (3.41)	0.26 (1.59)	0.34* (2.82)	0.36* (2.40)	-0.04 (-0.45)	-0.01 (-0.05)	-0.07 (-0.53)	-0.31 (-1.87)
Ethiopia	0.01 (0.08)	-0.02 (-0.10)	-0.29 (-1.81)	-0.04 (-0.21)	0.01 (0.19)	-0.63* (-3.51)	0.07 (0.38)	-0.28 (-0.99)	0.12 (1.18)	0.61* (2.66)	-0.11 (-0.50)	
Mali	-0.11 (-1.07)	0.01 (0.04)	-0.13 (-0.99)	-0.13 (-0.41)	0.09 (0.79)	0.40 (1.82)	0.10 (0.67)	0.08 (0.25)	-0.16 (-1.01)	-0.53 (-1.97)	-0.09 (-0.43)	-0.34 (-0.95)
Morocco	-0.19* (-2.88)	-0.34* (-2.21)	-0.34* (-3.68)	-0.42* (-2.20)	0.05 (0.73)	-0.08 (-0.49)	0.09 (0.88)	0.02 (0.12)	-0.07 (-0.75)	-0.12 (-0.63)	-0.07 (-0.53)	-0.17 (-0.76)
Nigeria	-0.15* (-3.94)	-0.20* (-2.46)	-0.23* (-2.18)	-0.34* (-3.00)	0.26* (6.07)	0.38* (4.29)	0.32* (2.82)	0.57* (4.72)	-0.20* (-3.64)	-0.28* (-2.74)	-0.13 (-0.89)	-0.38* (-2.64)
Rwanda	0.11 (1.98)	0.15* (2.11)	0.13 (1.90)	0.17 (1.76)	0.08 (1.16)	0.10 (1.25)	0.07 (0.86)	0.02 (0.20)	0.04 (0.42)	0.01 (0.12)	0.04 (0.39)	0.15 (1.05)
South Africa	-0.12* (-8.22)	-0.16* (-4.95)	-0.15* (-4.50)	-0.13* (-4.41)	0.17* (10.60)	0.23* (7.01)	0.18* (5.13)	0.16* (5.25)	-0.09* (-4.05)	-0.16* (-4.02)	-0.11* (-2.63)	-0.09* (-2.53)

Tanzania	-0.07 (-0.82)	-0.15 (-1.07)	-0.18 (-1.33)	-0.03 (-0.25)	0.26* (3.00)	0.48* (3.33)	0.15 (1.14)	0.34* (2.53)	-0.34* (-2.85)	-0.49* (-2.67)	-0.34 (-1.94)	-0.47* (-2.71)
Uganda	0.13 (1.47)	0.16 (1.11)	0.83* (2.30)	0.18 (1.38)	0.07 (0.67)	-0.08 (-0.51)	0.05 (0.12)	0.17 (1.14)	0.07 (0.49)			0.21 (1.06)
Zambia	-0.07 (-1.13)	0.01 (0.10)	-0.29* (-2.30)	-0.25 (-1.17)	-0.13 (-1.74)	0.04 (0.28)	-0.31* (-2.03)	-0.95* (-3.46)	0.00 (0.06)	0.02 (0.13)	0.27 (1.72)	0.61* (2.21)
Zimbabwe	-0.06 (-0.93)	-0.11 (-1.09)	-0.08 (-0.79)	0.01 (0.07)	0.16* (2.60)	0.08 (0.83)	0.06 (0.57)	0.24 (2.63)	-0.12 (-1.65)	-0.02 (-0.14)	-0.01 (-0.08)	-0.23* (-2.08)

Notes: 1. Based on probit results for extended model where z stats are displayed in parenthesis and * denotes statistical significance at the 5% level. For 1–10 and 0–1 definitions, a negative sign indicates that people who value their religion are happier. For 1–4 definition, a positive sign indicates people who value their religion are happier.
2. Variable dropped due to multicollinearity.

Table 3.22 Probit results for Africa – trust

	a170 (Scale 1–10)				a008 (Scale 1–4)				a008r (Scale 0–1)			
	Overall	Health Poor	Edn Poor	Income Poor	Overall	Health Poor	Edn Poor	Income Poor	Overall	Health Poor	Edn Poor	Income Poor
Algeria	−0.08 (−0.75)	−0.38* (−2.48)	−0.27 (−1.23)	−0.01 (−0.05)	0.13 (1.01)	0.00 (0.02)	0.20 (0.74)	0.19 (0.99)	0.30* (2.07)	0.49* (2.55)	0.23 (0.62)	0.21 (0.87)
Egypt	0.11* (3.35)	−0.08 (−1.32)	0.09 (1.91)	−0.10 (−1.44)	0.21* (5.24)	0.26* (3.93)	0.23* (4.19)	0.26* (3.12)	0.02 (0.46)	−0.11 (−1.44)	0.04 (0.63)	−0.24* (−2.31)
Ethiopia	−0.23* (−3.00)	−0.42* (−2.56)	−0.17 (−1.30)	0.27 (0.76)	0.14 (1.60)	0.10 (0.53)	0.08 (0.57)	−0.34 (−0.83)	−0.05 (−0.44)	0.15 (0.71)	−0.08 (−0.48)	
Mali	−0.19 (−1.75)	0.06 (0.29)	−0.04 (−0.31)	0.03 (0.10)	0.09 (0.79)	0.12 (0.58)	−0.09 (−0.60)	0.00 (−0.01)	0.23 (1.59)	0.14 (0.60)	0.46* (2.58)	0.19 (0.49)
Morocco	−0.29* (−5.19)	−0.29* (−2.39)	−0.35* (−5.21)	−0.40* (−2.55)	0.12 (1.94)	0.11 (0.84)	0.13 (1.78)	0.16 (0.95)	0.18* (2.27)	0.21 (1.43)	0.16 (1.76)	0.23 (1.18)
Nigeria	0.06 (1.55)	−0.11 (−1.13)	0.02 (0.21)	−0.04 (−0.36)	0.05 (1.16)	0.20 (1.94)	0.15 (1.57)	−0.07 (−0.59)	0.16* (2.91)	0.01 (0.13)	0.06 (0.51)	0.23 (1.73)
Rwanda	−0.18 (−1.37)	−0.05 (−0.29)	−0.16 (−1.01)	−0.27 (−1.31)	0.14 (0.93)	0.19 (0.99)	0.19 (1.06)	0.28 (1.24)	0.77* (5.07)	0.82* (4.57)	0.88* (4.95)	0.84* (3.90)
South Africa	−0.06 (−2.10)	−0.03 (−0.47)	−0.07 (−1.26)	−0.10 (−1.86)	0.05 (1.71)	−0.05 (−0.74)	0.07 (1.21)	0.14* (2.51)	0.05 (1.29)	0.14 (1.96)	0.03 (0.45)	0.05 (0.86)

Tanzania	-0.17	-0.75*	-0.21	-0.18	-0.02	-0.06	0.02	0.08	0.77*	0.64	0.46	0.82*
	(-1.19)	(-2.72)	(-1.08)	(-0.89)	(-0.13)	(-0.20)	(0.07)	(0.35)	(4.25)	(1.97)	(1.60)	(2.85)
Uganda	-0.10	0.00	-0.14	0.16	0.15	-0.60	-0.87	0.05	0.88*			0.91*
	(-0.57)	(0.01)	(-0.22)	(0.54)	(0.76)	(-1.25)	(-0.92)	(0.15)	(3.88)			(2.71)
Zambia	0.05	-0.28	-0.22	-0.36	-0.27*	-0.38	-0.44	-0.22	0.38*	0.23	0.40	0.26
	(0.49)	(-1.30)	(-1.02)	(-1.26)	(-2.24)	(-1.43)	(-1.56)	(-0.61)	(3.47)	(1.02)	(1.63)	(0.79)
Zimbabwe	-0.13	-0.32	-0.08	-0.15	-0.02	0.05	0.04	-0.12	0.10	-0.01	0.04	0.22
	(-1.11)	(-1.65)	(-0.49)	(-0.85)	(-0.12)	(0.23)	(0.23)	(-0.72)	(0.73)	(-0.06)	(0.20)	(1.12)

Notes: 1. Based on probit results for extended model where z stats are displayed in parenthesis and * denotes statistical significance at the 5% level. For 1–10 and 0–1 definitions, a negative sign indicates that people who trust others are happier. For 1–4 definition, a positive sign indicates people who trust others are happier.
2. Variable dropped due to multicollinearity.

Table 3.23 Probit results for Africa – confidence in civil services

	a170 (Scale 1–10)				a008 (Scale 1–4)				a008r (Scale 0–1)			
	Overall	Health Poor	Edn Poor	Income Poor	Overall	Health Poor	Edn Poor	Income Poor	Overall	Health Poor	Edn Poor	Income Poor
Algeria	-0.09* (-2.49)	-0.07 (-1.36)	0.10 (1.02)	0.02 (0.36)	0.14* (3.27)	0.14* (2.33)	0.22 (1.81)	0.15* (2.36)	-0.02 (-0.31)	-0.07 (-1.07)	-0.17 (-1.10)	0.01 (0.17)
Egypt	-0.04* (-2.41)	-0.04 (-1.44)	-0.02 (-0.80)	-0.04 (-1.18)	0.11* (5.76)	0.08* (2.61)	0.12* (4.51)	0.16* (4.27)	-0.08* (-3.22)	-0.05 (-1.28)	-0.08* (-2.25)	-0.17* (-3.73)
Ethiopia	-0.15* (-3.78)	0.01 (0.07)	-0.24* (-3.43)	-0.43* (-3.49)	0.31* (7.08)	0.39* (4.45)	0.36* (4.62)	0.65* (4.12)	-0.22* (-4.07)	-0.25* (-2.45)	-0.17 (-1.85)	
Mali	-0.04 (-0.94)	-0.09 (-1.15)	0.01 (0.12)	-0.05 (-0.41)	0.01 (0.26)	-0.15 (-1.78)	-0.04 (-0.69)	-0.28* (-2.34)	0.06 (0.89)	0.14 (1.31)	0.08 (1.03)	0.29 (1.92)
Morocco	-0.06* (-2.44)	0.01 (0.31)	-0.04 (-1.60)	0.02 (0.31)	0.13* (4.95)	0.01 (0.12)	0.14* (4.64)	0.00 (0.04)	-0.08* (-2.43)	0.01 (0.17)	-0.08 (-1.97)	-0.07 (-0.88)
Nigeria	-0.09* (-5.24)	-0.10* (-2.50)	-0.17* (-4.78)	-0.22* (-4.45)	0.04* (2.20)	0.04 (0.89)	0.09* (2.14)	0.10 (1.91)	0.01 (0.45)	0.00 (0.06)	-0.04 (-0.68)	-0.09 (-1.28)
Rwanda	0.06 (1.72)	0.15* (3.15)	0.06 (1.44)	0.17* (2.87)	0.08 (1.75)	0.09 (1.60)	0.10 (1.92)	0.13 (1.93)	0.00 (0.03)	0.06 (0.97)	-0.01 (-0.11)	-0.10 (-1.28)
South Africa	-0.07* (-5.50)	-0.08* (-2.94)	-0.05 (-1.81)	-0.04 (-1.59)	0.02 (1.55)	0.01 (0.23)	0.02 (0.81)	0.00 (-0.05)	0.01 (0.43)	0.01 (0.21)	0.01 (0.25)	0.04 (1.50)

Tanzania	-0.03	0.08	0.01	-0.05	0.13*	0.11	0.10	0.14*	-0.04	-0.08	0.06	-0.02
	(-0.76)	(1.09)	(0.22)	(-0.76)	(2.81)	(1.45)	(1.58)	(2.03)	(-0.53)	(-0.71)	(0.59)	(-0.14)
Uganda	0.00	0.12	0.19	0.08	0.12	-0.01	0.08	0.16	-0.06			0.01
	(-0.04)	(0.99)	(0.95)	(0.83)	(1.75)	(-0.05)	(0.32)	(1.49)	(-0.69)			(0.06)
Zambia	0.02	-0.12	-0.04	-0.16	-0.08	-0.13	-0.21	0.01	0.06	0.08	0.11	-0.05
	(0.60)	(-1.73)	(-0.49)	(-1.64)	(-1.87)	(-1.62)	(-2.30)	(0.06)	(1.46)	(1.03)	(1.26)	(-0.41)
Zimbabwe	-0.14*	-0.12	-0.13	-0.13	0.16*	0.17*	0.20*	0.21*	-0.13*	-0.16	-0.13	-0.15
	(-3.07)	(-1.72)	(-1.76)	(-1.81)	(3.51)	(2.28)	(2.67)	(2.81)	(-2.37)	(-1.88)	(-1.39)	(-1.72)

Notes: 1. Based on probit results for extended model where z stats are displayed in parenthesis and * denotes statistical significance at the 5% level. For 1–10 and 0–1 definitions, a negative sign indicates that people with confidence in civil services are happier. For 1–4 definition, a positive sign indicates people with confidence in civil services are happier.
2. Variable dropped due to multicollinearity.

status, and family and friends are statistically significant in a few cases, along with the social variables of trust, work, religion and civil services. The widespread incidence of HIV/AIDS is reflected throughout the probit results for Africa by the significance of the health variable for all poverty groups and also from the overall probit results.

3.3 Individual country analysis

For individual countries we look first at the countries of North Africa, Algeria, Egypt and Morocco. These countries have generally higher standards of living than countries in sub-Saharan Africa. They have a long colonial history with Europe and their pattern of trade and labor migration is more closely tied to Europe than to the rest of the African continent. They are also separated geographically by the Sahara desert. Not all the countries in North Africa are represented in the World Value Survey database – Libya is missing.

In **Egypt** the full sample results for the 1–10 designation for well-being show strong impacts for health, income and education. Women are happier, while married couples are happier than singles, widows and the divorced. Family is significant, while friends are significant with the wrong a priori sign – more friends results in greater unhappiness. Turning to the results for the three poverty groups, health and income are significant for all three groups while education is important for the health poor. It is significant with the wrong sign for the education poor. The control variable of gender is significant for all three poverty groups (women happier), and there is some evidence that age is nonlinear in well-being. Family is less important for the poor than for the entire sample, and friends has the wrong sign in all three poverty groups, mirroring the aggregate results. Trust is an important explanatory variable in Egypt for the 1 to 4 configuration of well-being for the overall sample and the health and education poor. Religion is also significant on the 1 to 10 and 1 to 4 satisfaction scales for some poor groups and the overall sample. Work is significant for the 1 to 10 configuration of well-being, while confidence in the civil service is important for the 1 to 4 designation of well-being.

In **Morocco**, for the full sample and 1–10 designation for well-being, health, income and education are all significant determinants of well-being. Age is not significant. Women are happier and friends are also important. Turning to the poverty groups, the results are similar. Women are happier and marriage improves well-being for all three poverty categories. Health, income and education are significant for two poverty groups (income and education), but only health is significant for the income poor. Family seems to be less important than friends, while the control variable of marital status supports the conclusion that marriage increases well-being. Furthermore, women are generally happier, and there is little evidence that well-being changes with age. Confidence in the civil service is significant, as is religion for the overall sample and some poverty groups, while trust and work are not.

Turning to the other countries in the region, we begin in the north and move south. For the full sample in **Ethiopia**, health and income are significant for the full sample while education is not. Gender is not significant and age has a moderate impact. There is no evidence that marriage increases well-being, and friends are important while family is not. Evidence from the three poverty groups suggests that health and income are important for all three poverty categories, while education is only significant for the health poor. Gender and marital status are not significant in any poverty category, nor is age, except in the health poor. Neither family nor friends are significant determinants of well-being. There is widespread confidence in the civil service across different definitions of well-being and poverty groups.

In **Mali**, health and income are significant in the full sample, while education is not. Friends are significant, while family is not. For the socioeconomic variables, age is significant, while marital status is not. For the health poor, all three policy variables are significant, with income being the most significant. Age enters in a nonlinear fashion, while gender and marital status are not significant. Neither family nor friends is significant with the proper sign. For the income poor, health is the only significant policy variable, and among the control variables only gender is statistically significant. Family and friends are not significant. For the education poor, health and income are significant. Among the socioeconomic independent variables, only age is significant. Friends is the only other significant variable. There are few significant coefficients for the other social variables in Mali.

In West Africa, sample results are only available for Nigeria. In **Nigeria**, the largest country in the sub-Saharan region, the pattern of well-being response is similar to that of Egypt. All three of the policy variables are significant, as well as the controls on age, gender and marital status. Other things equal, women are happier; there is a dip in well-being at midlife, and marriage increases well-being. Furthermore, family and friends are both significant determinants of well-being. Turning to the poverty categories, the health poor have their well-being raised by more income and better education. Nigeria is one of the few countries where health is not a significant determinant of well-being for the health poor. However, several of the control variables are significant. Age is significant and the response is nonlinear. Family is also significant. For the income poor, all three policy variables are statistically significant. Among the control variables, only marital status is significant, and Nigeria is one of the few instances where men are happier. Family and friends are important, although family just fails the significance level test. For the education poor, only health and income are significant policy variables. In addition, gender is significant, along with friends. Religion and confidence in the civil service are significant in Nigeria for the overall sample and the poor. Work and trust are not significant.

Rwanda, Zambia and Zimbabwe are all poor landlocked countries in central and southern Africa. The sample sizes for these three countries are relatively small, ranging from just over 1,000 for Zimbabwe to 1,507 for Rwanda. Only Algeria and the East African countries of Tanzania and Uganda have such small samples. As a result, the poverty groups number less than 500, constraining our ability to provide definitive answers to the poverty questions, as the power of the test of the statistical model is limited. In **Rwanda**, health and income are statistically significant policy variables, while none of the control variables or friends and family was statistically significant. For the health poor, health is the only significant variable, and for the income poor only health and education are significant policy variables. However, for the education poor all three policy variables (health, income and education) were statistically significant. The significance of the four other social variables in Rwanda is limited. Only a few coefficients are significant.

With the exception of education in **Zambia**, all three policy variables are significant in **Zambia** and **Zimbabwe**. Women are happier in both countries, and age has a nonlinear impact on well-being in both countries. Friends are significant in both countries, and marriage is associated with higher levels of well-being in Zambia. Turning to the results for the three poverty groups, only health has a significant impact on well-being in both countries. Several control variables are also significant (age, marital status, gender and family in Zimbabwe and friends in Zambia). The social variables are not important in Zambia and they often have the wrong a priori signs. In Zimbabwe, confidence in the civil service is marginally important.

South Africa has the largest sample size – more than twice that of Egypt and three times more than Nigeria. It is also the richest country in Africa. For the full sample, all of the independent variables, both policy and control, are statistically significant for the full sample. Women are happier, there is a dip in middle age, and family and friends are both significant. For the health poor, there were over 3,000 sample observations, and all three policy variables were statistically significant. Well-being is enhanced by more education, better health and more income. The control variables enter significantly and as expected. Age is nonlinear, marriage results in higher well-being, and having a good family relationship and friendships enhances well-being, although the latter is marginally important. For the other two poverty groups, the results are similar. For the income poor all variables are significant, except family, which is marginally significant. For the education poor all three policy variables are significant, although family enters at a low level. Religion is the only social variable that is significant with the right a priori sign in South Africa. There seems to be strong evidence that the sample size has an impact on the significance of the independent variables. For countries with large sample sizes the results are more compelling and levels of significance higher than for countries with smaller samples.

This is borne out for the final two countries, **Tanzania** and **Uganda**, both located in East Africa, the latter being another landlocked country.

In both cases health and income are statistically significant for the full sample. Education is significant only in Tanzania.

Gender and marital status are significant in both countries, but the unmarried are happier in Uganda. Neither family nor friends lifts well-being in these two countries. Turning to the three poverty groups, health is significant for the income poor in both countries. For the health and education poor, health is only significant in Tanzania. Income is important for the income and education poor in Tanzania but not in Uganda. Education does not lift well-being in either country's poverty groups. In fact, the sign of the education coefficient is perverse in both countries for the income poor, in Uganda for the health poor and in Tanzania for the education poor. These results bear out the possibility that small samples can lead to perverse and perhaps unreliable results when samples are small. Aside from religion in Tanzania, there are few significant social variables in either Tanzania or Uganda.

3. 4   Pooled results by region

We explored how the model of well-being in Africa is affected by regional aggregation. Using the United Nations definitions, we aggregate the African countries surveyed in the World Value Surveys into four regions. The results for the standard model are displayed in Table 3.24 for the full sample and the three poverty groups. For the sample as a whole, for

Table 3.24 Aggregated probit results for Africa

	a170 (Scale 1–10)				a008 (Scale 1–4)				a008r (Scale 0–1)			
	Overall	Health Poor	Edn Poor	Income Poor	Overall	Health Poor	Edn Poor	Income Poor	Overall	Health Poor	Edn Poor	Income Poor
STATE OF HEALTH												
North Africa	-0.16* (-11.54)	-0.28* (-5.50)	-0.16* (-8.24)	-0.21* (-7.20)	0.46* (27.05)	0.38* (6.61)	0.48* (20.55)	0.42* (12.01)	-0.35* (-16.25)	-0.21* (-3.82)	-0.38* (-13.08)	-0.41* (-9.85)
South Africa	-0.28* (-22.05)	-0.39* (-9.01)	-0.29* (-12.62)	-0.26* (-12.39)	0.41* (29.54)	0.34* (7.48)	0.39* (15.97)	0.40* (17.83)	-0.38* (-21.29)	-0.23* (-4.83)	-0.39* (-13.39)	-0.38* (-14.28)
East Africa	-0.24* (-14.16)	-0.55* (-9.56)	-0.26* (-9.88)	-0.23* (-7.58)	0.32* (17.56)	0.58* (9.44)	0.33* (11.54)	0.28* (8.93)	-0.31* (-14.12)	-0.46* (-8.26)	-0.33* (-9.63)	-0.27* (-7.14)
West Africa	-0.30* (-17.12)	-0.12 (-1.76)	-0.38* (-11.10)	-0.33* (-7.28)	0.49* (24.59)	0.16* (2.13)	0.58* (14.93)	0.52* (10.22)	-0.44* (-17.19)	-0.11 (-1.57)	-0.53* (-10.46)	-0.52* (-8.41)
Africa	-0.27* (-37.19)	-0.32* (-12.43)	-0.26* (-22.13)	-0.27* (-19.53)	0.43* (52.86)	0.36* (12.92)	0.41* (31.55)	0.37* (25.23)	-0.35* (-34.30)	-0.25* (-9.52)	-0.35* (-22.02)	-0.34* (-19.05)
INCOME												
North Africa	0.06* (11.41)	0.07* (7.84)	0.08* (9.49)	0.25* (4.76)	-0.09* (-13.20)	-0.08* (-6.98)	-0.11* (-10.98)	-0.25* (-4.25)	0.12* (13.82)	0.10* (7.45)	0.14* (10.50)	0.41* (6.02)
South Africa	0.12* (22.29)	0.11* (9.70)	0.16* (11.67)	0.10* (2.41)	-0.09* (-15.21)	-0.09* (-7.22)	-0.11* (-7.57)	0.00 (-0.09)	0.13* (15.91)	0.11* (7.55)	0.13* (6.97)	0.12* (2.33)
East Africa	0.11* (16.44)	0.11* (9.43)	0.12* (10.78)	0.11* (2.04)	0.02* (2.64)	0.00 (-0.26)	0.03* (2.36)	0.04 (0.66)	-0.02* (-2.35)	0.00 (-0.23)	-0.02 (-1.29)	0.07 (0.97)

West Africa	0.10* (13.58)	0.08* (5.53)	0.10* (7.54)	-0.10 (-1.13)	-0.07* (-8.40)	-0.10* (-6.24)	-0.09* (-6.04)	0.05 (0.53)	0.10* (9.49)	0.13* (6.71)	0.11* (5.39)	0.04 (0.31)
Africa	0.09* (32.91)	0.09* (17.18)	0.10* (18.99)	0.11* (4.16)	-0.06* (-19.92)	-0.07* (-11.21)	-0.07* (-11.64)	-0.03 (-1.18)	0.09* (20.36)	0.08* (11.71)	0.10* (14.32)	0.21* (6.57)
EDUCATION LEVEL												
North Africa	0.02* (3.70)	0.02 (1.76)	-0.05 (-1.08)	0.02 (1.92)	-0.02* (-2.84)	-0.03* (-3.19)	0.10* (2.11)	-0.04* (-2.95)	0.05* (6.23)	0.06* (5.13)	0.14* (2.23)	0.05* (2.96)
South Africa	0.03* (4.60)	0.04* (3.65)	0.06 (1.33)	0.05* (4.36)	-0.02* (-3.28)	-0.04* (-2.88)	-0.03 (-0.56)	-0.06* (-5.30)	0.06* (6.54)	0.07* (4.34)	0.09 (1.45)	0.08* (5.51)
East Africa	0.00 (-0.16)	-0.01 (-1.10)	-0.04 (-0.82)	-0.01 (-0.46)	-0.02 (-1.91)	0.01 (0.57)	-0.17* (-3.46)	0.00 (0.22)	0.02 (1.48)	0.00 (-0.16)	0.19* (3.31)	0.00 (-0.06)
West Africa	0.03* (3.89)	0.05* (3.15)	0.00 (0.01)	0.06* (3.01)	0.00 (0.20)	0.01 (0.47)	-0.14* (-2.08)	-0.05* (-2.30)	0.02 (1.85)	0.01 (0.26)	0.20* (2.24)	0.05 (1.64)
Africa	0.04* (13.70)	0.04* (6.38)	0.00 (0.03)	0.04* (5.78)	-0.03* (-8.02)	-0.02* (-2.75)	-0.12* (-4.71)	-0.03* (-4.17)	0.04* (9.51)	0.03* (4.64)	0.13* (4.25)	0.04* (4.61)
GENDER												
North Africa	0.11* (4.60)	0.11* (2.57)	0.07* (2.10)	0.12* (2.29)	-0.19* (-6.61)	-0.25* (-5.16)	-0.16* (-3.92)	-0.29* (-4.82)	0.40* (10.66)	0.39* (6.85)	0.37* (7.16)	0.48* (6.61)

(Continued)

Table 3.24 Continued

	a170 (Scale 1–10)				a008 (Scale 1–4)				a008r (Scale 0–1)			
	Overall	Health Poor	Edn Poor	Income Poor	Overall	Health Poor	Edn Poor	Income Poor	Overall	Health Poor	Edn Poor	Income Poor
South Africa	0.05* (2.11)	−0.04 (−0.80)	0.04 (0.98)	0.06 (1.33)	−0.11* (−4.48)	−0.07 (−1.43)	−0.07 (−1.34)	−0.11* (−2.47)	0.17* (5.12)	0.08 (1.34)	0.07 (1.26)	0.13* (2.55)
East Africa	0.14* (4.80)	0.15* (3.24)	0.15* (3.29)	0.17* (3.20)	0.04 (1.27)	0.06 (1.24)	0.16* (3.32)	0.04 (0.65)	0.07 (1.88)	0.06 (1.09)	−0.02 (−0.30)	0.14* (2.10)
West Africa	0.08* (2.57)	0.07 (1.02)	−0.01 (−0.16)	0.06 (0.67)	−0.11* (−3.26)	−0.11 (−1.55)	−0.10 (−1.61)	−0.36* (−3.79)	0.36* (7.72)	0.26* (3.05)	0.31* (3.68)	0.65* (5.62)
Africa	0.10* (8.03)	0.09* (3.66)	0.08* (3.50)	0.10* (3.85)	−0.09* (−6.77)	−0.08* (−3.33)	−0.05* (−2.24)	−0.13* (−4.65)	0.22* (12.27)	0.19* (6.45)	0.17* (5.92)	0.25* (7.52)
AGE												
North Africa	−0.17 (−1.79)	−0.18 (−1.00)	−0.20 (−1.43)	−0.03 (−0.13)	0.48* (4.23)	0.93* (4.54)	0.61* (3.70)	0.32 (1.35)	0.59* (4.73)	0.04 (0.20)	0.44* (2.54)	0.35 (1.49)
South Africa	−0.43* (−4.58)	−0.33 (−1.58)	−0.11 (−0.56)	−0.31 (−1.82)	0.56* (5.46)	1.00* (4.57)	0.31 (1.47)	0.69* (3.79)	0.23* (2.10)	−0.43* (−2.07)	0.49* (2.60)	0.07 (0.41)
East Africa	−0.31* (−2.50)	−0.40* (−2.06)	−0.14 (−0.77)	−0.02 (−0.09)	0.28* (2.09)	0.35 (1.72)	0.31 (1.53)	0.53* (2.20)	0.63* (4.69)	0.68* (3.21)	0.43* (2.14)	0.27 (1.11)
West Africa	−0.43* (−3.10)	−1.13* (−3.80)	−0.41 (−1.77)	−0.08 (−0.20)	0.62* (3.90)	0.89* (2.83)	0.63* (2.39)	0.50 (1.22)	0.35* (2.12)	−0.32 (−1.04)	0.35 (1.24)	0.56 (1.41)

Africa	-0.33* (-6.20)	-0.42* (-4.12)	-0.19* (-2.10)	-0.19 (-1.77)	0.52* (8.86)	0.84* (7.75)	0.51* (5.30)	0.67* (5.84)	0.41* (6.70)	-0.02 (-0.14)	0.40* (4.20)	0.17 (1.56)
AGE SQUARED												
North Africa	0.05* (2.11)	0.06 (1.40)	0.06 (1.77)	0.04 (0.78)	-0.15* (-5.15)	-0.25* (-5.17)	-0.19* (-4.80)	-0.10 (-1.75)	-0.10* (-3.04)	0.05 (0.89)	-0.04 (-0.91)	-0.04 (-0.71)
South Africa	0.13* (5.76)	0.11* (2.31)	0.06 (1.29)	0.11* (2.45)	-0.16* (-6.39)	-0.28* (-5.33)	-0.11* (-2.21)	-0.21* (-4.60)	-0.02 (-0.79)	0.16* (3.12)	-0.07 (-1.50)	0.02 (0.55)
East Africa	0.07* (2.12)	0.09 (1.78)	0.03 (0.53)	-0.02 (-0.27)	-0.08* (-2.22)	-0.09 (-1.69)	-0.08 (-1.51)	-0.12 (-1.91)	-0.15* (-4.11)	-0.16* (-2.95)	-0.11* (-2.02)	-0.08 (-1.18)
West Africa	0.11* (3.02)	0.27* (3.60)	0.11 (1.95)	0.05 (0.53)	-0.14* (-3.44)	-0.20* (-2.50)	-0.15* (-2.22)	-0.11 (-1.06)	-0.09* (-2.13)	0.06 (0.78)	-0.09 (-1.22)	-0.15 (-1.38)
Africa	0.10* (7.68)	0.12* (4.93)	0.07* (3.00)	0.07* (2.55)	-0.15* (-10.09)	-0.22* (-8.32)	-0.15* (-6.21)	-0.18* (-6.12)	-0.07* (-4.34)	0.04 (1.51)	-0.06* (-2.60)	-0.02 (-0.78)
MARITAL STATUS												
North Africa	0.12* (4.34)	0.11* (2.42)	0.11* (2.77)	-0.05 (-0.98)	-0.25* (-7.97)	-0.33* (-6.15)	-0.23* (-5.29)	-0.21* (-3.38)	0.28* (6.89)	0.29* (4.60)	0.30* (5.30)	0.21* (2.73)
South Africa	0.11* (4.40)	0.11* (2.15)	0.11* (2.32)	0.07 (1.63)	-0.13* (-4.65)	-0.18* (-3.45)	-0.11* (-2.25)	-0.10* (-2.11)	0.09* (2.51)	0.18* (2.86)	0.09 (1.50)	0.08 (1.35)
East Africa	0.02 (0.66)	0.04 (0.77)	0.04 (0.83)	0.11 (1.90)	-0.12* (-3.65)	-0.08 (-1.57)	-0.07 (-1.43)	-0.12* (-2.01)	0.16* (3.98)	0.12 (1.95)	0.14* (2.24)	0.21* (2.90)

(Continued)

Table 3.24 Continued

	a170 (Scale 1–10)				a008 (Scale 1–4)				a008r (Scale 0–1)			
	Overall	Health Poor	Edn Poor	Income Poor	Overall	Health Poor	Edn Poor	Income Poor	Overall	Health Poor	Edn Poor	Income Poor
West Africa	0.06 (1.65)	0.16 (1.83)	0.10 (1.44)	-0.05 (-0.46)	-0.05 (-1.15)	-0.03 (-0.37)	-0.13 (-1.54)	-0.04 (-0.32)	0.01 (0.16)	0.12 (1.11)	0.03 (0.28)	-0.19 (-1.41)
Africa	0.07* (4.93)	0.08* (3.23)	0.09* (3.68)	0.02 (0.55)	-0.14* (-9.00)	-0.17* (-6.12)	-0.16* (-6.16)	-0.13* (-4.35)	0.18* (8.94)	0.21* (6.25)	0.19* (5.77)	0.15* (4.22)
FAMILY												
North Africa	-0.06 (-1.25)	-0.12 (-1.39)	-0.06 (-0.81)	0.02 (0.14)	0.28* (4.89)	0.27* (2.92)	0.26* (3.30)	0.04 (0.32)	-0.10 (-1.59)	-0.20 (-1.88)	-0.11 (-1.23)	0.15 (1.08)
South Africa	-0.01 (-0.33)	-0.01 (-0.17)	-0.04 (-0.67)	-0.02 (-0.40)	0.09* (2.18)	0.02 (0.31)	0.09 (1.37)	0.05 (0.92)	0.06 (1.24)	0.07 (0.94)	-0.03 (-0.43)	0.03 (0.44)
East Africa	0.02 (0.60)	-0.03 (-0.47)	0.06 (0.93)	0.04 (0.54)	-0.02 (-0.38)	0.10 (1.78)	0.04 (0.59)	0.11 (1.60)	0.25* (4.74)	0.15* (2.17)	0.27* (3.41)	0.06 (0.68)
West Africa	-0.05 (-0.70)	-0.08 (-0.67)	-0.03 (-0.30)	-0.09 (-0.62)	0.19* (2.53)	0.25* (2.02)	0.11 (0.89)	0.09 (0.54)	0.18 (1.96)	0.05 (0.36)	0.13 (0.87)	0.25 (1.27)
Africa	-0.05* (-2.19)	-0.08* (-2.29)	-0.02 (-0.56)	-0.03 (-0.78)	0.06* (2.40)	0.04 (1.06)	0.03 (0.88)	0.01 (0.28)	0.12* (4.00)	0.11* (2.53)	0.10* (2.39)	0.11* (2.41)
FRIENDS												
North Africa	0.01 (0.33)	0.04 (1.39)	0.00 (0.10)	0.02 (0.51)	0.09* (4.89)	0.07* (2.24)	0.09* (3.81)	-0.02 (-0.64)	-0.07* (-3.02)	-0.04 (-1.04)	-0.09* (-3.04)	0.02 (0.42)

South Africa	-0.05* (-3.73)	-0.01 (-0.39)	-0.02 (-0.93)	-0.04 (-1.90)	0.09* (6.40)	0.08* (2.90)	0.06* (2.49)	0.06* (2.58)	-0.05* (-2.88)	-0.06* (-2.08)	-0.04 (-1.32)	-0.03 (-1.01)
East Africa	-0.11* (-5.38)	-0.11* (-3.36)	-0.11* (-3.15)	-0.15* (-3.78)	0.03 (1.18)	-0.08* (-2.12)	0.01 (0.19)	-0.05 (-1.24)	-0.08* (-3.11)	0.01 (0.15)	-0.12* (-2.86)	-0.04 (-0.80)
West Africa	-0.04* (-2.02)	0.00 (0.02)	-0.12* (-2.79)	-0.11 (-1.77)	0.09* (3.83)	0.01 (0.23)	0.12* (2.60)	0.05 (0.75)	-0.09* (-2.65)	0.02 (0.28)	-0.11 (-1.61)	-0.10 (-1.25)
Africa	0.00 (0.07)	0.03 (1.93)	-0.01 (-0.58)	-0.02 (-1.20)	0.08* (9.72)	0.06* (4.29)	0.10* (7.39)	0.07* (4.48)	-0.07* (-6.60)	-0.06* (-3.49)	-0.10* (-6.04)	-0.08* (-4.28)
WORK												
North Africa	0.03 (1.49)	0.11* (3.98)	0.05* (2.06)	-0.03 (-0.66)	0.05* (2.44)	-0.02 (-0.56)	0.03 (0.94)	0.08 (1.95)	0.02 (0.72)	0.05 (1.27)	0.04 (1.04)	-0.09 (-1.70)
South Africa	0.03 (1.94)	0.08* (2.22)	0.07* (2.00)	0.11* (3.20)	-0.07* (-3.48)	-0.10* (-2.63)	-0.13* (-3.20)	-0.12* (-3.21)	0.21* (7.04)	0.17* (3.60)	0.17* (3.41)	0.23* (4.69)
East Africa	0.12* (3.68)	0.15* (2.88)	0.18* (3.43)	0.02 (0.35)	0.00 (-0.12)	-0.11 (-1.89)	-0.04 (-0.74)	0.00 (-0.02)	0.06 (1.41)	0.08 (1.23)	0.07 (0.95)	0.06 (0.78)
West Africa	-0.03 (-1.04)	0.03 (0.44)	-0.08 (-1.38)	0.14 (1.32)	-0.05 (-1.30)	-0.06 (-0.71)	-0.05 (-0.80)	-0.09 (-0.73)	0.23* (3.86)	0.02 (0.23)	0.24* (2.33)	0.17 (1.08)
Africa	0.05* (4.59)	0.12* (6.54)	0.06* (3.60)	0.05* (2.11)	-0.02* (-2.11)	-0.07* (-3.66)	-0.03 (-1.52)	-0.04 (-1.60)	0.18* (10.71)	0.16* (6.32)	0.16* (6.54)	0.13* (4.26)
RELIGION												
North Africa	-0.09* (-2.06)	-0.13 (-1.46)	-0.19* (-2.75)	-0.29* (-3.14)	0.07 (1.50)	0.14 (1.44)	0.18* (2.34)	0.21* (2.06)	-0.05 (-0.75)	-0.03 (-0.32)	-0.04 (-0.50)	-0.17 (-1.51)

(Continued)

Table 3.24 Continued

	a170 (Scale 1–10)				a008 (Scale 1–4)				a008r (Scale 0–1)			
	Overall	Health Poor	Edn Poor	Income Poor	Overall	Health Poor	Edn Poor	Income Poor	Overall	Health Poor	Edn Poor	Income Poor
South Africa	−0.12* (−8.22)	−0.16* (−4.95)	−0.15* (−4.50)	−0.13* (−4.41)	0.17* (10.60)	0.23* (7.01)	0.18* (5.13)	0.16* (5.25)	−0.09* (−4.05)	−0.16* (−4.02)	−0.11* (−2.63)	−0.09* (−2.53)
East Africa	0.04 (1.38)	0.07 (1.90)	0.01 (0.14)	0.00 (0.09)	0.04 (1.41)	0.06 (1.39)	0.02 (0.45)	0.17* (3.42)	0.07* (2.01)	0.08 (1.65)	0.12* (2.09)	−0.04 (−0.69)
West Africa	−0.15* (−4.03)	−0.18* (−2.38)	−0.17* (−2.18)	−0.30* (−2.83)	0.25* (6.12)	0.38* (4.66)	0.25* (2.88)	0.52* (4.67)	−0.18* (−3.59)	−0.30* (−3.13)	−0.10 (−0.90)	−0.39* (−2.95)
Africa	−0.04* (−3.97)	−0.07* (−3.50)	−0.08* (−3.94)	−0.09* (−4.36)	0.10* (8.38)	0.14* (6.07)	0.10* (4.45)	0.16* (6.90)	−0.08* (−5.13)	−0.10* (−3.73)	−0.08* (−2.74)	−0.11* (−4.15)
TRUST												
North Africa	0.06* (2.12)	−0.10* (−2.10)	0.00 (−0.02)	−0.11 (−1.91)	0.14* (4.32)	0.19* (3.40)	0.16* (3.65)	0.17* (2.42)	0.09* (2.26)	0.02 (0.25)	0.09 (1.66)	−0.02 (−0.25)
South Africa	−0.06* (−2.10)	−0.03 (−0.47)	−0.07 (−1.26)	−0.10 (−1.86)	0.05 (1.71)	−0.05 (−0.74)	0.07 (1.21)	0.14* (2.51)	0.05 (1.29)	0.14 (1.96)	0.03 (0.45)	0.05 (0.86)
East Africa	−0.03 (−0.75)	−0.24* (−2.95)	−0.05 (−0.70)	−0.05 (−0.58)	−0.05 (−1.01)	−0.20* (−2.37)	−0.08 (−1.05)	−0.16 (−1.71)	0.36* (7.34)	0.55* (6.34)	0.40* (4.98)	0.53* (5.60)
West Africa	0.03 (0.76)	−0.09 (−1.06)	0.01 (0.09)	−0.04 (−0.36)	0.06 (1.50)	0.18* (2.03)	0.11 (1.35)	−0.06 (−0.56)	0.18* (3.41)	0.06 (0.59)	0.18 (1.85)	0.20 (1.63)

Africa	−0.02 (−1.04)	−0.13* (−4.08)	−0.03 (−1.20)	−0.12* (−3.59)	0.05* (3.15)	0.01 (0.33)	0.05 (1.66)	0.03 (0.84)	0.12* (5.65)	0.16* (4.27)	0.13* (3.77)	0.16* (4.07)

CIVIL SERVICES

North Africa	−0.05* (−3.94)	−0.04 (−1.87)	−0.02 (−1.28)	−0.03 (−1.24)	0.11* (8.02)	0.08* (3.42)	0.12* (6.46)	0.13* (4.56)	−0.08* (−4.43)	−0.05 (−1.68)	−0.08* (−3.44)	−0.11* (−3.30)
South Africa	−0.07* (−5.50)	−0.08* (−2.94)	−0.05 (−1.81)	−0.04 (−1.59)	0.02 (1.55)	0.01 (0.23)	0.02 (0.81)	0.00 (−0.05)	0.01 (0.43)	0.01 (0.21)	0.01 (0.25)	0.04 (1.50)
East Africa	−0.03* (−2.02)	0.01 (0.57)	−0.03 (−1.01)	−0.03 (−1.06)	0.19* (11.17)	0.16* (5.84)	0.19* (7.07)	0.20* (6.44)	−0.16* (−8.01)	−0.14* (−4.50)	−0.13* (−3.97)	−0.16* (−4.34)
West Africa	−0.08* (−5.32)	−0.10* (−2.85)	−0.12* (−3.98)	−0.19* (−4.21)	0.04* (2.27)	0.01 (0.20)	0.05 (1.49)	0.05 (1.13)	0.03 (1.03)	0.03 (0.60)	0.02 (0.36)	−0.03 (−0.58)
Africa	−0.06* (−8.81)	−0.05* (−3.90)	−0.05* (−4.37)	−0.06* (−4.41)	0.10* (13.21)	0.07* (5.26)	0.11* (9.54)	0.09* (6.24)	−0.06* (−6.27)	−0.05* (−3.24)	−0.06* (−3.88)	−0.04* (−2.53)

Notes: 1. Based on probit results for extended model where z stats are displayed in parenthesis and * denotes statistical significance at the 5% level.
2. North Africa includes Algeria, Egypt and Morocco.
3. East Africa includes Ethiopia, Rwanda, United Republic of Tanzania, Uganda, Zambia and Zimbabwe.
4. West Africa includes Mali and Nigeria.

all four regions, the results generally support the hypothesized model introduced in Chapter 1. Health, income and education are generally significant determinants of well-being. The only exception is education in East Africa. Women are happier in all regions, and age shows a midlife dip impacting on well-being. Aside from East Africa, marriage lifts well-being, and family and friends are important in three of the four regions (friends are not significant in North Africa and family is not significant in West Africa).

Turning to the poverty groups, the results are not quite as compelling, but still strongly supportive of the model of well-being. For the health poor, the three policy variables are significant in all but one region (education in East Africa). Well-being shows a dip in middle age for all regions but North Africa, women are happier in North and South Africa, and friends and family are important in these two regions respectively. For the poorly educated, the results suggest that family is not as important, although friends are in three of the four regions, that the other socioeconomic control variables have the right sign and are sometimes significant, and that health and income are more important policy variables than education. For the income poor, all three policy variables are important determinants of well-being, while family is not as significant as friends. The control variables generally have the expected sign and impact, although the levels of significance are not as high as the overall or the health poor probit regressions. Women are happier in three regions, those married are happier in two regions and there is no middle-age dip in well-being among the income poor in three of the four regions. Friends are more significant than family. We can conclude from these results that the policy variables of education, health and income are important determinants of well-being in country probit regressions as well as in regional subaggregate analysis. For individual countries, overall results show health and income to be more important than education. Gender and friends are highly significant in nine countries, while age and family are less important (six and five countries respectively). For the education poor, health and income are significant in most countries (eleven and ten respectively), followed by gender, marital status and friends (eight, five, six). Education, age and family are weak (three, three and two countries). For the health poor, health income and education are important in many countries (twelve, nine and seven respectively), while gender, age and marital status appear less often (six, six, five). Family and friends have weaker effects on well-being. For the income poor, health is again the strongest influence on well-being (11 countries), followed by income and education (six, four); marital status is less significant (four), while friends is also important (seven) and family is less so (three). These country results exhibit considerably more variation than the regional subaggregates, particularly regarding family and friends. However, health remains the most significant explanatory variable.

The results from pooling over African regions are consistent with earlier findings for Asia. Even partial pooling for subregions – as compared with no pooling and looking at individual countries – improves the statistical fit, sometimes dramatically. We will come back to this question of the appropriate level of pooling and aggregation once we have completed our analysis of Latin America in the next chapter.

A summary of the results from the regional analysis is displayed in Table 3.25. Compared with the individual country results, there are few significant coefficient differences – mainly income poverty, in which North Africa and West Africa show a significantly larger response of poverty to changes in income, health and education variables. Health is significant only in East Africa for the health poor.

To explore regional factors further, we present the results for the extended form of the model, in which we included the social variables for trust, confidence in the civil service, work and religion, and also including the results for the two other configurations of the well-being variable. We look at these results in detail variable by variable.

Health. Health is a significant determinant of well-being for all African regions, the full sample and for all poverty groups. This pattern reinforces the results from the country and independent variable assessment at the disaggregate level reported above.

Income. Income is less significant than health among the income poor, while retaining its overall level of significance as a determinant of well-being in all regions and for the overall sample and among the health and education poor.

Education. Education is a significant determinant of well-being in three of the four African regions as well as for Africa as a whole. However, in East Africa the education variable is statistically significant in two out of 12 possible cases, suggesting a lack of interest in education as a force for uplifting well-being. This lack of significance was also observed in the country probit results for the countries in this region, including Rwanda and Ethiopia, among others.

Gender. The gender results suggest that women are generally happier in North Africa and also in the probit results for Africa as a whole. Women are happier in the other regions a smaller number of times, particularly among the education poor. This doesn't mean that men are necessarily happier. It signifies that neither gender was significantly happier than the other.

Table 3.25 Significant differences between poverty coefficients and full sample coefficients in four African regions for probit analysis of determinants of well-being – scale of 1 to 10 for well-being

	Significant income poverty coefficient	Significant education poverty coefficient	Significant health poverty coefficient
Income poor sample	North Africa	West Africa	West Africa
Education poor sample			
Health poor sample			East Africa

Table 3.26 Effect of age on life satisfaction and well-being in Africa

	a170 (Scale 1–10)		a008r (Scale 0–1)	
Country	Overall	Health Poor	Overall	Health Poor
Ethiopia		1.65		
Mali		2.04		
Nigeria	2.00			
South Africa	1.65			1.34
Tanzania		1.97		
Zimbabwe			2.02	

Notes: 1. Age is defined as 1: 15–29, 2: 30–49 and 3: 50 years and above.
2. Data are shown only for available cases. The age at which the minimum occurs is given by the coefficient of linear age divided by twice the coefficient of age squared.

Age. Age enters in a nonlinear fashion in a few countries, and for the health poor more often than the other poverty groups. The details of the nonlinearity results are shown in Table 3.26. The results are similar to those reported for Asia. The inflection point occurs earlier in life, often in the 20s and early 30s. Shorter life expectancy and the possible impact of HIV/AIDS could explain this early onset of lower well-being. Further work needs to be done to explore this relationship, with particular reference to the impact of health and age on well-being.

Marital status. In North Africa and South Africa those who are married are happier than those who are not, but the coefficient is not significant in either West Africa or East Africa. These regional results mirror the findings for the country analysis reported above.

Family. Family is not generally significant, except in the aggregate results for the region as a whole, where the probit regression coefficient is significant in seven out of 12 cases, and in the full sample for the three different configurations of well-being, where it is significant in about half the cases. No region has particularly strong family coefficients, and South Africa is the weakest. The poverty results are weak, as the family variable is significant in nine out of a possible 45 cases.

Friends. The friends variable is significant for the full sample in all three configurations of well-being for the region as a whole.

For the regions, friends is strongest in East Africa. Friends is not significant for the majority of the poverty groups, although it is statistically significant for the health poor (four out of five times) in one case.

Turning to the social variables, **Work** is highly significant in South Africa and West Africa, for the full sample and for most of the poverty groups. It is also significant for Africa as a whole and for the poverty groups, but is less important for East Africa and West Africa, both for the overall sample and for the poverty groups.

Religion is significant for the African region as a whole, and for South Africa and West Africa for the full sample and all the poverty groups. The results for the other two regions are not nearly as strong.

Trust has many wrong signs and few significant results, either for the regions, for Africa as a whole or for the poverty groups in any region.

Civil service is very significant for all poverty groups and the overall sample when considering the African region as a whole. The results are also relatively strong for North Africa and East Africa but much weaker for South Africa and West Africa, where the poverty groups have significant coefficients in only a few poverty cases, mainly for the 1–10 configuration of well-being.

3.5 Extensions to the model

3.5.1 Probability of escape from poverty

We next explored an extension of the standard model (Equation 1.1) to include attitudes toward realizing a better lifestyle and how this impacted on the well-being of the poor. As noted in Chapter 2, the motivation for this exercise is the work of di Tella and MacCulloch (2006) who found a significant impact of beliefs on well-being using the third wave of the World Value Survey for 36 countries around the globe. The regression included all income levels and 43,700 sample observations.

Di Tella and MacCulloch found that lower income affects one's happiness in a negative way if it is accompanied by a belief that poverty tends to be a permanent state. They did this by using an interaction term of real income times the chance of escaping poverty. For the World Value Surveys we analyzed probit results for several countries where the question was part of several waves of the survey for individual countries. It seems to us that it is more useful to focus our attention on the poor rather than on all respondents, most of whom are nonpoor. We do not believe that the nonpoor know how the well-being of the poor would be impacted by responses to this variable. For brevity, only the coefficient and significance of the chance of escaping poverty variable are reported. The other variables are controls for personal characteristics. If the respondent thought there was a chance of escaping poverty a one (1) was recorded in the response sheet. If there was very little chance of escaping poverty the value was entered as two (2). Simply, if the coefficient on the variable is positive (negative) then the respondent's positive attitude about escaping has a negative (positive) impact on well-being for the 1 to 10 and 0 and 1 designations for well-being and a positive (negative) impact for the 1 to 4 designation.

For Africa we have a much smaller sample than for Asia. However, some analysis is possible by looking at a few economies. The results in Table 3.27 suggest that the escaping poverty variable has a definite positive impact on well-being in Nigeria for the health poor in all three versions of the well-being variable and for the overall sample and income poor in the 1–10 configuration of well-being. In South Africa there is no evidence that the escaping poverty variable has an uplifting impact on well-being. The two significant coefficients have the wrong sign. For the overall sample there is some evidence of uplifting well-being for the health poor in two versions of well-being (1–10 and 1–4). Two other significant coefficients have the wrong sign. Because of data limitations and the limited significance of the escape from poverty variable, it is difficult to draw any strong conclusions from these results.

3.5.2   Urban–Rural migration

As noted in Chapter 2, there are lots of reasons for migration from rural areas to cities, and one of them is income differentials. However, as migration continues, changes in migration and growth in income can lead to a shrinking of income differentials and happiness differentials (urban happier than rural) over time, and the allure of the city tends to fade.

According to Easterlin *et al.* (2010), this conclusion is consistent with happiness research, which finds well-being to be highly correlated with

Table 3.27 Significance of coefficient on chance to escape from poverty

	a170 (Scale 1–10)				a008 (Scale 1–4)				a008r (Scale 0–1)			
	Overall	Health Poor	Edn Poor	Income Poor	Overall	Health Poor	Edn Poor	Income Poor	Overall	Health Poor	Edn Poor	Income Poor
Nigeria	−0.22* (−3.53)	−0.40* (−3.06)	−0.13 (−0.79)	−0.68* (−3.26)	0.12 (1.69)	0.39* (2.83)	−0.05 (−0.26)	0.05 (0.21)	0.01 (0.09)	−0.43* (−2.76)	0.24 (1.02)	−0.09 (−0.31)
South Africa	0.05 (1.13)	−0.05 (−0.56)	0.00 (−0.01)	0.09 (1.46)	−0.08 (−1.73)	−0.03 (−0.36)	−0.01 (−0.17)	−0.06 (−0.98)	0.21* (3.35)	0.17 (1.62)	0.11 (1.15)	0.18* (2.39)
Overall	−0.05 (−1.37)	−0.17* (−2.53)	−0.05 (−0.67)	0.00 (0.04)	−0.01 (−0.23)	0.16* (2.15)	0.01 (0.16)	−0.05 (−0.91)	0.13* (2.64)	−0.07 (−0.92)	0.11 (1.31)	0.16* (2.25)

Notes: 1. Chance to escape from poverty ranges from 1 to 3. 1 indicates they have a chance. 2 indicates they have very little chance. 3 indicates other answer.

2. Based on probit results for Equation 2.2 where z stats are displayed in parenthesis and * denotes statistical significance at the 5% level. This is due to e132 data being available only in Wave 3 and hence not possible to incorporate other social variables as in the extended model.

Table 3.28 Probit results for Africa – rural–urban

	a170 (Scale 1–10)				a008 (Scale 1–4)				a008r (Scale 0–1)			
	Overall	Health Poor	Edn Poor	Income Poor	Overall	Health Poor	Edn Poor	Income Poor	Overall	Health Poor	Edn Poor	Income Poor
Egypt	−0.51* (−4.25)	−1.07* (−4.26)	−0.70* (−4.06)	−0.88* (−3.07)	0.29 (1.96)	0.42 (1.47)	0.44* (2.06)	0.15 (0.46)	0.00 (0.00)	0.01 (0.04)	−0.24 (−0.82)	−0.04 (−0.10)
Ethiopia	0.51 (0.73)								1.22 (0.84)			
Mali	1.81* (2.63)				0.10 (0.09)							
Morocco	0.32 (1.75)	0.57 (1.74)	0.48* (2.10)	0.68 (1.42)	0.13 (0.65)	−0.12 (−0.33)	0.03 (0.13)	−0.27 (−0.49)	0.23 (0.97)	0.12 (0.28)	0.25 (0.83)	−0.10 (−0.16)
Nigeria	−0.12 (−1.16)	−0.26 (−0.94)	−0.45* (−2.07)	−0.70* (−2.68)	−0.02 (−0.20)	0.24 (0.81)	0.33 (1.28)	0.34 (1.20)	0.02 (0.15)	−0.13 (−0.39)	−0.51 (−1.52)	−0.76* (−2.14)
South Africa	0.04 (0.55)	0.11 (0.86)	−0.07 (−0.63)	0.01 (0.14)	0.04 (0.58)	0.10 (0.72)	0.16 (1.28)	0.07 (0.78)	−0.05 (−0.49)	−0.08 (−0.52)	−0.22 (−1.42)	−0.08 (−0.67)
North Africa	−0.13 (−1.38)	−0.29 (−1.61)	−0.13 (−1.02)	−0.35 (−1.61)	0.17 (1.52)	0.18 (0.89)	0.21 (1.37)	0.13 (0.52)	0.01 (0.10)	0.07 (0.30)	−0.03 (−0.16)	−0.11 (−0.37)

West Africa	-0.04	-0.15	-0.21	-0.70*	-0.03	0.15	0.18	0.34	-0.03	-0.15	-0.60*	-0.79*
	(-0.47)	(-0.64)	(-1.10)	(-2.72)	(-0.26)	(0.60)	(0.85)	(1.21)	(-0.20)	(-0.50)	(-2.00)	(-2.25)
Overall	-0.04	-0.09	-0.08	-0.13	0.13*	0.05	0.19*	0.07	-0.06	-0.04	-0.11	-0.06
	(-0.96)	(-1.14)	(-1.17)	(-1.94)	(2.79)	(0.61)	(2.65)	(0.98)	(-1.11)	(-0.40)	(-1.24)	(-0.64)

Notes: * Denotes significance at 10% level.
1. The rural–urban variable ranges from 0: rural (2,000 and fewer residents) to 1: urban (500,000 and more residents). Under the 1–10 and 0–1 definitions of well-being, a positive sign indicates that urban residents are happier. Under the 1–4 definition, a negative sign indicates that urban residents are happier.
2. Based on probit results for inclusion of added dummy variable for rural–urban variable into original Equation 1.1 and z stats are displayed in parenthesis.
3. Data available for North African countries include Egypt and Morocco.
4. Data available for West African countries include Mali and Nigeria.
5. Variable dropped due to multicollinearity.

income, but not with growth in income above a certain point. However, the impact of urbanization on well-being in cross-section regressions remains high in some societies but not in others. This might be because, in a modern developed country setting, the disadvantages of living in a congested, noisy and polluted environment could outweigh any income advantage, and the retreat to the suburbs could be a way to bring about a partial return to a more relaxed and quiet lifestyle with less stress.

Certainly, the rapid and continued migration to the cities and the growing income differentials between the rural home base and the city should be reflected in higher levels of well-being if income and well-being are closely correlated and are not overwhelmed by other factors. This relationship could hold for many poorer countries and would tend to be moderated only after income has reached a certain level. However, it is not clear that the data support this conclusion, simply because there are so few studies of the impact of urbanization on well-being. It is clear that the pattern of migration in Africa differs from that of Asia, simply because of the more rapid economic growth in Asia. Nevertheless, economic forces still drive migration, and the pattern of migration has similarities to that of the other, richer regions. Young men are the most likely to migrate, along with a smaller proportion of young women, drawn by opportunities for household work. Those with some education are also more likely to migrate than those with limited skills.

The coefficients from the probit model displayed in Table 3.28 suggest that the results are more significant for the 1–10 definition of well-being than for the other definitions. In Egypt, the overall sample and all three poverty groups are happier in urban areas, and also the education poor in the 1–4 definition. In Mali, Morocco and Nigeria, as well as West Africa, urban residents are happier when well-being is defined on the 1–10 scale. The income and education poor are also happier in urban areas in West Africa and for the overall sample with the 1–4 definition of well-being. From these scattered results it is difficult to draw a general conclusion about the impact of rural to urban migration on happiness. Nevertheless, selected significance of results in some countries suggests that there are some gains in happiness for migrants in Africa.

4
Analysis for Latin America

As we did with Asia and Africa, we begin the discussion of Latin America with a review of health, education and income. Of the three regions, Latin America has the highest living standard, measured either by its ranking in human development or by the level of per capita income. Latin American economies in our sample rank in the top half of countries in the Human Development Index and (with one exception) also in terms of per capita income (see Table 4.1). The other regions cannot stake a similar claim, and Africa dominates the lower ranks of both the HDI and per capita income. Because of these rankings, we would expect that it would be more difficult for Latin America to make as much progress as the other regions, which started from a much lower base. Nevertheless, life expectancy increased by a few years between 1990 and 2008. See Table 4.2 for an overview of various health indicators for Latin American countries. The average increase for all countries combined is about four years, ranging from eight years in Guatemala to less than one year in Trinidad and Tobago. Life expectancy was over 69 for all countries in this region in 2008. Infant mortality and under-5 mortality also improved over the past 18 years. Infant mortality fell most dramatically in Peru, from 62 per thousand births in 1990 to 20 in 2008. Dramatic declines were also achieved in Brazil (46 to 18) and in Mexico (36 to 15), not the poorest countries in the region. Under-5 mortality also fell in Peru (78 to 22) and in Brazil (55 to 21) and the Dominican Republic (62 to 32). Peru ranks eighth in human development out of 12 countries and ninth in per capita income. This shows that progress in particular aspects of human development is not necessarily correlated with aggregate measures of well-being. The incidence of TB in Latin America is generally much lower than in the other regions (fewer than 100 cases per thousand households) compared with much

Table 4.1 Human development for Latin America

Country	Income share of lowest 10% (2006)	Income share of lowest 20% (2006)	early Gini –1992	later Gini after 2000–(2006)	Poverty rate National early 1998–2000	Poverty rate National later 2003–8	Rank of GDP per capita
Argentina	1.17	3.61	45.35	48.81			78
Brazil	1.06	2.97	57.37	55.80	22.00	21.50	103
Chile	1.59	4.10	55.52	52.00	17.00	19.00	72
Colombia	0.76	2.32	51.32	58.49	64.00	45.10	111
Dominican Republic	1.48	3.87	51.36	51.91	36.50	48.50	117
El Salvador	1.34	4.27	49.86	46.85	38.80	30.70	129
Guatemala	1.25	3.44	55.65	53.69	56.20	51.00	146
Mexico	1.81	4.64	51.06	48.11	24.20	17.00	85
Peru	1.45	3.88	43.87	49.55	54.30	22.00	115
Trinidad and Tobago			40.27				61
Uruguay	1.73	4.45	42.16	46.24			86
Venezuela	1.74	4.85	41.68	43.44	52.00		98

Source: *World Development Indicators*, OECD, *Latin American Outlook* 2011 and CIA Factbook.

Table 4.2 Health indicators in Latin American countries – life expectancy and mortality rates

Country	Life expectancy 1990	Life expectancy 2008	Infant mortality 1990 (per 1,000 live births)	Infant mortality 2008 (per 1,000 live births)	Under-5 mortality 1990 (per 1,000 live births)	Under-5 mortality 2008 (per 1,000 live births)
Argentina	71.55	75.33	25.00	13.60	27.90	14.70
Brazil	66.30	72.40	46.00	18.30	55.70	21.80
Chile	73.55	78.61	18.30	7.20	21.60	8.70
Colombia	68.30	72.98	28.10	16.70	35.00	19.60
Dominican Republic	67.74	72.57	48.20	27.20	62.30	32.60
El Salvador	65.98	71.26	48.20	15.60	62.30	17.90
Guatemala	62.24	70.34	57.00	33.30	76.10	40.70
Mexico	70.88	75.07	36.40	15.30	44.90	17.50
Peru	65.58	73.26	62.00	20.70	78.00	22.80
Trinidad and Tobago	68.98	69.34	30.40	31.10	34.40	35.30
Uruguay	72.62	75.98	20.50	11.70	23.90	13.90
Venezuela	71.25	73.55	26.50	15.80	31.70	18.10

Source: World Development Indicators, United Nations *Human Development Report 2011*.

Table 4.2 continued Health indicators in Latin American countries – health and sanitation indicators

Country	Access to improved water 1990	Access to improved water 2005	Access to improved sanitation 1990	Access to improved sanitation 2005	Health spending as % of GDP 2007	Health spending per capita $PPP 2007
Argentina	94.00	96.00	90.00	90.00	9.98	1,322.18
Brazil	88.00	95.00	69.00	78.00	8.44	798.58
Chile	90.00	96.00	84.00	96.00	6.24	767.85
Colombia	88.00	92.00	68.00	74.00	6.06	516.15
Dominican Republic	88.00	87.00	73.00	81.00	5.37	411.19
El Salvador	74.00	86.00	75.00	85.00	6.17	401.58
Guatemala	82.00	92.00	65.00	78.00	7.28	335.65
Mexico	85.00	93.00	66.00	82.00	5.86	823.10
Peru	75.00	81.00	54.00	66.00	4.26	326.87
Trinidad and Tobago	88.00	93.00	93.00	92.00	4.80	1,178.40
Uruguay	96.00	100.00	94.00	99.00	8.01	994.00
Venezuela	90.00	93.00	82.00	91.00	5.77	641.47

Source: World Development Indicators, United Nations Human Development Report 2011.

Table 4.2   continued Health indicators in Latin American countries

Country	Incidence of TB 2000 (per 1,000)	Incidence of TB 2008 (per 1,000)	Under-weight 2000-8 (%)	Population aged 5 suffering from stunting (%) 2000-8	Anemia under 5 1998-2008 (%)
Argentina	40.43	29.61	2.30	8.20	25.38
Brazil	60.35	46.47	2.20	7.10	29.12
Chile	19.45	11.47	0.60	2.10	28.33
Colombia	42.99	36.00	5.10	16.20	31.11
Dominican Republic	99.81	72.89	3.40	10.10	39.93
El Salvador	36.85	31.83	6.10	24.60	10.50
Guatemala	67.80	62.91	17.70	54.30	22.10
Mexico	31.70	18.69	3.40	15.50	20.60
Peru	180.00	120.00	5.40	29.80	42.70
Trinidad and Tobago	17.58	24.06	4.40	5.30	29.73
Uruguay	24.41	22.03	6.00	13.90	27.07
Venezuela	34.29	33.49			39.63

Source: World Development Indicators, United Nations *Human Development Report 2011.*

higher rates in Asia and Africa. Nevertheless, further progress has been made in reducing the incidence of TB, although Peru still has more than 100 cases per thousand. Access to safe water and good sanitation was high in 1990 and has improved further since then. With a few exceptions (Peru in particular), around 90 percent of households have access to safe water, and access to better sanitation has also increased, although it is still low in Peru (66 percent of households) and to a lesser extent in Colombia (74 percent) and Guatemala (78 percent).

Health spending as a percentage of GDP is also substantial, at over 5 percent of GDP for most countries in the region. This is somewhat higher than Asia but still lower than Africa, where several countries spend more than 6 percent of GDP on health (the impact of AIDS was noted in Chapter 3). The incidence of anemia and stunting varies from country to country in Latin America, perhaps more than we might expect given the generally higher health indicators noted above. Stunting is, nevertheless, much lower than in other regions, where rates of 30 percent or higher are commonplace (eight of 13 countries in Asia and nine of 12 in Africa). Only Guatemala has a stunting rate of over 30 percent. Similarly, the rates of anemia are lower than in the other regions; there are only a few countries where more than 30 percent of children under 5 are anemic. Spending on health averaged 6 percent of GDP in Latin America, and only two countries spent less than 5 percent of GDP. In Asia, spending on health was around 4.5 percent on average, and somewhat more in Africa, as noted above.

The average educational attainment is higher in Latin America than in the other regions. In 2008 all but one country in the region had net enrollment rates in primary education of over 90 percent, as can be seen in Table 4.3. These enrollment rates have risen steadily from 1991, when they were below 80 percent for several countries (Dominican Republic and El Salvador). With the exception of Guatemala and El Salvador, public spending per student in elementary and secondary schools was also higher – over $10 per head. Public spending per student in elementary schools has also increased in some countries, although it has fallen in Chile, Colombia, Peru, El Salvador, and Trinidad and Tobago. Male adult literacy and youth literacy are high – close to 100 percent for male youth literacy and slightly lower for the adult male population. However, continued efforts are needed to improve the delivery of primary education to the poor in order to provide a base for increasing earnings and living standards.

Poverty statistics take several forms in Latin America. These include the income share of the lowest 10 percent and lowest 20 percent of the population, Gini coefficients measuring the degree of inequality of the income distribution, and estimates of rates of poverty made by the national governments. These figures are augmented by rankings in the United Nations Human Development Index and the GDP per capita level, as well as ranking countries among 225 countries around the world. The income share of the lowest 10 percent and lowest 20 percent of the income distribution, as well as the Gini coefficients for the region, suggests a high level of income inequality. Gini coefficients are generally over 50; they have not fallen much, and in half of the countries have even increased, since the early 1990s.

The income shares of the lower income groups are consistent with this picture. Comparisons with other regions suggest a much less satisfactory state of affairs for the poor in Latin America. In Asia the income share of the poorest 10 percent averaged about 3.4 percent of total income, while in Latin America it was 1.4 percent, about 40 percent of the level for Asian economies! Comparisons for the lowest 20 percent are similar. These data are consistent with the levels of poverty in Latin America, which is higher than we might expect when compared with other regions. Since Latin America has substantially higher levels of income per capita and rankings on the human development scale than the other regions, it ought to have lower levels of poverty than the other regions. This is not the case. Adjusting for estimates at different times, poverty in the richer countries of Asia (Thailand, Malaysia) is lower than for comparable countries in Latin America. Thailand ranks 92 in HDI, 118 in income and had a poverty estimate in 1998 of 13.6 percent. Malaysia has an HDI ranking of 57, an income ranking of 76 and poverty of 15.5 percent in 1998. For both of these countries poverty has probably fallen by several percentage points since these estimates were made. A comparable Latin American country, Chile, had an HDI ranking of 40, an income ranking of 77 and a poverty level

Table 4.3 Education indicators for Latin American countries

Country	Primary completion rate 1991	Primary completion rate 2008	Male youth literacy 1990	Male youth literacy 2008	Male adult literacy
Argentina	100.22	102.44		99.00	97.60
Brazil	92.57	105.84		97.06	89.77
Chile	90.79	94.84		99.11	98.60
Colombia	72.85	110.47		97.55	93.32
Dominican Republic	61.05	90.74		94.63	88.21
El Salvador	65.02	89.35		95.41	87.05
Guatemala	47.95	80.01		88.50	79.50
Mexico	88.45	104.09		98.41	94.59
Peru	89.40	100.96		98.01	94.86
Trinidad and Tobago	101.62	91.78		99.50	99.10
Uruguay	93.80	103.62		98.63	97.83
Venezuela, RB	80.76	95.38		97.97	95.38

Source: World Development Indicators.

Table 4.3 continued Education indicators for Latin American countries

Country	Primary net enrollment rate 1999	Primary net enrollment rate 2008	Public spending per student elementary 1999	Public spending per student elementary 2007	Public spending per student secondary 1999	Public spending per student secondary 2008
Argentina	100.00	98.51	12.86	14.69	18.21	21.93
Brazil	91.28	94.16	10.81	17.72	9.51	18.46
Chile		94.38	12.06	11.93	13.79	13.45
Colombia	93.00	90.02	15.22	12.33	16.12	14.78
Dominican Republic	79.81	80.00	7.11	9.22		6.45
El Salvador	78.41	94.05	8.56	7.94	7.98	9.09
Guatemala	82.21	95.07	6.66	10.29	4.27	6.21
Mexico	97.25	98.05	11.69	13.29	14.22	13.48
Peru	97.64	94.44	7.57	7.31	10.80	9.98
Trinidad and Tobago	88.77	91.81	11.59	9.06	12.30	9.95
Uruguay	92.44	97.51	7.21	8.52	9.94	10.40
Venezuela, RB	85.57	90.08		9.10		8.11

Source: World Development Indicators.

of 17 percent estimated between 2003 and 2008. For Mexico, the HDI ranking was 46, income ranking 55 and poverty level either 24 percent or 47 percent, depending on the estimating agency. Even if we take the lower estimate, the level of poverty in both Latin American countries is higher than in the comparable Asian countries, yet their income and HDI rankings are stronger. As a result, we can make the inference that the higher rates of poverty are at least partially responsible for the result of poor income distribution in Latin America. The HDI in Latin America for 2010 bunches most of the countries in the range between 39 and the lower 60s. Only Guatemala, at 91, is outside that range. This is much better than Africa (where every country but Egypt is over 110) and Asia (where only Malaysia is in this range, the rest being 89 or over and bunched between 89 and 125).

From the Human Development (HDI) standpoint, the three regions are essentially nonoverlapping. Africa has the lowest HDI and Latin America the highest, with Asia in between. However, the annual changes in the HDI in Latin America since 1980 have been smaller than in the other two regions (less than 1 percent per annum in all but two cases compared with between 1 and 2 percent in both Asia and Africa). Part of this disparity could be explained by the fact that the HDI is bounded, so that large improvements are more difficult for the higher-ranking countries. Aside from Korea, none of the 42 highest-ranking countries had improvement of more than 1 percent per annum. Income rankings for the three regions are also pretty much distinct and not overlapping. For Latin America, the rankings were highest in 2010 (see CIA Factbook). All but two countries ranked between 61 and 117. This compared with all but one country ranked between 118 and 196 in Asia and all but three between 201 and 225 in Africa. Several additional features of the poor are of particular interest in Latin America. There has been high volatility in the growth rates in Latin America over the past few decades, which has hurt the poor, and there has been a high rate of unemployment in the lowest quintile of the population in several countries. In addition, the wage gap between the poor and the nonpoor is high and tax systems in the region are generally regressive. Furthermore, the direction of public spending is not well focused on the poor. Together, all of these factors have resulted in slow progress in reducing poverty over the past few decades in Latin America (see OECD 2011a and United Nations 2011 for more details).

Table 4.4 shows that life satisfaction appears to be generally quite high in Latin American countries, even more so than in the other two regions we looked at earlier. In general, eight out of 12 Latin American countries report life satisfaction levels above 7.0. El Salvador, Chile and Uruguay report life satisfaction of above 6.0, with Peru reporting the least at 5.9. The responses to job and living standard questions were correlated with life satisfaction. Satisfaction with living standards was ranked lower than job satisfaction. Venezuela reported the highest life satisfaction averages for overall and females. Mexico, Brazil and Dominican Republic followed closely behind. Data on other indicators, such as whether respondents felt that they led a purposeful life, being treated with respect, and had a social support system were also presented in Table 4.4.

Figure 4.1 shows the histograms of the well-being of the respective Latin American countries from the World Value Survey. Average well-being is considerably higher in Latin America than it is in the other regions. There are many peaks in well-being in the range of 8 to 10, and the average level of well-being for the 1 to 10 designation is much higher for Latin America than in the other two regions.

4.1   Well-being in Latin America

Who is poor ?

Before looking at the probit results for Latin America, we summarize the three different kinds of poverty for the Latin American economies. As with Asia and Africa, we have designated three poverty groups:

(1) Those who have limited education, i.e. respondents who reported that they either had no education or who have completed only elementary education as reported on the questionnaire.
(2) Those who have limited income, i.e. respondents who reported they are in the bottom quintile (20 percent) of the income distribution as reported on the questionnaire.
(3) Those who report being in poor health, i.e. respondents who reported they were in poor or very poor health on the questionnaire.

Note that all designations of poverty are taken from the distribution of responses to the questionnaire; income poverty from those who believe they are in the lowest 20 percent of the income distribution, education poverty from those who have completed primary education or less, and health poverty from those who reported being in either poor health or very poor health. All three variables are taken from the responses to questions contained in the World Value Survey. The data

Table 4.4 Life satisfaction, life purpose and satisfaction

Country	Life satisfaction		Purposeful life		Treated with respect		Social support network		Satisfied with job	Satisfied with living standard	Satisfied with health
	Total	Female	Total	Female	Total	Female	Total	Female			
Argentina	7.1	7.1	93	95	96	95	91	91	83	70	87
Brazil	7.6	7.6	96	97	94	95	91	91	86	74	82
Chile	6.3	6.2	90	88	93	91	83	83	81	68	73
Colombia	7.3	7.3	98	98	96	96	88	87	82	69	84
Dominican Republic	7.6	7.4	96	94	92	95	84	87	69	57	80
El Salvador	6.7	6.7	97	97	89	90	72	72	82	60	80
Guatemala	7.2	..	97	96	91	91	83	81	92	76	88
Mexico	7.7	7.9	93	93	91	91	86	84	88	69	82
Peru	5.9	5.8	96	95	89	88	79	78	74	54	72
Trinidad and Tobago	7.0	..	97	97	93	94	85	87	76	40	82
Uruguay	6.8	6.7	87	89	94	94	91	93	79	67	84
Venezuela	7.8	7.7	100	100	92	92	94	94	86	80	90

Source: United Nations Human Development Report 2011; raw data from Gallup Organization.

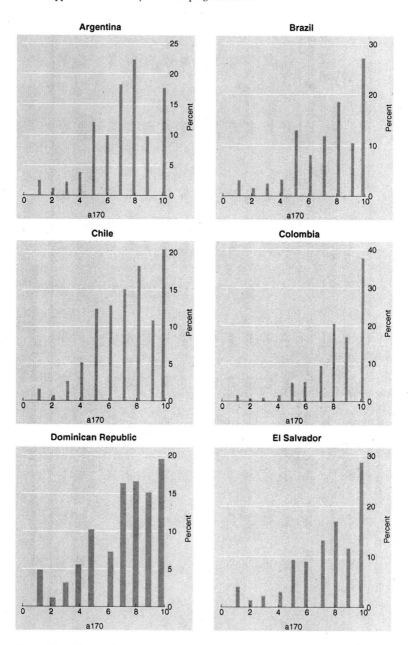

Figure 4.1 Life satisfaction in Latin America

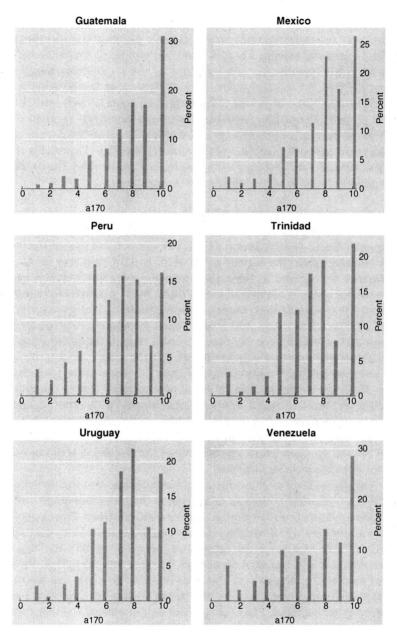

Figure 4.1   Continued

limitations are the same as mentioned earlier in Chapters 2 and 3 – generally fewer observations for health poor groups and difficulties in fitting into the extended model when the sample size is limited. For data on the income poor, the estimates of the respondents were reasonably close to the 20 percent poverty figure that the question was designed to elicit – Argentina (23 percent), Colombia (19 percent), Chile (28 percent), Dominican Republic (28 percent), Mexico (27 percent) and Peru (32 percent). For Brazil (49 percent) and Guatemala (65 percent), the responses were high, and slightly low for Uruguay (12 percent) and Trinidad and Tobago (14 percent). Despite these difficulties, the data do represent the spirit of identifying the income poor.

4.1.1 Sample size for Latin America

Overall sample size for Latin America is somewhat larger than the samples drawn from Asia and Africa. The summary of life satisfaction summarized from the various waves of the worldwide survey for Latin America is displayed in Table 4.5. However, once some variables have been dropped and the overall model fitted, many countries have fewer than 1,000 observations, mostly in the Caribbean, and some poverty groups have fewer than 100 observations. There are somewhat larger numbers of health poor than in Asia, even though the designation of health is the same and despite the fact that the Latin American region has higher average per capita income than the other two regions. Only in Africa did we put fair health in the poor category (due to the generally lower level of health standards as compared with other regions). The sample size for Guatemala and Mexico was also limited, which could have had an impact on the probit analysis of the determinants of well-being. Correlation results between the well-being scales of 1–10 and 1–4 are shown in Table 4.6.

The Venn diagrams show distinct differences between the three poverty groups and that there is more overlap than we observed in either Africa or Asia. The distribution and intensity of these three poverty groups for the Latin American region are reported in the Venn diagrams displayed in Figure 4.2. Education and income poor have the biggest overlap. It is still less than 50 percent for most countries. The overlap between the health poor and the other two poor groups is also not that large. In Brazil, Colombia and Chile, around half of the education poor are also income poor. The overlap is not as pronounced in other countries. In Mexico, for example, the overlap is about 30 percent.

As seen above, there is some overlap of the education and income poor in Latin America, but less between the health poor and either of

Table 4.5 Sample size by country and poverty group in Latin America (after fitting into model)

	Total	a170 (Scale 1-10)*				a008 (Scale 1-4)*				a008r (Scale 0-1)*			
		Overall*	Health Poor	Edn Poor	Income Poor	Overall*	Health Poor	Edn Poor	Income Poor	Overall*	Health Poor	Edn Poor	Income Poor
Argentina	5,368	1,976	145	695	468	1,972	145	694	464	1,989	147	701	469
Brazil	4,431	4,145	109	1,496	2,067	4,151	109	1,502	2,074	4,156	109	1,503	2,076
Chile	4,700	2,792	145	558	795	2,799	144	562	796	2,807	145	562	799
Colombia	9,050	2,918	57	690	569	2,919	57	690		2,919	57	690	569
Dominican Republic	417	286			81	285			79	287			81
El Salvador	1,254	992	72	413		1,005**		420**		1,006**	67**	421	
Guatemala	1,000	915		283	602	915		283	603	916		283	603
Mexico	8,827	4,256	255	1,248	1,140	4,278	258	1,273	1,164	4,307	264	1,285	1,172
Peru	4,212	3,607	101	600	1,662	3,608	101	603	1,671	3,622		603	1,672
Trinidad and Tobago	1,002	944		312	131	946		313	131	946	51**	313	131
Uruguay	2,000	1,685	46	645	211	1,681	47	644	210	1,689	47	646	211
Venezuela	2,400	1,042	47**	283	365	1,041	48	288	363	1,051		289**	335**
	44,661												

Note: *after fitting into the equation for the extended model (1.2).
**some variables dropped.

Table 4.6 Correlations for Latin America

	Correlation between 1–4 and 1–10 measures of life satisfaction and happiness	No. of observations
Andean	−0.3371	17,183
Mercosur	−0.4334	11,618
Caribbean	−0.3267	12,182
Latin America	−0.3620	40,983

Note: Andean includes Chile, Colombia, Peru and Venezuela; Mercosur includes Argentina, Brazil and Uruguay; and Mexico and Caribbean includes Mexico, Dominican Republic, El Salvador, Guatemala, and Trinidad and Tobago.

the other poverty groups. In the case of El Salvador, only 13 respondents believed they were in the lowest two deciles of the income distribution.

4.2 Probit regression analysis for Latin America

Variable definitions are shown in Table 4.7. We replicate Table 1.2 for ease of reference. We report the results by independent variable.

4.2.1 Policy variables

Health. State of health is an important explanatory variable in Latin America. All 12 countries had significant coefficients for each of the three configurations of well-being (Table 4.8). Health was by far the most important explanatory variable in lifting well-being in the probit regressions for this region. Furthermore, among the poor health was a powerful force lifting well-being in nearly all countries for the education and income poor. Even where the health outcomes were constrained (see explanation in Chapter 1), there were still a few cases in which health was significant. The strength of this result cannot be overestimated, since it was robust for changes in the form of well-being for the full sample and for the different poverty groups. There were also a few cases in which the size of the poverty coefficient was significantly larger than the coefficient for the full sample (Dominican Republic and Guatemala). This suggests an even greater impact of health on well-being for the poor in these countries.

Income. Income was also a significant force in uplifting well-being in most Latin American countries, although not as significant as health. Depending on the form of the well-being variable, income was a statistically significant variable in raising well-being in eight to 11 countries for the full sample (Table 4.9). For the poor subgroups, income was much less important than health in raising well-being. Income was significant in one to four countries out of 13, depending on the poverty group. There was greater significance for income among the poorly educated than the other two poverty groups.

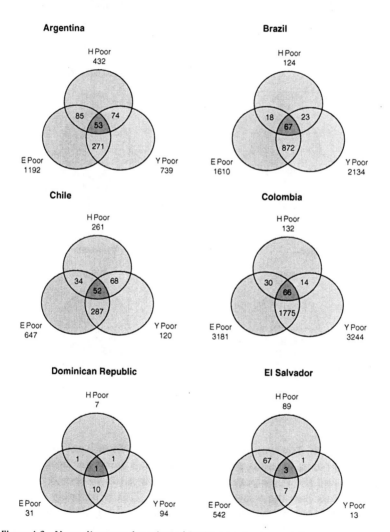

Figure 4.2 Venn diagrams for selected Latin American countries.

Note: H Poor stands for Health Poor, E Poor stands for Education Poor and Y Poor stands for Income Poor.

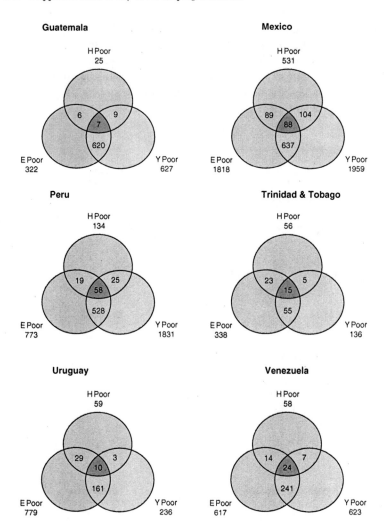

Figure 4.2   Continued

Education. The level of education was not a significant force in raising well-being in Latin America. This result holds for both the full sample and the three poverty groups (Table 4.10). In several cases the coefficients had the wrong a priori signs. This is probably a statistical artifact, but nevertheless a very strange and somehow disappointing outcome. Looking for an explanation for this result, it could be that the already high level of average education and the high cost of

Table 4.7 Definitions of selected World Value Survey indicators

a170 Satisfaction with your life
1: Dissatisfied
10: Satisfied
a008 State of happiness
1: Very happy
2: Quite happy
3: Not happy
4: Not at all happy
a008r
0: not very happy or not at all happy
1: happy or quite happy
State of Health
1: Very good
2: Good
3: Fair
4: Poor
5: Very Poor
1–3: Health Nonpoor
4–5: Health Poor (for Latin American countries)
Income level (country specific) 10th step
1st–2nd income decile: Income Poor
3rd–10th income decile: Income Nonpoor
highest level of education attained
1: Inadequately completed elementary education
2: Completed (compulsory) elementary education
3: Inadequately completed secondary education
4: Completed secondary education (technical, vocational secondary)
5: Inadequately completed secondary, university preparatory education
6: Completed secondary education: university preparatory
7: Some university without degree
8: University with degree/higher
1st–2nd level: Education Poor
3rd–10th levels: Education Nonpoor

Gender
1: Male
2: Female
Age (3 intervals)
1: 15–29
2: 30–49
3: 50 years and above
Marital Status (recoded)
0: Not Married
1: Married or Living Together
Family important in life
1: Very important
2: Rather important
3: Not very important
4: Not at all important
Friends important in life
1: Very important
2: Rather important
3: Not very important
4: Not at all important

Important in Life: Work
1: Very important
2: Rather important
3: Not very important
4: Not at all important
Important in Life: Religion
1: Very important
2: Rather important
3: Not very important
4: Not at all important
Most people can be trusted
1: Most people can be trusted
2: Can't be too careful
Confidence in the Civil Services
1: A great deal
2: Quite a lot
3: Not very much
4: None at all

Table 4.8 Probit results for Latin America – state of health

	a170 (Scale 1–10)				a008 (Scale 1–4)				a008r (Scale 0–1)			
	Overall	Health Poor	Edn Poor	Income Poor	Overall	Health Poor	Edn Poor	Income Poor	Overall	Health Poor	Edn Poor	Income Poor
Argentina	−0.26* (−9.36)	0.08 (0.19)	−0.29* (−6.36)	−0.31* (−5.71)	0.33* (10.90)	0.56 (1.21)	0.32* (6.56)	0.39* (6.63)	−0.29* (−7.39)	−0.35 (−0.96)	−0.25* (−4.15)	−0.30* (−4.27)
Brazil	−0.26* (−11.94)	−0.09 (−0.32)	−0.19* (−5.41)	−0.27* (−9.07)	0.42* (17.63)	0.66* (2.27)	0.35* (9.63)	0.42* (13.21)	−0.38* (−12.34)	−0.25 (−0.89)	−0.33* (−6.69)	−0.38* (−9.49)
Chile	−0.23* (−8.93)	−0.01 (−0.02)	−0.26* (−4.73)	−0.22* (−4.67)	0.39* (13.28)	−0.46 (−0.88)	0.38* (6.12)	0.46* (8.53)	−0.37* (−9.89)	0.08 (0.28)	−0.42* (−5.57)	−0.42* (−6.64)
Colombia	−0.36* (−12.38)	−0.40 (−1.01)	−0.45* (−8.05)		0.39* (12.47)	1.82* (3.64)	0.38* (6.74)		−0.40* (−9.69)	−1.24* (−2.17)	−0.44* (−5.88)	−0.47* (−5.37)
Dominican Republic	−0.41* (−4.71)			−0.46* (−2.51)	0.50* (5.20)			0.91* (4.05)	−0.55* (−4.50)			−0.88* (−2.88)
El Salvador	−0.31* (−7.27)	0.77 (1.60)	−0.32* (−5.47)		0.44* (8.98)		0.39* (5.85)		−0.36* (−4.78)	−0.45 (−0.97)	−0.35* (−3.53)	
Guatemala	−0.35* (−7.48)		−0.46* (−5.19)	−0.39* (−6.72)	0.51* (9.88)		0.76* (7.47)	0.53* (8.28)	−0.59* (−8.73)		−0.74* (−5.84)	−0.52* (−6.58)
Mexico	−0.24* (−11.85)	−0.35 (−1.73)	−0.16* (−4.47)	−0.25* (−6.84)	0.57* (24.44)	1.17* (4.87)	0.53* (12.68)	0.56* (13.64)	−0.55* (−17.61)	0.05 (0.28)	−0.52* (−9.47)	−0.48* (−9.52)
Peru	−0.24* (−9.55)	0.93 (0.82)	−0.29* (−4.63)	−0.25* (−6.64)	0.42* (14.87)	1.40 (1.12)	0.48* (6.96)	0.41* (9.96)	−0.39* (−11.87)		−0.38* (−4.94)	−0.35* (−7.53)

Trinidad and Tobago	−0.35* (−8.31)		−0.33* (−4.67)	−0.37* (−3.66)	0.47* (9.94)		0.40* (5.12)	0.51* (4.55)	−0.38* (−6.14)	−0.92 (−1.08)	−0.19* (−2.06)	−0.36* (−2.58)
Uruguay	−0.34* (−9.11)	1.05* (2.02)	−0.30* (−5.40)	−0.40* (−4.11)	0.44* (10.70)	1.27* (2.35)	0.45* (7.54)	0.32* (3.17)	−0.32* (−6.17)	−0.50 (−0.80)	−0.39* (−5.19)	−0.24* (−2.01)
Venezuela	−0.18* (−4.40)	−1.37 (−1.74)	−0.11 (−1.48)	−0.15* (−2.30)	0.43* (9.32)	1.88* (2.46)	0.33* (4.10)	0.39* (5.16)	−0.31* (−4.20)		−0.41* (−3.23)	−0.21 (−1.91)

Notes: 1. Based on probit results for extended model where z stats are displayed in parenthesis and * denotes statistical significance at the 5% level. For 1–10 and 0–1 definitions of well-being, a negative sign indicates healthier people are happier. For the 1–4 definition of well-being, a positive sign indicates healthier people are happier.
2. Variable dropped due to multicollinearity.

Table 4.9 Probit results for Latin America – income level

	a170 (Scale 1–10)				a008 (Scale 1–4)				a008r (Scale 0–1)			
	Overall	Health Poor	Edn Poor	Income Poor	Overall	Health Poor	Edn Poor	Income Poor	Overall	Health Poor	Edn Poor	Income Poor
Argentina	0.03* (3.34)	0.03 (0.86)	0.01 (0.74)	0.11 (1.09)	-0.02 (-1.48)	0.03 (0.87)	0.02 (1.20)	0.07 (0.63)	0.05* (3.88)	-0.01 (-0.25)	0.00 (0.09)	0.17 (1.34)
Brazil	0.01 (1.51)	0.18* (2.33)	0.02 (1.48)	-0.06 (-1.22)	-0.08* (-8.78)	-0.18* (-2.35)	-0.08* (-5.15)	-0.02 (-0.38)	0.10* (7.87)	0.19* (2.08)	0.14* (5.80)	0.16* (2.37)
Chile	0.07* (7.36)	0.06 (1.24)	0.02 (1.03)	0.01 (0.11)	-0.06* (-5.51)	-0.09 (-1.73)	-0.03 (-1.14)	0.06 (0.68)	0.10* (7.22)	0.08 (1.45)	0.02 (0.65)	0.06 (0.57)
Colombia	0.03* (2.41)	0.13 (1.15)	0.05 (1.45)		0.00 (-0.28)	-0.40* (-2.82)	-0.04 (-1.03)		0.07* (3.66)	0.70* (3.02)	0.08 (1.80)	1.62* (4.38)
Dominican Republic	0.05* (2.01)			-0.03 (-0.11)	-0.01 (-0.42)			-0.18 (-0.62)	0.04 (1.15)			0.26 (0.72)
El Salvador	0.14* (4.43)	0.07 (0.68)	0.09 (1.74)		-0.11* (-3.21)		-0.03 (-0.61)		0.11* (2.07)	-0.24 (-1.55)	0.04 (0.50)	
Guatemala	0.05 (1.77)		0.20* (2.91)	0.25 (2.83)	-0.07* (-2.09)		0.05 (0.72)	-0.09 (-0.94)	0.12* (2.59)		0.09 (0.99)	0.23 (1.91)
Mexico	0.05* (7.61)	0.10* (3.01)	0.06* (4.25)	-0.09 (-1.37)	-0.07* (-8.82)	-0.06 (-1.77)	-0.07* (-4.32)	-0.02 (-0.33)	0.12* (10.16)	0.07 (1.75)	0.08* (3.89)	0.23* (2.78)

Peru	0.06* (5.29)	0.18 (1.98)	0.04 (0.90)	0.08 (1.47)	−0.04* (−3.03)	−0.17 (−1.77)	−0.05 (−1.00)	−0.02 (−0.30)	0.09* (5.99)		0.11* (2.10)	0.12 (1.88)
Trinidad and Tobago	0.05* (2.85)		0.03 (1.18)	−0.27 (−1.36)	−0.05* (−2.40)		−0.03 (−1.03)	0.08 (0.36)	0.08* (2.81)	0.04 (0.35)	0.03 (0.77)	−0.10 (−0.36)
Uruguay	0.06* (4.29)	0.00 (0.00)	0.08* (3.35)	−0.31 (−1.85)	−0.03* (−2.32)	0.21 (1.92)	−0.08* (−3.16)	0.35 (1.99)	0.08* (3.76)	−0.24 (−1.59)	0.11* (3.03)	0.05 (0.23)
Venezuela	0.07* (3.13)	0.19 (1.53)	0.01 (0.25)	0.46* (2.94)	−0.02 (−0.74)	−0.16 (−1.18)	0.00 (−0.07)	−0.22 (−1.26)	0.11* (2.29)		0.03 (0.37)	0.39 (1.64)

Notes: 1. Based on probit results for extended model where z stats are displayed in parenthesis and * denotes statistical significance at the 5% level. For 1–10 and 0–1 definitions of well-being, a positive sign indicates that higher income results in higher well-being. For the 1–4 definition of well-being, a negative sign indicates higher income results in higher well-being.

2. Variable dropped due to multicollinearity.

Table 4.10 Probit results for Latin America – education level

	a170 (Scale 1–10)				a008 (Scale 1–4)				a008r (Scale 0–1)			
	Overall	Health Poor	Edn Poor	Income Poor	Overall	Health Poor	Edn Poor	Income Poor	Overall	Health Poor	Edn Poor	Income Poor
Argentina	-0.03	0.08	0.10	0.00	-0.02	-0.15*	-0.10	-0.02	0.07*	0.16*	0.21	0.07
	(-1.82)	(1.48)	(1.05)	(0.03)	(-1.58)	(-2.48)	(-1.02)	(-0.53)	(3.30)	(2.01)	(1.78)	(1.51)
Brazil	-0.05*	-0.14*	-0.10	-0.04*	0.03*	-0.06	0.12*	0.02	0.02	0.08	-0.04	0.03
	(-6.40)	(-2.16)	(-1.68)	(-2.49)	(3.37)	(-0.87)	(2.03)	(1.20)	(1.86)	(0.90)	(-0.50)	(1.63)
Chile	0.01	-0.02	-0.06	-0.02	0.00	0.05	0.04	0.02	0.05*	-0.02	-0.02	0.01
	(1.21)	(-0.41)	(-0.63)	(-0.91)	(-0.05)	(0.93)	(0.38)	(0.69)	(3.01)	(-0.41)	(-0.16)	(0.42)
Colombia	-0.05*	0.09	-0.01	0.00	0.00	0.00	-0.25*		0.05*	0.07	0.41*	0.02
	(-4.41)	(1.05)	(-0.08)	(0.15)	(0.15)	(-0.03)	(-2.78)		(3.13)	(0.47)	(3.49)	(0.65)
Dominican Republic	-0.02			0.02	-0.05			-0.10	0.15*			0.15
	(-0.41)			(0.29)	(-1.25)			(-1.45)	(3.03)			(1.55)
El Salvador	-0.06*	0.02	-0.04		0.03		-0.08		0.03	0.14	0.03	
	(-2.93)	(0.24)	(-0.37)		(1.28)		(-0.59)		(0.75)	(0.89)	(0.17)	
Guatemala	-0.03		-0.03	-0.02	-0.02		-0.13	-0.01	0.05*		0.02	0.05
	(-1.58)		(-0.19)	(-0.87)	(-0.91)		(-0.92)	(-0.31)	(2.04)		(0.12)	(1.69)
Mexico	-0.03*	-0.03	-0.07	-0.03	0.03*	-0.01	0.02	0.01	-0.01	0.00	0.17	0.02
	(-3.88)	(-1.06)	(-1.13)	(-1.51)	(3.02)	(-0.35)	(0.31)	(0.69)	(-0.43)	(-0.04)	(1.98)	(0.63)

Peru	-0.02	0.04	0.13	-0.04*	-0.01	-0.08	0.03	0.00	0.04*		-0.01	0.03
	(-1.62)	(0.63)	(1.54)	(-2.83)	(-1.33)	(-1.15)	(0.27)	(0.18)	(3.71)		(-0.07)	(1.66)
Trinidad and Tobago	-0.03		-0.08	-0.11	0.04		0.09	0.16*	0.04	-0.19	0.14	-0.16
	(-1.59)		(-0.53)	(-1.59)	(1.77)		(0.53)	(2.04)	(1.26)	(-1.17)	(0.65)	(-1.67)
Uruguay	-0.03	-0.07	-0.12	-0.09	0.03	-0.20	0.16	0.04	0.00	0.23	0.01	0.02
	(-1.98)	(-0.63)	(-1.34)	(-1.45)	(1.61)	(-1.61)	(1.64)	(0.56)	(0.19)	(1.49)	(0.04)	(0.31)
Venezuela	-0.01	0.12	0.04	-0.02	0.00	0.02	0.09	0.05	0.05		-0.20	0.01
	(-0.31)	(1.21)	(0.32)	(-0.49)	(0.25)	(0.20)	(0.58)	(1.25)	(1.56)		(-0.84)	(0.17)

Notes: 1. Based on probit results for extended model where z stats are displayed in parenthesis and * denotes statistical significance at the 5% level. For 1–10 and 0–1 definitions of well-being, a positive sign indicates that education results in higher well-being. For the 1–4 definition of well-being, a negative sign indicates education results in higher well-being.
2. Variable dropped due to multicollinearity.

additional education, as well as a high level of youth unemployment, could militate against the education variable having an uplifting impact on well-being. Other studies have also found a weak relationship between well-being and education, and Layard (2005) does not even consider it as an important explanatory variable, since it is closely related to income.

Difference between poverty and full sample coefficients for Latin America

This is very strong evidence, not only that well-being of the income and health poverty groups in Latin America could be uplifted by the provision of health and income services, but also that this response results in a significantly stronger response among the poor groups than it does for the full sample. See Table 4.11 for the analysis of significant differences between poverty group coefficients and the full sample coefficients, which were carried out for the 1–10 scale definition of well-being and yielded a few significant results for Venezuela and Uruguay. When the exercise was extended to the other two scales of well-being there were a few additional results, and these are added to the table, with asterisks showing the scale if it is different from 1 to 10. The probit regression coefficients for health and income for these two poverty groups are significantly larger than the coefficients for the full sample in several countries, notably Colombia, Mexico, Uruguay and Venezuela. This finding provides yet more evidence of the importance of delivering additional health services and more opportunities for boosting income for the poor.

4.2.2   Sociological and demographic variables

Gender.   There are only a few instances in which the evidence supports the hypothesis that gender affects happiness (Table 4.12). In Brazil, there is evidence that women are happier for the full sample and also for the education poor. In Mexico and Trinidad and Tobago, there is evidence that men are happier for the full sample. In the rest of Latin America, there are only a couple of significant coefficients for any country, either for the full sample or for the three poor subgroups. We draw the conclusion that gender does not have a significant impact on well-being in Latin America.

Age.   The relationship between age and well-being has been explored extensively for Asia and Africa, and also by other researchers for different countries and groups of countries (see Chapters 1, 2 and 3 and the work of Easterlin). See Tables 4.13 and 4.14. For Latin America there

Table 4.11 Significant differences between poverty coefficients and full sample coefficients in 13 Latin American countries for probit analysis of determinants of well-being – scale of 1 to 10 for well-being

	Significant income poverty coefficient	Significant education poverty coefficient	Significant health poverty coefficient
Income poor sample	Venezuela		
Education poor sample	Uruguay*		
Health poor sample	Colombia**, Dominican Republic*		Uruguay, Venezuela, Colombia**, Mexico*, Uruguay*, Venezuela*

*1 to 4 scale
**0 to 1 scale

is a good deal of support for a nonlinear relationship between well-being and age for the 1 to 10 scale (six countries) and the 0 to 1 scale (nine countries) of well-being. The midlife crisis point is displayed in Table 4.15. The evidence is stronger than for either of the other regions. Only two or three countries in Africa and Asia for the full sample, and also a few for the poor groups in Asia (but not Africa), had a nonlinear relationship between age and well-being. In Latin America, six countries had a nonlinear relationship between age and well-being. However, the inflection points were also at a very young age. In only three cases was the inflection point over 30. Most were in the late 20s.

Marital status. Married couples are often happier in Latin America than those who are not married, divorced or widowed. For the full sample, marriage raised well-being in more than half the countries for all three definitions of well-being. The results for the poor are less compelling. The married poor are happier in only a few cases for the 1 to 10 configuration of well-being for the three poverty groups. However, for the other two measures of well-being, marriage among the income poor is significant in about half the countries, but less significant for the education and health poor. In any event, marriage doesn't seem to have a large impact on well-being, certainly not as much as health or income (Table 4.16).

Table 4.12 Probit results for Latin America – gender

	a170 (Scale 1–10)				a008 (Scale 1–4)				a008r (Scale 0–1)			
	Overall	Health Poor	Edn Poor	Income Poor	Overall	Health Poor	Edn Poor	Income Poor	Overall	Health Poor	Edn Poor	Income Poor
Argentina	0.06 *(1.18)*	-0.03 *(-0.16)*	0.03 *(0.38)*	0.12 *(1.15)*	-0.04 *(-0.70)*	0.11 *(0.54)*	-0.01 *(-0.15)*	-0.15 *(-1.38)*	0.19* *(2.71)*	0.10 *(0.40)*	0.13 *(1.16)*	0.15 *(1.09)*
Brazil	-0.11* *(-3.31)*	-0.45* *(-2.01)*	-0.14* *(-2.51)*	-0.16* *(-3.30)*	0.06 *(1.62)*	0.33 *(1.44)*	0.14* *(2.39)*	0.09 *(1.74)*	-0.03 *(-0.74)*	-0.50 *(-1.82)*	-0.22* *(-2.76)*	-0.10 *(-1.61)*
Chile	0.02 *(0.50)*	0.16 *(0.86)*	0.07 *(0.78)*	-0.01 *(-0.11)*	-0.07 *(-1.66)*	-0.06 *(-0.31)*	-0.11 *(-1.12)*	-0.08 *(-1.01)*	0.10 *(1.83)*	-0.03 *(-0.13)*	0.16 *(1.36)*	0.18 *(1.82)*
Colombia	0.03 *(0.80)*	0.22 *(0.71)*	0.00 *(0.03)*		-0.06 *(-1.41)*	0.08 *(0.21)*	0.09 *(1.04)*		0.05 *(0.90)*	-0.08 *(-0.16)*	-0.22 *(-1.87)*	-0.19 *(-1.49)*
Dominican Republic	0.14 *(1.07)*			0.38 *(1.40)*	-0.12 *(-0.86)*			0.32 *(1.02)*	0.03 *(0.15)*			-0.07 *(-0.18)*
El Salvador	-0.04 *(-0.53)*	-0.05 *(-0.16)*	-0.02 *(-0.21)*		-0.03 *(-0.40)*		-0.16 *(-1.31)*		0.24 *(1.91)*	0.17 *(0.47)*	0.26 *(1.47)*	
Guatemala	-0.06 *(-0.89)*		-0.04 *(-0.31)*	0.02 *(0.22)*	0.07 *(0.84)*		0.08 *(0.55)*	0.13 *(1.33)*	-0.12 *(-1.24)*		0.06 *(0.37)*	-0.12 *(-0.98)*
Mexico	0.08* *(2.44)*	-0.02 *(-0.12)*	0.07 *(1.16)*	0.02 *(0.28)*	0.01 *(0.31)*	0.15 *(1.01)*	0.07 *(1.12)*	0.07 *(1.10)*	0.15* *(3.12)*	-0.20 *(-1.11)*	0.12 *(1.45)*	0.08 *(0.94)*

Peru	−0.02	−0.12	−0.12	−0.04	−0.01	−0.19	0.16	0.06	0.12*		−0.04	0.02
	(−0.56)	(−0.47)	(−1.33)	(−0.85)	(−0.30)	(−0.69)	(1.67)	(1.14)	(2.65)		(−0.33)	(0.30)
Trinidad and Tobago	−0.02		−0.25	−0.22	−0.28*		−0.27	−0.51*	0.31*	0.45	0.32	0.26
	(−0.31)		(−1.96)	(−1.11)	(−3.57)		(−1.85)	(−2.38)	(2.85)	(1.00)	(1.68)	(1.00)
Uruguay	0.00	0.22	−0.01	0.01	0.06	0.20	0.09	0.07	−0.04	−1.21*	−0.12	−0.02
	(0.04)	(0.50)	(−0.13)	(0.07)	(0.99)	(0.46)	(0.92)	(0.42)	(−0.50)	(−2.07)	(−0.99)	(−0.11)
Venezuela	0.06	0.26	0.05	0.05	−0.02	0.60	−0.07	−0.16	−0.02		0.07	0.27
	(0.92)	(0.71)	(0.37)	(0.40)	(−0.22)	(1.57)	(−0.46)	(−1.22)	(−0.19)		(0.30)	(1.36)

Notes: 1. Based on probit results for extended model where z stats are displayed in parenthesis and * denotes statistical significance at the 5% level. For 1–10 and 0–1 definitions, a positive sign indicates that women are happier. For 1–4 definition, a negative sign indicates women are happier.
2. Variable dropped due to multicollinearity.

Table 4.13 Probit results for Latin America – age

	a170 (Scale 1–10)				a008 (Scale 1–4)				a008r (Scale 0–1)			
	Overall	Health Poor	Edn Poor	Income Poor	Overall	Health Poor	Edn Poor	Income Poor	Overall	Health Poor	Edn Poor	Income Poor
Argentina	-0.58* (-2.80)	0.95 (1.00)	-0.73 (-1.74)	-0.47 (-1.03)	0.80* (3.53)	-0.22 (-0.21)	0.41 (0.92)	0.65 (1.32)	0.58* (2.45)	0.61 (0.55)	0.92* (2.31)	0.42 (0.92)
Brazil	-0.30* (-2.22)	0.67 (0.60)	-0.09 (-0.38)	-0.41* (-2.13)	0.33* (2.23)	-1.07 (-0.93)	0.38 (1.48)	0.12 (0.60)	0.56* (3.31)	2.04 (1.55)	0.84* (2.95)	0.41 (1.80)
Chile	-0.39* (-2.33)	-0.75 (-0.71)	0.53 (1.02)	-0.16 (-0.52)	0.67* (3.67)	-0.42 (-0.36)	0.26 (0.46)	0.71* (2.08)	0.61* (3.09)	0.09 (0.07)	1.33* (3.07)	0.70* (2.08)
Colombia	0.17 (0.99)	1.43 (1.02)	-0.14 (-0.38)		0.32 (1.80)	1.61 (0.98)	0.29 (0.75)		0.84* (4.14)	0.32 (0.17)	0.92* (2.29)	-0.06 (-0.11)
Dominican Republic	-0.29 (-0.40)			-0.62 (-0.42)	0.23 (0.30)			-0.45 (-0.29)	0.92 (1.14)			2.00 (1.10)
El Salvador	-0.55 (-1.94)	-0.59 (-0.40)	0.03 (0.07)		0.21 (0.64)		0.08 (0.16)		2.10* (4.43)	3.92* (2.19)	2.08* (3.22)	
Guatemala	0.20 (0.62)		0.66 (1.25)	0.19 (0.49)	0.26 (0.75)		0.26 (0.45)	0.52 (1.27)	0.84* (2.25)		0.82 (1.37)	0.58 (1.37)
Mexico	-0.52* (-3.77)	0.03 (0.05)	-0.65* (-2.31)	-0.32 (-1.24)	-0.18 (-1.16)	-0.10 (-0.16)	0.29 (0.95)	-0.24 (-0.87)	1.26* (7.60)	0.43 (0.66)	1.34* (4.55)	1.47* (5.08)

Peru	-0.52*	-0.63	-0.52	-0.44*	0.18	1.50	0.84	0.18	0.53*		0.71	0.57*
	(-3.53)	(-0.62)	(-1.28)	(-2.05)	(1.15)	(1.39)	(1.87)	(0.76)	(3.20)		(1.78)	(2.45)
Trinidad and Tobago	-0.25		-0.47	-0.11	0.45		0.42	0.05	0.26	3.30	0.99	1.76
	(-0.84)		(-0.69)	(-0.13)	(1.31)		(0.55)	(0.05)	(0.60)	(1.22)	(1.22)	(1.60)
Uruguay	-0.57*	-8.32*	-0.14	-2.17*	0.37	-0.86	0.68	2.29*	1.32*	7.69*	1.20*	0.17
	(-2.44)	(-2.03)	(-0.28)	(-3.07)	(1.47)	(-0.23)	(1.28)	(3.02)	(4.99)	(2.29)	(2.74)	(0.27)
Venezuela	0.05	-0.13	-0.20	-0.41	0.24	1.10	0.17	0.64	1.24*		1.65	0.82
	(0.19)	(-0.09)	(-0.31)	(-0.91)	(0.75)	(0.69)	(0.24)	(1.23)	(2.70)		(1.82)	(1.24)

Notes: 1. Based on probit results for extended model where z stats are displayed in parenthesis and * denotes statistical significance at the 5% level. For 1–10 and 0–1 definitions, a positive sign indicates that older people are happier and vice versa. For 1–4 definition, a negative sign indicates older people are happier.
2. Variable dropped due to multicollinearity.

Table 4.14 Probit results for Latin America – age squared

	a170 (Scale 1–10)				a008 (Scale 1–4)				a008r (Scale 0–1)			
	Overall	Health Poor	Edn Poor	Income Poor	Overall	Health Poor	Edn Poor	Income Poor	Overall	Health Poor	Edn Poor	Income Poor
Argentina	0.13* (2.55)	-0.19 (-0.83)	0.18 (1.81)	0.14 (1.25)	-0.17* (-3.05)	-0.01 (-0.05)	-0.09 (-0.90)	-0.17 (-1.47)	-0.14* (-2.40)	-0.05 (-0.20)	-0.21* (-2.11)	-0.07 (-0.59)
Brazil	0.11* (3.19)	-0.03 (-0.13)	0.06 (1.03)	0.15* (2.98)	-0.11* (-2.90)	0.17 (0.62)	-0.11 (-1.85)	-0.06 (-1.25)	-0.09* (-2.00)	-0.37 (-1.22)	-0.14* (-2.04)	-0.04 (-0.72)
Chile	0.10* (2.50)	0.19 (0.75)	-0.11 (-0.95)	0.04 (0.51)	-0.15* (-3.42)	0.16 (0.58)	-0.06 (-0.48)	-0.18* (-2.12)	-0.15* (-2.99)	-0.08 (-0.27)	-0.29* (-2.81)	-0.13 (-1.58)
Colombia	-0.03 (-0.76)	-0.28 (-0.86)	0.03 (0.34)		-0.07 (-1.49)	-0.16 (-0.43)	-0.08 (-0.85)		-0.19* (-3.58)	-0.14 (-0.29)	-0.17 (-1.74)	0.02 (0.15)
Dominican Republic	0.08 (0.38)			0.14 (0.31)	-0.06 (-0.29)			0.15 (0.33)	-0.23 (-0.94)			-0.58 (-1.05)
El Salvador	0.15* (2.07)	0.20 (0.60)	0.01 (0.10)		-0.04 (-0.51)		-0.03 (-0.25)		-0.53* (-4.42)	-0.93* (-2.31)	-0.48* (-2.99)	
Guatemala	-0.03 (-0.36)		-0.13 (-0.99)	-0.02 (-0.23)	-0.05 (-0.57)		-0.06 (-0.42)	-0.12 (-1.14)	-0.18 (-1.86)		-0.17 (-1.15)	-0.13 (-1.10)
Mexico	0.15* (4.31)	0.05 (0.33)	0.18* (2.65)	0.10 (1.57)	0.04 (1.02)	0.03 (0.21)	-0.04 (-0.62)	0.06 (0.92)	-0.30* (-6.88)	-0.09 (-0.56)	-0.32* (-4.29)	-0.35* (-4.63)

Peru	0.14* (3.81)	0.16 (0.65)	0.14 (1.49)	0.11* (2.03)	-0.02 (-0.56)	-0.32 (-1.27)	-0.14 (-1.38)	0.00 (-0.03)	-0.14* (-3.38)		-0.17 (-1.80)	-0.17* (-2.79)
Trinidad and Tobago	0.08 (1.01)		0.14 (0.86)	0.03 (0.16)	-0.11 (-1.35)		-0.12 (-0.67)	-0.03 (-0.15)	-0.06 (-0.52)	-0.80 (-1.24)	-0.19 (-0.98)	-0.42 (-1.57)
Uruguay	0.15* (2.70)	1.88* (2.07)	0.08 (0.74)	0.55* (3.25)	-0.07 (-1.13)	0.27 (0.33)	-0.13 (-1.07)	-0.51* (-2.84)	-0.34* (-5.19)	-1.82* (-2.30)	-0.28* (-2.59)	-0.03 (-0.17)
Venezuela	-0.01 (-0.18)	0.13 (0.36)	0.03 (0.22)	0.08 (0.68)	-0.05 (-0.68)	-0.26 (-0.69)	-0.02 (-0.11)	-0.15 (-1.11)	-0.28* (-2.39)		-0.35 (-1.61)	-0.18 (-1.03)

Notes: 1. Based on probit results for extended model where z stats are displayed in parenthesis and * denotes statistical significance at the 5% level.
2. Variable dropped due to multicollinearity.

Table 4.15   Effect of age on life satisfaction and well-being in Latin America

Country	a170 (Scale 1–10)			
	Overall	Health Poor	Edn Poor	Income Poor
Argentina	2.23			
Brazil	1.36			1.36
Chile	1.95			
Mexico	1.73		1.81	
Peru	1.86			2.00
Uruguay	1.90	2.21		1.97

Notes: 1. Age is defined as 1: 15–29, 2: 30–49 and 3: 50 years and above.
2. Data are shown only for available cases. The age at which the minimum occurs is given by the coefficient of linear age divided by twice the coefficient of age squared.

Family. Unexpectedly, family is of limited impact for most countries in Latin America, for both the full sample and the three poverty groups (see Table 4.17). For the overall sample, family was a significant variable in lifting well-being in nine out of 39 possible cases for the full sample and six out of 97 cases for the three poverty groups. These results are not dissimilar to the results for the other two regions. This is a very interesting and informative result, given the strong evidence from more aggregative studies of industrial countries reviewed in Chapter 1. It could be that aggregation over subregions or the region as a whole will confirm these more aggregative studies. However, that does not nullify the sample results from country probit analysis. More research needs to be undertaken to determine whether more aggregative studies are covering up more fundamental factors that have been discovered at the country level.

Friends. Friends are important in uplifting well-being about 40 percent of the time for the full sample in Latin America (Table 4.18). The impact is greater in the larger countries where there is a more substantial sample, particularly in Mexico and Brazil but also in Colombia, El Salvador and Peru. For the poor groups, the impact of friends is more muted, although friends are important in lifting well-being for the education and income poor in a few countries.

Table 4.16 Probit results for Latin America – marital status

	a170 (Scale 1–10)				a008 (Scale 1–4)				a008r (Scale 0–1)			
	Overall	Health Poor	Edn Poor	Income Poor	Overall	Health Poor	Edn Poor	Income Poor	Overall	Health Poor	Edn Poor	Income Poor
Argentina	0.22* (4.28)	0.35 (1.83)	0.04 (0.47)	0.02 (0.16)	−0.34* (−6.01)	−0.62* (−3.02)	−0.26* (−2.79)	−0.33* (−2.91)	0.37* (4.99)	0.42 (1.71)	0.18 (1.54)	0.22 (1.58)
Brazil	0.16* (4.62)	−0.44 (−1.87)	0.15* (2.53)	0.16* (3.29)	−0.20* (−5.25)	0.44 (1.81)	−0.16* (−2.55)	−0.24* (−4.55)	0.23* (4.55)	−0.18 (−0.63)	0.22* (2.65)	0.25* (3.75)
Chile	0.14* (3.20)	−0.05 (−0.26)	0.18 (1.89)	0.11 (1.36)	−0.24* (−5.04)	0.09 (0.45)	−0.10 (−0.98)	−0.17* (−2.05)	0.32* (5.13)	0.00 (−0.02)	0.20 (1.71)	0.27* (2.72)
Colombia	0.16* (3.55)	0.14 (0.42)	0.08 (0.81)		−0.17* (−3.56)	−1.03* (−2.57)	−0.19 (−1.87)		0.35* (5.44)	1.37* (2.46)	0.34* (2.68)	0.55* (4.17)
Dominican Republic	0.03 (0.25)			0.07 (0.24)	−0.02 (−0.11)			−0.41 (−1.24)	0.27 (1.34)			0.94* (2.21)
El Salvador	0.10 (1.43)	−0.06 (−0.19)	0.08 (0.70)		−0.22* (−2.67)		−0.36* (−2.79)		0.09 (0.70)	−0.20 (−0.47)	0.42* (2.30)	
Guatemala	0.01 (0.14)		−0.30 (−1.92)	−0.02 (−0.26)	−0.16 (−1.89)		−0.26 (−1.54)	−0.18 (−1.76)	0.23* (2.07)		0.35 (1.77)	0.24 (1.82)
Mexico	0.13* (3.75)	0.26 (1.87)	0.12 (1.66)	0.07 (1.07)	−0.10* (−2.47)	−0.14 (−0.99)	−0.26* (−3.42)	−0.21* (−2.86)	0.04 (0.71)	0.19 (1.10)	0.21* (2.11)	0.34* (3.82)

(Continued)

Table 4.16 Continued

	a170 (Scale 1–10)				a008 (Scale 1–4)				a008r (Scale 0–1)			
	Overall	Health Poor	Edn Poor	Income Poor	Overall	Health Poor	Edn Poor	Income Poor	Overall	Health Poor	Edn Poor	Income Poor
Peru	0.09* (2.38)	0.57* (2.30)	0.12 (1.12)	0.13* (2.24)	−0.19* (−4.31)	−0.47 (−1.79)	−0.26* (−2.36)	−0.23* (−3.71)	0.15* (2.93)		0.15 (1.17)	0.22* (3.06)
Trinidad and Tobago	0.28* (3.90)		0.14 (1.15)	0.56* (2.80)	−0.27* (−3.42)		−0.27 (−1.91)	−0.60* (−2.68)	0.17 (1.51)	−0.54 (−1.24)	0.20 (1.07)	0.44 (1.58)
Uruguay	0.20* (3.69)	0.46 (1.12)	0.23* (2.74)	0.31* (2.05)	−0.29* (−4.89)	0.18 (0.43)	−0.31* (−3.36)	−0.49* (−3.01)	0.36* (4.61)	0.06 (0.11)	0.43* (3.64)	0.48* (2.41)
Venezuela	0.11 (1.60)	−0.25 (−0.66)	0.23 (1.66)	0.03 (0.24)	−0.15 (−1.79)	0.73 (1.81)	−0.09 (−0.61)	−0.11 (−0.80)	0.06 (0.46)		−0.08 (−0.30)	0.10 (0.50)

Notes: 1. Based on probit results for extended model where z stats are displayed in parenthesis and * denotes statistical significance at the 5% level. For the 1–10 and 0–1 definitions of well-being, a positive sign indicates that married or living together couples are happier and vice versa. For 1–4 well-being, a negative sign denotes the positive effects of marriage/living together.
2. Variable dropped due to multicollinearity.

Table 4.17 Probit results for Latin America – importance of family

	a170 (Scale 1–10)				a008 (Scale 1–4)				a008r (Scale 0–1)			
	Overall	Health Poor	Edn Poor	Income Poor	Overall	Health Poor	Edn Poor	Income Poor	Overall	Health Poor	Edn Poor	Income Poor
Argentina	−0.13* (−2.06)	0.04 (0.16)	−0.06 (−0.58)	0.09 (0.84)	0.24* (3.59)	0.21 (0.83)	0.18 (1.62)	0.12 (1.04)	−0.13 (−1.57)	0.08 (0.23)	0.04 (0.28)	0.04 (0.29)
Brazil	−0.19* (−3.81)	−0.29 (−1.23)	−0.20* (−2.73)	−0.16* (−2.33)	0.25* (4.65)	0.46 (1.74)	0.18* (2.40)	0.29* (3.88)	−0.14* (−2.04)	−0.20 (−0.66)	0.03 (0.25)	−0.17 (−1.94)
Chile	−0.07 (−1.08)	−0.13 (−0.69)	0.09 (0.73)	0.00 (0.00)	0.30* (4.54)	0.14 (0.67)	0.38* (2.96)	0.24* (2.32)	−0.01 (−0.12)	0.15 (0.62)	−0.05 (−0.31)	0.13 (1.03)
Colombia	−0.07 (−1.33)	0.12 (0.30)	0.00 (0.04)		0.04 (0.66)	−0.44 (−0.93)	0.03 (0.30)		0.11 (1.44)	1.61* (2.12)	0.02 (0.17)	0.03 (0.25)
Dominican Republic	0.18 (0.87)			0.51 (1.35)	−0.04 (−0.19)			0.13 (0.31)	0.16 (0.56)			0.53 (1.03)
El Salvador	−0.08 (−0.53)	−0.18 (−0.70)	−0.31 (−1.66)		0.28 (1.76)		0.31 (1.67)		−0.21 (−1.03)	−0.71* (−2.13)	−0.38 (−1.63)	
Guatemala	0.30 (1.24)		−0.21 (−0.57)	0.32 (1.14)	0.15 (0.66)		0.35 (1.06)	0.15 (0.60)	0.35 (1.10)		0.24 (0.49)	0.26 (0.73)
Mexico	−0.09* (−2.32)	0.05 (0.48)	−0.13 (−1.86)	−0.10 (−1.66)	0.33* (7.95)	0.08 (0.66)	0.28* (3.90)	0.39* (5.93)	−0.33* (−6.64)	−0.35* (−2.23)	−0.22* (−2.56)	−0.33* (−4.24)
Peru	−0.03 (−0.66)	0.00 (0.01)	0.05 (0.46)	−0.05 (−0.92)	0.09* (2.04)	0.22 (0.81)	−0.04 (−0.39)	0.12 (1.96)	−0.04 (−0.71)		0.25* (2.00)	−0.01 (−0.21)

(Continued)

Table 4.17 Continued

	a170 (Scale 1–10)				a008 (Scale 1–4)				a008r (Scale 0–1)			
	Overall	Health Poor	Edn Poor	Income Poor	Overall	Health Poor	Edn Poor	Income Poor	Overall	Health Poor	Edn Poor	Income Poor
Trinidad and Tobago	0.00 (0.00)		0.17 (0.85)	0.02 (0.06)	0.28* (2.34)		0.32 (1.59)	0.31 (1.14)	-0.31* (-2.09)	0.12 (0.27)	-0.38 (-1.53)	-0.68 (-1.52)
Uruguay	-0.12 (-1.57)	0.06 (0.12)	-0.05 (-0.46)	0.01 (0.04)	0.15 (1.85)	0.15 (0.29)	0.10 (0.89)	0.03 (0.20)	0.00 (0.05)	0.03 (0.05)	-0.07 (-0.49)	0.03 (0.15)
Venezuela	-0.13 (-0.76)		-0.55 (-0.53)	-0.06 (-0.24)	0.05 (0.26)		0.70 (0.63)	-0.06 (-0.21)	0.25 (0.92)			-0.09 (-0.26)

Notes: 1. Based on probit results for extended model where z stats are displayed in parenthesis and * denotes statistical significance at the 5% level. For 1–10 and 0–1 definitions, a negative sign indicates that people who value family are happier. For 1–4 definition, a positive sign indicates people who value family are happier.

2. Variable dropped due to multicollinearity.

Table 4.18 Probit results for Latin America – importance of friends

	a170 (Scale 1–10)				a008 (Scale 1–4)				a008r (Scale 0–1)			
	Overall	Health Poor	Edn Poor	Income Poor	Overall	Health Poor	Edn Poor	Income Poor	Overall	Health Poor	Edn Poor	Income Poor
Argentina	0.02 (0.55)	−0.17 (−1.56)	−0.08 (−1.76)	−0.04 (−0.60)	0.02 (0.61)	0.13 (1.16)	0.07 (1.51)	0.06 (0.94)	−0.04 (−0.92)	−0.16 (−1.16)	−0.03 (−0.45)	−0.01 (−0.17)
Brazil	−0.07* (−3.03)	−0.09 (−0.67)	−0.08* (−2.14)	−0.08* (−2.33)	0.05 (1.99)	−0.19 (−1.35)	0.06 (1.49)	0.08* (2.33)	−0.03 (−0.95)	0.27 (1.52)	−0.08 (−1.44)	−0.05 (−1.24)
Chile	0.02 (0.71)	−0.07 (−0.71)	0.04 (0.84)	0.05 (1.21)	−0.04 (−1.71)	−0.01 (−0.14)	−0.08 (−1.63)	−0.04 (−0.84)	0.05 (1.45)	0.00 (−0.01)	0.03 (0.55)	−0.02 (−0.38)
Colombia	−0.06* (−2.31)	−0.21 (−1.16)	−0.10* (−2.03)		0.17 (6.19)	0.05 (0.21)	0.17* (3.18)		−0.11* (−3.02)	0.30 (1.02)	−0.16* (−2.40)	−0.27* (−3.57)
Dominican Republic	0.23* (2.33)			0.45* (2.53)	0.01 (0.09)			0.32 (1.55)	0.09 (0.70)			−0.08 (−0.28)
El Salvador	−0.10* (−2.02)	−0.39* (−2.12)	−0.16* (−2.20)		0.07 (1.29)		0.16 (1.98)		−0.08 (−0.87)	−0.18 (−0.68)	−0.08 (−0.70)	
Guatemala	0.12* (2.63)		0.14 (1.73)	0.16* (2.78)	0.02 (0.34)		0.07 (0.75)	0.03 (0.44)	0.09 (1.39)		0.04 (0.36)	0.09 (1.19)
Mexico	−0.05* (−2.56)	−0.16* (−2.16)	−0.03 (−0.82)	−0.05 (−1.25)	0.12* (5.11)	0.30* (3.84)	0.07 (1.84)	0.15* (3.76)	−0.08* (−2.73)	−0.21* (−2.13)	−0.14* (−2.95)	−0.19* (−3.72)

(Continued)

Table 4.18 Continued

	a170 (Scale 1–10)				a008 (Scale 1–4)				a008r (Scale 0–1)			
	Overall	Health Poor	Edn Poor	Income Poor	Overall	Health Poor	Edn Poor	Income Poor	Overall	Health Poor	Edn Poor	Income Poor
Peru	-0.04* (-2.06)	0.06 (0.45)	-0.06 (-1.25)	-0.03 (-0.97)	0.14* (5.98)	0.10 (0.74)	0.24* (4.55)	0.16* (4.94)	-0.13* (-4.82)		-0.27* (-4.44)	-0.17* (-4.46)
Trinidad and Tobago	-0.04 (-1.06)		-0.04 (-0.56)	0.09 (0.82)	0.11* (2.43)		0.15 (1.78)	0.09 (0.73)	-0.09 (-1.35)	-0.19 (-0.79)	-0.01 (-0.09)	-0.19 (-1.18)
Uruguay	0.02 (0.68)	-0.06 (-0.25)	-0.01 (-0.17)	-0.11 (-1.11)	0.02 (0.50)	-0.40 (-1.66)	0.05 (0.82)	0.02 (0.15)	-0.07 (-1.37)	0.28 (0.93)	-0.09 (-1.23)	0.00 (-0.02)
Venezuela	-0.06 (-1.53)	0.04 (0.26)	-0.26* (-3.47)	-0.13 (-1.94)	0.20* (4.42)	0.41* (2.21)	0.25* (3.05)	0.35* (4.51)	-0.25* (-3.59)		-0.36* (-2.95)	-0.49* (-4.26)

Notes: 1. Based on probit results for extended model where z stats are displayed in parenthesis and * denotes statistical significance at the 5% level. For 1–10 and 0–1 definitions, a negative sign indicates that people who value friends are happier. For 1–4 definition, a positive sign indicates people who value friends are happier.

2. Variable dropped due to multicollinearity.

4.2.3   Other social variables

Work. Work is important in uplifting well-being for the full sample only in Mexico and Chile, and to a lesser extent in Brazil (Table 4.19). For the poverty groups, there is scant evidence of the importance of work in lifting well-being anywhere in Latin America. These results are not dissimilar to those from Africa, where work was significant in a few countries, or in Asia, where the results were even less significant. With a few exceptions, the idea that work should be meaningful and uplifting has obviously not caught on in developing countries, either among the poor or in the general population. However, we do acknowledge the limitations of the work indicator, as it does not consider the characteristics of the job which could affect respondents' level of well-being.

Religion. Religion plays a significant and powerful role in raising well-being in Latin America (Table 4.20). In a predominantly Catholic society where church attendance continues to be very high, faith in God and religion are an important source of strength. It is also an uplifting force in people's lives. In all but a couple of countries, religion is significant for the full sample and two of the three definitions of well-being. Religion was also significant in half of the income poor countries for the 1 to 10 well-being definition, and also in a few cases for the education poor.

Trust. Having trust in others is not an important factor in uplifting the general well-being of Latin Americans (Table 4.21). It is significant infrequently, and in Brazil and Mexico enters with the wrong a priori sign in several instances. In the rest of the countries, it never appears as a significant variable in uplifting well-being either for the poor or for the general population.

Confidence in the civil service. Brazil is the only country where the civil service variable made a significant contribution to raising well-being in the probit analysis. This is a positive sign from the largest economy in the region. However, confidence in the civil service had a perverse sign several times in Mexico, suggesting that distrust in the civil service raised well-being. One explanation for this unexpected result is that the level of corruption is so high as to make the variable either not important or even a negative factor in Mexico. Furthermore, this variable had no impact on well-being elsewhere in the region (see Table 4.22).

Table 4.19 Probit results for Latin America – importance of work

	a170 (Scale 1–10)				a008 (Scale 1–4)				a008r (Scale 0–1)			
	Overall	Health Poor	Edn Poor	Income Poor	Overall	Health Poor	Edn Poor	Income Poor	Overall	Health Poor	Edn Poor	Income Poor
Argentina	0.04 (0.90)	−0.21 (−1.51)	−0.05 (−0.75)	−0.07 (−0.82)	0.04 (0.82)	0.31* (2.10)	0.15 (1.97)	0.12 (1.40)	0.05 (0.78)	−0.65* (−3.00)	−0.14 (−1.47)	−0.11 (−1.01)
Brazil	0.07 (1.86)	−0.25 (−1.35)	0.02 (0.31)	0.08 (1.47)	−0.01 (−0.22)	−0.18 (−0.95)	−0.03 (−0.58)	−0.05 (−1.00)	0.21* (3.94)	0.04 (0.19)	0.26* (3.22)	0.24* (3.26)
Chile	−0.08* (−2.66)	0.00 (0.01)	−0.11 (−1.65)	−0.01 (−0.24)	0.00 (−0.04)	0.36* (2.70)	0.05 (0.67)	−0.06 (−1.00)	0.09* (2.01)	−0.31* (−2.04)	0.01 (0.10)	0.13 (1.74)
Colombia	−0.01 (−0.25)	−0.46 (−1.42)	−0.01 (−0.08)	0.06 (1.17)	0.06 (1.17)	0.54 (1.27)	0.25* (2.40)		0.02 (0.28)	−0.35 (−0.58)	−0.14 (−1.07)	−0.05 (−0.40)
Dominican Republic	−0.11 (−1.04)			−0.30 (−1.37)	0.20 (1.69)			0.28 (1.18)	−0.07 (−0.50)			−0.21 (−0.71)
El Salvador	−0.11 (−1.04)	−0.26 (−0.24)	−0.08 (−0.44)		−0.12 (−0.93)		−0.12 (−0.63)		0.39 (1.52)		0.25 (0.76)	
Guatemala	−0.15 (−1.15)		0.11 (0.38)	−0.41* (−2.44)	−0.03 (−0.23)		0.09 (0.28)	0.17 (0.91)	0.19 (0.99)		−0.10 (−0.27)	0.07 (0.31)
Mexico	−0.09* (−3.08)	−0.20* (−2.21)	−0.04 (−0.69)	0.00 (0.08)	0.26* (8.00)	0.31* (3.18)	0.23* (4.03)	0.20* (3.74)	−0.18* (−4.24)	−0.33* (−2.67)	−0.07 (−0.91)	−0.11 (−1.60)

Peru	−0.06 (−1.79)	−0.12 (−0.60)	−0.05 (−0.62)	−0.06 (−1.22)	0.04 (1.25)	0.15 (0.71)	0.08 (0.89)	0.03 (0.49)	0.00 (−0.01)		−0.06 (−0.61)	0.02 (0.29)
Trinidad and Tobago	0.08 (1.42)		0.02 (0.22)	0.03 (0.24)	0.00 (−0.01)		0.07 (0.80)	0.06 (0.47)	0.09 (1.07)	0.39 (1.59)	−0.04 (−0.32)	0.05 (0.28)
Uruguay	−0.04 (−0.90)	0.62* (3.03)	−0.09 (−1.44)	0.13 (1.08)	0.05 (1.01)	0.05 (0.28)	0.02 (0.36)	0.00 (−0.02)	0.03 (0.46)	−0.03 (−0.11)	0.03 (0.34)	0.01 (0.05)
Venezuela	0.11 (1.16)	0.25 (0.55)	0.57* (2.27)	0.17 (1.10)	0.18 (1.62)	−0.31 (−0.44)	0.06 (0.25)	0.18 (1.07)	0.63* (2.21)		1.13 (1.51)	0.69 (1.91)

Notes: 1. Based on probit results for extended model where z stats are displayed in parenthesis and * denotes statistical significance at the 5% level. For 1–10 and 0–1 definitions, a negative sign indicates that people who value work are happier. For 1–4 definition, a positive sign indicates people who value work are happier.
2. Variable dropped due to multicollinearity.

Table 4.20 Probit results for Latin America – importance of religion

	a170 (Scale 1–10)				a008 (Scale 1–4)				a008r (Scale 0–1)			
	Overall	Health Poor	Edn Poor	Income Poor	Overall	Health Poor	Edn Poor	Income Poor	Overall	Health Poor	Edn Poor	Income Poor
Argentina	−0.09* (−3.43)	−0.04 (−0.39)	−0.10* (−2.07)	−0.06 (−1.03)	0.11* (3.91)	0.23* (2.14)	0.09 (1.75)	0.07 (1.23)	−0.02 (−0.54)	−0.11 (−0.83)	−0.06 (−0.99)	−0.06 (−0.77)
Brazil	−0.08* (−3.66)	0.01 (0.04)	−0.06 (−1.54)	−0.07* (−2.21)	0.13* (5.71)	0.27 (1.48)	0.18* (4.44)	0.14* (4.14)	−0.06* (−2.06)	−0.39 (−1.72)	−0.11* (−2.08)	−0.06 (−1.46)
Chile	−0.13* (−5.94)	−0.28* (−2.53)	−0.20* (−3.66)	−0.11* (−2.58)	0.13* (5.15)	0.05 (0.37)	0.03 (0.53)	0.10* (2.06)	−0.08* (−2.40)	−0.09 (−0.70)	−0.08 (−1.08)	−0.07 (−1.28)
Colombia	−0.08* (−3.21)	−0.06 (−0.25)	−0.05 (−0.67)		0.07* (2.60)	1.03* (3.31)	−0.02 (−0.35)		−0.03 (−0.81)	−1.15* (−2.61)	0.02 (0.21)	−0.22* (−2.37)
Dominican Republic	−0.22* (−2.84)			−0.37* (−2.34)	0.19* (2.23)			0.38 (1.97)	−0.16 (−1.48)			−0.48* (−2.13)
El Salvador	0.04 (0.65)	−0.70 (−1.38)	0.09 (0.93)		0.09 (1.33)		0.00 (−0.02)		−0.04 (−0.34)	0.51 (0.68)	0.28 (1.38)	
Guatemala	−0.04 (−0.57)		0.27 (1.82)	0.02 (0.18)	0.20* (2.78)		0.18 (1.20)	0.14 (1.49)	−0.14 (−1.60)		0.00 (0.02)	−0.11 (−0.95)
Mexico	−0.10* (−4.59)	0.05 (0.55)	−0.11* (−2.61)	−0.14* (−3.50)	0.14* (6.23)	0.08 (0.85)	0.19* (4.28)	0.20* (4.45)	−0.07* (−2.23)	−0.11 (−0.97)	−0.19* (−3.35)	−0.15* (−2.78)

Peru	-0.04 (-1.76)	-0.15 (-0.98)	-0.02 (-0.36)	-0.02 (-0.49)	0.11* (4.69)	0.25 (1.57)	0.10 (1.65)	0.09* (2.44)	-0.04 (-1.50)		0.01 (0.07)	-0.04 (-0.92)
Trinidad and Tobago	-0.10 (-1.90)		-0.20 (-1.92)	-0.31* (-2.19)	0.09 (1.55)		0.24* (2.16)	0.11 (0.72)	-0.06 (-0.76)	0.19 (0.72)	-0.12 (-0.92)	-0.09 (-0.47)
Uruguay	-0.06* (-2.51)	-0.05 (-0.29)	-0.07 (-1.61)	-0.11 (-1.53)	0.06* (2.12)	0.14 (0.76)	0.03 (0.58)	0.00 (0.06)	0.00 (-0.05)	-0.36 (-1.35)	0.06 (1.09)	0.09 (1.03)
Venezuela	-0.09* (-2.33)	0.09 (0.29)	-0.15* (-2.20)	-0.05 (-0.81)	0.11* (2.60)	-0.64 (-1.56)	-0.05 (-0.66)	0.02 (0.25)	0.06 (0.87)		0.12 (0.90)	0.06 (0.52)

Notes: 1. Based on probit results for extended model where z stats are displayed in parenthesis and * denotes statistical significance at the 5% level. For 1–10 and 0–1 definitions, a negative sign indicates that people who value their religion are happier. For 1–4 definition, a positive sign indicates people who value their religion are happier.
2. Variable dropped due to multicollinearity.

Table 4.21 Probit results for Latin America – trust

	a170 (Scale 1–10)				a008 (Scale 1–4)				a008r (Scale 0–1)			
	Overall	Health Poor	Edn Poor	Income Poor	Overall	Health Poor	Edn Poor	Income Poor	Overall	Health Poor	Edn Poor	Income Poor
Argentina	-0.11 (-1.64)	0.19 (0.67)	-0.03 (-0.28)	-0.22 (-1.57)	0.04 (0.58)	-0.12 (-0.38)	0.09 (0.67)	0.20 (1.37)	0.12 (1.40)	0.35 (1.01)	0.01 (0.08)	-0.13 (-0.78)
Brazil	-0.12 (-1.84)	-0.37 (-0.48)	-0.10 (-0.89)	-0.31* (-2.78)	0.14 (1.95)	0.78 (1.16)	0.13 (1.15)	0.10 (0.86)	0.37* (4.93)	-0.39 (-0.54)	0.29* (2.25)	0.40* (3.71)
Chile	0.02 (0.37)	-0.16 (-0.71)	0.00 (0.00)	-0.01 (-0.12)	0.07 (1.24)	0.02 (0.07)	0.03 (0.28)	0.01 (0.15)	0.11 (1.63)	0.11 (0.41)	0.15 (1.06)	0.15 (1.33)
Colombia	0.02 (0.37)	0.55 (0.83)	0.18 (1.29)		0.00 (0.05)	-0.06 (-0.07)	-0.02 (-0.11)		0.25* (3.05)	1.23 (1.26)	0.36* (2.09)	0.08 (0.35)
Dominican Republic	-0.24 (-1.63)			-0.55 (-1.48)	-0.05 (-0.33)			-0.29 (-0.68)	0.27 (1.37)			0.39 (0.73)
El Salvador	-0.02 (-0.17)	0.08 (0.14)	0.17 (1.11)		0.22 (1.96)		0.25 (1.42)		-0.32 (-1.70)		-0.42 (-1.43)	
Guatemala	-0.04 (-0.38)		-0.10 (-0.53)	-0.12 (-1.00)	0.05 (0.50)		-0.06 (-0.30)	0.09 (0.69)	0.13 (1.04)		0.32 (1.50)	0.20 (1.32)
Mexico	0.14* (3.74)	-0.07 (-0.48)	0.10 (1.28)	0.23* (3.16)	-0.16* (-3.75)	0.00 (-0.01)	-0.08 (-1.01)	-0.15 (-1.86)	0.49* (9.19)	0.12 (0.58)	0.34* (3.37)	0.39* (4.21)

Peru	-0.05	-0.91	-0.13	-0.09	0.02	0.33	0.17	-0.01	0.31*		0.34	0.42*
	(-0.84)	(-1.72)	(-0.74)	(-0.85)	(0.30)	(0.57)	(0.88)	(-0.11)	(4.39)		(1.75)	(3.95)
Trinidad and Tobago	0.16		0.06	1.24	0.09		-0.12	-1.19	0.30		-0.17	0.80
	(0.92)		(0.18)	(1.85)	(0.43)		(-0.33)	(-1.64)	(1.49)		(-0.42)	(1.43)
Uruguay	-0.02	-0.47	0.12	-0.35	0.07	0.16	-0.03	0.37	0.09	-0.73	0.14	0.00
	(-0.31)	(-1.07)	(1.19)	(-1.79)	(1.05)	(0.35)	(-0.28)	(1.78)	(1.12)	(-1.15)	(1.02)	(-0.02)
Venezuela	-0.15	0.65	-0.24	-0.44*	0.27*	-0.46	0.20	0.44	0.12		0.06	
	(-1.50)	(0.90)	(-1.24)	(-2.21)	(2.32)	(-0.59)	(0.86)	(1.74)	(0.67)		(0.17)	

Notes: 1. Based on probit results for extended model where z stats are displayed in parenthesis and * denotes statistical significance at the 5% level. For 1–10 and 0–1 definitions, a negative sign indicates that people who trust others are happier. For 1–4 definition, a positive sign indicates people who trust others are happier.

2. Variable dropped due to multicollinearity.

Table 4.22 Probit results for Latin America – confidence in civil services

	a170 (Scale 1–10)				a008 (Scale 1–4)				a008r (Scale 0–1)			
	Overall	Health Poor	Edn Poor	Income Poor	Overall	Health Poor	Edn Poor	Income Poor	Overall	Health Poor	Edn Poor	Income Poor
Argentina	0.01 (0.26)	0.02 (0.14)	0.04 (0.73)	0.01 (0.19)	0.05 (1.15)	-0.05 (-0.32)	0.02 (0.36)	-0.09 (-1.19)	0.01 (0.29)	0.06 (0.36)	0.00 (0.04)	0.15 (1.71)
Brazil	-0.09* (-4.98)	-0.12 (-1.08)	-0.10* (-3.43)	-0.09* (-3.77)	0.05* (2.42)	0.05 (0.41)	0.04 (1.50)	0.04 (1.47)	-0.02 (-0.73)	-0.04 (-0.25)	-0.04 (-0.93)	0.01 (0.44)
Chile	-0.01 (-0.56)	0.08 (0.83)	-0.04 (-0.79)	0.01 (0.27)	0.05 (1.77)	-0.01 (-0.09)	0.12* (2.12)	0.12* (2.64)	-0.01 (-0.43)	0.05 (0.40)	-0.13 (-1.98)	-0.10 (-1.83)
Colombia	-0.03 (-1.40)	-0.32 (-1.67)	-0.02 (-0.42)		0.04 (1.56)	0.48* (2.11)	0.04 (0.72)		-0.05 (-1.45)	-0.27 (-0.95)	-0.08 (-1.27)	-0.24* (-3.22)
Dominican Republic	-0.09 (-0.99)			0.05 (0.27)	0.29* (2.78)			0.16 (0.85)	-0.21 (-1.63)			-0.15 (-0.61)
El Salvador												
Guatemala	0.04 (0.94)		0.05 (0.58)	0.02 (0.26)	-0.03 (-0.51)		0.03 (0.28)	-0.01 (-0.19)	0.04 (0.68)		0.07 (0.68)	0.04 (0.47)
Mexico	0.03 (1.44)	-0.02 (-0.26)	0.06 (1.69)	0.01 (0.40)	-0.08* (-4.07)	-0.11 (-1.69)	-0.05 (-1.49)	-0.11* (-2.95)	0.16* (6.21)	0.15 (1.78)	0.14* (3.00)	0.10* (2.19)

Peru	0.02	0.24	−0.02	−0.05	0.06*	−0.08	0.00	0.06	0.02	0.08	0.02	−0.04
	(0.68)	(1.42)	(−0.33)	(−1.30)	(2.26)	(−0.44)	(−0.07)	(1.62)	(0.52)	(0.31)	(0.22)	(−0.82)
Trinidad and Tobago	0.03		0.00	−0.04	−0.03		0.03	0.32*	0.17*		0.09	−0.16
	(0.62)		(−0.03)	(−0.30)	(−0.57)		(0.42)	(2.18)	(2.59)		(0.88)	(−0.89)
Uruguay	0.02	−0.35	0.00	−0.02	0.00	0.35	0.04	−0.07	0.01	−0.21	−0.04	0.09
	(0.78)	(−1.56)	(0.06)	(−0.30)	(0.11)	(1.48)	(0.79)	(−0.85)	(0.24)	(−0.76)	(−0.55)	(0.94)
Venezuela	−0.05	−0.17	−0.01	−0.03	0.01	0.16	0.03	0.04	−0.10		−0.03	−0.02
	(−1.63)	(−0.97)	(−0.09)	(−0.53)	(0.30)	(0.85)	(0.45)	(0.65)	(−1.60)		(−0.25)	(−0.18)

Notes: 1. Based on probit results for extended model where z stats are displayed in parenthesis and * denotes statistical significance at the 5% level. For 1–10 and 0–1 definitions, a negative sign indicates that people with confidence in civil services are happier. For 1–4 definition, a positive sign indicates people with confidence in civil services are happier.
2. Variable dropped due to multicollinearity.

4.3   Individual country analysis

Next, we consider the results on a country-by-country basis to look at individual country determinants of well-being.

Argentina. Health is the most important explanatory variable in the probit regressions for Argentina. It is statistically significant in all three definitions of well-being for the full sample and also for the education and income poor. The coefficients for the poor are similar in size to those for the full sample. Income also has a significant impact on well-being for the full sample, but not for any of the poverty groups. Education, on the other hand, is not significant for the full sample or for the health poor in two out of three cases. Gender has a marginal impact on well-being, being significant once for the full sample and not at all for the poor groups. Marriage has a positive impact on well-being for the overall sample and also for the health and education poor in one case. For the full sample, age enters in a nonlinear fashion in two of the three well-being formulations and once for the education poor. Family has a significant positive impact on well-being in two of the three formulations. However, it is not a factor for any of the poverty groups. Friends are not significant for either the full sample or the poverty groups. Turning to the social variables, trust is not important, nor is confidence in the civil services. Work plays a role for the health poor in two out of three cases and not at all for the full sample or the other poor groups. Religion is important for the full sample in two out of three cases and for the education and health poor in a couple of cases.

Brazil. Brazil is the largest country in Latin America and the Caribbean, both in land area and in the size of the population. In land mass it is slightly smaller than the continental United States and its population is close to 200 million. In both respects it dominates the Latin American economy and general economic and social landscape. In terms of sample size available for analysis of well-being it ranks fourth, behind Mexico, Argentina and Colombia. This could explain the lack of significance of some of the social and policy variables. Turning to the results by variable, health is the most significant explanatory variable, being significant for the full sample and both education and income poor groups. Income is also an important factor uplifting well-being, although it is significant in only two of the three configurations of well-being for the full sample. However, income is significant for the health poor in all three cases and also for the education poor in two cases. Income is significant for the income poor only once, although this is not unexpected, given the truncated values of income for the income poor. Education is not significant with the correct a priori sign in any of the poverty groups or the full sample in any form. This is an unexpected and somewhat disturbing result. The sign of education is perverse and significant in several cases, suggesting that well-being is enhanced by lower educational attainment. This is most likely a statistical artifact. Nevertheless, combined with the other results, it does suggest that education is not a key determinant of well-being in Latin America. Alternatively, education could be acting through income or other social variables, having an indirect positive impact on well-being in Brazil. Turning to the demographic and social variables, gender has a strong impact on well-being in several cases; for the overall sample with the 1 to 10 scale and also for all three poor groups. Aside from the education poor, who had a significant coefficient for gender, there were few other significant coefficients for this variable. Marriage has an uplifting impact on well-being both for the full sample and among the income and education poverty groups. Age is significant and has a nonlinear impact on well-being in as many as nine of the countries sampled in Latin America, led by Brazil, Argentina, Mexico, Chile and Peru, and for all three definitions of well-being. Friends and family were significant for the full sample for all three definitions of well-being. This is a very encouraging result, showing that some developing countries value friends and family as important components of well-being and happiness. The education and income poor also had some significant coefficients for friends, but not so many for family. Turning to the four social variables, there are few encouraging results. Trust is significant only once for the income poor and not at all for the full sample or the other two poverty groups. Furthermore, it enters with the wrong sign three times. Work is not important as a factor uplifting well-being in Brazil, either for the poor or for the full sample. Confidence in the civil service is significant for the full sample and two poverty groups with the 1 to 10 measure of well-being, and also for the overall sample and the 1 to 4 well-being scale. This is an encouraging result and could build incentives for further improvements in the delivery of social services. Religion is an uplifting force for enhanced well-being in Brazil pretty much across the board aside from the health poor.

   Chile. The sample size in Chile, a little over 4,000 observations and about the same number as in Brazil and Peru, is not as large as some other countries in the region, but still large enough to give some insights into the motivations of its residents and how these forces impact well-being. As in many other countries in Latin America and the other developing regions, health plays a key role in uplifting well-being for the full sample and also for the income and education poor. In all cases the significance level of health is very high. The results for the health poor are constrained by their options, since their health is either poor or very poor. Income is significant as a determinant of well-being for the full sample but not for any of the poverty groups. This is quite surprising, although it echoes the results for some other countries. In any event, it undermines the idea that raising income will always increase well-being for the poor. Education is generally not significant for either the full sample or the poverty groups. The education variable is significant in the 0 to 1 form of well-being for the full sample. This result is not completely unexpected, given the lack of significance elsewhere in the region. Gender is not a factor in raising well-being. Being married does raise well-being for the full sample and also for the income poor. Perhaps having a second income is also a factor for some households. Age enters in a nonlinear fashion for the full sample and also for the income poor (see Table 4.15 for the timing of the midlife crisis). Friends is not a significant explanatory variable for the poor or the full sample. Family is significant in the 1–4 scale of well-being and also for the income poor. Turning to the social variables, trust and confidence in the civil service are not significant in any scale for the poor or the full sample. Religion is important for all three scales of well-being for the full sample, and also for the income poor in two out of three cases and for the health and education poor for the 1 to 10 scale. Work satisfaction also raises well-being for the full sample, and for the health poor in two definitions of well-being.

Colombia. Colombia has the fourth largest sample size for the overall probit regression and a large number of education and income poor. The number of health poor is much smaller, as it is in many other countries where respondents may be reluctant to admit they are not feeling well. Nevertheless, health is the most important independent variable, being significant for the full sample, all the education and income poor groups and even two of three health poor groups. Income is significant for the full sample and for two of three health poor groups. Income poor data is only available for the 0 to 1 scale, and it is significant. Education is not significant or has the wrong sign in two of the three configurations for the full sample and in two cases for the health poor. This result is not surprising, as education has not been significant in many countries in Latin America or, for that matter, in the other two regions. Marriage increases well-being for the full sample, and also for the health poor in two cases and the educated and income poor in one case. Age is linear, but not a strong factor in well-being. People get happier as they get older in one case for the full sample and in one case for the educated poor. For the rest, age is not significant. Work, civil service and trust are not important influences on well-being in Colombia. Religion is significant for the full sample and in two cases for the health poor.

Dominican Republic. There are few observations for the full sample in the Dominican Republic and limited reporting for the poor. Only the income poor were sampled. We can say briefly that health is important for the full sample and the income poor. Income is significant in one case for the full sample (1 to 10) and not at all for the income poor group. Education is significant in one case for the full sample and not for the income poor. Gender and age are not significant either for the full sample or the income poor. Marriage does not increase well-being except for one case of the income poor. Age has no impact on well-being and family is not significant. The friends variable is not statistically significant or has the wrong sign. Religion is important for well-being in all three cases and also among the income poor. Work, trust and civil service are not significant determinants of well-being in the Dominican Republic.

El Salvador. Although this is one of the smallest countries in the Caribbean and Latin America, there is still a substantial sampling set for well-being. Around 1,000 observations for the full sample are available for analysis. For the poverty groups there is less information. Results are available mainly for the education poor. Health is an important factor for raising well-being for the full sample and also for the education poor. Income is important in all three cases for the full sample, but not for the poverty groups. Education is not significant for El Salvador, either for the full sample or for the poor. The demographic control variables are not generally significant. Gender is not a factor in raising well-being, and neither is age, with the exception of the 0 to 1 version of well-being for the full sample, and the health and education poverty groups, also for the 0 to 1 configuration of well-being. Marriage raises well-being in one case for the full sample and in two cases for the educated poor. Family is not significant, but friends are, for the 1 to 10 scale of well-being for the full sample and also for the health and education poor. The health poor coefficient is also three times the size of the full sample coefficient, suggesting the strong importance of friends for the health poor in El Salvador. None of the social variables plays a role in raising well-being in El Salvador.

Guatemala Guatemala has a similar profile to El Salvador in terms of sample size and reporting for the poor. Education and income poor groups are reported but there is no evidence for the health poor. Health is the most significant variable in raising well-being for both the full sample and the income and education poor groups. All coefficients are significant in all three variations of well-being. Income also plays an important role for the full sample, as it is significant or nearly significant in all three cases. For the poverty groups, the results are less compelling. Income is significant only for the education poor in one case and not at all for the income poor. Education is significant for the full sample in only one case and not at all for the poverty groups. Turning to the demographic variables, gender is not significant, nor is marital status, with one exception for the overall sample. Age is not significant, suggesting that there is no discernible impact of age on well-being in Guatemala. Turning to the social variables, family and friends didn't have an impact on well-being, nor did trust or confidence in the civil service. Work had a significant impact on the income poor and religion in one case for the full sample.

Mexico. Mexico has the largest sample, of over 4,200 respondents, after dropping observations and fitting the model. It is also the most populous country in Central America. There are ample observations in all three poverty groups. The health poor number over 250, more than any other country in the region. Health is the most important explanatory variable and is significant for all three forms of the overall probit regression for the full sample. Health is also significant for all three poverty groups. In one case the health poor coefficient for health is more than twice the size of the coefficient for the full sample. Health is extremely important for the health poor, even when their options are limited by the nature of how they are selected. Income is significant for the full sample and also for the education poor in three cases and the health and income poor in one case each. The income coefficient for the income poor is twice the size of the income coefficient for the full sample, suggesting the strong importance of income for the income poor. As with so many other countries, education is either insignificant or has the wrong a priori sign in the probit regression. The reason for this result needs to be explored further. Turning to the demographic variables, gender is significant for the full sample. Men are happier than women. Gender is not significant for the poor groups. Marriage increases well-being both for the full sample and also for the poor, although the results are not quite as strong. Marriage is close to being significant in two cases and significant in four others. It is never significant among the health poor. Age has a nonlinear impact on well-being for both the education poor and the full sample. For details see Tables 4.13 and 4.14. Turning to the social variables, family and friends are both significant in Mexico, both for the full sample and for the poverty groups. Friends are significant in all three cases for the full sample, for all three health poor groups and for two of three income poor groups. Family is significant for the overall sample in all three cases, for the education and income poor in two of three and the health poor for one of three. These results for Mexico are encouraging support for the importance of friends and family in uplifting well-being. Trust is plagued by perverse coefficients for both the full sample and the poverty groups. The reason for this needs to be further investigated. Religion and work are both highly significant for both the full sample and the poverty groups. Religion lifts well-being for the full sample in all three of the well-being variables and also for the education and income poor. The health poor results are hampered by a small sample. For work, the results are also highly supportive of a positive impact on well-being for the full sample and also for the poverty groups, particularly the health poor in all three cases and the education and income poor to a lesser extent for one form of well-being. There is no support for the importance of confidence in the civil service in Mexico.

Peru. Peru has a very large sample of respondents, third in number behind Brazil and Mexico. However, the number of health poor is small, although still larger than in El Salvador, Colombia, Uruguay and Venezuela, where there were fewer than 100 respondents. Health is again the most important explanatory variable lifting well-being both for the full sample and for two of the three poverty groups. There are only a few observations for the health poor, whose health choices are constrained by the fact that they are health poor. Income is significant for the full sample, but for only one poverty group regression, a result observed for many other countries in Latin America. Education is not a strong factor in uplifting well-being in Peru, being significant for one of three cases for the overall sample and for none of the poverty groups. Turning to the demographic variables, age is significant and has a nonlinear impact on well-being in two or three cases for the full sample and also in one case for the income poor. Gender is not significant, with the exception of one full sample regression in which men are happier than women. Married couples are happier than singles and others not married for the full sample and also for some poverty groups. Turning to the social variables, family and friends are significant in a few cases (family in one of three for the full sample and one of three for the education poor group; friends for two of three full sample regressions, one education poor regression and two of three income poor regressions). The four other social variables were not particularly important; trust and work not at all, and religion and confidence in the civil service a few times.

Trinidad and Tobago. A small country in the Caribbean, Trinidad and Tobago has a small sample of fewer than 1,000 total observations, and only health and income poor statistics. Health is the most significant determinant of well-being for the overall probit regressions as well as for the education and income poor. Income is significant for the overall sample probit regressions but is not significant for any of the poverty groups, perhaps because of the small sample size. As in many countries in Latin America and the Caribbean, education is not significant for any of the overall regressions; it is significant for only one of the income poor equations and none of the education poor equations. Turning to the demographic variables, women are generally happier than men, in two of three overall regressions and one income poor regression. Age has no measurable impact on well-being either for the poor or for the full sample. Friends play a significant role in uplifting well-being in one of three overall regressions but not for any of the poor groups. Family is significant in two of three regressions of the full sample but not for any of the poverty groups. Turning to the social variables, only religion plays a significant role in uplifting well-being. It is significant in two of the three full sample equations and just fails to achieve significance in the third. Religion is also significant for the income poor and the education poor in one out of three cases and is nearly significant for the education poor in a second case. The other social variables of trust, work and confidence in the civil service are not significant for the full sample or for any of the poor groups.

Uruguay. Uruguay has a fairly large overall sample of 1,685 observations, a large proportion of which are education poor. It is quite surprising, then, that the education variable is not an important factor in lifting well-being. As in many countries, health is again the most significant factor in raising well-being for the full sample and all the poverty groups in Uruguay, including the health poor. Income is significant for the full sample (for all three definitions of well-being) and the education poor. The income variable does not affect well-being for either the health poor or the income poor group. For the demographic control variables, gender is not important in lifting well-being. Neither gender is significantly happier than the other. Marriage lifts well-being. Those who are married or living with a partner are happier than singles, divorced, and so on for the full sample and the education and income poor. Age exhibits a strong Easterlin effect for the full sample (two out of three definitions of well-being) and also for the health and income poor (two of three) and education poor (one of three). Turning to the social variables, friends and family are not significant factors in raising well-being, for either the poor or the full sample. Religion lifts well-being for the full sample but not for the poverty groups, although the income and education poor are close to statistical significance. As for the other three social variables of work, confidence in the civil service and trust, none are important in raising well-being.

Venezuela. Venezuela is an oil-rich country which has a strong political presence in Latin America. The overall sample size for the fitted model is just over 1,000 observations. There are few surprises, as the profile of significant variables that impact on well-being is similar to the other countries in the region. Health is the most important (in all cases but one for the full sample and all poverty groups), followed by income for the full sample (two of three) and the income poor (one of three). Education does nothing significant to lift well-being for the full sample or the three poverty groups. Age is not related to well-being, nor is marital status, and neither gender is significantly happier than the other. Friends are important for raising well-being for the full sample (two of three) and for the education poor group (two of three), health poor (one of two) and income poor (three of three). Family is not significant. Trust and confidence in the civil service are not important in lifting well-being, while work is significant for the full sample (one of three) and health poor (one of three). Religion was a strong factor in raising well-being, as we have seen from other country results in Latin America, particularly for the full sample (two of three) and also for the health poor (one of three).

4.4 Pooled results by region

We grouped Latin America into three different regions: (i) the Andean group, which includes Chile, Colombia, Peru and Venezuela, (ii) Mercosur, which includes Argentina, Brazil and Uruguay, and (iii) Mexico and the Caribbean, which includes Mexico, Dominican Republic, El Salvador, Guatemala, and Trinidad and Tobago. We analyze these regions by independent variable in much the same way as we proceeded with variables and countries in the earlier analysis with probit regression equations. We also ran probit regressions for regional groupings in Latin America in the same way as we proceeded with the other two regions. These results are reported in Table 4.23. In general, aggregation results in a better fit of the model and generally increases the significance of the independent variables, especially for marriage, family and work (which were less significant in the individual country analysis).

Health. With respect to health, the probit results for the three subregions of Latin America and the region as a whole are very strong. Well-being is uplifted by better health outcomes for all three poverty groups and the overall sample results for regions, with the exception of the health poor. As we have mentioned in previous chapters, this latter result could be due to the small sample size and a limited range of observation.

Income. The results for the Latin American region are strong for all regions, including Latin America as a whole, and also for the three poverty groups. There are only a few cases in which coefficients for any regression are not significant. This evidence supports our earlier conclusion about the importance of income as a force for uplifting well-being for the full sample and all the poverty groups throughout Latin America.

Table 4.23 Aggregated probit results for Latin America

	a170 (Scale 1–10)				a008 (Scale 1–4)				a008r (Scale 0–1)			
	Overall	Health Poor	Edn Poor	Income Poor	Overall	Health Poor	Edn Poor	Income Poor	Overall	Health Poor	Edn Poor	Income Poor
STATE OF HEALTH												
Andean	-0.27* (-19.10)	-0.12 (-0.49)	-0.27* (-9.07)	-0.23* (-9.84)	0.43* (27.87)	0.76* (2.90)	0.40* (12.61)	0.44* (16.69)	-0.41* (-20.63)	-0.02 (-0.09)	-0.41* (-10.30)	-0.38* (-12.37)
Mercosur	-0.27* (-17.37)	0.16 (0.82)	-0.23* (-9.59)	-0.28* (-11.29)	0.38* (22.87)	0.81* (3.92)	0.36* (13.85)	0.39* (14.76)	-0.34* (-15.79)	-0.33 (-1.78)	-0.32* (-9.57)	-0.34* (-10.42)
Mexico and Caribbean	-0.25* (-15.35)	-0.29 (-1.56)	-0.21* (-7.17)	-0.28* (-9.99)	0.53* (28.33)	0.96* (4.48)	0.51* (15.35)	0.53* (16.67)	-0.52* (-20.99)	-0.03 (-0.22)	-0.46* (-10.96)	-0.47* (-12.01)
Latin America	-0.26* (-29.65)	-0.02 (-0.17)	-0.23* (-14.56)	-0.26* (-18.14)	0.43* (44.85)	0.78* (6.32)	0.40* (23.84)	0.43* (27.07)	-0.42* (-34.03)	-0.10 (-1.05)	-0.39* (-18.31)	-0.40* (-20.68)
INCOME												
Andean	0.08* (14.25)	0.12* (3.51)	0.08* (5.02)	0.22* (5.74)	-0.04* (-6.50)	-0.15* (-4.26)	-0.07* (-3.89)	-0.09* (-2.22)	0.11* (13.79)	0.13* (3.19)	0.11* (5.28)	0.25* (5.17)
Mercosur	0.02* (4.26)	0.07* (2.35)	0.02 (1.98)	-0.07 (-1.79)	-0.06* (-9.97)	-0.02 (-0.58)	-0.04* (-4.39)	0.03 (0.72)	0.07* (9.56)	0.02 (0.71)	0.07* (5.14)	0.12* (2.25)
Mexico and Caribbean	0.04* (7.44)	0.07* (2.34)	0.05* (4.17)	0.02 (0.41)	-0.07* (-11.17)	-0.05 (-1.62)	-0.07* (-5.32)	-0.04 (-0.73)	0.11* (12.33)	0.05 (1.48)	0.09* (5.13)	0.23* (3.70)
Latin America	0.05* (15.65)	0.07* (4.26)	0.04* (5.89)	0.03 (1.27)	-0.06* (-16.81)	-0.07* (-3.75)	-0.06* (-8.12)	-0.07* (-2.69)	0.10* (21.63)	0.07* (3.35)	0.09* (9.40)	0.16* (5.45)

EDUCATION LEVEL

Andean	-0.01* (-2.39)	0.01 (0.25)	-0.02 (-0.48)	-0.05* (-5.26)	0.01 (1.64)	0.03 (0.89)	-0.03 (-0.52)	0.02 (1.89)	0.02* (3.00)	0.02 (0.44)	0.08 (1.38)	0.01 (1.08)
Mercosur	-0.04* (-6.16)	-0.02 (-0.63)	-0.08 (-1.99)	-0.02 (-1.85)	0.02* (3.27)	-0.08* (-2.07)	0.09* (2.05)	0.02 (1.12)	0.03* (3.32)	0.10 (1.97)	0.00 (-0.06)	0.05* (2.65)
Mexico and Caribbean	-0.03* (-3.81)	-0.01 (-0.25)	-0.16* (-3.12)	-0.02 (-1.62)	0.03* (3.40)	-0.03 (-0.95)	-0.01 (-0.23)	0.01 (0.68)	0.01 (0.84)	0.00 (-0.04)	0.12 (1.77)	0.03 (1.46)
Latin America	-0.02* (-5.61)	0.00 (0.13)	-0.08* (-2.93)	-0.04* (-5.46)	0.01* (2.55)	-0.03 (-1.33)	0.03 (1.17)	0.01 (1.46)	0.02* (3.30)	0.03 (1.33)	0.07* (2.09)	0.02* (2.44)

GENDER

Andean	0.00 (0.10)	0.10 (0.82)	-0.03 (-0.72)	-0.02 (-0.68)	-0.04 (-1.83)	0.05 (0.37)	0.06 (1.29)	-0.01 (-0.18)	0.13* (4.56)	-0.05 (-0.36)	-0.04 (-0.59)	0.09* (2.01)
Mercosur	-0.05* (-2.10)	-0.14 (-1.09)	-0.08 (-1.91)	-0.12* (-2.89)	0.03 (1.22)	0.14 (1.02)	0.10* (2.28)	0.04 (0.84)	0.02 (0.72)	-0.23 (-1.43)	-0.10 (-1.88)	-0.05 (-0.95)
Mexico and Caribbean	0.02 (0.64)	-0.09 (-0.79)	-0.03 (-0.54)	-0.04 (-0.73)	-0.02 (-0.68)	0.01 (0.10)	0.00 (-0.09)	0.05 (1.06)	0.11* (2.80)	-0.12 (-0.84)	0.14* (2.13)	0.03 (0.55)
Latin America	-0.02 (-1.69)	-0.06 (-0.86)	-0.05 (-1.99)	-0.07* (-2.92)	0.00 (-0.03)	0.04 (0.50)	0.06* (2.19)	0.03 (1.05)	0.09* (5.03)	-0.10 (-1.20)	-0.01 (-0.29)	0.04 (1.45)

AGE

Andean	-0.11 (-1.30)	-0.38 (-0.67)	-0.22 (-0.97)	-0.23 (-1.55)	0.32* (3.39)	0.82 (1.36)	0.40 (1.68)	0.29 (1.81)	0.91* (9.06)	0.11 (0.17)	1.25* (5.74)	0.83* (5.17)

Continued

Table 4.23 Continued

	a170 (Scale 1–10)				a008 (Scale 1–4)				a008r (Scale 0–1)			
	Overall	Health Poor	Edn Poor	Income Poor	Overall	Health Poor	Edn Poor	Income Poor	Overall	Health Poor	Edn Poor	Income Poor
Mercosur	−0.33* (−3.28)	0.26 (0.39)	−0.19 (−0.98)	−0.44* (−2.58)	0.38* (3.49)	−0.03 (−0.04)	0.37 (1.84)	0.31 (1.70)	0.85* (7.19)	1.10 (1.52)	1.10* (5.65)	0.55* (2.93)
Mexico and Caribbean	−0.39* (−3.52)	0.10 (0.19)	−0.37 (−1.64)	−0.19 (−0.97)	0.04 (0.29)	0.20 (0.37)	0.27 (1.10)	0.09 (0.40)	1.01* (7.62)	0.31 (0.53)	1.01* (4.31)	1.18* (5.40)
Latin America	−0.26* (−4.60)	0.02 (0.07)	−0.24* (−2.01)	−0.29* (−3.01)	0.28* (4.54)	0.36 (1.05)	0.32* (2.51)	0.23* (2.23)	0.92* (14.06)	0.40 (1.11)	1.12* (9.17)	0.85* (8.17)
AGE SQUARED												
Andean	0.04 (1.64)	0.11 (0.84)	0.04 (0.71)	0.05 (1.39)	−0.06* (−2.74)	−0.13 (−0.94)	−0.08 (−1.38)	−0.05 (−1.26)	−0.22* (−8.43)	−0.05 (−0.31)	−0.27* (−5.12)	−0.19* (−4.70)
Mercosur	0.10* (3.81)	−0.01 (−0.07)	0.07 (1.51)	0.14* (3.29)	−0.09* (−3.49)	−0.05 (−0.34)	−0.09 (−1.97)	−0.10* (−2.25)	−0.19* (−6.45)	−0.18 (−1.05)	−0.23* (−4.92)	−0.09 (−1.92)
Mexico and Caribbean	0.11* (3.84)	0.00 (−0.02)	0.10 (1.84)	0.06 (1.23)	−0.02 (−0.50)	−0.04 (−0.29)	−0.06 (−1.06)	−0.03 (−0.46)	−0.23* (−6.61)	−0.06 (−0.42)	−0.22* (−3.81)	−0.27* (−4.75)
Latin America	0.07* (5.04)	0.02 (0.21)	0.06* (2.18)	0.08* (3.41)	−0.06* (−4.05)	−0.08 (−1.02)	−0.07* (−2.29)	−0.06* (−2.19)	−0.21* (−12.63)	−0.07 (−0.82)	−0.24* (−8.12)	−0.18* (−6.88)
MARITAL STATUS												
Andean	0.12* (5.21)	0.09 (0.77)	0.17* (3.24)	0.10* (2.70)	−0.18* (−7.15)	−0.03 (−0.26)	−0.13* (−2.48)	−0.18* (−4.32)	0.20* (6.27)	0.14 (0.91)	0.15* (2.21)	0.21* (4.23)

Mercosur	0.19* (7.63)	-0.01 (-0.07)	0.16* (3.66)	0.18* (4.17)	-0.25* (-9.11)	-0.13 (-0.94)	-0.22* (-4.91)	-0.28* (-6.25)	0.30* (8.18)	0.16 (1.01)	0.27* (4.63)	0.29* (5.07)
Mexico and Caribbean	0.19* (6.50)	0.33* (2.77)	0.13* (2.37)	0.10* (2.03)	-0.14* (-4.45)	-0.08 (-0.63)	-0.25* (-4.20)	-0.21* (-3.79)	0.10* (2.47)	0.08 (0.54)	0.23* (3.13)	0.31* (4.51)
Latin America	0.16* (11.21)	0.12 (1.78)	0.16* (5.79)	0.13* (5.41)	-0.19* (-12.05)	-0.10 (-1.44)	-0.21* (-7.08)	-0.23* (-8.58)	0.20* (9.86)	0.13 (1.51)	0.22* (5.99)	0.25* (7.88)
FAMILY												
Andean	0.02 (0.86)	0.00 (-0.03)	0.14* (2.37)	0.00 (-0.05)	0.14* (4.60)	0.21 (1.48)	0.13* (2.18)	0.14* (3.04)	-0.03 (-0.76)	0.13 (0.77)	0.02 (0.32)	-0.01 (-0.18)
Mercosur	-0.14* (-4.20)	0.00 (-0.01)	-0.11* (-2.13)	-0.07 (-1.30)	0.22* (5.91)	0.20 (1.24)	0.16* (3.04)	0.21* (3.69)	-0.10* (-2.10)	-0.03 (-0.14)	0.03 (0.36)	-0.08 (-1.18)
Mexico and Caribbean	-0.06 (-1.59)	0.17 (1.62)	-0.08 (-1.21)	-0.07 (-1.20)	0.31* (8.37)	0.09 (0.82)	0.30* (4.55)	0.34* (5.66)	-0.30* (-6.76)	-0.33* (-2.33)	-0.24* (-3.10)	-0.26* (-3.66)
Latin America	-0.04* (-2.30)	0.11 (1.65)	-0.01 (-0.46)	-0.04 (-1.36)	0.21* (10.99)	0.17* (2.35)	0.20* (5.92)	0.21* (6.84)	-0.14* (-6.00)	-0.14 (-1.62)	-0.06 (-1.41)	-0.09* (-2.59)
FRIENDS												
Andean	-0.08* (-6.35)	-0.07 (-1.18)	-0.13* (-5.30)	-0.07* (-3.32)	0.13* (9.77)	0.13* (2.00)	0.15* (5.58)	0.16* (7.34)	-0.10* (-5.88)	-0.12 (-1.57)	-0.16* (-5.11)	-0.17* (-6.46)
Mercosur	-0.03* (-2.03)	-0.07 (-1.02)	-0.08* (-3.06)	-0.08* (-2.92)	0.03 (1.91)	-0.04 (-0.52)	0.05 (1.87)	0.06* (2.08)	-0.04 (-1.69)	0.02 (0.18)	-0.05 (-1.58)	-0.04 (-1.05)
Mexico and Caribbean	-0.02 (-1.45)	-0.11 (-1.69)	0.00 (0.06)	0.03 (0.95)	0.09* (5.16)	0.23* (3.39)	0.07* (2.24)	0.10* (3.27)	-0.04 (-1.62)	-0.17* (-2.07)	-0.07 (-1.76)	-0.08* (-2.20)

Continued

Table 4.23 Continued

	a170 (Scale 1-10)				a008 (Scale 1-4)				a008r (Scale 0-1)			
	Overall	Health Poor	Edn Poor	Income Poor	Overall	Health Poor	Edn Poor	Income Poor	Overall	Health Poor	Edn Poor	Income Poor
Latin America	-0.05* (-5.52)	-0.08* (-2.21)	-0.08* (-5.19)	-0.06* (-4.67)	0.07* (7.91)	0.13* (3.45)	0.07* (4.79)	0.10* (6.87)	-0.08* (-7.37)	-0.12* (-2.75)	-0.11* (-5.82)	-0.14* (-8.02)
WORK												
Andean	-0.06* (-2.97)	-0.07 (-0.74)	0.00 (-0.09)	-0.01 (-0.24)	0.07* (3.21)	0.27* (2.75)	0.13* (2.76)	0.02 (0.70)	0.02 (0.74)	-0.29* (-2.43)	-0.07 (-1.23)	0.05 (1.15)
Mercosur	0.03 (1.41)	-0.05 (-0.56)	-0.02 (-0.58)	0.05 (1.17)	0.01 (0.61)	0.17 (1.90)	0.03 (0.87)	0.00 (-0.05)	0.12* (3.50)	-0.26* (-2.37)	0.10 (1.98)	0.12* (2.25)
Mexico and Caribbean	-0.08* (-3.17)	-0.18* (-2.31)	-0.03 (-0.60)	-0.05 (-1.11)	0.19* (7.01)	0.22* (2.80)	0.15* (3.12)	0.17* (3.79)	-0.10* (-2.96)	-0.19 (-1.93)	-0.04 (-0.60)	-0.06 (-1.05)
Latin America	-0.04* (-2.84)	-0.07 (-1.38)	-0.02 (-0.79)	0.00 (-0.22)	0.09* (6.57)	0.22* (4.44)	0.10* (3.94)	0.06* (2.45)	0.01 (0.44)	-0.26* (-4.23)	0.00 (0.10)	0.04 (1.36)
RELIGION												
Andean	-0.10* (-8.19)	-0.12 (-1.65)	-0.15* (-5.11)	-0.08* (-3.35)	0.11* (8.46)	0.16* (2.01)	0.03 (0.84)	0.10* (4.01)	-0.03 (-1.68)	-0.11 (-1.16)	0.02 (0.39)	-0.05 (-1.63)
Mercosur	-0.08* (-6.50)	-0.07 (-1.08)	-0.10* (-4.48)	-0.10* (-4.04)	0.10* (7.05)	0.14* (2.01)	0.11* (4.54)	0.10* (3.71)	-0.04 (-1.97)	-0.12 (-1.48)	-0.06 (-1.95)	-0.05 (-1.66)
Mexico and Caribbean	-0.08* (-4.82)	0.01 (0.21)	-0.09* (-2.46)	-0.17* (-4.93)	0.14* (7.03)	0.10 (1.35)	0.18* (4.77)	0.17* (4.83)	-0.07* (-2.88)	-0.07 (-0.81)	-0.15* (-3.22)	-0.14* (-3.20)

Latin America	-0.11* (-14.60)	-0.07 (-1.86)	-0.13* (-8.38)	-0.12* (-8.00)	0.14* (16.44)	0.14* (3.34)	0.13* (7.67)	0.13* (8.10)	-0.04* (-3.93)	-0.11* (-2.14)	-0.06* (-2.74)	-0.06* (-3.40)
TRUST												
Andean	0.02 (0.63)	-0.12 (-0.72)	0.01 (0.16)	-0.05 (-0.88)	0.05 (1.42)	0.04 (0.21)	0.08 (0.98)	-0.03 (-0.46)	0.24* (6.01)	0.32 (1.51)	0.26* (2.94)	0.33* (4.83)
Mercosur	-0.05 (-1.28)	0.10 (0.46)	0.05 (0.89)	-0.23* (-2.95)	0.08* (2.03)	0.04 (0.20)	0.05 (0.77)	0.21* (2.55)	0.23* (5.04)	0.12 (0.48)	0.20* (2.71)	0.24* (2.93)
Mexico and Caribbean	0.04 (1.05)	-0.16 (-1.11)	0.00 (-0.03)	0.08 (1.38)	-0.11* (-3.12)	-0.05 (-0.32)	-0.07 (-0.99)	-0.08 (-1.28)	0.42* (9.52)	0.19 (1.05)	0.26* (3.13)	0.33* (4.48)
Latin America	-0.01 (-0.73)	-0.08 (-0.88)	0.01 (0.24)	-0.05 (-1.49)	0.01 (0.68)	-0.01 (-0.07)	0.03 (0.76)	0.04 (1.09)	0.32* (13.30)	0.23 (1.97)	0.26* (5.56)	0.33* (8.19)
CIVIL SERVICES												
Andean	-0.02 (-1.21)	0.02 (0.26)	0.00 (-0.09)	-0.03 (-1.31)	0.05* (3.99)	0.13 (1.86)	0.07* (2.36)	0.11* (4.54)	-0.04* (-2.37)	-0.08 (-0.99)	-0.09* (-2.58)	-0.10* (-3.77)
Mercosur	-0.07* (-5.36)	-0.09 (-1.34)	-0.09* (-4.18)	-0.10* (-5.06)	0.02 (1.07)	-0.06 (-0.86)	0.03 (1.24)	-0.01 (-0.50)	-0.02 (-1.05)	0.07 (0.80)	-0.05 (-1.84)	0.03 (1.00)
Mexico and Caribbean	0.05* (3.46)	0.05 (0.78)	0.08* (2.67)	0.03 (1.21)	-0.05* (-2.98)	-0.09 (-1.55)	-0.02 (-0.53)	-0.04 (-1.38)	0.13* (6.14)	0.12 (1.60)	0.10* (2.58)	0.06 (1.56)
Latin America	-0.02* (-2.28)	-0.03 (-0.83)	-0.02 (-1.37)	-0.04* (-3.00)	0.00 (-0.59)	-0.03 (-0.85)	0.01 (0.95)	-0.01 (-0.47)	0.01 (1.25)	0.06 (1.29)	-0.03 (-1.38)	-0.01 (-0.81)

Notes: 1. Based on probit results for extended model where z stats are displayed in parenthesis and * denotes statistical significance at the 5% level.
2. Andean includes Chile, Colombia, Peru and Venezuela.
3. Mercosur includes Argentina, Brazil and Uruguay.
4. Mexico and Caribbean includes Mexico, Dominican Republic, El Salvador, Guatemala, and Trinidad and Tobago.

Education. The probit regression results for education in Latin America are mixed. For the Latin American region as a whole, education plays a significant role in uplifting well-being for the overall sample, but not for all poverty groups. With the exception of Mercosur, well-being in most poverty groups is not significantly affected by the level of education.

Gender. There is little evidence to support the importance of gender differences in raising well-being in Latin America. Neither gender is happier in the sense that the coefficient is statistically significantly different from zero.

Age. There is some evidence of a nonlinear relationship of well-being with age for the 0 to 1 definition of well-being for the three regional groupings and for Latin America as a whole for all well-being definitions and the overall sample. There is also strong evidence of nonlinearities for two of the three poverty groups for Latin America as a whole (see Tables 4.13 and 4.14).

Marital status. Marriage generally has a positive impact on well-being for all regions, different definitions of well-being and poverty groups. The only exception is the health poor category, where the results are not strong.

Family. The importance of family in raising well-being is strongest for Latin America as a whole and for the overall sample in most regions. However, the impact of family on well-being is stronger in Mercosur and Mexico and the Caribbean than it is in the Andean region. The results for the poor are very weak. Only eight out of 45 coefficients are significant.

Friends. Friends are an important source of support for well-being in the probit regressions for Latin America as a whole and in the Andean region. The impact of friends is weakest in Mercosur, with Mexico and the Caribbean in between. The well-being of the income and education poor is more strongly impacted by having friends than the health poor.

Work. Work is important for well-being in the full sample for Latin America, and also for Mexico and the Caribbean and the Andean countries. The health poor are more responsive to the work variable than the income and education poor.

Religion. Religion is an important determinant of well-being for the full sample in all regions and for Latin America as a whole. Religion is generally uplifting for the poor, although the impact is weaker among the health poor, particularly in the 1 to 10 and 0 and 1 definitions of well-being.

Trust. Trust is not generally significant as a determinant of well-being except in the 0 and 1 definition and for the income poor in the Mercosur region.

Civil services. Confidence in the provision of civil services was not generally significant, aside from the full sample in the Andean and Mexico and Caribbean regions. Generally, the well-being of the poor was not raised by the confidence in better civil services.

4.5   Extensions to the model

4.5.1   Probability of escaping from poverty

Unlike previous results for Asia and Africa in Chapters 2 and 3, where the prospects of escaping poverty did not exert a strong influence on well-being, the results were highly significant on the 1–10 scale of well-being. This result supports the hypothesis that if Latin American respondents think they have a chance of escaping poverty their well-being will be uplifted. The significance of the coefficient for the chance of escaping poverty having an impact on well-being is displayed in Table 4.24. If the respondent thought there was a chance of escaping poverty, a one (1) was recorded in the response sheet. If there was very little chance of escaping poverty, the value was entered as two (2). A negative coefficient for the 1–10 and 0–1 scales signifies that having a chance to get out of poverty raises well-being, whereas a positive coefficient for the 1–4 scale signifies an increase in well-being.

This is particularly true for the 1–10 scale of well-being, less so for the 1–4 scale and not at all for the 0–1 scale. In general, the well-being of the education and income poor is more likely to be uplifted by chances of escaping poverty than the health poor, although there are several cases among the health poor in which the coefficients are close to statistical significance. Furthermore, the significance of the getting out of poverty variable is highest for the overall sample, perhaps reflecting the belief that a more mobile population generates opportunities for the nonpoor as well as the poor.

4.5.2   Urban–rural differences in happiness

There is virtually no evidence that urban dwellers are happier than those living in rural areas. There is only one significant coefficient for the five countries for which data is available, the results of which are displayed in Table 4.25. To understand this result, it is important to recognize that Latin America is more urbanized than Europe, Asia or Africa and, at 82.2 percent, nearly as urbanized as North America at 83.3 percent (see Cerrutti and Bertoncello 2003). Rural to urban migration took place in most of Latin America early in the twentieth century. Only a few countries are still in the state of urban transition, which we can define as having less than 65 percent urban population. These are the smaller and poorer countries in the Caribbean (Costa Rica, Guatemala, Haiti and Honduras), which still have significant movement from the countryside into the cities. The largest countries in the region – Brazil, Mexico, Colombia and Argentina – all have urbanization ratios of over 70 percent.

Table 4.24 Significance of coefficient on chance to escape from poverty for Latin America.

	a170 (Scale 1–10)				a008 (Scale 1–4)				a008r (Scale 0–1)			
	Overall	Health Poor	Edn Poor	Income Poor	Overall	Health Poor	Edn Poor	Income Poor	Overall	Health Poor	Edn Poor	Income Poor
Argentina	−0.28* (−3.46)	−0.48 (−1.71)	−0.30* (−2.17)	−0.55* (−3.52)	0.22* (2.50)	0.47 (1.58)	0.12 (0.83)	0.35* (2.12)	0.03 (0.22)		0.00 (0.03)	−0.20 (−1.00)
Brazil	−0.31* (−4.34)	−1.95 (−1.67)	−0.37* (−2.79)	−0.29* (−3.05)	0.23* (2.91)	1.38 (1.85)	0.11 (0.80)	0.35* (3.44)	−0.12 (−1.20)	−1.12 (−1.35)	−0.07 (−0.39)	−0.26 (−1.93)
Chile	−0.19* (−2.65)	−0.45 (−1.48)	−0.22 (−1.26)	−0.15 (−1.04)	0.17* (2.24)	0.17 (0.52)	0.26 (1.33)	0.52* (3.24)	−0.03 (−0.26)	−0.34 (−0.92)	−0.29 (−1.22)	−0.30 (−1.70)
Colombia	−0.11* (−2.83)	−0.23 (−0.72)	−0.01 (−0.10)	0.03 (0.33)	0.11* (2.61)	0.41 (1.16)	0.05 (0.56)		0.05 (0.87)	−0.39 (−0.99)	0.02 (0.17)	−0.08 (−0.60)
Dominican Republic	0.00 (0.03)		2.30 (1.97)	0.04 (0.16)	0.05 (0.40)			−0.12 (−0.45)	0.13 (0.86)		3.34 (1.44)	0.49 (1.64)
Mexico	−0.25* (−5.13)	−0.27 (−1.69)	−0.36* (−3.52)	−0.25* (−2.89)	0.15* (2.92)	0.32 (1.77)	0.38* (3.43)	0.15 (1.69)	0.06 (0.97)	−0.02 (−0.09)	−0.31* (−2.34)	−0.04 (−0.40)
Peru	−0.16* (−2.43)	−0.87 (−0.72)	−0.66* (−3.61)	−0.09 (−0.87)	0.04 (0.55)		0.18 (0.97)	0.07 (0.66)	−0.03 (−0.39)		−0.14 (−0.64)	−0.07 (−0.52)
Uruguay	−0.30* (−3.51)	0.62 (0.81)	−0.34* (−2.56)	−0.90* (−3.32)	0.16 (1.77)	0.05 (0.06)	0.05 (0.35)	0.10 (0.38)	0.16 (1.40)	0.01 (0.01)	0.26 (1.49)	0.01 (0.03)

Venezuela	0.05	0.53	0.13	0.09	0.07	−0.69	0.16	0.22	0.02		0.00	−0.19
	(0.68)	(1.56)	(0.98)	(0.82)	(0.98)	(−1.89)	(1.08)	(1.72)	(0.16)		(0.01)	(−0.92)
Overall	−0.18*	−0.24*	−0.18*	−0.13*	0.17*	0.32*	0.18*	0.19*	0.07*	−0.23	−0.03	0.00
	(−8.97)	(−2.44)	(−4.25)	(−3.35)	(7.58)	(3.10)	(4.05)	(4.87)	(2.54)	(−1.90)	(−0.59)	(0.10)

Notes: 1. Chance to escape from poverty ranges from 1 to 3. 1 indicates they have very little chance. 3 indicates other answer.

2. Based on probit results for Equation (2.2) where z stats are displayed in parenthesis and * denotes statistical significance at the 5% level. This is due to e132 data being available only in Wave 3 and hence not possible to incorporate other social variables as in the extended model.

Table 4.25 Probit results for Latin America – rural–urban

	a170 (Scale 1–10)				a008 (Scale 1–4)				a008r (Scale 0–1)			
	Overall	Health Poor	Edn Poor	Income Poor	Overall	Health Poor	Edn Poor	Income Poor	Overall	Health Poor	Edn Poor	Income Poor
Guatemala	0.09 (0.95)	-0.01 (-0.04)	-0.12 (-0.70)	0.21 (1.75)	-0.06 (-0.59)	-0.21 (-0.80)	-0.15 (-0.82)	-0.14 (-1.14)	-0.10 (-0.71)		-0.08 (-0.37)	-0.01 (-0.09)
Mexico	-0.10 (-1.50)		-0.22 (-1.95)	-0.08 (-0.68)	-0.05 (-0.70)		-0.14 (-1.20)	0.14 (1.15)	0.04 (0.36)	0.51 (1.50)	0.09 (0.55)	0.03 (0.16)
Uruguay	0.02 (0.12)		-0.05 (-0.29)	0.16 (0.35)	-0.04 (-0.24)	-0.05 (-0.02)	0.14 (0.74)	0.17 (0.35)	0.30 (1.58)		-0.09 (-0.35)	0.58 (1.02)
Venezuela	-0.34 (-1.23)		0.32 (0.70)		0.09 (0.29)		0.40 (0.83)		0.47 (1.13)			-0.19 (-0.31)
Overall	-0.07 (-1.93)	-0.01 (-0.03)	-0.11 (-1.85)	-0.06 (-0.99)	0.09* (2.15)	-0.07 (-0.41)	0.10 (1.56)	0.08 (1.28)	0.06 (1.09)	0.02 (0.11)	-0.05 (-0.63)	0.04 (0.51)

*Denotes significance at 10% level.

1. The rural–urban variable ranges from 0: rural (2,000 and fewer residents) to 1: urban (500,000 and more residents). Under the 1–10 and 0–1 definitions of well-being, a positive sign indicates that urban residents are happier. Under the 1–4 definition, a negative sign indicates that urban residents are happier.

2. Based on probit results for inclusion of added dummy variable for rural–urban variable into original equation (1.1) and z stats are displayed in parenthesis.

3. Variable dropped due to multicollinearity.

5
Conclusions from the Analysis of Probit Analysis for Asia, Africa and Latin America

The approach undertaken in this book enables a better understanding of the local factors that have a bearing on how well-being and happiness are uplifted in different countries and among different poverty groups. Insights have been gained by exploring the three alternatives suggested for measures of well-being and happiness as well as analysis by subregions. The life satisfaction ladder, with gradations from 1 to 10 which register a progression of life satisfaction from not at all satisfied to very satisfied, gives one perspective on which independent variables have the most significant impact on life satisfaction. The happiness definition, which varies between 1 and 4, gives a different perspective on well-being. Comparisons between the two ways to characterize well-being yield additional insights into behavior and how different forces work to uplift well-being and happiness. This approach contrasts with an analysis based on a single measure. Furthermore, a third variation, which collapses the 1 to 4 category into a binary choice of happy or unhappy, adds yet a further dimension to the analysis. With added insight come challenges. The introduction of several ways to measure well-being makes it more difficult to draw simple conclusions or to characterize the results for all countries and variables.

Table 5.1 presents aggregated probit results for the entire data set for all three regions, where there are easily over 75,000 observations for the entire sample set. From the aggregate results, it is not surprising that the statistical fit of the model improves dramatically with the pooling of observations and confirms the importance of the individual variables (as discussed earlier in our literature review).

Almost every variable is found to be significant. Health, income and education were extremely significant for all three configurations of well-being and across all poverty groups, with the slight exception of some

Table 5.1 Probit analysis

	a170 (Scale 1–10)				a008 (Scale 1–4)				a008r (Scale 0–1)			
	Overall	Health Poor	Edn Poor	Income Poor	Overall	Health Poor	Edn Poor	Income Poor	Overall	Health Poor	Edn Poor	Income Poor
Health	-0.25* (-54.47)	-0.04 (-0.68)	-0.24* (-30.53)	-0.25* (-28.30)	0.44* (85.31)	0.36* (5.24)	0.41* (48.22)	0.40* (42.14)	-0.38* (-57.61)	-0.01 (-0.24)	-0.39* (-36.06)	-0.37* (-32.33)
Income	0.06* (35.42)	0.10* (12.36)	0.06* (17.01)	0.04* (2.61)	-0.06* (-30.98)	-0.09* (-10.66)	-0.06* (-17.31)	-0.03 (-1.83)	0.10* (39.20)	0.10* (10.71)	0.11* (22.71)	0.16* (8.29)
Education	0.02* (14.26)	0.05* (5.57)	0.17* (11.94)	0.03* (7.85)	-0.01* (-3.91)	-0.02 (-1.85)	-0.13* (-8.57)	-0.02* (-4.95)	0.04* (14.52)	0.01 (1.44)	0.19* (9.98)	0.04* (8.71)
Gender	0.08* (11.22)	0.07* (2.07)	0.08* (6.16)	0.07* (4.21)	-0.07* (-8.80)	-0.04 (-1.28)	-0.03* (-2.00)	-0.06* (-3.83)	0.18* (17.18)	0.02 (0.51)	0.10* (5.56)	0.15* (7.56)
Age	-0.32* (-9.98)	-0.36* (-2.34)	-0.20* (-3.38)	-0.32* (-4.91)	0.35* (10.28)	0.51* (3.21)	0.36* (5.52)	0.41* (6.04)	0.73* (20.30)	-0.11 (-0.62)	0.63* (10.46)	0.55* (8.37)
Age squared	0.10* (12.81)	0.12* (3.32)	0.09* (6.14)	0.10* (6.47)	-0.10* (-11.28)	-0.13* (-3.55)	-0.11* (-6.91)	-0.11* (-6.45)	-0.16* (-16.89)	0.06 (1.38)	-0.12* (-7.92)	-0.11* (-6.47)
Marital status	0.11* (13.07)	0.16* (4.54)	0.12* (7.47)	0.12* (7.39)	-0.16* (-17.41)	-0.16* (-4.18)	-0.17* (-10.02)	-0.20* (-11.14)	0.20* (15.88)	0.20* (4.48)	0.21* (9.66)	0.22* (10.00)

Family	-0.02* (-2.01)	-0.03 (-0.86)	0.00 (-0.24)	0.00 (-0.16)	0.14* (12.44)	0.17* (4.70)	0.09* (4.73)	0.11* (5.29)	-0.05* (-3.72)	-0.18* (-4.12)	0.03 (1.29)	-0.03 (-1.03)
Friends	-0.02* (-3.67)	-0.02 (-0.92)	-0.04* (-5.36)	-0.04* (-4.81)	0.07* (13.58)	0.07* (3.75)	0.09* (10.20)	0.10* (10.08)	-0.07* (-10.77)	-0.05* (-2.35)	-0.10* (-8.98)	-0.12* (-10.11)
Work	-0.02* (-2.46)	0.00 (0.10)	-0.01 (-0.96)	0.00 (0.24)	0.04* (5.42)	0.05* (2.14)	0.04* (3.02)	0.01 (0.90)	0.09* (9.40)	-0.01 (-0.19)	0.09* (5.74)	0.08* (4.44)
Religion	0.00 (1.07)	0.01 (0.58)	0.02 (1.82)	-0.03* (-3.17)	0.09* (18.86)	0.05* (2.54)	0.07* (7.17)	0.10* (10.28)	-0.02* (-3.29)	-0.04 (-1.79)	-0.05* (-4.29)	-0.06* (-4.70)
Trust	0.01 (1.52)	-0.08 (-1.94)	0.05* (2.90)	0.01 (0.47)	0.02 (1.64)	0.07 (1.63)	0.01 (0.82)	-0.02 (-0.73)	0.13* (10.86)	-0.02 (-0.43)	0.11* (5.31)	0.22* (9.46)
Confidence in civil services	0.04* (9.06)	0.00 (-0.29)	0.05* (7.46)	0.06* (7.31)	0.01* (3.22)	0.05* (2.77)	0.02* (2.59)	0.00 (0.52)	-0.03* (-4.91)	-0.05* (-2.37)	-0.03* (-3.33)	-0.02 (-1.90)
Observations available	76588	3982	23342	18106	78638	4055	23939	185254	79007	4106	24062	18610

Note: 1. The definition of health poor was chosen as those who self-report to be in poor health and in very poor health. Due to the differences in the definition of health poor for African regions and those in the other two regions, we chose the narrower definition of health poor to run the results for the pooled sample set.

health poor. This again confirms the importance of these three variables to individual well-being, and to policymakers, who could adjust policy to achieve improvement in well-being. The importance of education to those who are education poor is especially striking – the size of the coefficient for the education poor is easily five to 13 times larger than for the overall sample. For sociological and demographic factors, marital status appears to be most important and is easily significant 12 out of 12 times, followed closely by age and age squared. Between family and friends, results appear to be tilted towards the importance of friends. Friends are significant in 11 out of 12 cases for the overall sample and the three poor groups, whereas family is only significant seven out of 12 times, and less significant for the 1–10 scale for the poor and the binary scale for education poor and income poor. Lastly, for the other social variables, the aggregate results appear to favor, in order, confidence in civil services (nine out of 12 cases), religion (eight out of 12 cases), work (seven out of 12 cases) and trust, which seems to be marginally significant (only four out of 12 cases were found to be significant). Given the importance of trust in the literature, it is surprising that it is not very significant for the three regions investigated here. For the sake of brevity, we have not included results for the nonpoor groups, since the results are very similar to the overall sample results.

As can be seen in Table 5.1, pooling by subregion – as compared with country or variable analysis alone – improves the statistical fit, sometimes dramatically. While it does not change the overall conclusion regarding the relative importance of the three policy variables, it does cover up the richness of individual nuanced results that are gained by a more micro orientation. At the same time, it reduces the significance of some variables or some countries where the sample size is small. Where there is sufficient data available, a disaggregate approach yields more insights into the nature of well-being among both the rich and the poor, and would be more useful to researchers and policymakers in understanding the determinants of well-being for individual countries and subregions.

Sections 5.1 to 5.3 look at the three regions separately and then draw some overall conclusions. Overall, Latin American countries are on average more developed, Asian countries are in the middle range of development and African countries least developed. However, it is to be acknowledged that there are major differences in the level of development within continents and regions and there are a myriad of factors that affect life satisfaction and well-being other than the level of economic development and income. Section 5.4 explores the importance of interaction effects for the three regions. Lastly, Section 5.5 concludes with a discussion of the importance of a global focus on health and education in improving life satisfaction.

5.1 Asia

Looking at Table 5.2, well-being in Asia follows a pattern that has been discussed for industrial countries and also for global data sets. Richer countries and regions, measured in per capita income terms, have higher levels of well-being than poorer countries and regions. East and

Table 5.2 Summary of life satisfaction and well-being in the three regions

	Life satisfaction (scale 1–10)	Well-being (scale 1–4)	Well-being (scale 0–1)	Data available	Total no. of observations
I. ASIA					
China	6.833	2.042	0.768	Waves 2–5	5,515
India	6.077	2.017	0.739	Waves 2–5	8,543
Indonesia	6.925	1.826	0.927	Waves 4–5	3,019
Bangladesh	6.092	2.041	0.811	Waves 3–4	3,025
Malaysia	6.839	1.689	0.948	Wave 5	1,201
Pakistan	4.851	2.016	0.764	Waves 3–4	2,733
Philippines	6.746	1.708	0.903	Waves 3–4	2,400
Thailand	7.213	1.676	0.924	Wave 5	1,534
Vietnam	6.863	1.748	0.915	Waves 4–5	2,495
Hong Kong	6.408	2.096	0.835	Wave 5	1,252
Singapore	7.235	1.689	0.949	Wave 4	1,512
Korea	6.433	2.043	0.878	Waves 2–5	3,649
Taiwan	6.623	1.892	0.874	Waves 3 and 5	2,007
South Asia	5.921	2.026	0.759	Waves 2–5*	14,301
East Asia and Southeast Asia	6.795	1.877	0.874	Waves 2–5*	24,584
Asia	6.480	1.932	0.831	Waves 2–5*	38,885

Table 5.2 Continued

	Life satisfaction (scale 1–10)	Well-being (scale 1–4)	Well-being (scale 0–1)	Data available	Total no. of observations
II. AFRICA					
Algeria	5.675	2.036	0.807	Wave 4	1,282
Egypt	5.564	2.009	0.866	Waves 4–5	6,051
Ethiopia	4.997	2.118	0.635	Wave 5	1,500
Mali	6.092	1.797	0.826	Wave 5	1,534
Morocco	5.781	1.966	0.812	Waves 4–5	3,464
Nigeria	6.705	1.656	0.829	Waves 2–4	5,019
Rwanda	4.965	2.048	0.849	Wave 5	1,507
South Africa	6.603	1.864	0.792	Waves 1–5	13,255
Tanzania	3.866	1.497	0.928	Wave 4	1,171
Uganda	5.651	1.994	0.776	Wave 4	1,002
Zambia	6.059	2.224	0.516	Wave 5	1,500
Zimbabwe	3.945	2.326	0.562	Wave 4	1,002
North Africa	5.647	1.998	0.842	Waves 4–5*	10,797
South Africa	6.603	1.864	0.792	Waves 1–5*	13,255
East Africa	4.973	2.038	0.707	Waves 4–5*	7,682
West Africa	6.569	1.689	0.828	Waves 2–5*	6,553
Africa	6.000	1.907	0.795	Waves 1–5*	38,287
III. LATIN AMERICA					
Argentina	7.193	1.918	0.804	Waves 1–5	5,368
Brazil	7.406	1.934	0.826	Waves 2–3 and 5	4,431
Chile	7.242	1.905	0.778	Waves 2–5	4,700
Colombia	8.306	1.673	0.856	Waves 3 and 5	9,050
Dominican Republic	7.127	1.949	0.726	Wave 3	417
El Salvador	7.496	1.533	0.920	Wave 3	1,254
Guatemala	7.951	1.769	0.787	Wave 5	1,000

Table 5.2 Continued

	Life satisfaction (scale 1–10)	Well-being (scale 1–4)	Well-being (scale 0–1)	Data available	Total no. of observations
Mexico	7.830	1.828	0.779	Waves 1–5	8,827
Peru	6.627	2.063	0.657	Waves 3–5	4,212
Trinidad and Tobago	7.260	1.659	0.855	Wave 5	1,002
Uruguay	7.296	1.923	0.831	Waves 3 and 5	2,000
Venezuela	7.122	1.550	0.895	Waves 3–4	2,400
Andean countries	7.575	1.813	0.792	Waves 2–5*	20,362
Mercosur countries	7.291	1.925	0.817	Waves 1–5*	11,799
Caribbean countries	7.737	1.783	0.798	Waves 1–5*	12,500
Latin America	7.545	1.836	0.801	Waves 1–5*	44,661

Notes: *Not all countries are represented for each wave, depending on the availability of data.
1. South Asia includes India, Bangladesh and Pakistan; East Asia includes China, Hong Kong, Korea and Taiwan; and South East Asia includes Indonesia, Malaysia, Philippines, Thailand and Vietnam.
2. North Africa includes Algeria, Egypt and Morocco; East Africa includes Ethiopia, Rwanda, Tanzania, Uganda, Zambia and Zimbabwe; and West Africa includes Mali and Nigeria.
3. Andean includes Chile, Colombia, Peru and Venezuela; Mercosur includes Argentina, Brazil and Uruguay; and Mexico and the Caribbean includes Mexico, Dominican Republic, El Salvador, Guatemala, and Trinidad and Tobago.
4. Wave 1: 1981–4, Wave 2: 1989–93, Wave 3: 1994–9, Wave 4: 1999–2004 and Wave 5: 2005–7. There is no information from 1985–8.

Southeast Asia have higher well-being levels than South Asia. Singapore has the highest level and Pakistan the lowest. Looking at Asia, all three measures result in a similarly strong valuation of the importance of health in raising happiness and well-being, This is followed by the importance of income and then education. The demographic control variables of gender, marital status and age are sometimes significant in particular countries or country groups. However, there does not seem to be a generally recognizable pattern as to their levels of significance. Moreover, there is considerable diversity of impacts from country to country, which is important to recognize. The conclusions drawn by Easterlin and others from a large sample for one country appear to be an oversimplification of the relationship between age and well-being. There is a "midlife crisis" in some countries and not in others. The pattern of statistical significance of the family and friends variables may have some relationship to the social and cultural relationships in the different parts of Asia. Family is important for life satisfaction (1 to 10 scale) in a few countries in East and Southeast Asia and also in India, whereas it is generally somewhat less important for happiness (the 1 to 4 and 0 to 1 scales). For friends, the pattern is reversed; seven countries, mostly in South and Southeast Asia, record significant happiness coefficients, and only three are significant for life satisfaction. Certainly, it is not possible to make any blanket statements regarding the importance of either variable for the Asian region as a whole.

Turning to the regional aggregation results, happiness and well-being are both uplifted by access to better health in all three regions of South Asia, East Asia and Southeast Asia, as well as Asia as a whole. There is a similar positive result for income in all subregions as well as Asia as a whole. Income is also significant in all regions as well as Asia. Education is less significant in East Asia and Southeast Asia than it is in South Asia, as noted in some country reports. The impact of demographic variables varies somewhat from region to region. Women are more often happier than men in East Asia compared with South Asia, while the impact of nonlinearities of the relationship between age and well-being is more pronounced for the 1 to 10 and 0 to 1 definitions of well-being, without much difference among regions or poverty groups. Women are generally happier than men in all three regions and in Asia as a whole. Friends are highly significant in South Asia and for the Asian region as a whole, while the impact of the family is more muted throughout the region. Family is not significant nearly as often as friends. More detailed studies are needed to explore these differences in greater depth. From the evidence for the four social variables, both life satisfaction and happiness are generally uplifted by religion, although the pattern is stronger for the happiness form of well-being, and also by trust. Confidence in the civil service improves well-being in about half the countries, and perhaps slightly more for the happiness form of well-being. Work does not uplift life satisfaction at all for any country, and only uplifts the happiness form of well-being in three countries out of 12. Turning to the poverty groups, health is the most significant variable for both forms of well-being, followed by income and education. As discussed above, education has a significant impact on well-being in South Asia, and the impact varies with the definition of the dependent variable.

It is important to recognize how the distinctive nature of the three different poverty groups impacts what they value and their levels of well-being. They are separate and distinct and respond to different independent variables, and much is to be gained by exploring them separately and in conjunction with the different poverty measures. The intersection of all three is very small (see Figure 2.4, Figure 3.2 and Figure 4.2) and there is less interaction between health and the other two poverty variables. This is because the health poor are self-selected. Nevertheless, the Venn diagram analysis highlights the importance of compiling and analyzing the three kinds of poverty.

A higher chance of escaping poverty lifts overall well-being for the entire sample in China, India, Bangladesh, Pakistan, the Philippines and Taiwan, and also the total sample for all countries aggregated. However, the effect is muted and more selective for the poor groups. A higher chance of escaping poverty raises well-being for education and income poor in China, and in Bangladesh for happiness and well-being and in all poverty groups. In the Philippines and Taiwan, where one might expect a significant response, the results were more muted. These results highlight again the importance of both aggregate and disaggregated data sets being analyzed together as well as separately.

An education is highly valued in South Asia, but less so in East and Southeast Asia, where levels of education are already high. However, health is highly valued everywhere in Asia and by the general population and all poverty groups. Income is also important, but not as generally significant as health. The control variables vary in importance, as noted above. A general conclusion about the importance of marriage, age or gender in raising well-being is difficult, although the general conclusions reached in other studies, that women and those who are married are happier and that there is a middle-age slump in well-being, is also supported.

5.2 Africa

The main conclusions regarding the determinants of well-being in Africa have already been summarized in Chapter 3, and these results echo the analysis for Asia. Better health is the most powerful and pervasive factor in raising well-being in the African region. Health is significant for all three configurations of the well-being variable, and in nearly all

African countries, for the sample as a whole and also for each of the poverty groups. Significantly, comparisons between the response of the poor and the full sample suggest that the health and income poor respond more strongly to improvements in health than the full sample. Table 3.13 shows that all three poverty groups would respond favorably to improvements in the provision of health services in several countries, and the strongest impact is for health, followed by income. Education is not generally as significant an explanatory variable in Africa as it was in Asia, and this holds for the overall sample as well as the poverty groups. While income is still important as a force to uplift well-being, we would argue that health should still take center stage in any strategy to address the well-being of those in all three poverty groups in Africa. This is basically the same message that we took away from the analysis in Asia. The results from pooling over African regions are consistent with earlier findings for the country reports and also with the aggregation results from Asia.

Africa is the poorest region in per capita income terms, and it also has the lowest well-being scores of the three regions. Generally, East Africa has the lowest well-being scores and South Africa and West Africa the highest well-being scores. Well-being in North Africa varies more than the other regions. Its well-being for the 0 to 1 scale is higher than any other region, but its ranking for the other two scales is lower. Pooling by subregion – as compared with country or variable analysis alone – improves the statistical fit, sometimes dramatically. While it does not change the overall conclusion regarding the relative importance of the three policy variables, it does cover up the nuances that are gained by a more micro orientation. At the same time, it reduces the significance of some variables or some countries where the sample size is small.

Health is still the number one variable influencing well-being, followed by income and education. Gender, marital status and age are important control variables that account for variations in socioeconomic characteristics and permit a generally more accurate and unbiased analysis of the policy variables of health, income and education that impact well-being. In the case of Africa, the findings for age, gender and marital status are similar to those from Asia and also observed by other researchers on well-being. Women are happier than men, those who are married are happier than those who are not, and there tends to be a dip in well-being in middle age, although not as dramatic as in some industrial countries. The finding that family and friends are not significant to the same extent that they are in industrial countries reinforces the conclusion drawn from the Asian experience. The muted importance of these two variables needs to be studied more carefully for the African region.

The importance of a strong civil service and a strong belief in religion are more important in Africa than a favorable work environment and a high level of trust. These conclusions are consistent with some of the results from other work on industrial countries and not consistent with some others, particularly the lack of importance of work and trust. Pooling by subregion improves the statistical fit and reinforces the conclusions from the more disaggregate country variable analysis. However, it tends to oversimplify the interplay of different forces, although it does serve to highlight how the different regions respond to the independent variables. These regional nuances are important to consider in making policy to improve the well-being of the poor.

Working with these general conclusions, both from the importance of the three policy variables and the demographic and social results, should provide some impetus for a modification of the policy stance in Africa. Aside from direct poverty reduction policies, these should create an environment where some rethinking of the appropriate policies needed to uplift well-being in the region can take place.

5.3 Latin America

Comparisons between the response of well-being and happiness to variations in the major policy variables of health, income and education in Latin America and in Asia and Africa bring a few surprises. One surprise is the near general failure of education to be a major factor in uplifting well-being and the strong importance of religion in raising well-being throughout the region. With regard to education, Latin America is more similar to Africa than to Asia. The lack of the desire for educational attainment and the commensurate lack of impact on happiness is a characteristic for both ends of the scale, the most educated continent and the least educated continent. Income is also a key policy variable, and is as important for the poor as for the full sample, although the coefficients are not as often significant because of some missing data problems. Age is nonlinearly related to well-being in more than half the countries in the region, more than in either of the other two regions. Marriage uplifts well-being on average, while gender makes little difference to well-being in Latin America, a different result from the other regions. As noted in the country reports and the general survey of the region above, family is significant for some countries in the full sample but not for the poverty groups. In comparison with friends, family is slightly more significant for the full sample, but friends is also weak for the poverty groups. The results for family and friends are slightly stronger than we concluded from Africa or Asia, but still not as important as previous research for industrial countries would lead us to believe. Religion is the most important of the four other social variables, for both the full sample and the poverty groups, particularly in the 1 to 10 and 1 to 4 scales for well-being. In this regard, religion is a much stronger force in raising happiness and well-being in Latin America than in the other two regions. Work is also significant in a few countries, as mentioned above, while there is little confidence in the civil service or trust in others as motivations for uplifting well-being. Analysis by region adds some insights, particularly with respect to the relative importance of friends and family in the different regions, with friends more important in the Andean region and family in Mercosur and Mexico. Also, the religion variable pointed out the importance of spiritual well-being for the region as a whole and the poverty groups in the three regions. The impact of the social variables also provides some scope for changes in policy, particularly in the provision of civil services. However, the impact of work varies rather dramatically by sub-region, being more important in South Africa and the region as a whole than in the other two regions. As far as public policy goes, these findings could have an important input into developing a framework to lift well-being by appropriate policies in the region, particularly for health and income and also for education and the provision of civil services.

5.4   Analysis of interaction effects

In addition to the direct impact of the major decision variables of health, education and income on well-being, it is possible for interaction effects among these variables to have an additional impact on well-being. For example, good health combined with higher income could provide a beneficial impact on well-being over and above the individual impacts of health and income. To reflect these possible interaction effects, we estimated a model containing three interaction effects in addition to the other explanatory variables for the three regions and corresponding subregions. These results are reported in Table 5.3.

Before summarizing the results, it should be noted that the expected sign of the interaction term will depend upon the relationship between the interacting variables and the selected index of well-being. In the case when the values of all three variables are positively related, i.e. when well-being increases so also do the policy variables, then the sign of the interaction term is a priori positive for the life satisfaction index coded from 1 to 10 and the binary happiness index coded from

0 to 1. This would be the case for the interaction of income and education. However, because of the definition of health, which is negatively related to well-being (i.e. good health is a smaller index number and poor health is a larger index number), the sign of the interaction terms involving the health variable would be ambiguous.

The results in Table 5.3 are based on probit results for the model in Equation 5.1:

$$WB = b_0 + b_1 \text{ Health} + b_2 \text{ Income} + b_3 \text{ Education} + b_4 \text{ Gender} +$$
$$b_5 \text{ Age} + b_6 \text{ Age Squared} + b_7 \text{ Marital status} + b_8 \text{ Family} +$$
$$b_9 \text{ Friends} + b_{10} \text{ Health*Income} + b_{11} \text{ Health*Education} +$$
$$b_{12} \text{ Education*Income} \tag{5.1}$$

In general, the results for Asia support the importance of interaction effects on well-being. Considering the full sample of all Asian economies, all three interaction terms are significant for all three definitions of well-being with the exception of the interaction of health and education for the 1–4 and 0–1 definitions. Considering the separate interaction impacts for the different regions and poverty categories, the impact of the health and income interaction on the education poor is significant in all three well-being definitions, while the health and income interaction is important in East and Southeast Asia but not South Asia. For the poor groups in Asia, the interaction effects of health and income are strongest for the education poor for the 1–10 and 1–4 scales and for the income poor for the 0 to 1 scale. Likewise, as with the health and income interactions, the education and income interactions appear to be significant in East and Southeast Asia and not South Asia. Lastly, health and education interactions tend to be weak for most poverty groups.

Turning to Africa, the interaction of health and income has more significant coefficients than the other two interaction terms.

Health and income interactions are particularly significant in North Africa and the African region as a whole. For the poverty groups, there are only a few cases in which the three interaction terms are significant, more often for the health poor and education poor than the income poor. The interaction of education and income follows next in order of importance, lastly followed by health and education. For the latter two interaction terms, they are particularly significant for the binary index of happiness.

For Latin America, the interaction term for health and income is again significant for the full sample for all three definitions of well-being. Among the poverty groups and regional aggregates, the interactions of

Table 5.3 Probit results for the three regions with interaction effects.

	a170 (Scale 1–10)				a008 (Scale 1–4)				a008r (Scale 0–1)			
	Overall	Health Poor	Edn Poor	Income Poor	Overall	Health Poor	Edn Poor	Income Poor	Overall	Health Poor	Edn Poor	Income Poor
I. ASIA												
HEALTH*INCOME												
South Asia	0.00 (0.52)	0.13 (1.88)	0.03* (3.27)	−0.02 (−0.48)	0.00 (0.38)	−0.07 (−1.01)	−0.01 (−1.30)	0.02 (0.37)	−0.05* (−6.84)	0.00 (−0.06)	−0.03* (−2.18)	−0.31* (−6.77)
East and Southeast Asia	0.03* (6.19)	0.02 (0.19)	0.03* (3.23)	0.02 (0.38)	−0.03* (−5.16)	−0.17 (−1.11)	−0.05* (−5.50)	−0.13* (−2.37)	−0.01 (−1.54)	0.05 (0.37)	0.02 (1.27)	−0.15* (−2.74)
East Asia and Singapore	0.02* (2.74)	0.05 (0.39)	0.01 (0.50)	0.05 (0.74)	−0.02* (−3.54)	−0.22 (−1.42)	−0.02* (−2.01)	−0.10 (−1.56)	−0.01 (−1.54)	0.12 (0.83)	−0.01 (−0.36)	−0.07 (−1.09)
Southeast Asia excluding Singapore	0.04* (5.31)		0.05* (3.55)	−0.09 (−0.94)	−0.02* (−2.17)		−0.06* (−4.12)	−0.14 (−1.36)	−0.01 (−0.94)		0.04 (1.82)	−0.30* (−2.84)
Asia	0.02* (4.88)	0.06 (0.99)	0.03* (4.65)	0.00 (−0.08)	−0.02* (−4.94)	−0.05 (−0.76)	−0.04* (−6.19)	−0.04 (−1.10)	−0.03* (−6.06)	−0.03 (−0.55)	0.00 (−0.54)	−0.25* (−7.23)
HEALTH*EDN												
South Asia	0.02* (3.89)	0.09 (1.53)	−0.04 (−0.85)	0.05* (4.86)	−0.02* (−4.03)	0.02 (0.39)	0.04 (0.89)	−0.03* (−2.89)	0.01* (2.11)	−0.02 (−0.43)	−0.20* (−4.16)	0.02 (1.83)
East and Southeast Asia	0.00 (−0.58)	−0.25 (−1.39)	0.02 (0.45)	−0.01 (−0.59)	0.02* (3.40)	0.17 (0.92)	0.02 (0.52)	−0.01 (−0.71)	−0.03* (−4.37)	−0.12 (−0.73)	−0.07 (−1.52)	−0.01 (−0.34)

East Asia and Singapore	0.00 (−0.19)	−0.24 (−1.30)	0.01 (0.26)	−0.02 (−1.34)	0.01 (1.67)	0.11 (0.59)	−0.05 (−1.01)	0.01 (0.91)	−0.02* (−2.81)	−0.06 (−0.36)	−0.03 (−0.51)	−0.01 (−0.65)
Southeast Asia excluding Singapore	0.00 (−0.72)		0.01 (0.24)	0.01 (0.49)	0.03* (3.78)		0.11 (1.79)	−0.05 (−1.98)	−0.05* (−4.02)		−0.04 (−0.58)	0.00 (−0.04)
Asia	0.01* (2.75)	0.09 (1.85)	0.00 (0.20)	0.02* (3.25)	0.00 (−1.01)	0.02 (0.40)	−0.04 (−1.34)	−0.02* (−2.97)	−0.01 (−1.27)	−0.01 (−0.25)	−0.09* (−3.01)	0.01 (1.22)

EDN*INCOME

South Asia	0.00 (−0.87)	−0.01 (−1.71)	0.03 (1.62)	0.00 (−0.25)	0.01* (3.17)	0.02* (2.22)	−0.02 (−0.90)	0.02 (0.92)	−0.02* (−7.29)	−0.01 (−1.08)	−0.01 (−0.29)	−0.05* (−2.37)
East and Southeast Asia	0.00* (−2.05)	0.00 (−0.22)	−0.05* (−3.11)	−0.03 (−1.34)	0.01* (5.35)	0.01* (2.13)	0.04* (2.55)	−0.01 (−0.35)	−0.02* (−9.58)	−0.03* (−3.28)	−0.07* (−3.45)	−0.01 (−0.29)
East Asia and Singapore	−0.01* (−2.88)	0.00 (−0.40)	−0.06* (−2.76)	−0.01 (−0.34)	0.01* (3.05)	0.00 (−0.23)	0.06* (2.56)	−0.05 (−1.71)	−0.02* (−5.22)	−0.01 (−1.40)	−0.06 (−1.98)	0.02 (0.68)
Southeast Asia excluding Singapore	0.00 (−0.40)		−0.04 (−1.76)	−0.05 (−1.47)	0.01* (3.12)		0.02 (0.64)	0.04 (1.04)	−0.03* (−6.30)		−0.07 (−1.86)	0.01 (0.14)
Asia	−0.01* (−6.45)	−0.01* (−2.13)	−0.01 (−0.70)	0.00 (−0.19)	0.01* (7.78)	0.02* (3.60)	0.01 (0.60)	0.00 (−0.35)	−0.02* (−12.70)	−0.02* (−3.56)	−0.02 (−1.62)	−0.03 (−1.71)

II. AFRICA

HEALTH*INCOME

North Africa	0.02* (3.47)	0.02 (0.78)	0.03* (2.97)	0.08 (1.50)	0.02* (3.02)	−0.07* (−2.65)	0.02* (2.34)	−0.19* (−3.12)	−0.03* (−3.78)	0.01 (0.24)	−0.01 (−0.59)	0.06 (0.97)

(Continued)

Table 5.3 Continued

	a170 (Scale 1–10)				a008 (Scale 1–4)				a008r (Scale 0–1)			
	Overall	Health Poor	Edn Poor	Income Poor	Overall	Health Poor	Edn Poor	Income Poor	Overall	Health Poor	Edn Poor	Income Poor
South Africa	0.00 (-0.23)	-0.01 (-0.48)	0.01 (0.87)	0.06 (1.76)	0.02* (2.68)	0.01 (0.44)	0.00 (0.03)	0.02 (0.54)	-0.02* (-3.17)	-0.04 (-1.57)	0.00 (-0.12)	-0.15* (-3.69)
East Africa	0.00 (0.21)	0.11* (4.04)	0.03* (2.85)	0.05 (0.94)	0.00 (-0.51)	-0.02 (-0.65)	0.00 (-0.08)	0.05 (0.87)	-0.02* (-2.30)	-0.10* (-3.37)	-0.03 (-1.81)	-0.23* (-4.15)
West Africa	0.00 (0.09)	0.00 (0.19)	0.03* (2.42)	0.05 (0.66)	-0.01 (-1.07)	0.00 (0.12)	-0.03* (-2.14)	0.01 (0.14)	-0.01 (-1.08)	-0.05 (-1.85)	0.03 (1.73)	-0.21* (-2.31)
Africa	0.00 (1.21)	0.04* (3.38)	0.02* (5.13)	0.06* (2.45)	0.02* (4.68)	-0.03* (-2.73)	0.01* (2.53)	-0.02 (-0.74)	-0.03* (-6.18)	-0.02* (-2.02)	-0.02* (-2.30)	-0.13* (-4.76)
HEALTH*EDN												
North Africa	-0.01 (-1.69)	-0.04 (-1.80)	-0.05 (-1.11)	-0.01 (-1.12)	-0.01 (-1.13)	0.07* (3.11)	-0.06 (-1.07)	0.01 (0.57)	-0.01 (-0.65)	-0.12* (-4.46)	-0.22* (-3.70)	-0.02 (-1.00)
South Africa	0.00 (0.58)	0.02 (1.21)	-0.06 (-1.37)	0.00 (0.36)	0.00 (-0.09)	-0.01 (-0.32)	0.08 (1.78)	0.01 (0.68)	-0.01 (-1.55)	-0.03 (-1.15)	-0.19* (-3.64)	-0.01 (-0.92)
East Africa	0.00 (-0.34)	0.01 (0.30)	0.09 (1.89)	0.03 (1.73)	0.01 (1.26)	-0.03 (-0.75)	0.06 (1.10)	0.00 (0.17)	-0.03* (-2.74)	-0.04 (-1.26)	-0.09 (-1.83)	-0.04 (-1.54)
West Africa	0.01 (1.15)	0.01 (0.36)	-0.01 (-0.19)	0.02 (1.20)	0.00 (-0.24)	-0.08* (-2.59)	0.02 (0.32)	-0.02 (-0.79)	-0.02* (-2.18)	0.04 (1.24)	-0.31* (-3.56)	0.00 (-0.13)
Africa	-0.01* (-2.30)	0.00 (0.33)	-0.05* (-2.31)	0.00 (-0.01)	0.00 (1.48)	-0.01 (-0.71)	0.04 (1.58)	0.01 (1.53)	-0.02* (-3.65)	-0.05* (-3.47)	-0.14* (-5.02)	-0.02 (-1.90)

EDN*INCOME

North Africa	0.00 (−1.49)	−0.01 (−1.82)	−0.01 (−0.64)	0.02 (0.73)	0.01* (2.74)	0.01 (1.99)	−0.02 (−0.84)	−0.03 (−1.38)	−0.01* (−3.74)	−0.01* (−2.97)	−0.02 (−0.58)	−0.05 (−1.61)
South Africa	−0.02* (−8.28)	−0.01* (−3.37)	0.01 (0.26)	0.01 (0.35)	0.01* (6.32)	0.01* (2.30)	−0.03 (−1.00)	0.00 (0.13)	−0.01* (−3.50)	−0.01 (−1.85)	0.02 (0.46)	−0.03 (−1.46)
East Africa	0.00 (−1.32)	−0.01* (−2.19)	0.02 (0.90)	0.07* (2.15)	0.00 (0.60)	−0.01 (−1.84)	0.08* (3.81)	−0.06 (−1.85)	−0.02* (−5.08)	−0.01 (−0.93)	−0.08* (−3.12)	0.04 (0.96)
West Africa	0.00 (0.25)	−0.01* (−2.13)	0.02 (0.66)	0.03 (0.78)	0.00 (1.59)	0.01 (1.67)	0.01 (0.29)	0.00 (0.09)	−0.01* (−2.39)	−0.01 (−1.82)	−0.07 (−1.96)	−0.03 (−0.70)
Africa	0.00* (−3.55)	−0.01* (−3.52)	0.01 (0.96)	0.01 (1.23)	0.00* (3.34)	0.00 (1.22)	0.03* (3.11)	−0.01 (−0.43)	−0.01* (−7.40)	−0.01* (−4.44)	−0.06* (−4.42)	−0.03* (−2.40)

III. LATIN AMERICA

HEALTH*INCOME

Andean	0.01 (1.56)	0.03 (0.26)	0.00 (0.06)	0.06 (1.21)	−0.03* (−4.08)	−0.08 (−0.59)	−0.04 (−1.99)	0.04 (0.67)	−0.03* (−2.62)	−0.09 (−0.70)	−0.05* (−2.06)	−0.27* (−5.63)
Mercosur	0.02* (2.55)	−0.11 (−1.21)	0.00 (−0.07)	0.05 (1.09)	−0.01 (−0.92)	0.01 (0.13)	0.01 (0.98)	−0.01 (−0.27)	−0.03* (−3.60)	−0.04 (−0.38)	−0.04* (−2.67)	−0.11 (−1.89)
Mexico and Caribbean	0.00 (0.62)	−0.09 (−0.86)	−0.01 (−0.67)	0.05 (0.99)	0.00 (−0.29)	−0.22 (−1.77)	−0.04* (−3.26)	−0.01 (−0.09)	−0.04* (−3.60)	−0.04 (−0.46)	0.03 (1.65)	−0.26* (−4.25)
Latin America	0.01* (3.82)	−0.04 (−0.77)	0.00 (−0.04)	0.08* (2.78)	−0.01* (−3.42)	−0.09 (−1.62)	−0.02* (−2.45)	0.02 (0.81)	−0.03* (−5.57)	−0.06 (−1.03)	−0.02 (−1.95)	−0.22* (−7.43)

(Continued)

Table 5.3 Continued

	a170 (Scale 1–10)				a008 (Scale 1–4)				a008r (Scale 0–1)			
	Overall	Health Poor	Edn Poor	Income Poor	Overall	Health Poor	Edn Poor	Income Poor	Overall	Health Poor	Edn Poor	Income Poor
HEALTH*EDN												
Andean	0.00 (0.44)	0.15 (1.33)	0.11* (2.00)	0.02 (1.71)	0.00 (0.72)	-0.18 (-1.45)	0.08 (1.44)	-0.02 (-1.31)	-0.04* (-5.15)	0.00 (0.02)	-0.33* (-5.32)	-0.01 (-0.78)
Mercosur	-0.01 (-1.56)	-0.02 (-0.20)	-0.07 (-1.48)	-0.01 (-1.00)	0.00 (-0.25)	-0.19 (-1.53)	-0.10* (-2.04)	0.01 (0.71)	-0.04* (-4.15)	0.10 (0.78)	-0.07 (-1.40)	-0.06* (-3.32)
Mexico and Caribbean	0.00 (0.58)	-0.22* (-2.99)	0.10 (1.97)	0.00 (-0.31)	0.00 (0.59)	-0.04 (-0.52)	0.13* (2.42)	-0.03* (-2.21)	-0.07* (-6.80)	-0.15 (-1.50)	-0.25* (-4.07)	0.00 (-0.26)
Latin America	0.00 (-0.84)	-0.07 (-1.27)	0.04 (1.41)	0.00 (-0.08)	0.01* (2.44)	-0.08 (-1.47)	0.01 (0.26)	-0.01 (-1.35)	-0.06* (-10.39)	-0.04 (-0.65)	-0.18* (-5.50)	-0.03* (-2.89)
EDN*INCOME												
Andean	0.00 (1.97)	-0.02 (-1.35)	0.02 (0.70)	0.00 (-0.17)	0.00 (1.06)	0.02 (1.52)	-0.04 (-1.19)	0.00 (-0.08)	-0.02* (-5.85)	0.00 (0.16)	0.03 (0.70)	-0.07* (-3.01)
Mercosur	0.00 (-0.24)	0.01 (0.67)	-0.04* (-2.04)	0.01 (0.49)	0.00 (0.09)	0.00 (-0.31)	0.00 (0.19)	-0.01 (-0.47)	-0.01* (-3.98)	0.00 (0.31)	-0.10* (-3.65)	-0.05 (-1.74)

Mexico and Caribbean	0.00 (0.79)	0.01 (0.89)	-0.01 (-0.45)	0.01 (0.31)	0.00 (0.82)	0.01 (1.28)	0.02 (0.68)	0.02 (0.66)	-0.01* (-3.60)	0.00 (-0.36)	-0.06 (-1.96)	-0.07* (-2.53)
Latin America	0.00* (3.46)	0.00 (0.43)	-0.02 (-1.78)	0.00 (-0.29)	0.00 (1.26)	0.01 (0.88)	0.00 (0.10)	0.00 (0.10)	-0.01* (-7.81)	0.00 (0.16)	-0.07* (-3.85)	-0.07* (-4.75)

Notes: 1. Based on probit results for the below model with interaction effects:

$WB = b_0 + b_1 \text{ Health} + b_2 \text{ Income} + b_3 \text{ Education} + b_4 \text{ Gender} + b_5 \text{ Age} + b_6 \text{ Age Squared} + b_7 \text{ Marital status} + b_8 \text{ Family} + b_9 \text{ Friends} + b_{10} \text{ Health*Income} + b_{11} \text{ Health*Education} + b_{12} \text{ Education*Income}$

z stats are displayed in parenthesis.

2. Health Poor is defined as 4–5 for Asia and Latin America. Health Poor is defined as 3–5 for African countries only.

3. South Asia includes India, Bangladesh and Pakistan; East Asia includes China, Hong Kong, Korea and Taiwan; and Southeast Asia includes Indonesia, Malaysia, Philippines, Thailand and Vietnam.

4. North Africa includes Algeria, Egypt and Morocco; East Africa includes Ethiopia, Rwanda, United Republic of Tanzania, Uganda, Zambia and Zimbabwe; and West Africa includes Mali and Nigeria.

5. Andean includes Chile, Colombia, Peru and Venezuela; Mercosur includes Argentina, Brazil and Uruguay; Mexico and Caribbean includes Mexico, Dominican Republic, El Salvador, Guatemala, and Trinidad and Tobago.

6. Variable dropped due to multicollinearity.

health and income and health and education are the most important (16 and 15 cases, respectively, out of 48 cases), while the interaction of income and education is less important (11 cases).

These results reinforce the importance of health by stressing its important interaction with the other two policy variables of income and education.

5.5 Global focus on health and education

Better health is the most important factor in raising well-being in all three regions, and we know that better public health brings with it a general uplifting impact on well-being and happiness. While not exhaustive, we summarize some of the successes that have been achieved in the field of public health and review the challenges to be faced in the future. The public health agenda has many components. One difficulty with the provision of more effective and well-focused public health is the inter-action between the demand for effective health services and the supply of these services. Modern medical practices call for particular protocols in dealing with different diseases. These approaches have been proven to be effective under different circumstances in both developed and developing countries. However, in many instances these practices have been adopted with lackluster enthusiasm, or sometimes even rejected more or less completely by different groups. A few examples put this critical interaction of supply and demand into focus. Sanitation and general cleanliness practices are often neglected even when facilities for clean water and proper sanitation are available. And even where latrines and outhouses are available outdoor defecation is still practiced. In this instance, the supply of facilities to increase the level of sanitation and cleanliness may not be sufficient. What needs to be changed is the level of awareness of disease and how diseases are spread. Public awareness campaigns are needed to increase this awareness in all three regions, but most critically in the poorest countries of Africa and Asia. Several other examples of the need for increased public awareness of important health practices come to mind. It is well known that breast feeding is the safest, cheapest and most nutritious way to feed infants. Yet as many as half of newly born infants in the developing world are not breast fed. Diarrhea is the leading cause of death of children before their fifth birthday. There are a series of protocols, any one of which could cut this mortality rate dramatically. The first is oral rehydration therapy (ORS), which is cheap and widely available. The second option is the life straw, which supplies safe drinking from a water source that is cleaned by a system that has been recently developed in Sweden. The third is using chlorine to purify drinking water. Yet only a few families in poor circumstances in the three regions use any of these methods for purifying water. In Zambia only 10 percent of families use ORS. In India, only one-third of children under 5 with diarrhea were given ORS, and the experience with the life straw has not yet been exhaustively investigated. Partly this is a result of lack of trust in these methods or belief that something else will do a better job. In their book *Poor Economics*, Banerjee and Duflo (2011) tell a story of health in western India, where nurses were not coming to work because the women who came to them for advice about diarrhea refused to give the ORS to their children and the nurses couldn't see the point of working when the patients paid them no heed. In Africa, bed nets to stop the transmission of malaria are widely distributed by charitable foundations. Research on the effectiveness of these bed nets showed significant economic returns in terms of less work loss, more energy and higher productivity. Yet the effectiveness of the nets requires that they be used every night and that they are replaced when the medication runs out. Despite best efforts of many donors, the malaria epidemic continues to claim 1.6 million lives per year. What is needed is a coordinated effort to use bed nets to treat the epidemic in the most heavily infected villages and for villagers to accept the need to achieve complete compliance with their use. TB and HIV/AIDS also present their own challenges. In both cases there is possible shame on the part of the patient and reluctance to seek the help of medical personnel. Again, greater awareness of the symptoms of the disease through greater public awareness could increase the probability of patients seeking help and reducing the spread of the disease. In all cases of communicable diseases the entry point is the health facility, and this is where traditional medicine continues to have a stranglehold on many households, preventing access to best practices and reducing the effectiveness of treatment, prolonging suffering and increasing mortality. Banerjee and Duflo note that in India, despite its being poor and densely populated, there are many health facilities with trained health care professionals. Yet in Udaipur, one of the poorer provinces,

the average adult we interviewed in an extremely poor household saw a health-care provider once every two months. Of these visits, less than one-fourth was to a public facility. More than one-half were to private facilities and the remainder was to *bhopas* – traditional healers who primarily offer exorcise from evil spirits. The poor in Udaipur seem to select the doubly expensive plan: cure, rather than prevention and cure from private doctors rather than from the trained nurses and doctors the government provides for free. (Banerjee and Duflo, 2011, p. 52)

What is needed is a public relations campaign to inform the public that the health care systems are working and that the doctors and nurses working in the public sector are competent, well informed and well trained. In India, and elsewhere in the developing world, many of the private doctors have no college or medical training, and there is no accrediting system in place so patients can tell what they are getting as they can with the public sector. These doctors tend to underdiagnose and overmedicate, which can be dangerous, particularly if needles are being used improperly.

There are shortages of medical personnel at all levels of training. According to Naicker *et al.* (2009), Africa has 2.3 healthcare workers per 1,000 population, compared with the Americas, which have 24.8 healthcare workers per 1,000 population. In Africa, 1.3 percent of the world's health workers care for people who experience 25 percent of the global disease burden. These shortages are compounded by the outmigration of trained health professionals, particularly to Europe and North America. The OECD estimates that 18 percent of all doctors in OECD countries are foreign born. There are push and pull factors that encourage migration of skilled health professionals, including lack of medical facilities in their home country and financial incentives to migrate. To exacerbate the shortages, the bulk of medical personnel in developing countries are concentrated in cities, creating additional shortages in rural communities which are already short of doctors and nurses. There are many approaches to dealing with these shortages, including providing more local facilities for medical training, limiting overseas visas to a certain time period, and required bonding of those who do go overseas to return and serve local communities. Money is also important. Poorer communities have smaller budgets, as we mentioned in our review of allocations for health and education in Chapters 2 to 4. We won't know exactly how resources can be reallocated in a more effective way until we analyze the feedback from randomized controlled trial (RCT) experiments and develop better systems to measure the effectiveness of poverty reduction and health intervention programs.

There are many communicable or infectious diseases. Globally, lower respiratory infections such as flu, pneumonia and bronchitis (3.9 million deaths in 2007) caused most infectious disease deaths, followed by

HIV/AIDS (2.8 million) and diarrheal disease (1.8 million), tuberculosis (1.6 million) and malaria (1.3 million). Davey (2000) provides a useful summary of ways to control infectious diseases in poor countries, along with many concrete country examples. There are several keys to success. First is to recognize the problem, and then to develop the appropriate tools and resources to deal with it. At the micro level, a few examples stand out. Malaria and tuberculosis are widespread and result in high rates of morbidity and mortality. Insecticide-treated bed nets have been effectively used to cut the risk of contracting malaria and to reduce the childhood death rate at minimal cost, yet only 1 percent of children currently sleep under bed nets in Africa. Anemia is often associated with malaria and can be treated with low-cost local programs that combine reducing the incidence of malaria along with vitamin-fortified diets and selective deworming of those at risk. TB can be effectively treated with Directly Observed Treatment, Short-course (DOTS), a five-pronged strategy for TB control. And new HIV cases could also be prevented by better programs spearheaded by better information for those at risk and distribution of condoms. Apart from lower respiratory infections like bronchitis and pneumonia, the world's most prolific killer is diarrheal disease from bacteria like typhoid, cholera, *E. coli*, salmonella and many others. Diarrhea is caused by unsanitary personal hygiene and contaminated water. Because over a billion people don't have safe water access and more than double that number don't have access to basic sanitation, diarrhea has reached epidemic proportions in many countries. Yet a coordinated program of personal hygiene and education at the village level, along with use of soap for hand washing, installation of latrines and water purification with cheap systems such as the life straw,[1] can save millions of lives and increase labor productivity as well as uplifting well-being for sufferers. In Bangladesh alone, diarrhea kills over 100,000 children under 5 annually and is the cause of one in four deaths of children under 5. Morbidity rates are much higher. An estimated 65 million episodes occur yearly among children under 5, three to four episodes a year. Coordinated programs at the village level can make a big difference. In Bangladesh, a community-led total sanitation (CLTS) program involves ending open defecation by the entire community. This is reinforced by a program to install and maintain latrines combined with lessons in personal hygiene. Such sanitation initiatives can be improved by providing safe water. Tube wells and water purification methods can be supplemented by new technology using a water purifying straw. At a cost of a dollar or two per year, one straw can provide an individual with safe drinking water for a year. Of course, the expense of distribution and education would raise the cost, but it is something to be considered for developing countries as an alternative to purification schemes that would be much more costly. Vietnam has made such a commitment to reducing malaria, and Thailand, Cambodia, Senegal and Uganda have made dramatic headway in reducing the spread of HIV through sex education and the widespread marketing of cheap condoms. In Kenya, employers are supplying bed nets to their workforce through payroll deductions. In Bangladesh, rural sanitation has improved as villages have ended the practice of open defecation and adopted the wider use of latrines. As a result, the proportion of households covered by proper sanitation practices has risen from close to zero in 1970 to 80 percent by 2010, and the incidence of diarrhea has declined. Where diarrhea still occurs, oral rehydration therapy is an effective tool for reducing the intensity of the episode and preventing the possibility of death. The key to success, as with any of these programs, is political commitment.

HIV/AIDS has spread throughout the globe over the last 30 years. The first recognized cases of AIDS occurred in the USA in the early 1980s, when gay men in New York and California developed rare opportunistic infections and cancers that were resistant to any treatment. As more was learned about the disease, it was discovered that these infections and cancers were caused by a virus, which was named HIV (Human Immunodeficiency Virus). Scientists discovered that HIV leads to and causes Acquired Immune Deficiency Syndrome (AIDS). At the time, AIDS did not yet have a name. Nevertheless, it became clear that all the men were suffering from a common syndrome. The discovery of HIV was made a short time later. Progress has been made with treatment so that patients with HIV can now live for some time without contracting AIDS. However, if HIV transmutes into AIDS, the disease is always fatal. HIV/AIDS has spread around the world and now infects over 30 million people worldwide. Vulnerable groups include sex workers, intravenous drug users, gay men, and women. The infection spreads through sexual contact and blood. There are an estimated 33 million cases of HIV/AIDS worldwide and around 22 million in sub-Saharan Africa. There are 4.1 million cases in Southeast and South Asia and 1.4 million cases in Latin America. To contain the spread of HIV/AIDS there are four suggested protocols: (1) promote the use of condoms for sex workers and bisexuals; (2) publicize the importance of condoms and of not sharing needles; (3) make condoms and needles available at reasonable prices or make them free; (4) promote HIV/AIDS awareness through the media and non-government organizations (NGOs). Antiretroviral drugs are medications for the treatment of HIV. It is often recommended to take several drugs in combination. There are different classes of antiretroviral drugs that act on different stages of the HIV life cycle. These treatments are expensive and beyond the reach of the poor in Africa and parts of Asia. Currently about 36 percent of patients in low and medium-income countries are receiving HIV/AIDS treatment. Those who do not receive treatment on a timely basis before HIV turns into AIDS face certain death. Over time, and without treatment, HIV gradually destroys the body's defenses against disease, leaving it vulnerable to many infections. Although some people living with HIV have no symptoms, others can develop severe health problems associated with AIDS. AIDS can be defined as the late stage of the HIV disease. By the time of an AIDS diagnosis, HIV has already seriously damaged the body's immune system. Often, a person living with AIDS will already have had life-threatening infections or cancers. It can take 10 years or more for an HIV infection to turn into AIDS. However, anti-HIV medications can radically interfere with HIV's destruction of the immune system and lengthen a person's life expectancy. With proper treatment, some people now living with HIV may never develop AIDS and may live a normal life span. Studies suggest that starting treatment early in the course of infection can significantly improve long-term treatment success. Nevertheless, the number of deaths from the disease between 1980 and 2007 now amounts to about 24 million people. By 2030 this total is projected to reach 75 million. However, the rate of new infections has peaked and is projected to decline as antiretroviral drugs are reaching more people and containment methods are being more widely adopted. Projections suggest that the number of AIDS deaths and the proportion of deaths due to AIDS will not increase (see Bongaarts *et al.* 2009 for more information about the projected pattern of AIDS deaths).

Many countries have food subsidy programs designed to aid the nutritional needs of the poor. There are many books and articles analyzing and critiquing these programs. This short summary is designed to highlight some successes and challenges. A good starting point is the work of the International Food Policy Research Institute, published by Johns Hopkins University Press and edited by Per Pinstrup Anderson (1988). The benefits and costs of food subsidies will depend upon many factors, and budget implications have to be considered. The challenge is to identify programs in which consumer-focused subsidies are appropriate policy measures and are cost effective. Such policies should be useful in reducing the insecurity of access to food at the household level and by increasing the purchasing power of the poor. However, such programs need to be assessed in the light of other government programs and the need to be cost effective. There are several modalities.

Direct cash transfers are made by direct cash payments, issuance of food stamps or a voucher system. These programs are all designed to increase the calories and nutrition of poor families. As we noted in Chapters 2, 3 and 4 the incidence of being underweight, having stunted growth or being anemic is quite high in some parts of Asia and Africa. Over 30 percent of children under 5 were anemic in 10 out of 12 African countries and in eight of 12 Asian countries. Over 40 percent of children had stunted growth in six Asian countries and five African countries. These deficiencies can be directly addressed by appropriate targeted interventions to these groups.

Subsidized food is another way to deliver nutrition to the poor through rationing of highly subsidized food, mainly grains and some oils.

A third initiative to help the poor is through public works programs, sometimes called workfare. The program in India guaranteeing 100 days' work per year has received widespread news coverage. These programs have three objectives. The first is to provide income for the poor in exchange for work contributed to a government project. The second is that the worker in the project can benefit from the project through skill enhancement and experience. If so, it is possible for him to leverage this to obtain a better job once his workfare is completed. The third objective is to work on projects that will benefit the wider community, such as roads, schools, irrigation systems, sewage and primary health care facilities. To the extent that the income from these workfare jobs is spent on food and health care, these programs meet the stated objective.

Conditional cash transfers (CCT) are programs designed to offer a subsidy to families if they send their children to school. The subsidy is conditional upon school attendance, which is monitored. The subsidies from these programs are not directly seen as health subsidies. However, if they are properly targeted to poor families the bulk of the subsidy will be spent on food. The effectiveness of CCT programs has been evaluated, and they have generally been found to be an effective use of resources. For example, in Mexico CCT programs were 10 times more effective than school building programs that took place simultaneously (see Dowling and Yap 2009, Chapter 4 and Morley and Coady 2003, as well as the next section on the use of CCTs as a means to provide educational subsidies).

The important lessons gained from a review of these various initiatives to increase nutrition are threefold: target the recipients of the subsidy carefully, make sure the leakage to administrative or other costs is small, and carefully assess whether private distribution is a better alternative than public distribution. The former has been implemented effectively in the Philippines and Egypt (see Pinstrup-Anderson 1988, p. 336). There is, however, a cost to achieving better targeting, including identification of target households, which must be weighed against the targeting goal.

Turning to education, the issue of the balance between supply and demand arises again. The Millennium Development Goals stress the importance of education in the second and third objectives, namely to ensure that every child completes primary school by 2015 and that gender discrimination ends, also by 2015. Compliance with these objectives seems to be one of the objectives of many national governments. Enrollment rates in primary schools have increased dramatically between 1999 and 2006 in sub-Saharan Africa, from 54 percent to 70 percent, and in East Asia, from 75 percent to 88 percent (see Banerjee and Duflo 2011, p. 73). Certainly, getting children into school is important. What they learn is equally important, and here there are no directions from the Millennium Development Agenda. Unfortunately, there are wide discrepancies between what might be expected of students at the end of primary school and what is being achieved. There are discrepancies in what is expected of teachers and also of their students. A survey on national absence rate conducted by the World Bank in 2003 concluded that teachers in six countries in Africa, Asia and Latin America (Bangladesh, Ecuador, India, Indonesia, Peru and Uganda) miss one day a week out of five on average, and this is even higher in Uganda and India. In India further evidence suggests that teachers spend a lot of time drinking tea and reading the newspaper when they should be teaching. Furthermore, this lack of teacher discipline and neglect of their students is widespread throughout the developing world. In Kenya a survey found that 27 percent of students in the fifth grade could not read a simple paragraph, and in Pakistan 80 percent of children in the third grade could not read a first grade level paragraph. In India only 30 percent of students in higher grades could do basic division, a skill supposedly taught to second graders (see Banerjee and Duflo 2011, p. 75).

Looking at the policies that can be adopted in the education sector to resolve the gap between the demand for good education and the seemingly endless supply of bad education, some observers have simply said that the educational system has broken down because parents don't care about it. In their view, the current benefits to public education are not high enough to warrant any changes in the system. When rates of return and the perceived benefits to education increase, the demand for the state to improve its delivery of educational services will also increase. The growth of call centers in India and the Philippines reflects these changes for one small sector of the labor force. Recognizing that girls can earn an income from answering the phone, they started caring about the education that their girls were getting. Only when the demand for an educated labor force increases will the demand for quality education increase. Little is achieved by simply increasing the supply of low-quality education. But this is a policy that is short-sighted at best. Children are entitled to a good education, irrespective of the whims of their parents and/or society. Is there a way around this impasse? In western countries children have to be sent to school until a certain age, and efforts are made to see that they are getting a good education. Such an approach is not working in poorer countries around the world. One new approach that is working in many countries is to pay parents for sending their children to school.

Rather than pay to send their children to inferior but free public schools, parents receive payments for sending their children to school. However, they receive these "conditional cash transfers" only if the children show up for school. As noted above in the discussion of health subsidies, these programs were started in Mexico in the late 1990s and have been successfully adopted in many developing countries around the world. Their viability and sustainability have been proven, initially through randomized trials and eventually by the overwhelming success in raising school attendance and performance as well as children's health. Many of the programs have tied school attendance to preventative health care for their families. Further randomized trials to test the efficacy of new programs in other countries have brought about modifications and improvements in programs, particularly in other Latin American and Asian countries. The CCT program should be extended to better reach the chronically poor, who may find it too costly to send their children to school (see Dowling and Yap 2009, Chapter 4 and Banerjee and Duflo 2011, Chapter 4). CCT programs have not generally been effective in Africa, despite the demand for better education among some poor groups (see Chapter 4, this volume). However, a program begun in Malawi demonstrated that transfers don't have to be conditional on school attendance. Parents generally want to send their children to school if the school is doing a good job of teaching. A direct transfer is enough to provide some additional income to facilitate sending children to school rather than sending them out to work in some menial job or having them stay at home as a domestic helper. In the case of Africa, it is the grinding poverty that needs to be lifted to enable families to send their children to school. Remember that CCT programs originated in Mexico, one of the richer Latin American countries, and spread to the rest of the region, where incomes are still much higher than in Africa. Even though CCT programs have been adopted in parts of Asia, it seems that the quality of the schools had something to do with poor attendance and that CCT was an effective way to improve student attendance as well as teacher quality. Even in the poor countries of Asia, then, levels of human development are still generally higher than in Africa. Recall the comparisons of the HDI discussed in Chapter 4, where the three regions are generally separable on the HDI index scale, with Latin America on top, Asia second and Africa at the bottom.

Public policies for health and education designed to lift well-being and happiness will depend upon the level of economic development and the pattern of poverty in individual countries. Policies that might be appropriate in Latin America might not work in Africa or Asia. The best mix of policies will depend upon the needs and constraints in each country and region. It is important to realize that a one-size-fits-all strategy is not appropriate and results in a poor allocation of resources and continued lack of understanding of who is in need and what is needed. The only way this imbalance can be redressed is with more resources, research and careful analysis of the options available and the potential returns to medical treatment, given local conditions and budget constraints.

Notes

1 Introduction

1. The impact of changes in status seems to last longer than changes in income (see Di Tella and MacCulloch, 2006).
2. Note that these are estimates made by respondents regarding their relative income status. World Value Survey data don't contain actual income and distributions of income data. Compared with the rest of the sample, we can judge how accurate these estimates of relative income poverty are by comparing the relative frequency of responses to this question with the size of the total sample. This is explored for the three regions in Chapters 2, 3 and 4.

2 Analysis for Asia

1. The fact that the Gallup results were for rankings from 0 to 10 while the World Value Surveys were from 1 to 10 could impart a small bias to the comparisons but is unlikely to have a significant impact on the comparisons since it is probably reflected in the intercept term.
2. From a z test of differences between the overall and poverty coefficients in the regression equation, and also reflected in their appearing in Table 2.12.
3. Data on the confidence in civil services variable is not available for Singapore.
4. There are two cases when the family or friends variable has the wrong a priori sign; family and friends reduces well-being.
5. It is important to note the limitation of the income data here, where the individuals self-report on their level of income by reporting on their income decile. The caveat is that self-reporting must be a reliable and accurate assessment of own placing within the income distribution. If respondents do not accurately assess their place in the income distribution, this might not be appropriate for policy analysis which focuses on raising the level of incomes. Respondents could be in self-denial, feeling that they are not in the lowest income decile, and as a result report they are in a higher decile. Alternatively, respondents may be in a higher income decile but feel extremely deprived and report that they are in the poorest income decile.
6. Again, the limitation of health data has to be noted. Recall could be a potential problem, and respondents may have a distorted view of their own health status.
7. The *hukou* system of residence permits dates back to ancient China. Households were required to register by law. The hukou system requires a person as a resident of an area and includes name, parents, spouse and date of birth.

3 Analysis for Africa

1. This is a simplified version of a statistical test of difference between means.

Bibliography

African Development Bank (2009). *African Development Report 2009: Conflict, Resolution, Peace and Reconstruction in Africa.* New York: Oxford University Press.

Albert, C. and M. A. Davia (2005). *Education, wages and job satisfaction.* Paper presented at the Epunet Conference 2005, Colchester, UK.

Alesina, A., R. Di Tella and R. McCulloch (2004). Inequality and happiness: Are European and Americans different? *Journal of Public Economics,* 88, 2009–2042.

Arbache, J., D. S. Go and J. Page (2008). *Is Africa's Economy at a Turning Point.* Policy Research Working Paper 4519. World Bank.

Argyle, M. (1999). Causes and correlates of happiness. In *Well-being: the foundations of hedonic psychology,* eds. D. Kahneman, E. Diener and N. Schwarz. New York: Russell Sage Foundation.

Aristotle. http://happinessisbetter.com/2008/12/04/what-determines-happiness/

Aristotle (1985). *Nichomachean Ethics.* Translated by Terence Irwin. Indianapolis: Hackett Publishing Co.

Arrindell, W. A., C. Hatzichristou, J. Wensink, *et al.* (1997). Dimensions of national culture as predictors of cross-national differences in subjective well-being. *Personality and Individual Differences,* 23, 37–53.

Baldacci, E., G. Callegari, D. Coady, *et al.* (2010). *Public Expenditures on Social Programs and Household Consumption in China.* IMF Working Paper No. 10/69. Washington, DC: International Monetary Fund.

Banerjee, A. and E. Duflo (2011). *Poor Economics: a radical rethinking of the way to fight global poverty.* New York: Public Affairs.

Barnett, S. and R. Brooks (2010). *China: Does Government Health and Education Spending Boost Consumption?* IMF Working Paper No. 10/16. Washington, DC: International Monetary Fund.

Bauer, A., R. Hasan, R. Magsombol and G. Wan (2008). *The World Bank's New Poverty Data: Implications for the Asian Development Bank.* ADB Sustainable Development. Working Paper Series No. 2. Manila: ADB.

Baumeister, R. F. and M. R. Leary (1995). The need to belong: Desire for interpersonal attachments as a fundamental human motivation. *Psychological Bulletin,* 117, 497–529.

Baumeister. R. F. and D. M. Tice (1990). Anxiety and social exclusion. *Journal of Social and Clinical Psychology,* 9(2), 165–195.

Becker, G. (1994). *Human Capital: A Theoretical and Empirical Analysis With Special Reference to Education.* Chicago: The University of Chicago Press.

Berry, B. J. L. and A. Okulicz-Kozaryn (2009). Dissatisfaction with City Life: A New Look at Some Old Questions. *Cities,* 26, 117–124.

Bidani, B. and M. Ravallion (1997). Decomposing social indicators using distributional data. *Journal of Econometrics,* 77, 125.

Blanchflower, D. G (2009). International Evidence on Well-Being. NBER Chapters. In *Measuring the Subjective Well-Being of Nations: National Accounts of Time Use and Well-Being,* pages 155–226. National Bureau of Economic Research, Inc.

Blanchflower, D. G. and A. J. Oswald (1994). Estimating a wage curve for Britain. *The Economic Journal*, 104, 1025–1043.

Blanchflower, D. G. and A. J. Oswald (2004a). Well-being over time in Britain and the USA. *Journal of Public Economics*, 88(7), 1359–1386.

Blanchflower, D. G. and A. J. Oswald (2004b). Money, sex and happiness: An empirical study. *Scandinavian Journal of Economics*, 106, 393–415.

Bongaarts, J., F. Pelletier and P. Gerland (2009). Global Trends in AIDS mortality. Chapter prepared for *International Handbook of Adult Mortality*, eds. R. Rogers and M. Crimmins. New York: Springer.

Brickman, P., D. Coates and R. Janoff-Burlam (1978). Lottery Winners and Accident Victims: Is Happiness Relative? *Journal of Personality and Social Psychology*, 36, 917–927.

Brockmann, H., J. Delhey, C. Welzel and Hao Yuan (2009). The China Puzzle: Falling Happiness in a Rising Economy. *Journal of Happiness Studies*, 10(4), 387–405.

Caldes, N., D. Coady and J. A. Maluccio (2004). *The Cost of Poverty Alleviation Transfer Programs: A Comparative Analysis of Three Programs in Latin America.* Food Consumption and Nutrition, FCND Discussion Paper 172. Washington, DC: International Food Policy Research Institute.

Campbell, A., P. E. Converse and W. L. Rodgers, eds (1976). *The Quality of American Life. Perceptions, Evaluations and Satisfactions.* New York: Russel Sage Foundation.

Campbell III, C. (1993). Do Firms Pay Efficiency Wages? Evidence with Data at the Firm Level. *Journal of Labor Economics*, 11, 442–470.

Cantril, H. (1965). *The Pattern of Human Concerns.* New Brunswick, New Jersey: Rutgers University Press.

Castriota, S. (2006). *Education and Happiness: A Further Explanation to the Easterlin Paradox?* Departmental Working Papers 246. Tor Vergata University, CEIS.

Cerrutti, M. and R. Bertoncello (2003). *Urbanization and Internal Migration in Latin America.* Paper presented at Conference on African Migration in Comparative Perspective, Johannesburg, South Africa, June 2003.

Chappel, S., M. Forster and J. P. Martin (2009). *OECD Inequality and well-being in OECD countries: What do we know?* The 3rd OECD World Forum on "Statistics, Knowledge and Policy" *Charting Progress, Building Visions, Improving Life.* Busan, Korea, 27–30 October 2009.

Checchi, D. (2006). *The Economics of Education.* Cambridge: Cambridge University Press.

CIA Factbook. www.cia.gov/library/publications/the-world-factbook (8 July 2011).

Clark, A. E. and A. J. Oswald (1994). Unhappiness and unemployment. *The Economic Journal*, 104, 648–659.

Clark, M. S. (1984). Record Keeping in Two Types of Relationships. *Journal of Personality & Social Psychology*, 47, 549–557.

Clark, M. S. and J. Mills (1979). Interpersonal attraction in exchange and communal relationships. *Journal of Personality and Social Psychology*, 37(1), 12–24.

Corey, G. (2009). *Theory and practice of Counseling and Psychotherapy*, Part Two, Belmont, California: Thomson Brooks/Cole.

Csikszentmihalyi, M. and J. Hunter (2003). Happiness in everyday life: the uses of experience sampling. *Journal of Happiness Studies*, 4(2), 185–199.

Davey, S. (2000). *Health, a key to prosperity: success stories in developing countries.* Geneva, Switzerland: World Health Organization, Communicable Diseases (CDS). http://www.who.int/inf-new/dnldpdf/preface.pdf

Deaton, A. (2008). Income, Health and Well-being around the world: evidence from the Gallup world poll. *Journal of Economic Perspectives*, 22(2), 53–72. http://www.gallupworldpoll.com/content/24046/About.aspx.

Deiner, E. and M. E. Seligman (2002). Very happy people. *Psychological Sciences*, 13(1), 81–84.

Deiner, E., J. F. Helliwell and D. Kahneman, eds (2010). *International Differences in Well-Being.* New York: Oxford University Press.

Deininger, K., D. Byerlee, J. Lindsay, *et al.* (2011) *Rising global interest in farmland: Can it yield sustainable and equitable benefits?* Washington, DC: World Bank.

Diener, E. and M. E. P. Seligman (2004). Beyond money: Toward an economy of well-being. *Psychological Science in the Public Interest*, 5, 1–31.

Diener, E., M. Diener and C. Diener (1995). Factors Predicting the Subjective Well Being of Nations. *Journal of Personality and Social Psychology*, 69(5), 851–864.

Diener, E., S. Oishi and R. E. Lucas (2003). Personality, culture, and subjective well-being: Emotional and cognitive evaluations of life. *Annual Review of Psychology*, 54, 403–425.

Diener, E., R. E. Lucas and C. N. Scollon (2006). Beyond the hedonic treadmill: Revisions to the adaptation theory of well-being. *American Psychologist*, 61, 305–314.

Di Tella, R. and R. J. MacCulloch (2006). Some uses of happiness data in economics. *Journal of Economic Perspectives*, 20, 25–46.

Di Tella, R. and R. J. MacCulloch (2008). *Happiness Adaptation to Income beyond Basic Needs.* NBER Working Papers 14539. National Bureau of Economic Research, Inc.

Di Tella, R., R. J. MacCulloch and A. J. Oswald (2001). Preferences over inflation and unemployment: Evidence from surveys of happiness. *American Economic Review*, 91, 335–341.

Di Tella, R., R. J. MacCulloch and A. J. Oswald (2003). The Macroeconomics of Happiness. *Review of Economics and Statistics*, 85, 793–809.

Dolan, P., T. Peasgood and M. White (2006). *Review of research on the influences of personal well being and applications to policy making.* Project Report for Department of Environment Food and Rural Affairs (DEFRA). London: DEFRA.

Dowling, J. M. and Yap Chin-Fang (2007). *Modern Developments in Behavioral Economics.* New Jersey: World Scientific.

Dowling, J. M. and Yap Chin-Fang (2009). *Chronic poverty in Asia: Causes, Consequences and Policies.* New Jersey: World Scientific.

Doyle, G. (2002). Media Ownership – The Economics and Politics of Convergence and Concentration in the U.K. and European Media. *Journal of Cultural Economics*, 27(3), 290–293.

Dunn, E. W., D. T. Gilbert and T. D. Wilson (2011). If money doesn't make you happy, then you probably aren't spending it right. *Journal of Consumer Psychology*, 2011, 115–125.

Dusenberry, J. S. (1949). *Income, Saving and the Theory of Consumer Behaviors.* Cambridge: Harvard University Press.

Easterlin, R. A. (2001). Income and Happiness: Toward a Unified Theory. *Economic Journal*, 111, 465–484.

Easterlin, R. A. (1974). Does Economic Growth Improve the Human Lot? In *Nations and Households in Economic Growth: Essays in Honor of Moses Abramovitz*, eds P. A. David and M. W. Reder. New York: Academic Press, Inc.

Easterlin, R. A., L. Angelescu McVey, M. Switek, *et al.* (2010). The Happiness–Income Paradox Revisited. *Proceedings of the National Academy of Sciences of the United States of America*, 107(52), 22463–22468.

Easterlin, R. A., L. Angelescu McVey and J. S. Zweig (2011). The Impact of Modern Economic Growth on Urban-Rural Differences in Subjective Well-Being. *World Development*, 39(12), 2187–2198.

Eifert, B., A. Gelb and V. Ramachandran (2005). *Business Environment and Comparative Advantage in Africa: Evidence from the Investment Climate Data*. Working Paper No. 56. Washington: Center for Global Development.

FIDH (2011). http://www.fidh.org/Situation-of-minorities-remains.

Frank, R. H. (1988). *Passion within reason. The strategic role of the emotions*. New York: Norton.

Frank, R. H. (1999). *Luxury Fever: why money fails to satisfy in an era of excess*. New York: Norton.

Frey, B. S. and A. Stutzer (2000). Happiness, Economy and Institutions. *The Economic Journal*, 110, 918–938.

Frey, B. S. and A. Stutzer (2002a). *Happiness and Economics: How the economy and institutions affect well-being*. Princeton and Oxford: Princeton University Press. 220 pp.

Frey, B. S. and A. Stutzer (2002b). What Can Economists Learn from Happiness Research? *Journal of Economic Literature*, 40(2), 402–435.

Friedman, M. (1957). *A Theory of the Consumption Function*. Princeton: Princeton University Press.

Future Agricultures Consortium. http://www.future-agricultures.org/index.php (15 July 2011).

Gerlach, K. and G. Stephan (1996). A Paper on Unhappiness and Unemployment in Germany. *Economics Letters*, 52(3), 325–330.

Gilovich, T. (1991). *How We Know What Isn't So: The Fallibility of Human Reason in Everyday Life*. New York: The Free Press.

Graham, C. (2009). *Happiness Around the World: the paradox of happy peasants and miserable millionaires*. New York: Oxford University Press.

Graham, C. (2010). *The Challenges of Incorporating Empowerment into the HDI: Some Lessons from Happiness Economics and Quality of Life Research*, United Nations Development Programme Human Development Reports Research Paper.

Gupta, S., M. Verhoeven and E. Tiongson (2001). *Public Spending on Health Care and the Poor*. IMF Working paper WP/01/127. Washington, DC: IMF.

Hagerty, M. (2000). Social comparisons of income in one's community: Evidence from national surveys of income and happiness. *Journal of Personality and Social Psychology*, 78, 764–771.

Hayo, B. and W. Seifert (2003). Subjective economic well-being in Eastern Europe. *Journal of Economic Psychology*, 24(3), 329–348.

Helliwell, J. (2003). How's life? Combining individual and national variables to explain subjective well-being. *Economic Modelling*, 20, 331–360.

Helliwell, J. (2005). *Well-Being and Social Capital: Does Suicide Pose a Puzzle?* NBER Working Paper 10896. National Bureau of Economic Research, Inc.

Helliwell, J. (2008). *Life Satisfaction and Quality of Development*. NBER Working Papers 14507. National Bureau of Economic Research, Inc.

Hirsch, F. (1976). *Social Limits to Growth*. Cambridge, MA: Harvard University Press.

Herodotus, *The History*. Translated by George Rawlinson, http://classics.mit.edu/Herodotus/history.html

Holmes, T. H. and R. H. Rahe (1967). The social readjustment rating scale. *Journal of Psychosomatic Research*, 11, 213–218.

Inglehart, R. (1990). *Cultural Shifts in Advanced Industrial Society*. Princeton: Princeton University Press.

Inglehart, R. and H.-D. Klingemann (2000). Genes, culture, democracy and happiness. In *Culture and Subjective Well-being*, eds E. Diener and E. M. Suh. Cambridge, MA: MIT Press.

International Monetary Fund (2010). *Macro-Fiscal Implications of Health Care Reform in Advanced and Emerging Economies*. Fiscal Affairs Department, 28 December 2010.

Iwao, S. (1993). *The Japanese Woman: Traditional Image and Changing Reality*. New York: The Free Press.

Journal of Economic Perspectives, 20, 3–24.

Kabat-Zinn, J. 1994. *Wherever You Go, There You Are: Mindfulness Meditation in Everyday Life*. New York: Hyperion.

Kahneman, D (2011). *Thinking, Fast and Slow*. New York: Farrar, Straus and Giroux.

Kahneman, D. and A. Deaton (2010). High income improves evaluation of life but not emotional well-being. *Proceedings of the National Academy of Sciences of the United States of America*, 107(38), 16489–16493.

Kahneman, D. and A. B. Krueger (2006). *Developments in the Measurement of Subjective Well being*.

Kahneman D. and J. Riis (2005). Living, and thinking about it: Two perspectives on life. In *The science of well-being*, eds F. A. Huppert, N. Baylis and B. Keverne. Oxford: Oxford University Press.

Kahneman, D. and A. Tversky (1979). Prospect theory: An analysis of decision under risk. *Econometrica*, 47, 263–291.

Kahneman, D. and A. Tversky (1982). The psychology of preferences. *Scientific American*, 246, 160–173.

Kahneman, D. and A. Tversky (1983). Choices, values and frames. *American Psychologist*, 39, 341–350.

Kahneman, D., P. P. Wakker and R. Sarin (1997). Back to Bentham? Explorations of experienced utility. *Quarterly Journal of Economics*, 112, 375–405.

Kahneman, D., A. B. Krueger and D. A. Schkade *et al.* (2004). A Survey Method for Characterizing Daily Life Experience: The Day Reconstruction Method, *Science*, 306(5702), 1776–1780. http://www.sciencemag.org/content/306/5702/1776.short – corresp-1

Kaiser Family Foundation website. http://kff.org/

Kasser, T. and A. D. Kanner (2004). *Psychology and consumer culture: The struggle for a good life in a materialistic world*. Washington, DC: American Psychological Association.

Lane, R.E. (2000). *The Loss of Happiness in Market Democracies*. London: Yale University Press.

Layard, R. (2005). *Happiness: Lessons From A New Science.* New York: Penguin Press.

Leary, M. R. (1990). Reponses to social exclusion: Social anxiety, jealousy, loneliness, depression, and low self-esteem. *Journal of Social and Clinical Psychology,* 9(2), 221–229.

Levinger, B. (1986). *School Feeding Programs in Developing Countries: An Analysis of Actual and Potential Impact.* Aid Evaluation Special Study No. 30. US Agency for International Development. http://www.schoolsandhealth.org/sites/ffe/Needs%20Assessment/pnaal060.pdf

Lucas, R. E. (2007). Adaptation and the Set-Point Model of Subjective Well-Being: Does Happiness Change After Major Life Events? *Current Directions in Psychological Science,* 16(2), 275–279.

Lykken, D. and A. Tellegen (1996). Happiness is a stochastic phenomenon. *Psychological Science,* 7, 186–189.

McAdams, D. P. (1985). Motivation and Friendship. In *Understanding Personal Relationships: An Interdisciplinary Approach,* eds S. Duck and D. Perlman. London: Sage Publications.

McKinsey Global Institute (2010). *Lions on the move: The progress and potential of African economies.* McKinsey & Company.

McMahon, D. M. (2004). The History of Happiness: 400 B.C. – A.D. 1780, *Daedalus Journal,* Spring 2004.

Miner, A., T. M. Glomb and C. L. Hulin (2005). Experience sampling mood and its correlates at work. *Journal of Occupational and Organizational Psychology,* 78(2), 171–193.

Minority Rights Group International (2012). *World Directory of Minorities and Indigeneous Peoples. Overview of Asia and Oceania.* http://www.minorityrights.org/?lid=499

Morley, S. and D. Coady (2003). *From Social Assistance to Social Development: A Review of Targeted Education Subsidies in Developing Countries.* Washington, DC: International Food Policy Research Institute.

Naicker, S., J. Plange-Rhule, R. C. Tutt and J. B. Eastwood (2009). *Ethnicity and Disease,* 19, 60–64, Spring. http://www.ishib.org/journal/19-1s1/ethn-19-01s1-60.pdf

New York Times (April 16, 2008). "Maybe Money Does Buy Happiness After All".

Ng, Yew-Kwang (2002). The East-Asian Happiness Gap: Speculating on Causes and Implications. *Pacific Economic Review,* 7(1), 51–63.

OECD (2011). *Compendium of OECD well-being indicators* http://www.oecd.org/document/28/0,3746,en_2649_201185_47916764_1_1_1_1,00.html (5 October 2011)

OECD (2011a). *Latin American Economic Outlook 2011.* Paris: OECD Development Centre.

Packer, S., J. Husted, S. Cohen and G. Tomlinson (1997). Psychopathology and quality of life in schizophrenia. *Journal of Psychiatry Neuroscience,* 22(4), 231–234.

Pinstrup-Andersen, P., ed. (1988). *Food Subsidies in Developing Countries Costs, Benefits and Policy Options.* Baltimore: Published for the International Food Policy Research Institute by Johns Hopkins University Press.

Price, S. J. and P. C. McKenry (1988). *Divorce.* Newbury Park, CA: Sage.

Psychiatric Times (2002), 19(1), January.

Putnam, D. (2001). *Bowling Alone: The Collapse and Revival of American Community.* New York: Simon and Schuster.

Quibria, M. G. (2002). *Growth and Poverty: Lessons from the Asian Miracle Revisited.* ADB Institute Research Paper 33. Tokyo: Asian Development Bank Institute.

Rojas, M. (2004). *Well-being and the Complexity of Poverty: A Subjective Well-being Approach.* UNU-WIDER Research Paper. United Nations University World Institute for Development Economics Research.

Ryff, C. D. (1995). Psychological well-being in adult life. *Current Directions in Psychological Science,* 4(4), 99–104.

Samuelson, P. A. (1937). A Note on Measurement of Utility. *Review of Economic Studies,* 4(2), 155–161.

Scheier, M. F., K. A. Matthews, J. F. Owens, *et al.* (1989). Dispositional optimism and recovery from coronary artery bypass surgery, the beneficial effects of physical and psychological well being. *Journal of Personality and Social Psychology,* 57(6), 1024–1040.

Spector, P. E. (1997). *Job Satisfaction, Application, Assessment, Cause and Consequences.* California: Sage Publications.

Stearns, J. (2011). *Dancing in the Glory of Monsters: The Collapse of the Congo and the Great War in Africa.* New York: Public Affairs Press.

Sternberg, R. J. (1986). A Triangular Theory of Love. *Psychological Review,* 93, 119–135.

Stiglitz, J. E., A. Sen and J.-P. Fitoussi (2010). *Mismeasuring our Lives Why GDP doesn't add up.* New York and London: The New Press.

Subramanian, U. and M. Matthijs (2007). *Can Sub-Saharan Africa Leap into Global Network Trade?* World Bank Policy Research Working Paper 4112. World Bank.

Swinyard, W. R., A. K. Kau and H. Y. Phua (2001). Happiness, Materialism and Religious Experience in the US and Singapore. *Journal of Happiness Studies,* 2(1), 13–32.

Tellegen, A., D. T. Lykken, T. J. Bouchard, *et al.* (1988). Personality similarity in twins reared apart and together. *Journal of Personality and Social Psychology,* 54, 1031–1039.

Thaler, R. and C. Sunstein (2009). *Nudge: Improving Decisions about Health, Wealth, and Happiness.* New Haven: Yale University Press.

The Economist, 31 July 2010.

Thompson, S. and N. Marks (2008). *Measuring Well-Being in policy issues and applications.* Report commissioned by the Foresight Project on Mental Capital and Well-being, UK government office for Science. London: nef and the Foresight Commission.

Triandis, H. C. (1994). *Culture and Social Behavior.* New York: Mc Graw Hill.

Triandis, H. C. (1995). *Individualism and collectivism.* Boulder, Colorado: Westview Press.

United Nations (2011). *Economic Survey of Latin America and the Caribbean 2009–2011.* Santiago: Economic Commission for Latin America and the Caribbean (ECLAC).

United Nations Development Programme (2010). *Human Development Report 2010 – The real wealth of nations: pathways to human development.* New York: UNDP.

United Nations Development Programme (2011). *Human Development Report 2011 – Sustainability and Equity: Towards a Better Future for All.* Basingstoke, England: Palgrave Macmillan.

Veenhoven, R. (1994). *Correlates of Happiness: 7837 Findings from 603 Studies in 69 Countries 1911–1994*. 3 vols. Rotterdam: Erasmus University Press.

Veenhoven, R. (2001). Are the Russians as Unhappy as they say they are? Comparability of Self Reports Across Nations. *Journal of Happiness Studies*, 2, 111–136.

Warr, P. (1990). The measurement of well-being and other aspects of mental health. *Journal of Occupational Psychology*, 63, 193–210.

Weiss, R. S. (1973). *Loneliness: The Experience of Emotional and Social Isolation*. Cambridge, MA: MIT Press.

Weiss, R. S. (1979). The Emotional Experience of Marital Separation. In *Divorce and separation: Context, Causes and Consequences*, eds G. Levinson and O. C. Moles. New York: Basic Books.

Wilson, T. P. and D. T. Gilbert (2003). Affective Forecasting. *Advances in Experimental Social Psychology*, 35, 345–411.

World Bank (2005). *The Gap Matters: Poverty and Well being of Afro-Columbians and Indigenous Peoples*. Environmentally and Socially Sustainable Development Unit: Latin America and The Caribbean Region.

World Bank (2011). *World Development Indicators*. Washington, DC: World Bank.

World Database of Happiness. http://worlddatabaseofhappiness.eur.nl/

World Values Study Group (1994). *World values survey, 1981–1984 and 1990–1993*. Ann Arbor, MI: Institute for Social Research, University of Michigan.

World Values Survey. http://worldvaluessurvey.org/

Zak, P. and S. Knack (2001). Trust and Growth. *The Economic Journal*, 111(4), 295–321.

Index

CPSIA information can be obtained at www.ICGtesting.com
Printed in the USA
LVOW10*1621210514

386771LV00013B/306/P